The Bhagavad Gita

With the complete story of the

Mahabharata

Published 2025
FINGERPRINT! CLASSICS
Prakash Books

Fingerprint Publishing
@FingerprintP
@fingerprintpublishingbooks
www.fingerprintpublishing.com

ISBN: 978 93 6214 663 2

The Bhagavad Gita

with Sanskrit text, translation, notes, comments and complete story of the Mahabharata

by

Swami Nikhilananda

FP CLASSICS

PUBLISHER'S NOTE

According to the renowned Indic scholar, Sri Ananda Coomaraswamy "The Bhagavad Gita or Gita is considered to be the apogee of Indian philosophical thought. The Bhagavad Gita is probably the most important single work ever produced in India."

He further maintains that "the Gita, consisting of eighteen chapters, is not, as it has been sometimes called, a 'sectarian' work, but one universally studied and often repeated daily from memory by millions of Indians of all persuasions; it may be described as a compendium of the whole Vedic doctrine to be found in the earlier Vedas, Brahmanas and Upanishads, and being therefore the basis of all the later developments in the field of Hindu religion. It can be regarded as the focus of all Indian religious and philosophical activities of that time."

The aim of this new translation of the Bhagavad Gita is to present the book to the world as a manual of Hindu religion and philosophy.

The present volume of the Bhagavad Gita by Swami Nikhilananda is unique in many ways: an authentic text in Sanskrit is being added so that the reader has a feel of our sastras. It has an excellent commentary and word-meaning by none other than Swami Nikhilananda, who was a renowned Indic scholar of Ramakrishna order and headed its Vedanta Centre at New York for long. There has also been included the story of the Mahabharata, which will acquaint the reader of the Gita with its background and with the character of Sri Krishna.

The bewilderment many feel at the choice of a battlefield for the unfolding of a scheme of the highest good and liberation will, it is hoped, be removed by a perusal of the story of the Mahabharata which has been included.

It has been our constant endeavour to bring out important texts on religion which are long out of print or very difficult to acquire but are of great significance for their transcendental and intrinsic value. We hope that our present volume will add to the knowledge about Hindu religion and help the reader to comprehend the true spirit of the Bhagavad Gita.

FOREWORD

No translation of Plato is definitive; no translation of the Tao Teh King; no translation of the Bhagavad Gītā. The more searching and impressive a work, the more it is impossible to convey, in any one version in another tongue, its full meaning. For that reason, the great classics of meditation require ever new translations, and each one adds a facet to the total sense. A new translation is always sufficiently formidable a task to deter anyone lacking in devotion, especially if he is familiar with the labors of his predecessors. A new translation of a great work, by a competent scholar, is therefore to be received with gratitude. It is especially to be welcomed if he has avoided, as I think Swami Nikhilananda has avoided, the warping of new translations by old: where a previous translator has hit upon a happy expression, a later translator is often constrained to avoid that expression, to seek the different solely for the sake of differing. The translation. here given seems to me to be natural and direct, conveying the sense in admirably idiomatic English. At the same time, there has been no hesitation about using a few Sanskrit terms, such as dharma, yoga, mays, essentially untranslatable, whose meaning the reader readily acquires.

No one who desires to grasp the spirit of religious aspiration of India can afford to remain unacquainted with this, "The Lord's Song." It is, in a sense, the New Testament of Hinduism. It had an important message to a people whose religious ideal tended to be contemplative and mystical, who had the genius to reveal to the world that ultimate goal for thought and reverence sometimes called "The Absolute," the One without a second. Its message was the meaning, of action, the justification even of warfare in the light of union with the Ultimate.

It is therefore the direct answer to those who identify the Indian spirit with that sort of mysticism which involves retreat from the world of affairs. Its position, as that one of the world's classics most intimately known by so many millions, is assurance that its temper is indicative of the inner quality of modern India.

This fact lends a special interest to the commentary which accompanies the text. It is an adaptation from the extended commentary of Śaṅkarācārya, the greatest exponent of the Vedānta system of philosophy in its strictly monistic form. There can be no doubt about the profundity of Śaṅkara's work, its great philosophical importance, and its permanent message to a world tempted to the distractions of pluralism. In my personal judgment, Śaṅkara missed the peculiar message of the Bhagavad Gītā above referred to: his comments attempt to bring the Gītā back to the supremacy of meditation over action as the condition of union with God. (p. 102) To scholars, this tug between differing points of view will add a spice of historical piquancy to the work. To the average reader, the effect of the difference may be confusing. Many of these comments, moreover, directed as they are to an India of the ninth century of our era, may appear either unnecessary or unenlightening to the man of today. If so, let him consider that the service to American scholarship in presenting Śaṅkara's view of the Gītā in such close relation to the text will surely justify a hurdle so easily taken.

May this majestic poem find its way into the familiar literary friendship of many readers, and contribute to the sense of spiritual kinship with the most gifted people of Asia, akin to us both in blood and in language.

William Ernest Hocking

PREFACE

The aim of this new translation of the Bhagavad Gītā is to present the book to the English-speaking public of the Western world as a manual of Hindu religion and philosophy. To achieve that purpose, notes and explanations have been added to the text, and the connexion of thought between the verses has been shown, wherever that seemed necessary. The explanations follow, in the main, the commentary on the Gītā by Śaṅkarācārya. Abstruse and technical portions of the commentary have been omitted as of no particular interest to most readers of the book.

There has also been included the story of the *Mahābhārata,* which will acquaint the student of the Gītā with its background and with the character of Śrī Kṛṣṇa. The bewilderment many students feel at the choice of a battle-field for the unfolding of a scheme of the Highest Good and liberation will, it is hoped, be removed by a perusal of the story.

In the Introduction the translator has made an attempt to explain some of the philosophical concepts of the Gītā, such as the meaning of duty, its place in the moulding of the spiritual life, and the meaning of action and actionlessness from the relative and the absolute standpoint.

The diacritical table will help Occidental students in the pronunciation of unfamiliar Sanskrit words. The glossary will enable them to understand the meaning of Sanskrit expressions left in the text and notes for want of equivalents in English. It is hoped that they will simplify the problems faced by Westerners in studying the Bhagavad Gītā.

There are in existence many English translations of the Bhagavad Gītā. The present translator has profitably consulted two of these, one by D.S. Sarma and the other by A. Mahādeva Śāstri. In addition, he has looked into *Essays on the Gītā* by Śrī Aurobindo. The works of Margaret E. Noble (Sister Nivedita) and Dr. Ānanda Coomaraswāmy have proved useful in the writing of the story of the *Mahābhārata.* He has also received invaluable help from Mr. Denver Lindley and Mr. Joseph Campbell, who revised the manuscript. It is a real pleasure to acknowledge the translator's indebtedness to them all.

Humanity is now passing through a critical stage of transition. Many branches of physical science, psychology, sociology, and humanism are placing every day at our disposal a wealth of facts of which hitherto we have been unaware. They need collation and synthesis in order to be useful to the life of the individual and society. There is also the primal antithesis between this world and the other world, between secular duties and spiritual values. Men are confused and picture life as full of shreds and patches. But they feel a profound need of seeing life as a seamless garment. To those who sincerely seek, the Bhagavad Gītā may be a means of coordinating these apparently contradictory facts.

New York
November 1, 1943

Swami Nikhilananda

NOTE ON THE PRONOUNCIATION OF SANSKRIT WORDS

a	has the sound of	*u* in b*u*t
ā	has the sound of	*a* in f*a*ther
ai	has the sound of	*ai* in *ai*sle
au	has the sound of	*ow* in c*ow*
c	has the sound of	*ch* in *ch*urch
d	has the sound of	*th* in *th*em
ḍ	has the sound of	*d* in har*d*
e	has the sound of	*a* in m*a*te
ī	has the sound of	*ee* in t*ee*th
jñ	has the sound of	hard *gy* in English[1]
o	has the sound of	*o* in m*o*de
u	has the sound of	*u* in p*u*t
ś	has the sound of	*sh* in *sh*ut
ū	has the sound of	*oo* in m*oo*d

1 jñāna is pronouinced as gyāna.

sh	may be pronounced as in Engli*sh*
ṭ	has the sound of *t* in *t*rump

Other consonants appearing in the transliteration may be pronounced as in English

CONTENTS[1]

1 In the original every chapter of the Bhagavad Gītā is called a yoga, or way of union with God.

INTRODUCTION

The Bhagavad Gītā, popularly known as the Gītā, comprises eighteen chapters—the twenty-fifth through the forty-second—of the section on Bhīṣma in the *Mahābhārata*. It takes the form of a dialogue between Śrī Kṛṣṇa and Arjuna on the battle-field of Kurukṣetra. The setting of the battle-field contributes a dramatic element to the book and relates religion to the realities of life.

The Gītā is one of the most important religious classics of the world. Hindus of all sects and denominations revere the book. It is read daily by unnumbered Hindus for spiritual inspiration and is held in the highest esteem by all—men and women, young and old, householders and monks.

The teacher of the Gītā is Kṛṣṇa, who is regarded by the Hindus as the supreme manifestation of the Lord Himself. Ideal friend, wise teacher, far-seeing statesman, devout yogi, and invincible warrior, Kṛṣṇa harmonizes in His character the various conflicting activities of life. He is the most highly esteemed religious prophet in India.

From the human standpoint Kṛṣṇa and Arjuna are friends and companions; but in a deeper sense they are one soul in two bodies, two aspects of the one Reality, each incomplete without the other. Their conjoined forms are still worshipped in India under the name of Pārtha-sārathī, Kṛṣṇa as Arjuna's charioteer. Again, at the shrine of Badrī-Nārāyaṇa, in an almost inaccessible part of the Himalayas, they are worshipped as Nara-Nārāyaṇa, Arjuna as Nara, Man, and Kṛṣṇa as Nārāyaṇa, God. The two, God-Man, form the total picture of the Godhead.

There are many who regard the story behind the Gītā not as historical fact but as an allegory. To them Arjuna represents the individual soul, and Śrī Kṛṣṇa the Supreme Soul dwelling in every heart. Arjuna's chariot is the body. The blind King Dhṛtarāṣṭra is the mind under the spell of ignorance, and his hundred sons are man's numerous evil tendencies. The battle, a perennial one, is between the power of good and the power of evil. The warrior who listens to the advice of the Lord speaking from within will triumph in this battle and attain the Highest Good.

The Upaniṣads, the Gītā, and the Brahma-sūtras—technically known as the three prasthānas—form the bed-rock of Vedānta philosophy. These religious classics are, as a rule, read by the monks of the Vedānta school, who have renounced the world in quest of Truth. Many commentaries have been written on these texts by the celebrated philosophers of India. According to Hindu tradition, a philosopher or sage seeking to preach a new doctrine must gain his support from the Upaniṣads, the Gītā, and the Brahma-sūtras, which alone are the valid authorities on super-sensuous truths. Among the most important commentators on these books may be counted Śaṅkarācārya (AD 788-820), Rāmānujācārya (AD 1017-1137), and Madhvācārya (AD 1199-1276), generally known as Śaṅkara, Rāmānuja, and Madhva. Each of them has explained the ancient teaching differently. The soul and the world are spoken of by the non-dualist Śaṅkara as one with Brahman, or Ultimate Reality; by Rāmānuja, the upholder of Qualified Non-dualism, as parts of Reality; and by the dualist Madhva, as different from Reality. According to the commentators themselves, these views are mutually incompatible and exclusive. Nevertheless they need not be; for man's relationship with Ultimate Reality is relative to his conception of himself. When he identifies himself with the body, then he is certainly different from God. (Dualism.) When he regards himself as a living being, then he is a part of the Universal Life. (Qualified Non-dualism.) But when he realizes that he is incorporeal Spirit, beyond time, space, and causality, then he is one with the Universal Spirit. (Non-dualism.) Apparently the Gītā accepts all three views as pertaining to man's various stages of spiritual evolution.

The present translator, in his notes and comments, has followed, in the main, Śaṅkara's commentary. Śaṅkarācārya, called Śaṅkara for short, is one of the brightest stars in the firmament of India. He is one of the pillars of the Eternal Religion of the Hindus. Unfortunately, very little is known of the life of this wonderful man. The scholars are by no means unanimous about the date of his birth. According to one celebrated Hindu scholar[1] he was born about the middle or the end of the sixth century, and according to another[2] in AD 680 or a few years earlier. According to some European scholars[3] he was born in AD 788 and died in 820.

Śaṅkara belonged to the simple, scholarly, and industrious Nāmbudri sect of brāhmins of Malabar in south India. The village of Kālādi, on the west coast of the peninsula, is pointed out as his birth-place. Even while a boy he showed utter indifference to material pleasures and renounced the world at an early age in quest of Truth. He found his teacher, Govindapāda, on the bank of the river Narmadā and was initiated by him into the life of a wandering monk. Soon he completely mastered the sacred lore of the Vedas, the Upaniṣads, and the other scriptures of Hinduism. He wrote commentaries to elucidate the texts of the Bhagavad Gītā, the Brahma-sūtras, and the ten principal Upaniṣads. He became the personification of Vedic wisdom and a strong upholder of the Non-dualistic system of Vedānta.

It was the twilight of Buddhism. Various superstitious practices and corrupt rituals passed as religion. Śaṅkara travelled over the length and breadth of India, challenging the heretics and engaging in discussion with the leaders of the rival schools. Everywhere he was triumphant. He practised yoga and came to possess many supernatural powers. He reformed the monastic order of Hinduism and established four monasteries, the chief of which is at Śrīṅgerī in Mysore. The others are at Purī in the east, Dwārakā in the west, and Badrīnātha in the Himalayas. Though an ascetic, he was nevertheless full of the milk of human kindness and filial affection. In open defiance of the rules that govern the order of saṃnyāsis, Śaṅkara performed the funeral rites of his mother and thus incurred the serious displeasure of his community. Though an uncompromising non-dualist and an upholder of the nameless and formless Absolute, yet, out of deference to the feelings of ordinary devotees, he composed many soul-stirring hymns in praise of different gods and goddesses of popular Hinduism, never failing to point out that these deities are manifestations of the great, all-pervading Spirit. The life of Śaṅkara in an inexplicable manner reconciles contraries. He was a philosopher and a poet, a savant and a saint, a mystic and a religious reformer, a lover of God and a debater

1 Telang.
2 Sir R.G. Bhāndārkār.
3 Max Müller and Professor Macdonell.

of rare forensic power. According to tradition, this great man died at Kedārnātha, in the Himalayas, at the age of thirty-two.

One may read the Gītā without the help of any commentary, comprehend its meaning in a general way, and feel its uplifting influence; but the commentaries reveal much of the subtlety, grandeur, depth, and sublimity that would otherwise remain hidden. Without the help of the commentaries it is sometimes impossible to discover the thread that connects the verses and the chapters. The text of the Gītā well serves the purpose of daily devotional reading; but the commentaries help one to sound its depths.

No amount of critical study, however, will enable a reader to grasp the real meaning of the Gītā unless he is equipped with the four qualifications laid down for the spiritual aspirant. He must possess the power of discriminating between the Real and the unreal; he must cultivate will to renounce the unreal; he must be endowed with the "six spiritual virtues," namely, control of the senses, control of the mind, forbearance, withdrawal from the distracting objects of the world, faith, and one-pointedness of minds lastly, he must have an intense longing for liberation from the illusory experiences of the relative world. Equipped with these four qualifications, he may come to understand the profound meaning of the scripture. Spirituality is the transformation of life, not the satisfaction of intellectual curiosity. It is being and becoming; not mere knowing. Really to know God is to be God.

The story is told of an illiterate farmer who one day was listening to a learned exposition of the Gītā apparently without understanding a word of the interpretation. But tears flowed down his cheeks. On being asked the cause of his emotion, the farmer said that while the pundit was explaining the Gītā he clearly saw Arjuna's chariot on the battle-field of Kurukṣetra and the Lord instructing him in divine wisdom. It was true that he did not grasp the scholar's interpretation. Nevertheless his ignorance of the letter did not stand in the way of his understanding the spirit of the book. The inwardness of mind necessary to probe the meaning of the Gītā is acquired through the practice of self-control and contemplation.

What are the form and content of the book? The Bhagavad Gītā, which literally means the Song of the Lord, is not a formal theology or a cut-and-dried system of philosophy. One does not find in the book consistency even in the use of certain important words, such as yoga,

Brahman, and Ātman. The Gītā is written in the form of an inspired dialogue; it is that living dialogue which the discerning man finds going on constantly in his own heart between his everyday worldly self and his higher Self. To such a student it appears that he himself is raising the questions, which are then answered by the Lord within. The book's power of suggestion is without limit if it is approached in the proper spirit. One feels that Arjuna's dilemma and confusion are one's own and that the Lord's words are addressed to oneself from the continuous revelation going on within every human heart.

The Gītā is a yogaśāstra, a scripture on yoga. The word "yoga," still much abused in Europe and America, denotes the union of individual soul with Universal Soul, and also the means to such union. Hence yoga is the goal of all religions and the basis of all religious practices. It implies much more than religion in its usual sense. Instead of laying down creeds and doctrines for acceptance by religious aspirants, it emphasizes the psychological approach to self-unfoldment. Thus yoga takes into consideration the different types of human minds—the active, the philosophical, the emotional, and the psychic—and expounds for them, respectively, the path of work (karmayoga), the path of knowledge (jñānayoga), the path of love or devotion (bhaktiyoga), and the path of concentration and self-control (rājayoga). Each of these paths opens upon the infinite horizon of Truth and effects the union of man with God. The Gītā describes them all.

The Gītā is called the Brahmavidyā, the Science of the Absolute, and the mokṣaśāstra, the scripture dealing with liberation. Though its immediate purpose is to persuade Arjuna to follow the path of a worldly duty, yet its message is the message of Truth and salvation. The problems discussed are philosophical and metaphysical: God, the soul, the hereafter, evolution, matter, Spirit, duty, social service, and the rest. Man is understood as an integral whole whose activities and feelings are not to be departmentalized. Even his most trivial work cannot be understood or evaluated unless it is related to the very root of his being. The aim of Kṛṣṇa's teachings is to remove the doubts and delusions that overpower man in everything, great or small; but these can be removed only through a realization of Truth. Thus alone can a man be prepared to face the world and his duty with the strength and understanding derived from the consciousness of God dwelling in his heart.

The Gītā is a compendium of the essential meaning of the Vedas, India's Book of Wisdom. Here one finds the fairest flowers of the Vedas cleared of the weeds and underbrush of rituals, ceremonies, and myths. The aphoristic nature of the Gītā makes it easy for the student to recall its teachings for the purpose of meditation or for inspiration at critical moments of indecision and bewilderment.

The God preached by the Gītā is universal and all-inclusive. "Its hands and feet are everywhere; Its eyes, heads, and faces are everywhere; Its ears are everywhere; Its existence envelops all." Yet to Him we look for succour in time of need. "I am the Goal and the Support; the Lord and the Witness; the Abode, the Refuge, and the Friend; I am the origin and the dissolution; the ground, the storehouse, and the Imperishable Seed." He is the impersonal Power behind the universe. "The Light even of lights, It is said to be beyond darkness. As knowledge, the object of knowledge, and the goal of knowledge, It is set firm in the hearts of all." "The light that is in the sun and illumines the whole universe, the light that is in the moon and is likewise in fire—know that light to be Mine." He animates the whole of Nature. As He sustains the macrocosm, so also does He sustain the microcosm. Nevertheless His true nature is transcendent and beyond human comprehension. Only a portion of Him is manifest in the universe. The all-pervading, incomprehensible, transcendental Consciousness appears to man as a Personal God and requires from him single-minded love unstained by worldliness. "Whosoever offers Me, with devotion, a leaf, a flower, a fruit, or water—that I accept, the pious offering of the pure in heart."

That religion is an opiate—a frequent criticism—is refuted by the Gītā. The spiritual aspirant must work, and work incessantly, both for individual liberation and for the stability of the world order. "Neither let your motive be the fruit of action, nor let your attachment be to non-action"—is Śrī Kṛṣṇa's warning to those who mistake inertia for spirituality. Inertia, indolence, and inadvertence are the three worst enemies of spiritual life and are more harmful than the majority of the notorious sins. The aim of Śrī Kṛṣṇa's teachings was to rescue Arjuna from his dreamy ideal of a recluse's life and make him plunge into a whirl of activity, where the grimmest facts of existence were to be faced and accepted. From the sequel we know that Śrī Kṛṣṇa did not sow His seed on barren soil. After listening to the instruction Arjuna said: "My delusion is gone. I have regained my memory through Your grace, O Kṛṣṇa. I am firm; I am free from doubt. I will act according to Your word." Work, or duty, is not the enemy of spiritual life; the real enemy is ignorance, the mother of attachment and delusion. "May He awaken our understanding," one of the earliest prayers of the Vedas, is still repeated every day by millions of Hindus.

Throughout the Gītā, Śrī Kṛṣṇa urges Arjuna to perform his duty on the battle-field. The warrior was confused regarding the nature of duty. Must a man cling to his worldly duties even if they bring suffering and pain to himself and others? Does not duty often create friction and irritation? Is it not our true duty to cast off duties and follow the line of least resistance in a life of non-activity? This was Arjuna's dilemma; and this is the dilemma we often face in our everyday life. Arjuna's confusion was due to his attachment and egotism. And also, he was frightened, to some extent, by the presence of the powerful combatants on the opposing side. Śrī Kṛṣṇa points out to Arjuna the imperative nature of duty and its usefulness as a spiritual discipline, But not the Stoic ideal of duty for duty's sake that Śrī Kṛṣṇa preaches, rather the spiritual ideal of duty for God's sake. Duty must be performed to please God alone; brooding over the result has nothing to do with the performance of duty. God is immanent in the universe. He is the indwelling Soul of all beings. Therefore the Upaniṣad says: "The husband is dear to the wife, not for the sake of the husband, but for the sake of the Lord in the husband. The wife is dear to the husband, not for the sake of the wife, but for the sake of the Lord in the wife." So every duty is an act of worship. Duty performed in this spirit confers joy upon the doer irrespective of success or failure. There is a joy in being made an instrument of God, there is a joy in being used by Him, and there is a joy in being set aside when the instrument is broken or has served its purpose.

Here we come to the main discipline of the Gītā for the attainment of liberation. It is karmayoga, or the performance of work as a yoga, a method of communion with the Godhead. Everyone must work. Inactivity is impossible for an embodied being. His eating, his moving, and even the functioning of his bodily organs, mean action. Work is the effective means of self-expression. in the relative world. Even God Himself is an ever active Power. "I have, O Pārtha, no duty; there is nothing in the three worlds that I have not gained and nothing that I have to gain. Yet I continue to work." But behind a man's work there may be different motives. He may work for his own satisfaction, or he may work to please God. In the former case he regards his individualized self as the doer, is elated by success and depressed by failure, and clings to the result, which is the satisfaction of the doer himself. In the latter case he knows that the Lord alone is the Doer, and himself only His instrument; he then works viewing alike success and failure, for the fruit of the action belongs to God alone. Ego-centric action creates bondage for the doer, whereas action performed to please God leads to liberation. Through such action the heart becomes pure, and the man of pure heart acquires the fitness to cultivate Self-knowledge. Through Self-knowledge he attains liberation. This is called karmayoga, the performance of duty as a yoga. Yoga is the secret of work. To remain unperturbed in success and failure is yoga.

All actions can be performed as yoga. Even an apparently violent action, inflicting suffering on others, as on a battle-field, can be a yoga and therefore spiritual, if the motive is not the aggrandizement of the individual or communal or national ego, but the establishment of truth and justice.

The relative universe consists of pairs of opposites, good and evil, pain and pleasure, virtue and vice, life and death. They are like the two sides of the same coin and are indispensable to complete the picture of the world. A perfect world, containing goodness or happiness alone, is a contradiction in terms; an undisturbed balance is possible only in the state of dissolution. The act of creation begins precisely when that balance is lost. When everybody will be perfect the world will cease to exist. The only active and intelligent Agent behind these ceaseless activities of the universe is the Lord Himself. His will alone is operative in every action. He is the only conscious Entity that exists; but He acts through embodied beings, using them as His instruments. In His foreordaining mind everything that is to be accomplished has already been accomplished. Both past and future are only a present moment in His infinite Consciousness. For the purpose of carrying out His plans in the relative world, He chooses different beings for different actions, apparently good or evil, according to their inborn dharmas. He expects them to be conscious of their instrumental nature. Men suffer because they regard themselves as doers. When once they realize that the Lord alone is the Doer, then their duty, whatever its nature may be, will bring them joy and satisfaction. It will bring them spiritual success. "By worshipping Him through the performance of duty does a man attain perfection." Man is essentially of the nature of God. Therefore any work done for the satisfaction of God must also satisfy man's true Self.

In the Gītā, Śrī Kṛṣṇa emphasizes svadharma, one's own dharma. The word "dharma" is really untranslatable. "Religion," "duty," "righteousness," and the other English equivalents give only a partial meaning. Dharma is derived from the root *dhṛ,* meaning to hold or sustain. The word signifies the attitude behind a man's action or duty that sustains him in his present stage of evolution and also helps him to realize his ultimate destiny. The dharma of a man is determined by his past experiences and tendencies. The beginningless Soul assumes different forms in different births for the gaining of experience. The works performed in every birth leave impressions, which are stored up in the subconscious mind and are not destroyed with the death of the body. When the Soul assumes a new body, these impressions begin to operate. Thus they form his svabhāva, or character; they determine his dharma—his duty, his religion, his sense of right and wrong. Education and environment only help a man to manifest what he has inherited from his own past. Heredity supplies him with the physical means of working out his dharma. So a man's dharma is the basis of his thought and action; he cannot get rid of it any more than a dreaming person can get rid of his dream. To try to act against one's dharma is to do violence to one's nature. The duty determined by a man's dharma is his natural duty. That is the only real thing for him; all other duties are alien to his nature, imposed from outside and therefore sources of confusion. Kṛṣṇa asks to Arjuna to cling to his kṣatriya dharma though it does not seem perfect from other standpoints. "Better is one's own dharma, though imperfectly performed, than the dharma of another well performed. Better is death in the doing of one's own dharma: the dharma, of another is fraught with peril." "He who does the duty ordained by his own nature incurs no sin." As a poisonous substance does not injure the worm born in that substance, so he who acts according to his inborn dharma does not incur evil.

Dharma impels a man to righteous or unrighteous actions, which produce good or evil results. Both the evil and the good operate as barriers to the Knowledge of Reality, which is transcendent and beyond such pairs of opposites. Dharma and adharma, righteousness and unrighteousness, may be compared to clouds of different thickness that hide the resplendent sun: what is called good is only a lesser evil. The light of the sun is seen in its full brilliance only when the clouds are totally removed. Likewise, the true glory of the Self is perceived only when the mind remains free from all the tendencies created by its good as well as its evil actions. This condition of mind is produced when a man acts according to his dharma in a spirit of utter detachment. The organs may then be active, but the mind does not retain the slightest impression of the action. This is the meaning of Śrī Kṛṣṇa's advice to Arjuna to work and surrender the results to the Lord. It is the only way to exhaust the past tendencies and at the same time prevent the formation of new ones. By freeing the mind of attachment and delusion a man ultimately realizes that his supreme dharma is to worship God, and God alone. "Abandon all dharmas and come to Me alone for shelter. I will deliver you from all sins; do not grieve." Thus, through our worldly dharma, we acquire fitness to perform the supreme duty of human evolution, which is the attainment of Self-knowledge.

The great Śaṅkara, in his commentary on the Gītā, describes perfection, or liberation, as a state of actionlessness or non-activity. He repeatedly asserts, throughout the book, that action and Self-knowledge are incompatible. This philosophical position taken by him has created a great deal of controversy in East and West alike. It would seem that this confusion is mainly due to a misunderstanding of "inactivity" and "Self-knowledge" as used by Śaṅkara. He nowhere denies the place of action for the security of the world order. He clearly says in his Introduction to the Gītā that, after creating the world, the Lord taught men both the dharma of action and the dharma of renunciation in order to ensure the stability of society; for both are necessary to man's welfare. Through action man attains worldly well-being, and through renunciation the Highest Good. But a man will not seek the Highest Good unless, through experience, he has realized the illusory nature of worldly prosperity. Action becomes, for a spiritual aspirant, a dharma, or means of Self-knowledge, only when he performs it in a spirit of detachment, knowing that God alone is the Doer and man His instrument. Otherwise action feeds greed and lust, produces chaos and confusion, and ultimately brings about the destruction of the world.

According to Śaṅkara, the Ātman, or Soul, in Its essential nature, is one with Brahman, the Absolute. It is pure, luminous, eternal, and free. Birthless and deathless, It is beyond time, space, and causality.

It is Spirit and Consciousness, and One without a second. Being the embodiment of Perfection, Bliss, and Peace, It neither changes nor acts. But Brahman, or Ātman, *appears* to be active on account of the inscrutable māyā—a mysterious power, inhering in Brahman, which makes the One appear to have become many, the Absolute to have become the relative. The creation and multiplicity are due to māyā. Through its influence names and forms are falsely superimposed upon Brahman. As long as one sees the slightest trace of duality, one is dwelling in the realm of ignorance, or māyā.

Action, described in the Gītā as incompatible with Self-knowledge, or perfection, is always associated with the triple consciousness of a doer, an instrument, and a result. In every action undertaken by an unillumined or ignorant person these three factors are inevitably present. The knowledge of the non-dual Soul, or Brahman, is incompatible with the knowledge of multiplicity. According to Śaṅkara a knower of Brahman cannot perform any action characterized by, multiplicity. That is why Self-knowledge is incompatible with activity.

Furthermore, a man endowed with Self-knowledge feels no incentive to action, such as the attainment of the desirable, the relinquishment of the undesirable, the reforming of the impure, or the changing of one substance into another. All these incentives are found only in the relative world characterized by good and evil, pain and pleasure, and the other pairs of opposites. An illumined person sees Brahman, or Perfection, everywhere—both within and without. There exists for him no imperfection or evil that he might change or destroy; for if he sees anywhere even a trace of evil, he has not attained the Knowledge of Brahman.

Other motives of action, such as inner restlessness, boredom, a haunted conscience, the desire for name and fame, and the desire for "self-expression," are totally absent in a man of Knowledge, who has found peace within and without and is constantly aware of the blissful nature of the Soul.

In his commentaries on the Gītā, the Upaniṣads, and the Brahma-sūtras, Śaṅkara often says that action is proper only for an ignorant person. He uses the words "ignorant" and "action" in a special sense. The word "ignorant" (avidyā) does not have the connotation "uneducated," but applies to a person who has not realized the complete identity of his soul with Brahman, or the Absolute. According to Śaṅkara, the knowledge of Non-duality is the only real knowledge. All other forms of knowledge, associated with duality, are ignorance. Consistent with his theory of Non-dualism, which also is corroborated by the inner experience of many seers of Truth, Śaṅkara characterizes even the highest experience of dualism as stained by ignorance. The word "action" in this connexion refers only to that action which recognizes the multiplicity of a doer, an instrument, and a result.

It seems to be the consensus of opinion of Indian spiritual teachers that an unillumined or ignorant person, for the purification of his heart, follows karma-yoga, that is to say, performs action looking upon himself as an instrument of the Lord and surrendering to Him the fruits of action. As a result of karma-yoga he gradually frees himself from ego, greed, and passion. As his heart becomes purer, he takes less interest in outside activities and pays more heed to meditation and contemplation. His attention is diverted from the outer life to the inner life. His outer activities are confined to the bare maintenance of the body, the entire mind being directed to contemplation of the Lord. Through such intense spiritual practice his heart becomes entirely pure, and the purity of heart is instantaneously followed by the attainment of Knowledge. Thus karmayoga plays a vital part in the realization of Self-knowledge. Śaṅkara nowhere shows disdain for karmayoga.

Does a man endowed with Self-knowledge, then, remain inactive or inert like an inanimate object? That would be absurd. Inertia is a condition of weariness, indolence, or sleep. It is utterly absent in Brahman, or Ātman, which is all Knowledge-Existence-Bliss Absolute. No two beings are further apart than a seer of Truth and a stone. As dualistic action is incompatible with Brahman, so too is inertia. As a knower of Brahman cannot work from any external motive, neither can he remain actionless, like a stone or stump. Then how does he move and live in the world? All this has been vividly described by Śrī Kṛṣṇa in the Gītā. (II, 55-72; XIV, 22-27)

What Śaṅkara emphasizes is that a man endowed with Self-knowledge is free from all trace of duality—the illusory notions of a doer, an instrument, and a result of action. His activity is really the same as his Knowledge of Reality. In every phase of action, in its every accessory, he sees nothing but Infinite Brahman. The action that is free from the notion of a doer, an instrument, and a result is Knowledge itself. "He who sees inaction in action, and action in inaction, he is wise among men, he is a yogi, and he has performed all action."

The important thing to remember here is that the emphasis is laid on the knowledge that inspires the action and not on the outer action itself. An ignorant person and a knower of Brahman may seem to engage in the same kind of work, for instance, eating or sleeping; but whereas the former may see in his action the presence of the ego or various material factors, the latter sees in it only Brahman. It is Knowledge that distinguishes a wise man from an ignorant.

In a man endowed with Self-knowledge, eternal peace and eternal action are harmonized in an inexplicable manner. Such a man works as God Himself works. The whirlwind activities of the universe touch only the periphery of the Godhead, whose inner being is of the nature of Peace. Śaṅkara himself is an example of this. A knower of Brahman, he was far from being an inactive man. As from a higher standpoint of physical science one cannot distinguish matter from energy, so also from the standpoint of the Absolute, one cannot distinguish non-activity from activity. The most intense form of movement often creates an illusion of immobility. Any discussion of the Absolute or attempt to understand It through the dialectics of the relative world will bristle with contradiction.

Śaṅkara knows the value of action in the unfoldment of spiritual life. He recommends again and again the path of work for the ignorant and the beginners, for those in whose minds the idea of multiplicity is firmly impressed. Those who see the duality of good and evil must work to eliminate evil till they realize that good and evil are two inseparable entities, two inescapable factors of the relative world. They may engage, according to their temperaments, in ritualistic worship or philanthropic action. Those conscious of worldly responsibilities may do their duties to their family, community, or country. But the Gītā enjoins workers to perform their duties in a spirit of detachment, surrendering the results to God. Then alone does a work, or karma, become dharma and purify the mind by removing the illusory notion of duality. The man of pure mind sees the blissful Brahman within, without, and everywhere. His fear and expectation give place to an inner calmness and self-assurance, his longing and restlessness to unruffled peace. More and more he becomes engrossed in the contemplation of Reality. If his mind is diverted outward by any lingering desire for work, he is admonished by an inner voice:

"Follow me; and let the dead bury their dead." (Bible: *Matthew* 8:22) "Ye have the poor always with you; but me ye have not always." *(Matthew* 26:11) Such a person may not fit into any scheme of social service or patriotic endeavour; he may not be utilized to promote worldly culture; yet he is the salt of the earth.

Such a person also desists from ritualistic action—which is, in general, the meaning of the action denounced by Śaṅkara in his commentary on the Gītā—in order to secure happiness in heaven, as promised by religion. Discovering the Self to be the abode of real happiness, he renounces all the illusory happiness of the relative world. That is why the organized religions often disapprove his conduct and denounce him as a rebel.

Thus, when the mind and senses are completely withdrawn from the outside world and freed from all desires, and when they are directed to the Eternal Reality, there comes the Great Revelation, the Knowledge of Truth, which destroys the ignorance and delusion of the relative world. The dreamer wakens from sleep and enters a world of a new dimension. The timid and hesitant fledgling jumps from the nest into the crisp autumn air and flies toward the dome of heaven. It is a new life with its own beauty and grandeur. The old slough is discarded; there is no more return to the world of ignorance. The Gītā often declares that a man of Self-knowledge is not born again. This birth refers to birth in ignorance as a slave of māyā. To this birth the illumined man does not return. But by no means can he be said to be annihilated: he has become one with Sat, Existence Itself. By transcending the relative life, which is the same as death, he regains Everlasting Life.

The physical body may not survive the impact of such realization. Very often it falls off like a dry leaf. The body, in this case, is, immaterial. It has served its purpose: through its help the bound soul has regained its freedom. After the image is made, it matters little whether the mould be kept or thrown away. But if the body survives—as is the case with Divine Incarnations and other souls born with a special mission for humanity—the seer by no means remains inactive. He engages in an intense type of activity notwithstanding his apparent calmness. Through his every thought and every action he devotes himself to the welfare of the world. Any personal motive behind his work, either for worldly enjoyment or spiritual felicity, is out of the question. Even while engaged in the most intense action, he finds that the Self is immersed in peace and blessedness and that it is only the senses and their objects that busy themselves in the world. (III, 28; V, 8-9) The ego, the notion of being a doer, is totally absent; it has been either burnt in the Knowledge of Brahman or melted in the love of God. The life of an illumined person is a perfect example of dedication and unselfishness. Truly unselfish action is not possible without the Knowledge of Self. True dedication is impossible without the Knowledge of God. Whatever he may do or however he may comport himself, the man of Self-knowledge sees Brahman in all the phases and accessories of action. "To him Brahman is the offering and Brahman is the oblation, and it is Brahman who offers the oblation in the fire of Brahman. Brahman alone is attained by him who thus sees Brahman in action."

When a man does not identify himself with the body, when he has known the Supreme Self, and when all notions of multiplicity have dropped away from him, he experiences total communion with the Absolute in every action he undertakes. Such a man, in the expressive words of Śrī Rāmakṛṣṇa, works "keeping in his pocket the Knowledge of Non-duality."

As a pitcher immersed in water is filled with water inside and surrounded with water outside, above and below and on every hand, so also the man endowed with Knowledge is filled with God-consciousness inside and surrounded with it outside, above and below and on every hand. Again, as an empty pitcher suspended in the air has nothing within or without, above or below or on any hand, so also the man devoid of worldliness has nothing within or without, above or below or on any hand. As the flying bird leaves no footprint in the air, and the swimming fish no track in the water, so also the knower of Truth leaves no track or footprint on earth. He is known only to himself and to those who have attained Self-knowledge.

THE STORY OF THE MAHĀBHĀRATA

The *Mahābhārata* is one of the two great epics of India. The other is the *Rāmāyaṇa,* which deals with the life and exploits of Rāma, regarded by the Hindus as an Incarnation of God. The *Mahābhārata* contains the story of the great descendants of Bharata, the son of Duṣyanta and Śakuntalā. The scene of the epic is northern India. The *Mahābhārata,* more than any other book, has influenced the lives of the millions of Hindus for the last two thousand years. It is, still read with unabated zeal by Hindu men and women all over the country. In the course of time, more and more matter has been added to the original book, until it has assumed its present huge form containing about a hundred thousand couplets. The book contains all sorts of tales, legends, myths, philosophical discussions, and scraps of history. It is a mine of knowledge, secular and spiritual. But throughout the endless chapters and many digressions runs the old, original story—the fratricidal war between the two branches of a royal kṣatriya family.

In ancient times, long before the Christian era, there lived in India two royal families of cousins, known as the Kauravas and the Pāṇḍavas. The Kauravas were the sons of Dhṛtarāṣṭra and the Pāṇḍavas of his brother Pāṇḍu. The former was the elder, but being blind from birth, he was debarred from the throne in accordance with Āryan law; whereupon Pāṇḍu became the ruler of the ancestral kingdom, which comprised a great part of northern India.

Pāṇḍu had two wives, Kuntī and Mādrī. By the first he had three sons: Yudhiṣṭhira, Bhīma, and Arjuna; and by the second he had twins: Nakula and Sahadeva. Dhṛtarāṣṭra's queen, Gāndhārī, a princess of Gāndhāra, the modern Kāndāhār in Afghanistan, bore him one hundred sons. At the time of her marriage, when she had learnt of her husband's blindness, she had bandaged her own eyes with many layers of cloth, and taken a vow not to remove the bandage as long as he lived, so that she might not enjoy the light that was denied to him.

Pāṇḍu died a premature death, and his five young children were placed under the loving care of their blind uncle. Their education was supervised by Bhīṣma affectionately addressed by all as the "grand-sire."

Bhīṣma is one of the noblest characters of the *Mahābhārata,* the personification of statesmanship, wisdom, and knightly valour, all crowned by the example of utter selflessness. He was a prince in his own right. When Bhīṣma was very young, his father had fallen in love with a beautiful maiden belonging to a low caste. But the maiden's father, a very proud and sensitive man, forbade her marriage to the king except on certain conditions. He knew that Bhīṣma would inherit the kingdom after the king's death; so one of the conditions of the marriage was that Bhīṣma must for ever give up his claim to the throne. And to this was added another, a rigorous vow to be taken by Bhīṣma to remain unmarried as long as he lived, so that any future offspring of the maiden should have no rival for the throne. The king hesitated to ask his son to sacrifice all his future happiness; but Bhīṣma of his own accord went to his father and vowed to relinquish his claim to the throne and remain a life-long celibate. Deeply touched by his son's nobility, the king blessed him with a boon, namely, that death should never snuff out his life without first obtaining Bhīṣma's consent. The king married the beautiful maiden and a son was born to them. Many years later Bhīṣma won two lovely princesses in a joust of arms. They became wives of his half-brother and the mothers of Dhṛtarāṣṭra and Pāṇḍu. Bhīṣma was an ideal knight errant of his time, always lending his services for the cause of righteousness, giving wise counsel to kings, crowning them, and protecting them from enemies abroad and anarchy within. So unyielding did he remain in his vows that even now an inflexible vow in India is often called "Bhīṣma's vow."

Bhīṣma took charge of training the children of Pāṇḍu and Dhṛtarāṣṭra The brāhmin archer Droṇa was appointed as their military teacher. Yudhiṣṭhira, the eldest of all, was marked as the future king. The cousins received impartial treatment from the elders and grew up side by side. As time went on, their latent tendencies began to manifest themselves. Yudhiṣṭhira was found to be endowed with gentleness, piety, righteousness, and, especially, an undeviating regard for truth, and such other qualities as befit the ruler of a kingdom. Great physical courage and an almost superhuman strength were Bhīma's special traits; and with them he exhibited bluntness, recklessness, and utter disregard for personal comfort. Arjuna was the pattern of the chivalric ideal of his time. Devotion to duty, proficiency in archery, indomitable courage, remarkable self-control, tenderness of feeling, generosity to the weak, loyalty to friends, and other knightly qualities, marked him as a born leader of men. All the five brothers cultivated a keen sense of manliness, princely deportment, respect for sacred things, and nobility of character.

In striking contrast stood Duryodhana, the eldest son of Dhṛtarāṣṭra. Undoubtedly, he was loyal to his friends and efficient in the military arts; but he was cruel, malicious, deceitful, and selfish. Even as a boy he had become aware that Yudhiṣṭhira was an obstacle in his way to the throne and that Bhīma and Arjuna were more than his match in physical strength. Once he poisoned Bhīma in an attempt to remove him from his path.

Soon Yudhiṣṭhira was publicly declared the heir apparent, and the event was solemnized with appropriate ceremonies. He began to discharge many important functions of state with the counsel of Bhīṣma, Drona, and the other elders. He endeared himself to all by his patience, forbearance, uprightness, and benevolence.

But all this only served to inflame the jealousy of Duryodhana, who was ever on the lookout for a means of destroying him and his brothers. Dhṛtarāṣṭra, no doubt, tried his utmost to treat alike his own children and his nephews, but he did not altogether succeed in keeping under control a special affection for his eldest son. Thus many a time Duryodhana wrung from his father grudging consent to things that might harm or destroy his five cousins. With the connivance of the blind father he succeeded in trapping the five brothers and their mother in a house built of lac and other inflammable materials. But through the timely warning of a well-wisher they escaped being burnt alive. They left the house through a subterranean passage and, to ensure their safety, disguised themselves as brāhmin beggars and went into hiding.

At that time it was proclaimed that the princess Draupadī, a noted beauty of northern India, would celebrate her svayaṃvara, or bridal-choice ceremony. The kings, princes, and knights of the land responded to the invitation of her father, King Drupada, and assembled in his capital, each cherishing the desire to win the noble lady in the tournament. The Pāṇḍava brothers, too, attended the festival in their brāhmin guise. The winning of the bride was to be decided by shooting at a difficult target, the eye of a fish hung in the air. Five arrows must pass in succession through a swiftly revolving wheel before striking the target, and the archer must aim at the fish by looking down in a dish of water in which it was reflected.

Duryodhana, who was present with his friends, stepped forward. But he failed to pierce the target and was jeered by the crowd. The same fate met the efforts of the other princes. At last Arjuna came forward. Everyone tittered at what appeared an unseemly greed on the part of a brāhmin beggar. But, to the surprise of all, he pierced the eye of the fish, thus fulfilling the condition of winning Draupadī's hand.

At the festival were Kṛṣṇa and Balarāma, two brothers related to Draupadī. They were also distant cousins of the Pāṇḍava brothers. The sharp eye of Kṛṣṇa did not fail to recognize them in their disguise. He and Balarāma followed them and Draupadī to the hut where Mother Kuntī was eagerly awaiting the arrival of her sons with their daily alms. That day they were unusually late and she was worried. At last she heard their footsteps in the dark and was greeted by them in rather hilarious fashion. Even before being apprized of their day's earning, she asked them to share it among themselves. The five brothers decided to marry Draupadī. Kṛṣṇa gave them His blessing.

Kṛṣṇa, in whose veins flowed royal blood, was born in the clan of the Vṛṣṇis. His father, Vāsudeva, was a nobleman in the court of Kaṃsa, to whose sister, Devakī, he was married. Kaṃsa, the king of Mathurā, was a great tyrant. He was cruelty and unrighteousness personified. After the wedding of his sister, as he was driving her and his brother-in-law to Vāsudeva's palace, he heard a voice from heaven saying, "The eighth child of this couple, O tyrant, will be a boy and your slayer." The king, enraged, drove back with Vāsudeva and Devakī, and imprisoned them in a dungeon of his palace. They were heavily shackled and their prison was watched day and night by armed sentries. In course of time were born to them seven children, who, with the exception of one, were killed by the vicious Kaṃsa. The one child, Balarāma, was secretly carried away, and the king was informed that he was dead.

Now the time arrived for the great event, and Vāsudeva and Devakī expectantly awaited the birth of the Saviour, the Deliverer of the people from the oppression of the tyrant. Kaṃsa himself saw many omens of his oncoming doom and doubled the sentries about the prison-house. It was a stormy night. Blinding rain and a violent storm raged outside. Now and then lightning illumined the dark sky. At midnight Devakī gave birth to a boy, and from all the miracles that happened at the time, it became apparent to the joyous parents that the child was none other than Viṣṇu, the Supreme Lord, born to relieve the earth of sin and unrighteousness. Soon, however, the veil of māyā clouded their vision, and the Saviour appeared to them as their own babe. As they remembered the fate of the other children, their hearts were filled with unspeakable sadness, when they heard a voice saying, "Take the child to the house of Nanda, in the village of Gokul, and bring here the girl who has just been born to him."

Overpowered by an irresistible impulse, Vāsudeva resolved to act according to the revelation. When lo, the chains fell from his hands and feet, the bolts slipped back, the heavy doors swung open, and the watchful sentries suddenly fell into a deep slumber. The bewildered father took the child in his arms and went forth from the dungeon. The darkness parted before him; the rain offered no obstacle; and he came to the river Jamunā, across which lay Gokul, the village of the cowherds. Safely he forded the river and arrived at Nanda's house. A light was burning in a room, and Vāsudeva saw Yaśodā, Nanda's wife, in deep sleep, with the newly born girl by her side. The children were exchanged and Vāsudeva hurried back with the girl to the prison. Then instantly, as if by magic, the doors closed again, the irons shackled his limbs, and the watchman resumed guard of the dungeon with fixed arms.

In the morning the people of Gokul were pleasantly surprised to discover that it was a boy, and not a girl, that had been born to their beloved chieftain. Nanda and Yaśodā, though puzzled, accepted the child as their own and named Him Kṛṣṇa, the Dark One; for His complexion was deep blue, like a dark rain-cloud, or like the tamāla tree, or like the dark waters of the Jamunā.

Kaṃsa came to learn of the birth of a child to his sister. He hurried to the prison, determined to kill it with his own hands. The tyrant found that it was only a girl, but remembering the prophecy, seized her. The babe miraculously slipped from his hands and, ascending into the sky, declared mockingly, "He who shall slay you, O wicked man, is even now growing up in the village of Gokul on the other side of the Jamunā."

Kaṃsa's heart was filled with fear. He seethed with rage to see how he had been outwitted by the gods. With the counsel of his vicious ministers, the king ordered the slaughter of all the babies of Mathurā and its neighbourhood. Himself an incarnation of evil, he had in his employ many evil creatures whose cruelty stopped at nothing and who, it is said, could, like magicians, assume diverse forms to fulfil their diabolical purpose. Some of these emissaries came to Gokul to trap the child Kṛṣṇa; but they were all annihilated by Him in what seemed a playful mood. The villagers discovered, to their great delight and surprise, that the powerful demons were no match for Him.

Kṛṣṇa began to grow into a mischievous child. His charm was simply irresistible. The villagers never tired of watching Him. But His roguery was also without limit. The little pest would stealthily enter the homes of the cowherds and steal their cream, butter, and milk, and then entertain with all these His friends and His pet monkeys and birds. Though this sweet mischief delighted the hearts of the cowherd girls, still they were anxious lest he should grow into a thief. One day they complained to His mother, and she determined to punish the culprit. She procured a cord to bind Him, but found it was not long enough. She added more and more cord, but again and again found it insufficient to bind Kṛṣṇa. All at once she discovered that she was trying to bind with an ordinary cord the all-pervading and omnipresent Lord, who can be bound only with the cord of His devotees' love. She was dumbfounded and stood with folded hands before the Universal Form of Kṛṣṇa. Soon the vision passed and the Child laughingly submitted to her chastisement. Her heart overflowed with motherly love and she dismissed the miracle as mere fancy.

Another day Kṛṣṇa, in a playful mood, ate some earth. His angry mother made Him open His mouth, and saw there the whole universe, with the heavens, the earth, and the nether world. As she recoiled from this wondrous sight, Kṛṣṇa laughed and resumed His natural form.

And so the seasons passed. When Kṛṣṇa was seven or eight years old, Nanda and his cowherd friends moved to the forests of Vṛndāvan. Balarāma and Kṛṣṇa accompanied them and were allowed to go with the other lads to the pastures to tend the herds.

These were delightful years that Kṛṣṇa spent with the herd-boys and herd-girls of Gokul and Vṛndāvan in the forests and pastures and along the bank of the Jamunā. He was particularly fond of the herd-girls, called gopīs. He was their playfellow and special pet. Their mutual love was deep and intense, but singularly free from any worldly stain. Their love-episodes in the woods and dales and meadows of Vṛndāvan are still cherished by millions of Hindus and form an important part of India's mystical literature.

One of Kṛṣṇa's favourite pastimes was to play His flute. The music would draw the gopīs to the forest from their hearths and homes. To the Hindus Kṛṣṇa's flute-note signifies the call of the Absolute, God's summons to men to leave behind their earthly ties and attachments. Under the blossom-laden trees, and with the south wind blowing gently, Kṛṣṇa and His friends would put up swings and play all day long. Sometimes the girls would form a ring around a great tree and try to capture Kṛṣṇa as He went darting in and out under their arched arms. Even the beasts of the herd had for Him a special love, and the cows would gaze at Him or low happily when He caressed them. No eyes ever had enough of the exquisite beauty of Kṛṣṇa, the dark-blue form clad in a yellow robe, a garland of wild flowers hanging from His neck, and a peacock feather adorning His crest.

Kṛṣṇa's favourite spot was a kadamba tree on the bank of the Jamunā. Perched on a high branch, He would play His magic flute, and the spellbound girls would rush from home, the river would cease to flow, and nature would be hushed in silence. The joy of the gopīs and Kṛṣṇa would reach its climax in the vernal season on the night of the full moon, when the mango blossom filled the air with its fragrance, red flowers covered the aśoka tree, and the long, delicate buds of the leaf-almond were about to burst into tender green. All would play and swing and dance in a rhapsody of joy; the touch of Kṛṣṇa would transport their minds far away from the dual world and plunge them in divine ecstasy. Immediately they would experience God, the Embodiment of love and beauty.

The chief among the gopīs was Rādhikā, called Rādhā for short, who realized in the companionship of Kṛṣṇa the most intense sweetness. Her sorrow at her separation from Him was excruciating, but the yearning and longing of her heart reunited her with her Beloved, filling her mind with delight. To the Hindus, Rādhikā's ardent desire typifies the passionate love of the human soul for the ineffable Divine Spirit.

When Kṛṣṇa was twelve years old, all the attempts of Kaṃsa to destroy Him having failed, the vile king tried a ruse to bring his nephew to Mathurā in order to destroy Him. He arranged a royal sacrifice to be celebrated with appropriate games and feats of strength. Invitations to attend the festival were sent to Kṛṣṇa and Balarāma and they accepted.

The chief event on the program was a tournament. The galleries and seats were occupied by the nobles, officers, invited guests, holy men, humble folk, and the cowherd boys and girls of Mathurā and Vṛndāvan. They sat according to their social position, and Kaṃsa, seated on his high throne in the middle, dominated the whole scene.

Kṛṣṇa entered the arena accompanied by Balarāma, both attired according to their true rank, like noblemen to be presented to the court. They were very handsome and all eyes were fixed on them. And how various were the emotions evoked at that moment by the sight of Kṛṣṇa! The mighty wrestlers saw in Him a death-dealing thunderbolt. Women saw the god of love. The sages saw the Supreme Lord. The common people saw simply a great man. Nanda and his friends saw the beloved Cowherd of Vṛndāvan. Vāsudeva and Devakī saw their loving child, born on a stormy night twelve long years before. And Kaṃsa trembled on his seat to see before him his own inescapable doom.

After the first flurry of excitement, the chief of the court wrestlers came forward and challenged Kṛṣṇa and Balarāma to a mock contest for the entertainment of the spectators. But the bout was only a pretext; for the wrestler had been instructed. to kill Kṛṣṇa at an appropriate moment. Kṛṣṇa discovered the trap. He manifested superhuman strength and killed the court wrestler as if in mere play. Whereupon Kaṃsa sprang to his feet and fell upon Kṛṣṇa. In the twinkling of an eye Kaṃsa lay dead on the ground.

As the whole assembly was quaking with consternation at the death of the mighty Kaṃsa, Kṛṣṇa and Balarāma walked calmly to their parents and reverently saluted them. Devakī and Vāsudeva saw in Kṛṣṇa the Lord Himself and began to worship Him. But the inscrutable māyā covered their eyes with a veil, and they were overjoyed to be united with Kṛṣṇa and Balarāma whom they had not seen since their births.

Kṛṣṇa never returned to Vṛndāvan. He felt the call of a new mission. The complex national life of India summoned Him to new activities. After slaying Kaṃsa He gave the kingdom to Kaṃsa's father, Ugrasena. Soon after, He founded the city of Dwārakā, on the sea-coast of Gujrat, and placed it, with the surrounding kingdom, in the hands of His kinsmen, the Vṛṣṇis.

From now on He dwelt in palaces of kings and princes. The sweet episode of Vṛndāvan was tucked away in a niche of His mind as a pleasant dream. He promised the heartbroken and wailing gopīs that He would reveal Himself in their hearts whenever they longed to see Him; but it would be only a revelation of His Spirit-form.

Though Kṛṣṇa became the adviser of kings and princes in matters of diplomacy, war, and statecraft, He occupied no throne Himself. He would create or conquer kingdoms but then give them over to others. Everybody noticed that, though intensely busy with the affairs of the world, He never identified Himself with any action. He was always a detached witness of events. He showed utter impassivity in the midst of a whirlwind of activity. On the highways of the world He moved, taking interest in every event, great or small, yet was never stained by worldliness. Though His hands and feet were ever busy in the world, yet His mind seemed to be fastened upon something not of this world. He looked on the world and its movement as a dream unfolding at the bidding of a Higher Will and regarded Himself as a mere spectator. Even while mingling with kings, He never actually interfered with their work. He did not impose His will upon others. His very presence would reveal what was right and what was wrong, but He would leave it to the individual to decide what he should do. Sometimes, at most, He would remove an obstacle so that the will of man might have unimpeded play. Thus He permitted events to take their own shape. and strove always to aid the course of destiny, even though destiny might lead in the end to the self-destruction of all things.

Now, when Kṛṣṇa had given the five Pāṇḍava brothers His blessing on the occasion of their marriage to Draupadī, they, strengthened by their new friendship with the Divine Youth and the matrimonial alliance with King Drupada, at last came out of hiding. Dhṛtarāṣṭra was told of their reappearance and, at the insistence of Bhīṣma agreed to give them half their kingdom, but stipulated that the other half should be set aside for his own sons. With the advice of Kṛṣṇa and the indefatigable labours of his brothers, King Yudhiṣṭhira laid the foundations of his new capital at Indraprastha, adjacent to modern Delhi. The foundations of the city were so soundly constructed that even today, after ages, its walls are shown to visitors; and its site was so well chosen that India's imperial capital has ever since been either that city itself or a place near by.

The new kingdom was administered with remarkable efficiency. There was no misery in the kingdom; peace and prosperity were visible everywhere. Kṛṣṇa became the close friend and adviser of the Pāṇḍava brothers. He and Arjuna became almost inseparable companions. In all affairs of state Yudhiṣṭhira consulted Kṛṣṇa.

Under the management of Kṛṣṇa the coronation ceremony of Yudhiṣṭhira was celebrated with great pomp. India's kings and princes participated in it. The happy event came to a termination with the performance of the rājasūya sacrifice, in which many princes acknowledged the lordship of Yudhiṣṭhira.

King Duryodhana and his brothers attended the festival. He was smitten with jealousy at the splendour of the new kingdom and the honour shown to his royal cousin. He resolved to bring about the destruction of the Pāṇḍavas and found an able accomplice in his uncle Śakuni. This man, sly as a fox, was a brother of Duryodhana's mother and a gambler very skillful with the dice.

King Yudhiṣṭhira, for all his noble qualities, had one weakness. He could not refuse a game of dice when challenged. It was to him a challenge to battle; true kṣatriya knight that he was, he could never decline. Duryodhana, counselled by Śakuni, prevailed upon his blind father to invite Yudhiṣṭhira to a game of dice. Yudhiṣṭhira knew that he gambled badly; furthermore, as a game would approach its height, he would completely lose his head and bet wildly. Therefore he always tried to avoid outright challenges to play. This time, however, he was summoned by his elder, and his chivalrous nature could not refuse the invitation. He saw bad omens and felt certain premonitions regarding the outcome of the game. He declared as he set forth with his brothers and wife: "I think it is the call of fate. Who is man to fight against destiny?"

The Pāṇḍava brothers and their wife were royally received by Duryodhana. Soon the fateful game began. King Dhṛtarāṣṭra Bhīṣma Droṇa, Karṇa, and the whole court, besides Duryodhana and his brothers, were the spectators. Yudhiṣṭhira was to play with Śakuni, and Duryodhana had promised to pay the stakes that the latter might lose.

The dice were loaded. From the very beginning Yudhiṣṭhira began to lose. and Śakuni to win. Yet each time he lost, the king shouted for higher stakes. Thus were lost his jewels and royal treasures, lost the wardrobes and precious banners, lost the royal stables and chariots, and lost even the weapons with which he had fought on the battle-field, and finally his kingdom itself. The king was now nearly insane and beyond all reasoning. At a critical moment of the play he staked his brothers, himself, and their wife—and lost!

Duryodhana's jubilation knew no bounds. He ordered one of his brothers to bring the wife, Draupadī, to court. She was dragged there by the hair. She was informed that thenceforward she would be a slave of Duryodhana and must obey all his commands. To make her humiliation complete, an attempt was made to snatch away her clothes; but she called on Kṛṣṇa, the Protector of His devotees in the hour of their shame, and behold! the scarf and veil that were snatched from her body were miraculously replaced, and the queen was not for a moment disrobed. The elders shuddered at this humiliation of womanhood. King Dhṛtarāṣṭra trembled with fear and begged Draupadī to ask of him three boons to allay her wrath.

For the first boon she asked the freedom of Yudhiṣṭhira, and for the second, the freedom of the four other brothers with all their weapons. When asked about the third boon, she flung back with pride and scorn: "Nay, I ask no more! The Pāṇḍavas, being free, can right themselves—they need owe no man anything!"

The Pāṇḍavas were now free to return to their own kingdom. But the wily Duryodhana, finding his purpose unaccomplished, persuaded the blind and weak king to invite Yudhiṣṭhira for another game of dice. Dhṛtaraṣṭra again sent an invitation to Yudhiṣṭhira, who could not refuse it, since to him it was a point of honour. This time the stake was that the loser should retire into the forest for twelve years, to lead the austere life of a hermit, and pass the thirteenth year unrecognized in some city, or, if recognized, pass another twelve years in the forest as forfeit. The dice were thrown and Yudhiṣṭhira of course lost again. The Pāṇḍava brothers, with their wife, made ready to go into the forest. They took leave of the elders, who were sad to see them go. They saluted the blind king, who assured them, "If Duryodhana fails to discover your hiding-place, then, on the day that ends the thirteenth year, you will return to your home and your kingdom as free men and princes, precisely as when you came to this place to play dice."

Duryodhana showed his irritation at this uncalled for generosity of his father; but the pledge had been given by the king and could not be taken back. The five brothers and Draupadī went into exile.

During their twelve years in the forest the Pāṇḍavas lived as hermits. They practised austerities, mingled with holy men, and received from them spiritual enlightenment. The tedium of their wandering life was mitigated by the loyal devotion of Draupadī and the indissoluble bond of friendship among the brothers themselves. During this period Kṛṣṇa and Arjuna spent a great deal of time together, discussing God, the soul, and the hereafter. The thirteenth year of their exile was spent in a city, where the five brothers worked as menials of King Virāṭa. This critical year passed without their being recognized.

When the period of exile was over, a delicate situation arose. For thirteen years Duryodhana had enjoyed unrivalled lordship of northern India. He had consolidated his position by forming alliances with many kings. He controlled the army and the treasury. And the five brothers were practically beggars when they returned from the forest. Naturally Duryodhana was loath to part with his ill-gotten power and possessions. The elders, however, wanted a peaceful settlement between the Pāṇḍavas and the Kauravas. The restoration of their legitimate kingdom to the five sons of Pāṇḍu was the minimum demand of justice. And Yudhiṣṭhira was willing to make peace on these terms, forgiving and forgetting all the insults inflicted by Duryodhana on him, his brothers, and their wife. Bhīṣma and Droṇa wholeheartedly supported this policy of reconciliation, and everyone emphasized the evils of a fratricidal war. Kṛṣṇa, too, strongly urged Duryodhana to return to Yudhiṣṭhira his rightful kingdom. The plighted word of King Dhṛtarāṣṭra on the eve of the Pāṇḍavas' departure was recalled. Duryodhana had no just claim in denying the Pāṇḍavas their legitimate kingdom.

To all the requests of the elders and the wise, the wicked prince gave only one reply. In his opinion Yudhiṣṭhira had lost his kingdom in an honourable game as though he had lost it on the battle-field. The whole country now belonged to Duryodhana alone, and he was capable of defending it. In case he died on the battle-field, defending his own rights, he would go straightway to heaven. In his view the ancestral kingdom could be enjoyed either by the Pāṇḍavas or by the Kauravas, but never by both. One party must live like beggars; both could not rule at the same time—To Kṛṣṇa's repeated requests to concede half the kingdom, or five villages at the least, Duryodhana stubbornly replied that he would not relinquish even as much land as could be lifted on the point of a needle.

Nothing more could be said. War became inevitable. Destiny must be fulfilled. The wicked counsellors of Duryodhana were jubilant, for they were certain of the annihilation of the Pāṇḍavas. The wise, however, had not the slightest doubt that in the end righteousness would triumph; and they knew, too, which side was righteous.

The Pāṇḍavas and the Kauravas appealed to their friends and relatives to support them in what each described as a just war. To this appeal in the name of knighthood all the kings and princes responded. Feverish preparations were in progress.

Kṛṣṇa was the natural friend and ally of Arjuna; but Duryodhana, too, coveted His friendship. Both went to Kṛṣṇa's palace to seek His help, and were told that He was asleep. Duryodhana entered the bedroom and sat on a high stool near Kṛṣṇa's head. Arjuna followed and sat in a humble manner at Kṛṣṇa's feet. They awaited His awakening from sleep. As Kṛṣṇa opened His eyes, His glance fell on Arjuna. Duryodhana declared that he had entered the bedchamber first and therefore had the first claim on Kṛṣṇa's friendship. Kṛṣṇa said, with a smile, that He had seen Arjuna first. But He did not want to disappoint either of them and had in His mind two proposals. He could give to one party His own picked soldiers, tens of thousands in number, fully armed and equipped. To the other He could promise His own mere presence, being Himself unarmed and resolved not to fight. Under no condition, He said, would He handle a weapon in this war or take any active part in it. The rival cousins were asked to make their choice. He had foreseen that Duryodhana, blinded by greed and lust, would never seek the presence of the Divine Kṛṣṇa. Arjuna, in a voice choked with emotion, asked for His presence near him as his unarmed charioteer, and Duryodhana, on his part, was delighted to avail himself of the service of His brave fighting-men. Asked by Kṛṣṇa why he was satisfied with His useless presence, Arjuna said: "I know that You alone are able to kill all our enemies. But I myself want to destroy the forces of evil and earn the glory. So I accepted You and not your battalions. It is my desire that You remain always with me as my charioteer."

Yudhiṣṭhira could not easily reconcile himself to this war among brothers. But Kṛṣṇa said to him: "I have tried My utmost to establish peace, but I have not succeeded. Duryodhana is under the power of unrighteousness. People will not blame you for this war; you are guiltless before God and dharma."

King Dhṛtarāṣṭra accepted the decision of his sons to fight as the unalterable decree of destiny. He saw that before God's will human power was futile.

Both Bhīṣma and Droṇa had been for many years in the service of King Dhṛtarāṣṭra, Karṇa, though a half-brother of the Pāṇḍavas, had been the recipient of many favours from Duryodhana. Further, he bore a grudge against Arjuna, because the two were almost peers in the military arts. Thus, at the call of duty and honour, these three great warriors espoused the side of Duryodhana, though to the insight of Bhīṣma and Droṇa the outcome of the battle could not have remained hidden.

At last the fateful day arrived. Both sides assembled on the historic plain of Kurukṣetra, hallowed from time out of mind by many religious sacrifices and selected again and again, in the subsequent history of India, as a battle-field for the control of the political destiny of the country. Bhīṣma became the generalissimo of Duryodhana, and Dhṛṣṭadyumna commanded the Pāṇḍava army. The military leaders, according to their rank and position, mounted chariots or elephants or horses. Each warrior waved his pennon carrying his own cognizance. Everyone was equipped with his own favourite weapon—a bow or a sword or a club—and each carried in his hand a conch-shell with which he sounded the call to battle. The mighty armies drawn up against each other were like two vast oceans of human heads.

King Dhṛtarāṣṭra wanted to be informed of the events on the battle-field. The blind king was offered special sight by the sage Vyāsa; but he refused the boon, for he knew that the deaths of his near and dear ones would be more than he could bear. Therefore Sañjaya acted as his reporter. Since the battle-field was too vast for any mortal eye and too complex for any human mind, Sañjaya was given supernatural vision, by a boon of Vyāsa, to see and hear all that happened there.

It was indeed a wondrous sight. The best of India's manhood was there. Banners of various hues waved in the wind. The garments of the combatants were colourful and variegated. The sound of conchs and drums was like a tempest sweeping over the forests or a tidal-wave in the ocean. The trumpeting of elephants, the neighing of horses, the blare of trumpets and clash of cymbals, created a tumult too great for human ears. The warriors had staked their lives to win victory for their respective sides. And who were these warriors? In happier days they had been friends, comrades, and playfellows. Now confronted each other youths who were as brothers, and elders venerated by all for their age and wisdom.

As the combatants stood poised, Arjuna asked Kṛṣṇa to drive his chariot into the space between the armies—a sort of no-man's-land. Casting his eyes around him, he saw assembled the very flower of India's knighthood, those to whom he was bound by a thousand ties of love, respect, and affection. He must wade through their blood in order to regain the kingdom. Eyes swimming in tears and voice faltering, he said to Kṛṣṇa, his charioteer:

"O Kṛṣṇa, at the sight of these my kinsmen, assembled here eager to give battle, my limbs fail and my mouth is parched. My body is shaken and my hair stands on end. The bow Gāṇḍīva slips from my hand. and my skin is on fire. I cannot hold myself steady; my mind seems to whirl. O Keśava, I see omens of evil.

"Nor do I perceive, O Kṛṣṇa, any good in slaughtering my own people in battle. I desire neither victory nor empire nor even any pleasure . . . .

"These, O Madhusūdana, I would not kill, though they should kill me, even for the sake of sovereignty over the three worlds—how much less for this earth!"

Arjuna enumerated to Kṛṣṇa all the evils that befell society from war—perfect arguments used by pacifists even of modern times. He concluded:

"Far better would it be for me if the sons of Dhṛtarāṣṭra, weapons in hand, should slay me in the battle, unarmed and unresisting."

Kṛṣṇa instantly perceived Arjuna's temporary confusion, which any mortal might feel when faced with such an overwhelming situation. The Pāṇḍava warrior had forgotten where the path of duty lay. But Kṛṣṇa, great psychologist that He was, knew it was no time for platitudes. The depressed soul must be lashed into action. Striking Arjuna at his most sensitive point, the honour of a kṣatriya, Śrī Kṛṣṇa said:

> "In this crisis, O Arjuna, whence comes such lowness of spirit, unbecoming to an Āryan, dishonourable, and an obstacle to the attaining of heaven?"

The real cause of Arjuna's confusion was his ignorance—his lack of discrimination between the Real and the unreal, Spirit and matter, Soul and body. Such darkness of ignorance can be removed only by the light of knowledge. Śrī Kṛṣṇa instructed Arjuna about the nature of the Soul and the meaning of death:

> "Even as the embodied Self passes, in this body, through the stages of childhood, youth, and old age, so does It pass into another body. Calm souls are not bewildered by this.
>
> "The unreal never is. The Real never ceases to be. The conclusion about these two is truly perceived by the seers of Truth.
>
> "That by which all this is pervaded know to be imperishable. None can cause the destruction of that which is immutable.
>
> "Only the bodies, of which this eternal, imperishable, incomprehensible Self is the indweller, are said to have an end. Fight, therefore, O Bhārata.
>
> "He who looks on the Self as the slayer, and he who looks on the Self as the slain—neither of these apprehends aright. The Self slays not nor is slain.
>
> "It is never born, nor does It ever die, nor, having once been, does It again cease to be. Unborn, eternal, permanent, and primeval, It is not slain when the body is slain. . . .
>
> "Even as a person casts off worn-out clothes and puts on others that are new, so the embodied Self casts off worn-out bodies and enters into others that are new.
>
> "Weapons cut It not; fire burns It not; water wets It not; the wind does not wither It."

Kṛṣṇa explained to His royal disciple the meaning of action and non-action, the nature of the Godhead and Its manifestation, the different paths of liberation, and the way to the *summum bonum*.

Throughout the Bhagavad Gītā, Śrī Kṛṣṇa addresses Arjuna by different epithets, each one bearing a special meaning. The purpose of the Teacher is to remind Arjuna either of his royal lineage or noble ancestry or physical might or great power of self-control or the like. Thus Kṛṣṇa seeks to stir up noble feelings in the mind of His dejected disciple. Arjuna, too, while addressing Śrī Kṛṣṇa, uses different epithets associated with the spiritual nature of the Divine Teacher.

The setting of the magnificent dialogue could not have been more appropriate and sublime—a battle-field, where all are on the borderline between life and death and where one realizes the transitory nature even of the most cherished objects in the world. The moment could not have been more auspicious: Arjuna's mind was one-pointed, in view of the imminent crisis, and eager to know what lay beyond.

Even after three thousand years it is not difficult for a modern man to visualize Arjuna's chariot in that no-man's-land, his snow-white horses impatient to plunge into the fray, but restrained by the strong muscles of Kṛṣṇa's arm so that they are drawn back almost on their haunches; Arjuna, drooping and dejected, in bewilderment of spirit, supplicating the Divine Teacher to show him the path of duty; and Śrī Kṛṣṇa, with the forefinger of His free hand raised, His face calm, His eyes full of compassion, and His lips parted in a faint smile.

The great Master, the embodiment of His own teaching, says:

> "He who sees inaction in action, and action in inaction, he is wise among men, he is a yogi, and he has performed all action."

The Teacher goes on instructing Arjuna that the Lord alone is the Doer and the Master. All things, great and small, are done at His supreme command. Men are but instruments in His hands. It is futile to try to oppose His will. Life and death, good and evil, light and darkness, though opposed to each other on the relative plane, are synthesized in the Reality of the Godhead. Things are accomplished first in the foreordaining mind of the Lord, and then men are used as His instruments to demonstrate their accomplishment in the outside world. The combatants on the battle-field of Kurukṣetra have already been slain by the Lord to fulfil His divine purpose on earth; it is now Arjuna's duty, nay, his privilege, to be the Lord's instrument in the manifested world.

> "Therefore stand up and win glory; conquer your enemies and enjoy an opulent kingdom. By Me and none other have they already been slain; be an instrument only, O Arjuna."

The instruction is accompanied by an unprecedented revelation—the vision of the Lord's Universal Form, embodying all created beings, all pairs of opposites, all events of the past, present, and future. Such a staggering sight, including everything in one sweeping vision, can be seen only through the Lord's grace.

Arjuna's hesitation melts away. He springs to his feet fearlessly, sounds the war-cry of the Pāṇḍavas, and flings himself into the fortunes of battle; for when a man sees God, he feels strong to face the world and do his duty.

The dialogue between Kṛṣṇa and Arjuna, and the revelation of the Godhead—what Kṛṣṇa taught in a few moments and Arjuna saw in a flash—were expressed by the sage Vyāsa in seven hundred verses, entitled the Śrīmad Bhagavad Gītā, the Song of the Blessed One.

Then followed a terrible slaughter. No quarter was asked and none given. The heroes of both sides fell one by one. After eighteen days of unceasing battle Duryodhana was killed by Bhīma's club. The war ended with the victory of the five brothers, although they too lost their friends, relatives, and children.

When the dead, once bejewelled kings and princes, lay mangled on the battle-field, covered with dust, there approached the procession of royal women of the Kurus, with Gāndhārī as their leader, to identify their husbands, children, and relatives. Their cries were lifted to the sky. They were accompanied by the Pāṇḍava brothers and Śrī Kṛṣṇa. At the sight of her dead sons, one hundred in number, Gāndhārī's grief knew no bounds. Bitterly she cursed Kṛṣṇa:

> "Two armies, O Kṛṣṇa, have been consumed. Whilst they thus put an end to one another, why were Thine eyes closed? Thou who couldst have done either well or ill, as pleased Thee—why hast Thou allowed this evil to come upon all? I shall now, in virtue of the truth and purity of womanhood, pronounce Thy doom. Thou, O Kṛṣṇa, because of Thine indifference to the Kurus and the Pāṇḍavas whilst they killed one another, shalt Thyself become the slayer of Thine own kinsmen. In the thirty-sixth year from now, O Kṛṣṇa, having brought about the destruction of Thy sons and kindred, Thou shalt Thyself perish by woeful means, alone in the wilderness. And the women of Thy race, deprived of sons, kindred, and friends, shall weep in their desolation as do now these women on the battle-field of Kurukṣetra!"

When she had finished her imprecations, Kṛṣṇa said with a smile:

"May all blessings fall upon you, O Gāndhārī, in thus aiding Me in the ending of My task. Verily are My people, the Vṛṣṇis, incapable of defeat. Therefore must they needs die by the hands of one another. Behold, O Queen, I accept your curse."

"Arise, awake, O Gāndhārī," Kṛṣṇa went on, "and set not your heart on grief. By indulging in sorrow man increases it twofold. Remember, O My daughter, that the brāhmin woman bears children for the practice of austerity, the cow brings forth offspring for the bearing of burdens, the labouring woman adds, by child-bearing, to the ranks of the workers, but those of royal blood are destined from their birth to die in battle."

Queen Gāndhārī listened to these words in silence and realized that they were true. The great events happening before her very eyes had purified her mind, and she found that everything in the material universe is unreal. In this world there is a Will higher than man's, and it must be fulfilled. Through pleasure and pain, grief and sorrow, the Lord chastens man's spirit and helps him to attain illumination. She and Dhṛtarāṣṭra restrained their grief and, accompanied by the Pāṇḍavas, went to the Ganges to perform the last rites for the dead.

King Yudhiṣṭhira ascended the throne and ruled his subjects for thirty-six years, justifying his appellation, the "embodiment of righteousness." The people had never been happier. His rule was based on dharma. Soon the country recovered from the ravages of war, and prosperity was seen on all sides. For the first fifteen years of his reign Yudhiṣṭhira regarded himself as the viceroy of Dhṛtarāṣṭra Then the blind king withdrew into the forest, accompanied by Gāndhārī, and both lived as ascetics, absorbed till the last moment of their lives in contemplation of God.

Now the time arrived for the fulfilment of Gāndhārī's curse on Kṛṣṇa and His relatives. A civil war broke out in Dwārakā. The members of the Vṛṣṇi clan fell upon one another and perished. Kṛṣṇa looked on as a detached witness, seeing in all the fulfilment of destiny. He sent word to the Pāṇḍavas to come to Dwārakā and take charge of the women and the old. Then He beheld Balarāma give up his body. Realizing that the time of His departure was near at hand, He restrained His mind and senses in yoga and lay down on the bare earth under a tree. He was thus rapt in Self-communion when a hunter, seeing the red soles of His feet from a distance, thought that a deer lay crouching there and aimed an arrow, which struck the Lord in the heel. As the hunter drew near, he realized his mistake and was beside himself with grief. Kṛṣṇa blessed him with a smile and soon thereafter gave up His body.

Arjuna arrived in Dwārakā but found complete desolation reigning in that once prosperous place. Mournfully he conducted thence the kinsmen of Kṛṣṇa, the women and the old who had survived. On the road a band of warriors fell upon the miserable company and carried away a large number of the women. Arjuna could not muster strength to lift his mighty bow Gāṇḍīva with which he had slain many demons and powerful warriors. It became apparent to him that with the passing away of Kṛṣṇa his own strength, too, had gone.

The five royal heroes now came to realize that the time of their end had arrived. They chose a grandson of Arjuna, Parikshit by name, as the successor to the throne, and set forth on their last solemn journey. Their aim was to climb the Himalayas and reach heaven. Queen Draupadī and a dog joined the procession. For their last act of royal grace, they circumambulated their kingdom and then proceeded toward the Himalayas. As they climbed the lofty mountains, peak by peak, Draupadī, the twins Nakula and Sahadeva, the mighty Arjuna, and Bhīma, one by one, fainted, fell by the roadside, and died. But Yudhiṣṭhira did not flinch or look back or utter a groan or sigh. The faithful dog was by his side.

As he ascended the topmost peak, Indra, king of heaven, arrived with his chariot to escort the pious king to the celestial realm among the stars. After the first greeting Yudhiṣṭhira inquired about his brothers and wife and was assured that they had preceded him to heaven. They could not go to heaven in their mortal bodies because each one had committed a sin while on earth. Thus assured, the king stepped aside to let the dog climb into the chariot first. But Indra objected. It was absurd that an unclean animal should enter the abode of the gods. He begged Yudhiṣṭhira to send the dog away. But the king refused to get into the chariot alone. His personal pride and honour were involved. The dog had been his loyal and devoted friend the whole course of the journey. Even while on earth the king had never failed to give shelter to one who sought it. The dog with wistful eyes looked on. No, even the happiness of heaven would be gall to him should he have to remember that he had cast away a true friend.

Yudhiṣṭhira stood at the portal of heaven, resolved not to enter it alone. And lo, in the twinkling of an eye, the dog was transformed into a shining deity, Dharma Himself, the god of righteousness. The king came through the final ordeal triumphant. As he walked into heaven he experienced, for a brief moment, a vision of hell in punishment for an equivocal sentence he had uttered, in a critical hour, on the battle-field of Kurukṣetra. Then the pious king, first among mortals, entered heaven in a human body.

INTRODUCTION BY ŚAṄKARĀCĀRYA

Om. *Nārāyaṇa*[1] *is beyond the Unmanifest;*[2] *the Golden Egg*[3] *is produced from the Unmanifest. The earth*[4] *with its seven islands, and all other worlds, are in the Egg.*

The Lord created the earth and desired its continuance. With that aim He first created the Prajāpatis[5]*—Marīci and the rest—and taught them the dharma characterized by pravṛtti, or activity,*[6] *as described in the Vedas. He then created others—Sanaka, Sanandana, and the rest*[7]*—and taught them the dharma of nivṛtti, or renunciation, characterized by knowledge and dispassion.*

Of two kinds is the dharma dealt with in the Vedas: the one characterized by activity and the other by renunciation. This twofold dharma, the cause of the stability of the world order and also the

---

1 An epithet of the Supreme Lord, on account of His lying on the waters (nārā) of the Great Cause before the beginning of a cycle.

2 The first manifestation of the Absolute conditioned by māyā. In this state the names and forms of the relative universe are not evolved but remain in latent form, like the future tree in a seed.

3 In this state of manifestation the five subtle elements of matter are evolved.

4 The earth and other material objects consist of the five gross elements of matter, which are formed by a particular combination of the five subtle elements. *See* note on VII, 4.

5 *Lit.*, lords of created beings.

6 The purpose of which is the attainment of worldly well-being.

7 From their very birth they were without desire or passion. They could not be persuaded to perpetuate the creation by begetting children.

direct means by which men attain prosperity and the Highest Good,[1] *was followed by members of the different castes—the brāhmin, kṣatriya, and the rest—and of the different āśramas,*[2] *desirous to secure their welfare.*

People practised the Vedic dharma for a long time. Then lust arose among them; discrimination and wisdom declined. Unrighteousness began to outweigh righteousness. Thus, when unrighteousness prevailed in the world, Viṣṇu,[3] *the First Creator, also known as Nārāyaṇa, wishing to ensure the continuance of the universe, incarnated Himself, in part,*[4] *as Kṛṣṇa. He was born to Devakī and Vāsudeva for the protection of the brāhmins on earth and their spiritual ideal. By the protection of the brāhmin ideal the dharma of the Vedas is preserved,*[5] *since all the, different castes and āśramas are under its control.*

The Lord, the eternal Possessor of Knowledge, Sovereignty, Power, Strength, Energy, and Vigour, brings under His control māyā—belonging to Him[6] *as Viṣṇu—the primordial Nature, characterized by the three guṇas. And then, through that māyā, He is seen as though born, as though endowed with a body, and as though showing compassion to men; for He is; in reality, unborn, unchanging, the Lord of all created beings, and by nature eternal, pure, illumined, and free.*

Though the Lord had no purpose of His own to serve, yet, with the sole desire of bestowing favour on men, He taught this twofold Vedic dharma to Arjuna, who was deeply sunk in the ocean of grief and delusion; for a dharma spreads and grows when accepted by high-minded persons.

---

1 Liberation.

2 The āśramas denote the four stages of life, namely, the stage as a religious student practising austerity, the stage as a householder, the stage as a contemplative, when husband and wife retire from active life, and the stage as a saṃnyāsī, or monk.

3 *Lit.*, the All-pervading Spirit; the Lord.

4 In an illusory form created by His own will.

5 The brāhmins explain the Vedas and officiate as priests in the sacrifices.

6 Māyā cannot exist or act independently of Brahman. It is an inscrutable power inhering in Brahman. Though the Lord creates the universe, with the help of māyā, yet He is not under its control. The ordinary living being is under the control of māyā.

It is this dharma taught by the Lord that the omniscient and venerable Vyāsa, the compiler of the Vedas, embodied in seven hundred verses under the name of the Gītā.

This scripture, the Gītā, is a compendium of the essential teachings of the whole of the Vedas; its meaning is extremely difficult to grasp. Many commentators, desiring to present a clear idea of that meaning, have explained the words, and the meaning of the words and of the sentences, and also the arguments. But I find that, to people of ordinary understanding, these explanations convey diverse and contradictory meanings. Therefore I intend to write a brief commentary on the Gītā, with a view to determining precisely what it signifies.

The ultimate aim of the Gītā is, in a word, the attainment of the Highest Good, characterized by the complete cessation of relative existence and its cause. This is realized by means of that dharma whose essence is devotion to Self-knowledge attained through the renunciation of all action. With reference to this dharma laid down in the Gītā, the Lord says in the Anugītā:

> *"That dharma is quite sufficient for the Knowledge of Brahman." (Mahābhārata, Chapter on the Aśvamedha, xvi, 12)*

In the same treatise it is said:

> *"He is without righteousness and without unrighteousness—he who is absorbed in the one Goal, silent, and without thinking."*

> *"Knowledge is characterized by renunciation."*

In the concluding chapter of the Bhagavad Gītā, Śrī Kṛṣṇa says to Arjuna:

> *"Abandon all dharmas and come to Me alone for shelter." (XVIII, 66)*

The dharma characterized by activity and prescribed for the different castes and āśramas is, no doubt, a means of securing worldly welfare and also of attaining the regions of the gods; but when it is practised in a spirit of complete self-surrender to the Lord, and without desire for fruit, it leads to the purification of the mind. A man of pure mind becomes fit to acquire devotion to the path of knowledge and attains Knowledge. Thus, by means of the dharma of activity, one ultimately realizes the Highest Good. With this view in mind the Lord says in the Gītā:

> *"He who works without attachment, resigning his actions to Brahman." (V, 10)*

> *"The yogis act, without attachment, for the purification of the heart." (V, 11)*

The purpose[1] *of the twofold dharma described in the Gītā is the attainment of the Highest Good. The subject-matter of the treatise is Supreme Reality, known as Vāsudeva the Ultimate Brahman. It expounds both in a special manner. Thus the Gītā treats of a specific subject, with a specific end in view, and there is a specific relation between the subject-matter and the object.*

Knowledge of the Gītā enables one to attain the goal of all human aspiration. Hence my attempt to explain its teachings.

---

1 A Vedantic treatise must contain, at the very outset, a statement of the following: the subject-matter of the book, its object or purpose, the relationship of the book to the subject-matter and the object, and the qualifications of those who may hope to study it. The subject-matter of the Gītā is Brahman, and the object is mokṣa, or liberation. It is related to the subject-matter as the exposition thereof and to the object as the means of attaining it. The four qualifications of the student are: discrimination between the Real and the unreal; renunciation of the unreal; cultivation of the six virtues, consisting of control of the senses and of the mind, forbearance, withdrawal of the mind from external objects, faith, and one-pointedness of the mind; and the desire for liberation.

MEDITATION

Om. O Bhagavad Gītā, it was through Thy help that Nārāyaṇa, the Lord Himself, brought enlightenment to Arjuna. Afterwards Vyāsa, a sage of ancient times, incorporated Thee in the Mahābhārata. O Goddess, through Thy eighteen chapters Thou showerest the immortal nectar of the wisdom of Non-duality and destroyest man's rebirth in this mortal world. O Mother, I meditate on Thee.

I salute you, O Vyāsa, the possessor of great wisdom. Your beautiful eyes are large as the petals of a full-blown lotus. You have lighted the lamp of Knowledge, filling it with the oil of the Mahābhārata.

I salute Thee, O Kṛṣṇa! Thou art the Wish-fulfilling Tree for those who take refuge at Thy feet. Thy one hand holds a staff for driving cows, and the other is raised—the thumb touching the tip of the forefinger—as imparting the Divine Knowledge. Thou art the Milker of the ambrosia of the Gītā.

The Upaniṣads are as a herd of cows; Kṛṣṇa, the Son of a cowherd, is their Milker. Arjuna is the calf, the supreme ambrosia of the Gītā the milk, and the wise man the drinker.

I salute Thee, O Divine Kṛṣṇa, Teacher of the universe! Thou art the Son of Vāsudeva the Giver of supreme delight to Mother Devakī and the Destroyer of the demons Kaṃsa and Cāṇūra.

With the help of Kṛṣṇa the five sons of Pāṇḍu emerged victorious from the battle of Kurukṣetra. He acted as the Ferryman on the terrifying river of the battle-field, of which Bhīṣma and Droṇa formed the high banks, Jayadratha the water, the king of Gāndhāra the blue lotus, Śalya the shark, Kṛpa the current, Karṇa the breakers,

Aśvatthāmā and Vikarṇa the alligators, and Duryodhana the whirlpool.

May the impeccable lotus of the Mahābhārata, which grows in the water of Vyāsa's words and destroys the sins of the Kaliyuga; of which the Gītā forms the irresistible fragrance, and many noble tales of heroes the stamens; which is enlightened by discourse on the Lord Hari; and on which light, seeking its nectar, a swarm of black bees, the joyous men of piety—may that Mahābhārata bestow on us the Highest Good!

I salute Kṛṣṇa, the Embodiment of Supreme Bliss, through whose grace the mute become eloquent and the lame scale mountains.

I salute the Shining One, whose praise is sung in diverse hymns by Brahmā, Varuṇa, Indra, Rudra, and the Maruts; whose glories are proclaimed by the bards in the verses and chapters of the Vedas; whom the yogis see when their minds are absorbed in contemplation; and whose limit is not known by the hosts of gods or demons.

ŚRĪMAD BHAGVAD GĪTĀ

CHAPTER 1

ARJUNA'S GRIEF

[अर्जुनविषादयोगः]

धृतराष्ट्र उवाच।

धर्मक्षेत्रे कुरुक्षेत्रे समवेता युयुत्सवः।
मामकाः पाण्डवाश्चैव किमकुर्वत सञ्जय॥ १॥

1. *Dhṛtarāṣṭra said:* 1. O Sañjaya, what did Pāṇḍu's sons and mine do when, desirous to fight, they assembled on the sacred plain of Kurukṣetra?

Pāṇḍu—Younger brother of Dhṛtarāṣṭra and father of the Pāṇḍavas: Yudhiṣṭhira, Bhīma, Arjuna, Nakula, and Sahadeva.

Mine—The hundred sons of Dhṛtarāṣṭra of whom the eldest was King Duryodhana; the antagonists of the Pāṇḍavas.

Sacred plain-Kurukṣetra is sacred to the Hindus because here, from very ancient times, holy men have practised spiritual disciplines. In and around Kurukṣetra lie battlefields where several times the fate of India has been decided and where, in obedience to their dharma, the kṣatriyas unsheathed their swords to protect the spiritual culture of their motherland.

Dhṛtarāṣṭra was born blind; hence he inquires of Sañjaya concerning the progress of the battle.

सञ्जय उवाच।

दृष्ट्वा तु पाण्डवानीकं व्यूढं दुर्योधनस्तदा।
आचार्यमुपसङ्गम्य राजा वचनमब्रवीत्॥ २॥

2. *Sañjaya said:* On seeing the Pāṇḍava army arrayed for battle, King Duryodhana went to his teacher and spoke these words:

Pāṇḍava army—The army of Pāṇḍu's sons.

Teacher—The military teacher of the royal children of Pāṇḍu and Dhṛtarāṣṭra is a brāhmin named Droṇa. Droṇa knows that King Duryodhana upholds an unrighteous cause, yet fights for him in obedience to his duty to the reigning king.

पश्यैतां पाण्डुपुत्राणामाचार्य महतीं चमूम्।
व्यूढां द्रुपदपुत्रेण तव शिष्येण धीमता॥ ३॥

3. O teacher, behold the great army of the sons of Pāṇḍu arrayed by your talented disciple, the son of Drupada.

Dhṛṣṭadyumna, the son of Drupada, is the official commander-in-chief of the Pāṇḍavas. Drupada is the father-in-law of the Pāṇḍava brothers.

अत्र शूरा महेष्वासा भीमार्जुनसमा युधि।
युयुधानो विराटश्च द्रुपदश्च महारथः॥ ४॥

धृष्टकेतुश्चेकितानः काशिराजश्च वीर्यवान्।
पुरुजित्कुन्तिभोजश्च शैब्यश्च नरपुङ्गवः॥ ५॥

युधामन्युश्च विक्रान्त उत्तमौजाश्च वीर्यवान्।
सौभद्रो द्रौपदेयाश्च सर्व एव महारथाः॥ ६॥

4-6. In that army are mighty archers and heroes, in battle equal to Bhīma and Arjuna: Yuyudhāna, Virāṭa, and Drupada, each a mahāratha;

Heroic Dhṛṣṭaketu, Cekitāna, and the king of Kāśī; Purujit, Kuntībhoja, and Śaivya, all the best of men;

Powerful Yudhāmanyu, brave Uttamaujā, Subhadra's son, and the sons of Draupadī—all mahārathās indeed.

Mahāratha—One able to fight single-handed ten thousand archers.

Draupadī—The wife of the five Pāṇḍava brothers.

अस्माकं तु विशिष्टा ये तान्निबोध द्विजोत्तम।
नायका मम सैन्यस्य संज्ञार्थं तान्ब्रवीमि ते॥ ७॥

7. O best of the twice-born, let me also recount to you the leaders of my own army, those distinguished amongst ourselves. I shall name them, that you may know them all:

Twice-born—The word "dvija" refers to men belonging to the three higher castes among the Hindus, whose second birth is said to take place when they are initiated into spiritual life with the investiture of the sacred thread. Here the word denotes only the brāhmins

भवान्भीष्मश्च कर्णश्च कृपश्च समितिञ्जयः।
अश्वत्थामा विकर्णश्च सौमदत्तिस्तथैव च॥८॥

8. Yourself and Bhīṣma and Karṇa; Kṛpa, who is ever victorious in war; Aśvatthāmā, Vikarṇa, Jayadratha, and Somadatta's son;

Aśvatthāmā is Droṇa's son.

अन्ये च बहवः शूरा मदर्थे त्यक्तजीविताः।
नानाशस्त्रप्रहरणाः सर्वे युद्धविशारदाः॥९॥

9. And many other heroes besides, armed with many weapons, each well skilled in battle, and all resolved to lay down their lives to serve my cause.

अपर्याप्तं तदस्माकं बलं भीष्माभिरक्षितम्।
पर्याप्तं त्विदमेतेषां बलं भीमाभिरक्षितम्॥१०॥

10. But this army of ours, protected by Bhīṣma is inadequate, and that army of theirs, protected by Bhīma, is adequate.

The verse is also interpreted to mean that the army under Bhīṣma is *unlimited*, whereas that under Bhīma is *limited.* Bhīṣma the grandsire of the sons of Pāṇḍu and of Dhṛtarāṣṭra has impartial love for them all and wishes the welfare of both sides. But Bhīma, the protector of the Pāṇḍava army, naturally wants the victory of his side alone. He can be expected to show more zeal in winning the battle, whereas Bhīṣma the protector of Duryodhana's army, is not especially eager to annihilate the opposing side. Hence Duryodhana's pessimistic note, as interpreted in the text. The army of Duryodhana exceeds, in actual numbers, the army of his opponents.

अयनेषु च सर्वेषु यथाभागमवस्थिताः।
भीष्ममेवाभिरक्षन्तु भवन्तः सर्व एव हि॥११॥

11. Now take your proper places in front of your marshalled troops and protect Bhīṣma alone.

No harm must befall Bhīṣma the commander-in-chief, from the enemy.

तस्य सञ्जनयन्हर्षं कुरुवृद्धः पितामहः ।
सिंहनादं विनद्योच्चैः शङ्खं दध्मौ प्रतापवान् ॥ १२ ॥

12. Bhīṣma the grandsire, the courageous, the oldest of the Kurus, gave forth a lion-roar and blew his conch, causing joy to Duryodhana.

Lion-roar—A common expression in Sanskrit for a triumphant, confident, or exulting declaration.

Droṇa coldly receives the words of Duryodhana, and Bhīṣma wants to whip up the enthusiasm of his king and grandson. The blowing of the conch, indicating a challenge, opens the fight. Thus Duryodhana's side becomes the aggressor, responsible for the battle.

ततः शङ्खाश्च भेर्यश्च पणवानकगोमुखाः ।
सहसैवाभ्यहन्यन्त स शब्दस्तुमुलोऽभवत् ॥ १३ ॥

13. Then conchs and kettle-drums, tabors and trumpets and cow-horns suddenly blared forth; and the sound was stupendous.

The noise arises on Duryodhana's side.

ततः श्वेतैर्हयैर्युक्ते महति स्यन्दने स्थितौ ।
माधवः पाण्डवश्चैव दिव्यौ शङ्खौ प्रदध्मतुः ॥ १४ ॥

14. Whereupon Mādhava and Pāṇḍava seated in their magnificent chariot yoked to white horses, also blew their celestial conchs.

Mādhava—A name of Kṛṣṇa.

Pāṇḍava—*Lit.*, son of Pāṇḍu the epithet here is applied to Arjuna.

Arjuna accepts the challenge of Duryodhana.

पाञ्चजन्यं हृषीकेशो देवदत्तं धनञ्जयः ।
पौण्ड्रं दध्मौ महाशङ्खं भीमकर्मा वृकोदरः ॥ १५ ॥

15. Hṛṣīkeśa blew His conch, the Pāñcajanya; Dhanañjaya, the Devadatta; and Vṛkodara, the doer of fearful deeds, blew his great conch, the Pauṇḍra.

Hṛṣīkeśa—*Lit.*, the Lord, or Director, of the senses; a name of Kṛṣṇa, the Godhead.

Dhanañjaya—A name of Arjuna, given in honour of his having subdued the kings of India and acquired their wealth. Vṛkodara—*Lit.*, one having the belly of a wolf; a name of Bhīma, given because of his enormous appetite.

अनन्तविजयं राजा कुन्तीपुत्रो युधिष्ठिरः।
नकुलः सहदेवश्च सुघोषमणिपुष्पकौ॥ १६॥

16. King Yudhiṣṭhira, the son of Kuntī, blew his conch, the Anantavijaya; and Nakula and Sahadeva blew the Sughoṣa and the Maṇipuṣpaka.

काश्यश्च परमेष्वासः शिखण्डी च महारथः।
धृष्टद्युम्नो विराटश्च सात्यकिश्चापराजितः॥ १७॥

द्रुपदो द्रौपदेयाश्च सर्वशः पृथिवीपते।
सौभद्रश्च महाबाहुः शङ्खान्दध्मुः पृथक्पृथक्॥ १८॥

17-18. The great archer, the king of Kāśī; the great warrior Śikhaṇḍī; Dhṛṣṭadyumna and Virāṭa; the unconquered Sātyaki;

Drupada, and the sons of Draupadī, and the mighty son of Subhadrā, O Lord of the Earth, each blew his own conch.

Son of Subhadrā—Abhimanyu; Subhadrā is Arjuna's wife.

Lord of the Earth—Dhṛtarāṣṭra

स घोषो धार्तराष्ट्राणां हृदयानि व्यदारयत्।
नभश्च पृथिवीं चैव तुमुलोऽभ्यनुनादयन्॥ १९॥

19. And that tumult, resounding through heaven and earth, rent the hearts of Dhṛtarāṣṭra's followers.

Verses 14-19 contain several hints by Sañjaya regarding the superiority of the Pāṇḍava army and the ultimate defeat of the sons of Dhṛtarāṣṭra

अथ व्यवस्थितान्दृष्ट्वा धार्तराष्ट्रान् कपिध्वजः।
प्रवृत्ते शस्त्रसम्पाते धनुरुद्यम्य पाण्डवः॥ २०॥

हृषीकेशं तदा वाक्यमिदमाह महीपते।

अर्जुन उवाच।
सेनयोरुभयोर्मध्ये रथं स्थापय मेऽच्युत॥२१॥

यावदेतान्निरीक्षेऽहं योद्धुकामानवस्थितान्।
कैर्मया सह योद्धव्यमस्मिन् रणसमुद्यमे॥२२॥

20-22. Then, O Lord of the Earth, seeing Dhṛtarāṣṭra's army standing in battle array and the clash of arms about to begin, Arjuna, whose ensign bore the device of a monkey, spoke as follows to Kṛṣṇa:

Arjuna said: O Acyuta, between the two armies. draw up my chariot, that I may behold those who stand there eager to fight, and may know, on the eve of battle, with whom I must contend.

Acyuta—*Lit.*, the Changeless One; an epithet of Kṛṣṇa.

योत्स्यमानानवेक्षेऽहं य एतेऽत्र समागताः।
धार्तराष्ट्रस्य दुर्बुद्धेर्युद्धे प्रियचिकीर्षवः॥२३॥

23. I would observe those who are gathered here to fight, desiring on the field of battle the welfare of the evil-minded son of Dhṛtarāṣṭra

सञ्जय उवाच।
एवमुक्तो हृषीकेशो गुडाकेशेन भारत।
सेनयोरुभयोर्मध्ये स्थापयित्वा रथोत्तमम्॥२४॥

भीष्मद्रोणप्रमुखतः सर्वेषां च महीक्षिताम्।
उवाच पार्थ पश्यैतान्समवेतान्कुरूनिति॥२५॥

24-25. *Sañjaya said:* O Bharata, thus addressed by Guḍākeśa, Kṛṣṇa drew up the excellent chariot between the two armies, facing Bhīṣma, Droṇa, and all the rulers of the earth, and said, "Behold, O Pārtha, all the Kurus here assembled !"

Bharata—*Lit.*, a descendant of Bharata; here it refers to Dhṛtarāṣṭra

Guḍākeśa—*Lit.*, one who has controlled sleep; an epithet of Arjuna.

Pārtha—*Lit.*, the son of Pṛthā; an epithet of Arjuna,

तत्रापश्यत्स्थितान्पार्थः पितृनथ पितामहान्।
आचार्यान्मातुलान्भ्रातृन्पुत्रान्पौत्रान्सखींस्तथा॥२६॥

26. Then Pārtha saw, arrayed in both the armies, fathers and grandfathers, maternal uncles and brothers, sons and grandsons, comrades and friends, fathers-in-law and teachers.

Fathers—Uncles, revered as fathers.

The leaders of the two armies are first cousins; therefore Arjuna sees on both sides kinsmen and relatives united by bonds of blood and love.

श्वशुरान्सुहृदश्चैव सेनयोरुभयोरपि।
तान्समीक्ष्य स कौन्तेयः सर्वान्बन्धूनवस्थितान्॥ २७॥

27. Casting his eyes on all these kinsmen stationed on opposing sides, the son of Kuntī was overcome with deep pity and sorrowfully spoke.

Kuntī—Arjuna's mother.

कृपया परयाविष्टो विषीदन्निदमब्रवीत्।

अर्जुन उवाच।
दृष्ट्वेमं स्वजनं कृष्ण युयुत्सुं समुपस्थितम्॥ २८॥

सीदन्ति मम गात्राणि मुखं च परिशुष्यति।
वेपथुश्च शरीरे मे रोमहर्षश्च जायते॥ २९॥

गाण्डीवं स्रंसते हस्तात्त्वक्चैव परिदह्यते।
न च शक्नोम्यवस्थातुं भ्रमतीव च मे मनः॥ ३०॥

28-30. *Arjuna said:* O Kṛṣṇa, at the sight of these my kinsmen, assembled here eager to give battle, my limbs fail and my mouth is parched. My body is shaken. and my hair stands on end. The bow Gāṇḍīva slips from my hand and my skin is on fire. I cannot hold myself steady; my mind seems to whirl. O Keśava, I see omens of evil.

Gāṇḍīva—The mighty bow of Arjuna.

Keśava—An epithet of Kṛṣṇa.

निमित्तानि च पश्यामि विपरीतानि केशव।
न च श्रेयोऽनुपश्यामि हत्वा स्वजनमाहवे॥ ३१॥

31. Nor do I perceive, O Kṛṣṇa, any good in slaughtering my own people in battle. I desire neither victory nor empire nor even any pleasure.

न काङ्क्षे विजयं कृष्ण न च राज्यं सुखानि च।
किं नो राज्येन गोविन्द किं भोगैर्जीवितेन वा॥३२॥

येषामर्थे काङ्क्षितं नो राज्यं भोगाः सुखानि च।
त इमेऽवस्थिता युद्धे प्राणांस्त्यक्त्वा धनानि च॥३३॥

आचार्याः पितरः पुत्रास्तथैव च पितामहाः।
मातुलाः श्वशुराः पौत्राः श्यालाः सम्बन्धिनस्तथा॥३४॥

32-34. O Govinda, of what avail to us is empire, of what avail are enjoyments and even life itself? Our fathers and uncles, sons and grandsons, fathers-in-law and brothers-in-law, teachers and other relatives, for whose sake we desire kingdom, enjoyments, and pleasures, are arrayed here in battle, having staked their wealth and lives.

Govinda—An epithet of Kṛṣṇa.

एतान्न हन्तुमिच्छामि घ्नतोऽपि मधुसूदन।
अपि त्रैलोक्यराज्यस्य हेतोः किं नु महीकृते॥३५॥

35. These, O Madhusūdana, I would not kill, though they should kill me, even for the sake of sovereignty over the three worlds—how much less for this earth!

Madhusūdana—*Lit.*, the Slayer of the demon Madhu; an epithet of Kṛṣṇa.

Three worlds—Heaven, earth, and the nether world.

निहत्य धार्तराष्ट्रान्नः का प्रीतिः स्याज्जनार्दन।
पापमेवाश्रयेदस्मान्हत्वैतानाततायिनः॥३६॥

36. O Janārdana, what joy can be ours in killing these sons of Dhṛtarāṣṭra Sin alone will possess us if we kill these felons.

Janārdana—*Lit.*, the Destroyer of the demon Jana, or, according to Śaṅkara, He who is prayed to for prosperity and liberation; an epithet of Kṛṣṇa.

Felons—The Sanskrit word describes one who sets fire to the house of another person or poisons him or falls on him, sword in hand, to kill him or steals his wealth, land, or wife. According to law, such a criminal can be killed with impunity. The sons of Dhṛtarāṣṭra are guilty of all these crimes; but Arjuna's argument is based on the injunction. of the higher religion, according to which killing of any kind is sinful.

तस्मान्नार्हा वयं हन्तुं धार्तराष्ट्रान्स्वबान्धवान्।
स्वजनं हि कथं हत्वा सुखिनः स्याम माधव॥ ३७॥

37. Therefore we ought not to kill our kinsmen, the sons of Dhṛtarāṣṭra for, O Mādhava, how can we ever be happy by killing our own people?

यद्यप्येते न पश्यन्ति लोभोपहतचेतसः।
कुलक्षयकृतं दोषं मित्रद्रोहे च पातकम्॥ ३८॥

कथं न ज्ञेयमस्माभिः पापादस्मान्निवर्तितुम्।
कुलक्षयकृतं दोषं प्रपश्यद्भिर्जनार्दन॥ ३९॥

38-39. Though they, their understanding overcome by greed, perceive no evil in the decay of families and no sin in hostility to friends, why, O Janārdana, should not we, who clearly perceive the evil in the decay of families, learn to refrain from this sin?

They—Duryodhana and his friends.

Decay of families—The inevitable result of a civil war.

कुलक्षये प्रणश्यन्ति कुलधर्माः सनातनाः।
धर्मे नष्टे कुलं कृत्स्नमधर्मोऽभिभवत्युत॥ ४०॥

40. With the decay of a family, perish its dharmas, which have existed from time out of mind. With the ending of the dharmas, adharma overwhelms the whole family.

Dharmas—Duties, rites, and ceremonies practised by the family in accordance with religious injunctions.

Perish its dharmas—Owing to the death of the elders, who are the custodians, instructors, and transmitters of the religious traditions of the family.

Adharma—The opposite of dharma; impiety and unrighteousness.

अधर्माभिभवात्कृष्ण प्रदुष्यन्ति कुलस्त्रियः।
स्त्रीषु दुष्टासु वार्ष्णेय जायते वर्णसङ्करः॥ ४१॥

41. When adharma overwhelms the family, O Kṛṣṇa, the women of the family become corrupt; and when, O Kṛṣṇa, the women are corrupt, there arises a mixing of castes.

Become corrupt—As a result of an internecine war the number of men is depleted. In civilized societies men generally act as guardians of the weaker sex.

Mixing of castes—One of the evil consequences of the depletion of the number of men in society is that the women break the caste rules and traditions as regards marriage. Marriage outside one's caste is considered irregular by the Hindu law-givers.

सङ्करो नरकायैव कुलघ्नानां कुलस्य च।
पतन्ति पितरो ह्येषां लुप्तपिण्डोदकक्रियाः ॥४२॥

42. This mixture leads into hell the family itself as well as those who destroy it; for their ancestors fall, deprived of the offerings of rice-balls and water.

Rice-balls and water—The reference is to the Hindu religious rites for the dead, known as the śrāddha ceremony, in which rice-balls and water are offered by the eldest son for the satisfaction of the soul of the deceased. This ceremony cannot be performed by children born of irregular marriages, that is to say, marriages in which husband and wife belong to different castes. Deprived of the rice-balls and water, the soul of the deceased, according to Hindu tradition, goes to hell. The offering of rice-balls and water is a symbol of loving and reverent thoughts for the dead, which help to foster a feeling of close relationship between the living and their forebears.

According to the Hindu religious injunctions a son serves two purposes. First, he assures the continuity of the family; and second, he preserves the family tradition through his reverence for the ancestors. These purposes are served only through legitimate children. When women become corrupt, illegitimacy increases.

दोषैरेतैः कुलघ्नानां वर्णसङ्करकारकैः।
उत्साद्यन्ते जातिधर्माः कुलधर्माश्च शाश्वताः ॥४३॥

43. By these evil deeds of the destroyers of families, which result in the mixing of castes, the eternal dharmas of caste and family are uprooted.

उत्सन्नकुलधर्माणां मनुष्याणां जनार्दन।
नरके नियतं वासो भवतीत्यनुशुश्रुम ॥४४॥

44. We have heard it said, O Janārdana, that inevitably the men whose family dharmas are destroyed dwell in hell.

अहो बत महत्पापं कर्तुं व्यवसिता वयम्।
यद्राज्यसुखलोभेन हन्तुं स्वजनमुद्यताः ॥ ४५ ॥

45 Alas, we are resolved to commit a great sin, in that we are ready to slay our kinsmen to satisfy our greed for the pleasure of a kingdom!

Kingdom—The reason for the battle of Kurukṣetra is Duryodhana's refusal to give back to the Pāṇḍava brothers their legitimate kingdom.

यदि मामप्रतीकारमशस्त्रं शस्त्रपाणयः।
धार्तराष्ट्रा रणे हन्युस्तन्मे क्षेमतरं भवेत् ॥ ४६ ॥

46 Far better would it be for me if the sons of Dhṛtarāṣṭra, weapons in hand, should slay me in the battle, unarmed and unresisting.

Arjuna has turned a complete pacifist and adopted the policy of non-resistance to evil. But this policy is wrong, inasmuch as if one sees evil one must resist it. The real attitude of non-violence follows from the perception of God in all beings. Only the man whose mind has gone beyond good and evil does not resist evil, for he does not see evil, Further, Arjuna is a kṣatriya; hence it is his duty to fight in a righteous cause.

सञ्जय उवाच।
एवमुक्त्वार्जुनः सङ्ख्ये रथोपस्थ उपाविशत्।
विसृज्य सशरं चापं शोकसंविग्नमानसः ॥ ४७ ॥

47 *Sañjaya said:* Arjuna, having spoken thus on the battlefield, cast aside his bow and arrow and sank down on his chariot-seat, his mind overcome with grief.

ॐ तत्सदिति श्रीमद्भगवद्गीतासूपनिषत्सु
ब्रह्मविद्यायां योगशास्त्रे श्रीकृष्णार्जुनसंवादे
अर्जुनविषादयोगो नाम प्रथमोऽध्यायः ॥ १ ॥

Thus in the Bhagavad Gītā, the Essence of the Upaniṣads, the Science of Brahman, the Scripture of Yoga, the Dialogue between Śrī Kṛṣṇa and Arjuna, ends the First Chapter, entitled: ARJUNA'S GRIEF

CHAPTER 2

THE WAY OF ULTIMATE REALITY

[साङ्ख्ययोगः]

सञ्जय उवाच।

तं तथा कृपयाविष्टमश्रुपूर्णाकुलेक्षणम्।
विषीदन्तमिदं वाक्यमुवाच मधुसूदनः॥ १॥

1. *Sañjaya said:* To Arjuna, who was thus overwhelmed with pity, and whose troubled eyes were filled with tears, Madhusūdana spoke these words:

श्रीभगवानुवाच।

कुतस्त्वा कश्मलमिदं विषमे समुपस्थितम्।
अनार्यजुष्टमस्वर्ग्यमकीर्तिकरमर्जुन॥ २॥

2. *The Lord said:* In this crisis, O Arjuna, whence comes such lowness of spirit, unbecoming to an Āryan, dishonourable, and an obstacle to the attaining of heaven?

Crisis—When the highest standard of chivalry, honour, and discrimination is demanded.

Unbecoming to an Āryan—Non-Āryans are generally insensitive to the finer feelings of righteousness and nobility.

Heaven—A life of well deserved happiness and enjoyment in heaven is a kṣatriya's goal after death.

With words of biting reproach Kṛṣṇa tries to rouse Arjuna's drooping spirits.

क्लैब्यं मा स्म गमः पार्थ नैतत्त्वय्युपपद्यते।
क्षुद्रं हृदयदौर्बल्यं त्यक्त्वोत्तिष्ठ परन्तप॥३॥

3. Do not yield to unmanliness, O son of Pṛthā. It does not become you. Shake off this base faint-heartedness and arise, O scorcher of enemies!

Unmanliness—Arjuna has covered his momentary weakness with a mask of religious feeling.

Scorcher—A well chosen word to remind Arjuna of his kṣatriya heritage.

Kṛṣṇa, great psychologist that He is, knows very well that soft expressions of sympathy do not invigorate a drooping soul. Lashing words of strength are needed to rouse its forgotten manliness. Compare what the Lord said, under similar circumstances, to Job: "Gird up now thy loins like a man." (Bible: *Job* 38:3)

अर्जुन उवाच।
कथं भीष्ममहं सङ्ख्ये द्रोणं च मधुसूदन।
इषुभिः प्रतियोत्स्यामि पूजार्हावरिसूदन॥४॥

4. *Arjuna said:* But how, O Destroyer of Madhu, O Slayer of enemies, can I fight with arrows on the battlefield against Bhīṣma and Droṇa, who are worthy of my worship?

Bhīṣma and Droṇa are Arjuna's grandsire and teacher.

गुरूनहत्वा हि महानुभावान्
श्रेयो भोक्तुं भैक्ष्यमपीह लोके।
हत्वार्थकामांस्तु गुरूनिहैव
भुञ्जीय भोगान् रुधिरप्रदिग्धान्॥५॥

5. It would be better, indeed, to live on alms in this world rather than to slay these high-souled teachers. But if I kill them, even here I shall enjoy wealth and desires stained with their blood.

Even here—This world will be turned into hell.

न चैतद्विद्मः कतरन्नो गरीयो
यद्वा जयेम यदि वा नो जयेयुः।

यानेव हत्वा न जिजीविषाम-
स्तेऽवस्थिताः प्रमुखे धार्तराष्ट्राः ॥ ६ ॥

6. We do not know which would be the better for us: that we should conquer them or they should conquer us. Arrayed against us stand the very sons of Dhṛtarāṣṭra, after slaying whom we should not wish to live.

That we should conquer—We should enjoy wealth and desires, but stained with blood, and our victory would be turned into a defeat.

They should conquer—We should then live on alms without slaying the enemy, and our defeat would be a triumph of spirituality.

कार्पण्यदोषोपहतस्वभावः
पृच्छामि त्वां धर्मसम्मूढचेताः ।
यच्छ्रेयः स्यान्निश्चितं ब्रूहि तन्मे
शिष्यस्तेऽहं शाधि मां त्वां प्रपन्नम् ॥ ७ ॥

7. Overpowered in the very essence of my being by this evil of commiseration, my mind confused about dharma, I supplicate You: tell me in sooth which is the better. I am Your disciple. Instruct me, who have taken refuge in You.

Evil of commiseration—Commiseration is for Arjuna an evil because it has confused his judgement.

Dharma—*Lit.*, that which holds together. As such, it means the inmost constitution of a thing, the law of its inner being, which hastens its growth and without which it ceases to exist. The secondary meaning of the word is duty, religion, righteousness. The dharma of a man is not imposed from outside; it is acquired by him as a result of his actions in his past lives. Every action leaves behind a tendency or impression in the subconscious mind. A man's character is the sum-total of these tendencies. Death cannot destroy them. It is these tendencies that determine his dharma, or duty. In order to be true to himself he must act according to his dharma. Fighting in a just cause is the dharma of a kṣatriya, while the same thing is a sin for a brāhmin, for it is contrary to the law of his being. To mould one's action according to the law of one's own being is therefore the dharma, the religion or way to liberation, of every individual. It acts as the wind that blows away the cloud of ignorance, created by man's past actions, which hides the sun of his divine heritage. Any action contrary to a man's dharma only makes the cloud thicker.

Disciple—Until the seeker acknowledges himself to be a disciple, the teacher may not impart the highest Knowledge.

न हि प्रपश्यामि ममापनुद्याद्
यच्छोकमुच्छोषणमिन्द्रियाणाम्।
अवाप्य भूमावसपत्नमृद्धं
राज्यं सुराणामपि चाधिपत्यम्॥ ८॥

8. Indeed, I see naught to destroy the grief that is drying up my very senses—even the attainment of unrivalled and flourishing dominion on earth and lordship over the gods in heaven.

सञ्जय उवाच।
एवमुक्त्वा हृषीकेशं गुडाकेशः परन्तप।
न योत्स्य इति गोविन्दमुक्त्वा तूष्णीं बभूव ह॥ ९॥

9. *Sañjaya said:* Having spoken thus to Hṛṣīkeśa, Arjuna, scorcher of foes, said to Govinda, "I will not fight," and fell silent.

तमुवाच हृषीकेशः प्रहसन्निव भारत।
सेनयोरुभयोर्मध्ये विषीदन्तमिदं वचः॥ १०॥

10. O descendant of Bharata, to him grieving in the midst of the two armies Hṛṣīkeśa, smiling, spoke these words:

Descendant of Bharata—Refers to Dhṛtarāṣṭra

With the next verse begin the instructions of Kṛṣṇa and the philosophy of the Gītā. Arjuna's grief is caused by delusion in the form of attachment to his kinsmen, friends, and so on. The delusion is based on the egotistic notion: "I am theirs and they are mine." Of his own accord he has come to the battle-field to fulfil his dharma, or duty, as a kṣatriya: to fight in a righteous cause when all efforts at appeasement have failed. But under the influence of this inscrutable delusion he now wants to abstain from his proper duty and lead a mendicant's life. All people under the influence of delusion want to give up their own duties and assume those of others. Delusion, based on ego and attachment, is the cause of saṃsāra, the incessant round of birth and death in the relative world. Only by the Knowledge of Reality can it be destroyed. Kṛṣṇa desires to teach the whole world this Knowledge through Arjuna.

Since Śrī Kṛṣṇa has discovered that the deep-seated delusion and grief of Arjuna cannot be removed without the knowledge of Reality, He immediately starts His discourse on the immortality of the Soul.

श्रीभगवानुवाच।

अशोच्यानन्वशोचस्त्वं प्रज्ञावादांश्च भाषसे।
गतासूनगतासूंश्च नानुशोचन्ति पण्डिताः ॥ ११ ॥

11. *The Lord said:* You have been mourning for those who should not be mourned for; yet you speak words of wisdom. Neither for the living nor for the dead do the wise grieve.

Should not be mourned for—Because they are eternal in their real nature.

Words of wisdom—A reference to Chapter I, 35-45.

Wise—They alone are wise who know the true nature of the Self.

The cause of Arjuna's grief is lack of discrimination between the body and the Soul,

Why do they deserve no grief? Because they are eternal.

न त्वेवाहं जातु नासं न त्वं नेमे जनाधिपाः।
न चैव न भविष्यामः सर्वे वयमतः परम् ॥ १२ ॥

12. Never was there a time when I did not exist, nor you, nor these kings of men. Never will there be a time hereafter when any of us shall cease to be.

Obviously Śrī Kṛṣṇa does not mean that our bodies, subject to birth and death, are eternal. As the Ātman, the Self, we exist in all three periods of time: past, present, and future.

That the Self is eternal is expounded by an illustration:

देहिनोऽस्मिन्यथा देहे कौमारं यौवनं जरा।
तथा देहान्तरप्राप्तिर्धीरस्तत्र न मुह्यति ॥ १३ ॥

13. Even as the embodied Self passes, in this body, through the stages of childhood, youth, and old age, so does It pass into another body. Calm souls are not bewildered by this.

Embodied Self—The Soul assuming a physical body.

Calm souls—Their calmness is due to Self-knowledge.

This—Death.

The transition from childhood to youth is not marked by any change in the identity of the Soul. This is also true of the transitions to middle age, old age, and senility. The Soul remains unchanged through all the variations that take place in the body. Just so, the Soul passes unchanged into another body after death. Birth and death are spoken of with regard to the body and not the Soul.

It may be true that a man of Self-knowledge is not deluded by death; but how should ordinary people conduct themselves, people who believe in the happiness and suffering of the Soul due to contact with the pairs of opposites, such as heat and cold, pleasure and pain?

मात्रास्पर्शास्तु कौन्तेय शीतोष्णसुखदुःखदाः।
आगमापायिनोऽनित्यास्तांस्तितिक्षस्व भारत॥ १४॥

14. Notions of heat and cold, of pain and pleasure, arise, O son of Kuntī, only from contact of the senses with their objects. They come and go; they are impermanent. Endure them, O Bhārata.

They come and go—As distinguished from the Permanent Self.

Endure them—Do not give yourself to joy or grief on their account.

The two epithets by which Arjuna is addressed point to his noble lineage on both his mother's and his father's side.

What good comes to him who endures heat and cold, and the like?

यं हि न व्यथयन्त्येते पुरुषं पुरुषर्षभ।
समदुःखसुखं धीरं सोऽमृतत्वाय कल्पते॥ १५॥

15. That calm man who remains unchanged in pain and pleasure, whom these cannot disturb, alone is able, O greatest of men, to attain immortality.

Calm—Śrī Kṛṣṇa is not speaking of the Stoic calmness, in which agitation of feeling is not outwardly expressed. The calmness of which He speaks is based on the knowledge of the Soul's immortality.

Remains unchanged etc.—Neither exults in pleasure nor feels dejected in pain.

Endurance, coupled with discrimination between the Real and the unreal, and detachment from worldly objects and pleasures, prepare the aspirant for right knowledge, which alone leads to liberation. Vedānta defines endurance as the bearing of all afflictions without wishing to redress them, while being free from all anxiety or regret on their account.

An additional reason is given for abandoning grief and delusion:

नासतो विद्यते भावो नाभावो विद्यते सतः।
उभयोरपि दृष्टोऽन्तस्त्वनयोस्तत्त्वदर्शिभिः॥ १६॥

16. The unreal never is. The Real never ceases to be. The conclusion about these two is truly perceived by the seers of Truth.

The determination of the nature of Reality is the quest of philosophy. The Real is that which is always the same, and the unreal is that which does not remain the same. The Real remains the same through past, present, and future. It always is. Any object conditioned by the law of cause and effect is not absolutely real; for every effect is a change brought about by a cause, and every cause is temporary.

The unreal never remains the same for two successive moments. The whole of the phenomenal world is unreal. ("Whatever did not exist in the past or will not exist in the future cannot really exist in the present."—Gauḍapāda) Names and forms, which constitute the phenomenal world, did not exist before the Soul came under the influence of ignorance; they will disappear with the destruction of ignorance. Like the objects seen in a dream, names and forms. are perceived only when the Soul is overpowered by ignorance. The only Reality is the Ātman, Consciousness, which is the unchanging Witness of the changes in the relative world. The Absolute Reality is not conditioned by causality.

What, then, is that which is always real?

अविनाशि तु तद्विद्धि येन सर्वमिदं ततम्।
विनाशमव्ययस्यास्य न कश्चित्कर्तुमर्हति॥ १७॥

17. That by which all this is pervaded know to be imperishable. None can cause the destruction of that which is immutable.

That—Brahman, or the unchangeable Consciousness. It is the Self of all.

All this—The world of names and forms.

Pervaded—Brahman is the Witness and the inmost Essence of the changeable world.

Cause the destruction etc.—For Brahman is without parts and is One without a second. Destruction of an object is caused by the loss of its parts, as in the case of the body, or by the loss of something belonging to it.

The immutable Consciousness, or Ātman, in the individual is the same as the all-pervading Consciousness, or Brahman, in the universe.

What is the unreal, whose nature is subject to change?

अन्तवन्त इमे देहा नित्यस्योक्ताः शरीरिणः।
अनाशिनोऽप्रमेयस्य तस्माद्युध्यस्व भारत॥ १८॥

18. Only the bodies, of which this eternal, imperishable, incomprehensible Self is the indweller, are said to have an end. Fight, therefore, O Bharata.

Eternal, imperishable—The physical body may be injured or destroyed by illness or death. The Self is subject to neither of these.

Incomprehensible—It is not comprehended by the senses, by the mind, or by any other instrument of knowledge. The Self is *svataḥ-siddha,* determined by Itself. Being the knowing Consciousness, It cannot be known by any other instrument. Everything else is known by the Self. The immediate and direct experience of "I am I" is the basis of all cognition. The statements of the scriptures regarding the Self do not serve the purpose of directly revealing Its true nature; they only eliminate all the attributes falsely superimposed upon It.

Fight—Kṛṣṇa is not really commanding Arjuna to fight. Arjuna, following his dharma, had come to the battle-field determined to fight. He refused to fight on account of his ignorance about the true nature of the Soul. The Lord wants to remove this ignorance and leave him free to do what he, Arjuna, considers to be right.

That Bhīṣma Droṇa, and the others are going to be killed by Arjuna is a false notion on his part.

य एनं वेत्ति हन्तारं यश्चैनं मन्यते हतम्।
उभौ तौ न विजानीतो नायं हन्ति न हन्यते॥ १९॥

19. He who looks on the Self as the slayer, and he who looks on the Self as the slain—neither of these apprehends aright. The Self slays not nor is slain.

The agent of slaying is the ego (ahaṃ) and the object of slaughter is the body; therefore the Self, which is different both from the ego and from the body, is neither the slayer nor the slain. For verses 19 and 20, compare *Kaṭha Upaniṣad,* I, ii, 18-19.

Why is the Self immutable?

न जायते म्रियते वा कदाचिन्
नायं भूत्वा भविता वा न भूयः।

अजो नित्यः शाश्वतोऽयं पुराणो
न हन्यते हन्यमाने शरीरे ॥२०॥

20. It is never born, nor does It ever die, nor, having once been, does It again cease to be. Unborn, eternal, permanent, and primeval, It is not slain when the body is slain.

This verse describes the absence of the six kinds of modification inherent in every living thing: birth, subsistence, growth, transformation, decay, and death. The Self is altogether changeless.

The proposition stated in verse 19 is that the Self is neither the agent nor the object of slaying; the reason for this, given in verse 20, is Its immutability. Now the proposition is concluded:

वेदाविनाशिनं नित्यं य एनमजमव्ययम्।
कथं स पुरुषः पार्थ कं घातयति हन्ति कम्॥२१॥

21. He who knows the Self to be indestructible, eternal, unborn, and immutable—how can that man, O son of Pṛthā, slay or cause another to slay?

By denying the act of slaying to the Soul, all actions are denied to It. An enlightened man, possessing Self-knowledge, renounces all action associated with the idea of a doer, an instrument of action, and a result of action. The unenlightened man performs action in accordance with the scriptural injunctions in order to purify his mind. The pure mind alone knows the Truth.

The indestructibility of the Soul is expounded by an illustration:

वासांसि जीर्णानि यथा विहाय
नवानि गृह्णाति नरोऽपराणि।
तथा शरीराणि विहाय जीर्णा-
न्यन्यानि संयाति नवानि देही॥२२॥

22. Even as a person casts off worn-out clothes and puts on others that are new, so the embodied Self casts off worn-out bodies and enters into others that are new.

In the act of giving up the old body or entering into the new body, the real Self does not undergo any change whatsoever. According to Vedānta, Brahman, through Its inscrutable māyā, creates a body, identifies Itself with it, and regards Itself as an individual, or embodied, soul. Its purpose in assuming innumerable bodies is to rediscover ultimately Its transcendental nature. Through innumerable births in the relative world It gains experience, from experience It derives Knowledge, and through Knowledge It ultimately attains freedom. But during the state of self-forgetfulness the true nature of the Self never changes, just as the sun, though hidden by a cloud, never loses its splendour, or as the desert, in spite of the appearance of water in the mirage, remains always dry.

Why is the Self altogether changeless?

नैनं छिन्दन्ति शस्त्राणि नैनं दहति पावकः ।
न चैनं क्लेदयन्त्यापो न शोषयति मारुतः ॥ २३ ॥

23. Weapons cut It not; fire burns It not; water wets It not; the wind does not wither It.

Weapons can destroy an object by cutting it into parts; but the Self is without parts and is therefore indestructible. The same applies to the other methods of destruction. Only a material object consists of parts and is therefore destructible.

For this reason,

अच्छेद्योऽयमदाह्योऽयमक्लेद्योऽशोष्य एव च ।
नित्यः सर्वगतः स्थाणुरचलोऽयं सनातनः ॥ २४ ॥

24. This Self cannot be cut nor burnt nor wetted nor withered. Eternal, all-pervading, unchanging, immovable, the Self is the same for ever.

Eternal—Because water, fire, wind, and all other agents of destruction cannot destroy the Self, which is infinite and hence without parts.

It is extremely difficult to understand the mystery of the Self. Therefore *Śrī* Kṛṣṇa describes It again and again, so that in some way or other Its nature may be grasped.

Furthermore,

अव्यक्तोऽयमचिन्त्योऽयमविकार्योऽयमुच्यते ।
तस्मादेवं विदित्वैनं नानुशोचितुमर्हसि ॥ २५ ॥

25. This Self is said to be unmanifest, incomprehensible, and unchangeable. Therefore, knowing It to be so, you should not grieve.

Unmanifest—Inaccessible to the senses.

Incomprehensible—Inaccessible to the mind. The mind can think only about an object perceived by the senses. The Self, however, can be known by the pure mind, that is, by the mind totally free from greed, lust, and ego. The pure mind is the same as the Self.

Unchangeable—Because the Self is infinite. Being without parts, It cannot change.

Therefore Arjuna should not cherish the idea of the Self as slayer or slain and on that account grieve.

Assuming, for the sake of argument, that the Self is not eternal, Śrī Kṛṣṇa proceeds:

अथ चैनं नित्यजातं नित्यं वा मन्यसे मृतम्।
तथापि त्वं महाबाहो नैवं शोचितुमर्हसि॥ २६॥

26. But if you think the Self repeatedly comes into being and dies, even then, O mighty one, you should not grieve for It.

Repeatedly comes into being etc.—According to the materialistic view, the Self is born with the body and dies with the body.

From the materialistic standpoint, grief for the Self is senseless, for Its birth and death are inevitable. Further, the Self, being impermanent, cannot have any hereafter and therefore cannot suffer from sin and hell.

जातस्य हि ध्रुवो मृत्युर्ध्रुवं जन्म मृतस्य च।
तस्मादपरिहार्येऽर्थे न त्वं शोचितुमर्हसि॥ २७॥

27. For to that which is born, death is certain, and to that which is dead, birth is certain. Therefore you should not grieve over the unavoidable.

It is not proper to grieve for beings, which are mere combinations of cause and effect.

अव्यक्तादीनि भूतानि व्यक्तमध्यानि भारत।
अव्यक्तनिधनान्येव तत्र का परिदेवना॥ २८॥

28. All beings are unmanifest in their beginning, O Bharata, manifest in their middle state, and unmanifest again in their end. Why, then, lament for them?

All beings—As physical entities, which are mere combinations of material elements correlated as cause and effect.

Unmanifest—Non-perceptible.

Beginning—Before birth.

Middle state—After birth and before death.

End—After death.

Anything whose existence is not perceived in the beginning or end cannot be real, as is the case with magic or dreams. If it is perceived in the middle, it is only an illusory perception, like a dream. Such a thing should not disturb one's mind.

आश्चर्यवत्पश्यति कश्चिदेन-
माश्चर्यवद्वदति तथैव चान्यः।
आश्चर्यवच्चैनमन्यः शृणोति
श्रुत्वाप्येनं वेद न चैव कश्चित्॥ २९॥

29. Some look on the Self as a wonder; some speak of It as a wonder; some hear of It as a wonder; still others, though hearing, do not understand It at all.

Wonder—As an object unseen, strange, or suddenly perceived.

A man, on account of his ignorance, is unaware of his Self, the inmost Reality. Though the Self is of the nature of Spirit, yet It is confused with body, mind, sense-organs, relatives, and worldly possessions. Though changeless, It appears to change. Though of the nature of Light, illumining the mind and the senses, It remains hidden to man. Though one with Brahman, It appears to have a separate existence. Though always beyond time and space, It appears to be bound by them. Therefore the true nature of the Self is a great mystery. Wonderful seems to be the nature of the Self when described or taught by a teacher. True Knowledge makes a man realize that he is the Soul and has a body, not that he is the body and has a soul.

The verse may also be interpreted in this way: He who sees the Self is himself something of a wonder. He who hears and speaks of the Self is also a wonder; for among many thousands of men only one will be found endowed with Self-knowledge. Thus the Self is difficult to understand.

Śrī Kṛṣṇa concludes the topic:

देही नित्यमवध्योऽयं देहे सर्वस्य भारत।
तस्मात्सर्वाणि भूतानि न त्वं शोचितुमर्हसि॥ ३०॥

30. The Self, which dwells in all bodies, can never be slain, O Bhārata. Wherefore you should not mourn for any creature.

The Self is immortal, though the body may be slain. Therefore grief on account of death is improper.

Grief is improper for other reasons besides those of Truth.

स्वधर्ममपि चावेक्ष्य न विकम्पितुमर्हसि।
धर्म्याद्धि युद्धाच्छ्रेयोऽन्यत्क्षत्रियस्य न विद्यते॥ ३१ ॥

31. Considering, also, your own dharma, you should not waver; for to a kṣatriya nothing is better than a righteous war.

Fighting is natural for Arjuna because he is a kṣatriya. "Heroism, high spirit, firmness, resourcefulness, dauntlessness in battle, generosity, and sovereignty—these are the duties of a kṣatriya, born of his own nature." (Gītā, XVIII, 43) But the kṣatriya, before unsheathing his sword, must be convinced that the purpose of the war is to uphold law, justice, and righteousness.

Arjuna must not hesitate to accept the great boon that has presented itself to him unsought.

यदृच्छया चोपपन्नं स्वर्गद्वारमपावृतम्।
सुखिनः क्षत्रियाः पार्थ लभन्ते युद्धमीदृशम्॥ ३२ ॥

32. Happy indeed are the kṣatriyas, O Pārtha to whom comes such a war, offering itself unsought, opening the gate to heaven.

Unsought—Arjuna's enemies had precipitated the war by their own indiscretion.

According to the Hindu scriptures, a kṣatriya who gives up his life in a righteous war goes to heaven.

Evil results will befall Arjuna if he refuses to fight.

अथ चेत्त्वमिमं धर्म्यं सङ्ग्रामं न करिष्यसि।
ततः स्वधर्मं कीर्तिं च हित्वा पापमवाप्स्यसि॥ ३३ ॥

33. But if you refuse to wage this righteous war, then, renouncing your own dharma and honour, you will certainly incur sin.

अकीर्तिं चापि भूतानि कथयिष्यन्ति तेऽव्ययाम्।
सम्भावितस्य चाकीर्तिर्मरणादतिरिच्यते॥ ३४ ॥

34. People, too, will recount for ever your infamy. And to a man who has been honoured, dishonour is worse than death.

With these stinging words Kṛṣṇa seeks to stiffen Arjuna's spirit.

भयाद्रणादुपरतं मंस्यन्ते त्वां महारथाः।
येषां च त्वं बहुमतो भूत्वा यास्यसि लाघवम्॥ ३५॥

35. The great warriors will think you have withdrawn from the battle through fear; and you will go down in the esteem of those who have thought much of you.

Great warriors—Duryodhana and the others.

अवाच्यवादांश्च बहून्वदिष्यन्ति तवाहिताः।
निन्दन्तस्तव सामर्थ्यं ततो दुःखतरं नु किम्॥ ३६॥

36. Your enemies will speak many a word that should not be uttered, scorning your prowess. Could anything be more bitter than that?

Referring to Arjuna's confusion, described in the sixth verse of the present chapter, the Lord says:

हतो वा प्राप्स्यसि स्वर्गं जित्वा वा भोक्ष्यसे महीम्।
तस्मादुत्तिष्ठ कौन्तेय युद्धाय कृतनिश्चयः॥ ३७॥

37. If you are killed in the battle, you will go to heaven; if you win, you will enjoy the earth. Therefore arise, O son of Kuntī, resolved to fight.

Whatever may be the outcome of the war, Arjuna will be the gainer.

Arjuna will not incur any sin

सुखदुःखे समे कृत्वा लाभालाभौ जयाजयौ।
ततो युद्धाय युज्यस्व नैवं पापमवाप्स्यसि॥ ३८॥

38. Regarding alike pleasure and pain, gain and loss, success and defeat, prepare yourself for battle. Thus, you will incur no sin.

Regarding alike pleasure and pain, etc.—Not being exalted by the one and depressed by the other.

It is desire for and attachment to the result of an action that create bondage; but when an action is performed without any such desire, it leads to freedom of the soul. The injunction to fight is only incidental.

The Lord explains Self-knowledge from the standpoint of karmayoga:

एषा तेऽभिहिता साङ्ख्ये बुद्धिर्योगे त्विमां शृणु।
बुद्ध्या युक्तो यया पार्थ कर्मबन्धं प्रहास्यसि॥ ३९॥

39. What has been declared to you is the wisdom of sāṅkhya. Now listen to the wisdom of yoga, armed with which, O son of Pṛthā, you will break through the bonds of karma.

Sāṅkhya—The true nature of the Absolute Reality. This wisdom refers to jñānayoga, the path of knowledge, which teaches discrimination between the Real and the unreal and urges renunciation of the unreal. The Knowledge of Reality directly destroys ignorance, which is the cause of birth and death in the relative world, and of the grief and delusion inevitably associated with it.

Yoga—Karmayoga, or the path of action. The follower of this path engages in action without any desire for or attachment to the result. He regards himself as an instrument of God. It is desire and attachment that create the subtle impressions in the mind which are the seeds of future action. Action performed without attachment or care for the result does not create new karma, but leaves the will free to devote itself to the achievement of Self-realization. Here is the secret of karmayoga.

Bonds of karma—Merit and demerit, virtue and sin, pain and pleasure, and the other pairs of opposites constitute the bondage of all action performed with a motive.

Sāṅkhyayoga, or the path of knowledge, which directly reveals the true nature of the Self, is meant for very rare seekers, endowed with keen intellect for discrimination and undaunted will-power for renunciation. Other seekers must first of all purify their minds through the disciplines of karmayoga; only then will they become fit to follow the path of knowledge. The pure in heart attain Self-knowledge through the grace of God."

Arjuna can qualify for the highest Knowledge only through performance of his duty. Śrī Kṛṣṇa gives various arguments to persuade him of this. In verses 11-25 of the present chapter Śrī Kṛṣṇa speaks of the highest Knowledge as it is described in the Upaniṣads by the knowers of Brahman. In verses 26 and 27 He discourses from a purely materialistic standpoint. Verses 31-37 develop the attitude of a man of the world. In verse 39 and those that follow, Śrī Kṛṣṇa describes karmayoga, which is the special contribution of the Gītā to the philosophy of life.

The special merit of karmayoga:

नेहाभिक्रमनाशोऽस्ति प्रत्यवायो न विद्यते।
स्वल्पमप्यस्य धर्मस्य त्रायते महतो भयात्॥४०॥

40. In this no effort is ever lost and no harm is ever done. Even very little of this dharma saves a man from the Great Fear.

This—Karmayoga.

Ever lost—A religious rite or ceremony undertaken for a definite object, if left uncompleted, is wasted, like an incomplete house, which is neither serviceable nor enduring.

No harm—In the case of sickness the use of the wrong medicine may result in death. Likewise, certain forms of worship, if carelessly performed or left unfinished, produce positive loss instead of gain.

Dharma—Karmayoga.

Great Fear—Caused by the unending wheel of birth and death.

Karmayoga leads to the Highest Good.

व्यवसायात्मिका बुद्धिरेकेह कुरुनन्दन।
बहुशाखा ह्यनन्ताश्च बुद्धयोऽव्यवसायिनाम्॥४१॥

41. In this, O scion of Kuru, there is only one resolute and unwavering thought; but the thoughts of the irresolute are many-branched and unending.

In this—That is to say, in karmayoga, characterized by devotion to God and firm conviction that Self-realization will be achieved through His grace.

Thought—Self-realization.

Irresolute—Those who perform action with a desire for results.

Those who crave results from their action are naturally assailed by many thoughts and are born in innumerable bodies. But those whose action consists in worship of God alone, and that also for His satisfaction, acquire the purity of mind and one-pointedness of aim that lead to Self-knowledge.

Selfish action motivated by a desire for enjoyment of happiness, such as is described in the ritualistic section of the Vedas, is condemned:

यामिमां पुष्पितां वाचं प्रवदन्त्यविपश्चितः।
वेदवादरताः पार्थ नान्यदस्तीति वादिनः॥४२॥

कामात्मानः स्वर्गपरा जन्मकर्मफलप्रदाम्।
क्रियाविशेषबहुलां भोगैश्वर्यगतिं प्रति॥४३॥

भोगैश्वर्यप्रसक्तानां तयापहृतचेतसाम्।
व्यवसायात्मिका बुद्धिः समाधौ न विधीयते॥४४॥

42-44. O Pārtha no resolute and unwavering thought is formed in the minds of those who are deeply attached to pleasure and power; who allow their discrimination to be stolen away by the flowery words of the unwise; who permit their souls to be ridden with desires; who regard the attainment of heaven as the highest goal; and who take great delight in quoting the panegyric texts of the Vedas and declare that besides these there is nothing. These texts promise rebirths as the reward of their action and lay down specific rites for the attainment of pleasure and power.

Panegyric texts—The karmakāṇḍa, or ritualistic section, of the Vedas, which lays down specific rules for specific sacrifices and extols highly the results of these actions, namely, the enjoyment of pleasures in heaven.

Nothing—They ignore the philosophical section of the Vedas leading to liberation.

Rebirths—On earth, for the enjoyment of more pleasure and power.

All religions promise the beginners great power and pleasures in the after-life as a reward for their devotions and meritorious acts. The Vedas are divided into two sections. One section deals with rites and sacrifices, which promise their performers happiness in heaven and pleasure and power in their next birth on earth. The other section deals with the Knowledge of the Self, which leads to liberation. The results of the rites and sacrifices performed with desires are ephemeral, for they are limited by time, space, and the law of causation. But when performed without desire for results, these religious rites purify the mind.

The practice of the Vedic rites does not lead to liberation.

त्रैगुण्यविषया वेदा निस्त्रैगुण्यो भवार्जुन।
निर्द्वन्द्वो नित्यसत्त्वस्थो निर्योगक्षेम आत्मवान्॥४५॥

45. The Vedas deal with the three guṇas. Be free, O Arjuna, from the three guṇas. Be free from the pairs of opposites. Be always established in sattva. Do not try to acquire what you lack or preserve what you have. Be established in the Self.

Vedas—Refers to the karmakāṇḍa, or ritualistic section, of the Vedas.

Guṇas—The word "guṇa" is a technical term of Sāṅkhya philosophy, also accepted by Vedānta. According to Sāṅkhya, the two principal categories are Puruṣa and Prakṛti. The former denotes the Soul, or Consciousness, and the latter, Nature, or matter, which is dull and insentient. Prakṛti consists of the three guṇas, namely, sattva, rajas, and tamas. Rajas, denoting restlessness, is the active principle in Nature. Tamas is the principle of inertia. And sattva, serenity and harmony, is the equilibrium between rajas and tamas. As Prakṛti consists of the three guṇas, every object in Prakṛti is compounded of these three elements. Saṃsāra, or relativity, is the realm of the guṇas. Freedom is beyond them. Even the highest experiences of heaven come within the realm of the guṇas and are therefore limited by the laws of Nature or matter.

Free from the three guṇas—Free from all desires.

Pairs of opposites—All correlated ideas and sensations, for instance, good and evil, pleasure and pain, heat and cold, light and darkness.

Be always established in sattva—Be always balanced; do not be swayed by either extreme. Sattva enables an aspiring soul to go beyond the guṇas and attain freedom.

Do not try to acquire etc.—Striving people are restless. and unfit for the highest Knowledge.

Be established in the Self—Be on guard and do not yield to the objects of the senses.

Arjuna is asked to follow these injunctions while engaged in the performance of his duty.

What is the use of the Vedas?

यावानर्थ उदपाने सर्वतः सम्प्लुतोदके।
तावान्सर्वेषु वेदेषु ब्राह्मणस्य विजानतः ॥४६॥

46. To the enlightened Brāhmin all the Vedas are of as much use as a pond when there is everywhere a flood.

Enlightened Brāhmin—One who has realized Brahman, or the truth concerning Absolute Reality.

The various purposes of a pond, a well, and other reservoirs are more than served by an all-encompassing flood. Likewise, the various pleasures that result from the performance of the works enjoined in the Vedas are included in the Bliss enjoyed by a Brāhmin enlightened with Self-knowledge. All kinds of limited bliss are included in the Infinite Bliss. A knower of the Self does not need to follow the Vedic injunctions. This does not mean, however, that the Vedas are useless. They serve the purpose of the unenlightened. Through the performance of the works prescribed by the Vedas one becomes fit for the path of knowledge.

For Arjuna the performance of action is imperative.

कर्मण्येवाधिकारस्ते मा फलेषु कदाचन।
मा कर्मफलहेतुर्भूर्मा ते सङ्गोऽस्त्वकर्मणि॥४७॥

47. To work, alone, you are entitled, never to its fruit. Neither let your motive be the fruit of action, nor let your attachment be to non-action.

Work, alone—Arjuna is not ready for the path of knowledge.

Never to its fruit—If a man longs for the fruit of action, he will have to reap it in the future. An action produces bondage when it is performed with a desire for its fruit.

Non-action—Non-action is possible only for the lowest being or the highest saint.

The word "karma" (work) has different meanings. It primarily means action. It also means the tendencies, impulses, habits, characteristics, and so on, formed by action, and thus it denotes the subtle impressions of action, which determine the future embodiment, environment, and, in short, the whole future life, whether on earth or in any other plane of existence. A third meaning of karma, often used in reference to one's caste or position in life, is duty, the course of conduct one ought to follow in pursuance of the tendencies acquired as a result of past actions, with a view to working them out and regaining the pristine purity of the Self.

If a man ought not to be impelled to an action by desire for its results, how, then, should he perform it?

योगस्थः कुरु कर्माणि सङ्गं त्यक्त्वा धनञ्जय।
सिद्ध्यसिद्ध्योः समो भूत्वा समत्वं योग उच्यते॥४८॥

48. Being established in yoga, O Dhanañjaya, perform your actions, casting off attachment and remaining even-minded both in success and in failure. This evenness is called yoga.

Yoga—The state of being an instrument in the hand of God, having given up even the desire that through our action we shall please Him. Only thus can one remain unconcerned as to success and failure.

Attachment—The notion that arises when a man regards himself not as the instrument but as the doer of an action.

Success—Including the attainment of knowledge as the result of the mind's having achieved purity through works performed without any longing for result.

The secret of karmayoga is complete effacement of one's individuality and total identification with God's will. Thus alone does the worker become free from the joys or griefs that result from the success or failure of his works; thus alone does he enjoy peace while performing his duties.

An action performed with a view to the result is of very inferior value.

दूरेण ह्यवरं कर्म बुद्धियोगाद्धनञ्जय।
बुद्धौ शरणमन्विच्छ कृपणाः फलहेतवः ॥४९॥

49. Far inferior, indeed, is mere action, O Dhanañjaya, to action performed with evenness of mind. Seek refuge in this evenness. Wretched are they who work for results.

Mere action—Action performed to gain a result. Such action is the cause of future birth and death, and hence creates bondage.

Evenness—The state of not being exalted or depressed by success or failure. It is not callousness or indifference, but a total devotion of the worker to his duty, whereby he regards himself as an instrument of God. One attains true evenness only as a result of the Knowledge of the Supreme Reality. This Knowledge alone, not any incidental result, should be the goal of work.

Wretched are they etc.—They are wretched indeed who busy themselves with calculation of the gains or losses resulting from their action and thus depart from the world without realizing the Supreme Reality.

The result of performing one's duty with evenness of mind:

बुद्धियुक्तो जहातीह उभे सुकृतदुष्कृते।
तस्माद्योगाय युज्यस्व योगः कर्मसु कौशलम्॥५०॥

50. Endued with evenness of mind, one casts off, in this very life, both good deeds and evil deeds. Therefore strive for yoga. Yoga is skill in action.

Good deeds and evil deeds—These are responsible for one's birth in a higher or a lower world.

Yoga—That is to say, evenness through the realization of God.

Skill in action—If a man performs his duties, maintaining this evenness, then his mind rests on God all the while. Hence evenness is the source of

power. Work that otherwise enslaves becomes a means to freedom when performed with evenness of mind.

It is a mistake to think that pleasure is the aim of action. Pleasure is of a transitory nature. The real aim of action is knowledge. Through knowledge one attains detachment and ultimate freedom.

How does action lead to liberation?

कर्मजं बुद्धियुक्ता हि फलं त्यक्त्वा मनीषिणः ।
जन्मबन्धविनिर्मुक्ताः पदं गच्छन्त्यनामयम् ॥५१ ॥

51. The wise, of even mind, renounce the fruit of action. Freed from the fetters of birth, they attain the state that is beyond all evil.

Fetters of birth—Birth in the relative world, associated with suffering and death, is a form of bondage. It is the result of action in a previous life,

State—That is to say, liberation.

According to the Hindu view, the life of the world, with its many happy moments, is a bondage and hence not desirable. According to the materialistic view, the life of the world, in spite of its many attendant evils, is very much worthwhile.

The "evenness" (buddhi) of verses 48-51 can also mean the sāṅkhya wisdom, the Knowledge of the Absolute Reality, which is compared in verse 46 to a flood. This flood arises when the mind has been purified by karmayoga.

When does one attain the wisdom that is the result of the purity of mind induced by karmayoga?

यदा ते मोहकलिलं बुद्धिर्व्यतितरिष्यति ।
तदा गन्तासि निर्वेदं श्रोतव्यस्य श्रुतस्य च ॥५२ ॥

52. When your mind has crossed the slough of delusion, you will achieve indifference regarding things already heard and things yet to be heard.

Slough of delusion—Which causes non-discrimination between the Self and the non-Self, or ego, and turns the mind toward the objects of the senses.

Things already heard etc.—Being finite in nature, these things are considered futile. The text does not refer to the injunctions of the scriptures regarding the Knowledge of Ātman, the Self.

It may be asked, how long does one take to attain freedom? This is not a question of time. Freedom refers to an experience that denotes

"timelessness." It can be attained at any moment, the only condition being the desirelessness of the aspirant. One must be free from attachment to objects attainable in this world or in heaven.

When does one attain the true yoga, or the Knowledge of the Supreme Truth?

श्रुतिविप्रतिपन्ना ते यदा स्थास्यति निश्चला।
समाधावचला बुद्धिस्तदा योगमवाप्स्यसि॥५३॥

53. When your mind—now perplexed by what you have heard—stands firm and steady in the Self, then you will have attained yoga.

What you have heard—The conflicting views of the various religious books, regarding happiness and the other ends of life.

Firm and steady—Free from distraction and doubt.

Yoga—Complete absorption in God-consciousness, or samādhi, which is the result of discrimination between the Real and the unreal.

What are the characteristics of one who has attained wisdom through samādhi?

अर्जुन उवाच।
स्थितप्रज्ञस्य का भाषा समाधिस्थस्य केशव।
स्थितधीः किं प्रभाषेत किमासीत व्रजेत किम्॥५४॥

54. *Arjuna said:* What, O Keśava, is the description of the man of steady wisdom merged in samādhi? How does the man of steady wisdom speak, how sit, how move?

Steady wisdom—The wisdom that makes a man realize that he is Brahman.

Merged in samādhi—Fully conscious of his identity with Brahman.

The two questions asked by Arjuna are: (1) How is a man of steady wisdom described by others? (2) How does the influence of wisdom manifest itself when the man comes out of samādhi? The answer runs from verse 55 to the end of the chapter. It includes the characteristic attributes of a man of steady wisdom and also the means of attaining such wisdom. These attributes apply to one in whom dispassion for work and devotion to knowledge (jñāna) are innate, and also to one who, as the result of the practice of karmayoga, has become ready for the practice of jñāna.

The means of attaining Knowledge are also the characteristic attributes of the man who has attained Knowledge. In this discipline the means and the end are the same.

श्रीभगवानुवाच।

प्रजहाति यदा कामान्सर्वान्पार्थ मनोगतान्।
आत्मन्येवात्मना तुष्टः स्थितप्रज्ञस्तदोच्यते॥५५॥

55. *The Lord said:* O Pārtha when a man completely casts off all the desires of the mind, his Self finding satisfaction in Itself alone, then he is called a man of steady wisdom.

Itself—The innermost Self of man, which is the same as the Supreme Reality.

Such a man does not long for external possessions, for he enjoys the Supreme Bliss of Self-knowledge. A man of steady wisdom has renounced all cravings for progeny, wealth, and attainment of heaven, and enjoys the bliss of communion with the Self. This answers the first part of Arjuna's question.

Moreover,

दुःखेष्वनुद्विग्नमनाः सुखेषु विगतस्पृहः।
वीतरागभयक्रोधः स्थितधीर्मुनिरुच्यते॥५६॥

56. He who is not perturbed by adversity, who does not long for happiness, who is free from attachment, fear, and wrath, is called a muni of steady wisdom.

Adversity—Men may be victims of three kinds of adversity: ādhyātmika, arising from disorder of the body; ādhibhautika, arising from external objects, such as tigers or snakes; ādhidaivika, arising from the action of great cosmic forces, such as those that cause rain, storms, or earthquakes.

Long for happiness—Fire flares up when fuel is thrown upon it; but in the case of a man of wisdom, his happiness does not create a longing for more happiness.

Attachment—To outward objects.

Fear—He is free from fear because of his constant communion with the inner Self.

Wrath—He is free from wrath because he regards all beings as his own Self.

Muni—A man given to meditation and contemplation.

This and the two following verses answer the second part of Arjuna's question, as to the conduct of one of steady wisdom

Moreover,

यः सर्वत्रानभिस्नेहस्तत्तत्प्राप्य शुभाशुभम्।
नाभिनन्दति न द्वेष्टि तस्य प्रज्ञा प्रतिष्ठिता ॥५७॥

57. He who is not attached to anything, who neither rejoices nor is vexed when he obtains good or evil— his wisdom is firmly fixed.

Anything—Such as his body, children, friends, and so on.

Who neither rejoices nor is vexed—Consequently does not praise or blame anything. This answers Arjuna's query: "How does he speak?"

Moreover,

यदा संहरते चायं कूर्मोऽङ्गानीव सर्वशः।
इन्द्रियाणीन्द्रियार्थेभ्यस्तस्य प्रज्ञा प्रतिष्ठिता ॥५८॥

58. When he completely withdraws the senses from their objects, as a tortoise draws in its limbs, then his wisdom is firmly fixed.

Withdraws—This is the process of pratyāhāra, described in Yoga. According to this discipline the mind is fixed on the Self; in the absence of attention the sense-organs are withdrawn from their objects.

The tortoise, when frightened, draws in its limbs instantly and without effort. Likewise, a man of steady wisdom can at any moment enter into samādhi without the least effort. Then his mind is completely withdrawn from the outer world.

It is seen that the senses of ignorant, sick, or infirm persons, too, are withdrawn from their objects. But such persons retain their taste for those objects. How can the taste be withdrawn?

विषया विनिवर्तन्ते निराहारस्य देहिनः।
रसवर्जं रसोऽप्यस्य परं दृष्ट्वा निवर्तते ॥५९॥

59. The objects of the senses fall away from a man practising abstinence, but not the taste for them. But even the taste falls away when the Supreme is seen.

A man practising abstinence—An unillumined person practising austerity for a worldly goal and abstaining from sense-enjoyments. The phrase can refer also to a sick person or an imbecile, who is incapable of enjoying sense-pleasures. These all retain the longing for enjoyment.

Repression or inhibition due to illness or selfish causes is completely different from the self-control practised by yogis. In the former case there is only a physical abstention, but the mind retains its longing. In the latter case the subtle desire disappears as well, on account of the yogis' attainment of the Supreme Bliss in communion with the Self. This Bliss is like an all-encompassing flood, which removes the need for wells or ponds.

The uncontrolled senses injure aspirants seeking spiritual illumination.

यततो ह्यपि कौन्तेय पुरुषस्य विपश्चितः ।
इन्द्रियाणि प्रमाथीनि हरन्ति प्रसभं मनः ॥ ६० ॥

60. The turbulent senses, O son of Kuntī, violently carry off the mind even of a wise man striving for perfection.

Even a man of discrimination falls prey to the temptation of the world. Therefore the aspirant must not relax his effort for self-control.

Wherefore,

तानि सर्वाणि संयम्य युक्त आसीत मत्परः ।
वशे हि यस्येन्द्रियाणि तस्य प्रज्ञा प्रतिष्ठिता ॥ ६१ ॥

61. The yogi restrains them all and remains intent on Me. His wisdom is steady whose senses are under control.

Me—The Supreme Lord, who is the innermost Self of all.

The turbulent senses can be brought under control only by love of God and through His grace. It is impossible to subjugate the senses through one's own efforts, unaided by prayer. The difference between the moral path of the agnostic and the religious path of the devotee is that the former emphasizes self-effort, and the latter, humility and surrender to God.

The very thought of sense-objects causes future misfortune.

ध्यायतो विषयान्पुंसः सङ्गस्तेषूपजायते ।
सङ्गात्सञ्जायते कामः कामात्क्रोधोऽभिजायते ॥ ६२ ॥

क्रोधाद्भवति सम्मोहः सम्मोहात्स्मृतिविभ्रमः ।
स्मृतिभ्रंशाद् बुद्धिनाशो बुद्धिनाशात्प्रणश्यति ॥ ६३ ॥

62-63. When a man dwells on objects, he feels an attachment for them. Attachment gives rise to desire, and desire breeds anger.

From anger comes delusion; from delusion, the failure of memory; from the failure of memory, the ruin of discrimination; and from the ruin of discrimination the man perishes.

Objects—Any thing or person that is perceived.

Failure of memory—Regarding the lessons learnt from the scriptures and the teacher, and also from past experience.

Perishes—Is unable to attain the spiritual goal.

"A beautiful image appears. The tendency of the mind is to repeat it. Then, if the image is allowed to recur, a liking grows. With the growth of liking the wish to come close, to possess, appears. Any obstacle to this produces wrath. The impulse to anger throws the mind into confusion, which casts a veil over the lessons of wisdom learnt by past experience. Thus deprived of his moral standard, he is prevented from using his discrimination. Failing in discrimination, he acts irrationally, on the impulse of passion, and paves the way to moral death. Thus Kṛṣṇa traces moral degradation to those first breaths of thought, that come softly and almost unconsciously to the mind."—Swāmi Swarūpānanda's commentary on the Gītā.

If thinking of objects leads to suffering, what leads to peace?

रागद्वेषविमुक्तैस्तु विषयानिन्द्रियैश्चरन्।
आत्मवश्यैर्विधेयात्मा प्रसादमधिगच्छति॥ ६४॥

64. The man of self-control, moving among objects with his senses under restraint, and free from attachment and hate, attains serenity of mind.

The man of self-control—He who has controlled the mind.

Objects—Such objects as are indispensable for preserving one's life.

Free from attachment and hate—Attachment and hate are natural in the presence of pleasant and unpleasant objects.

The seeker after God, with a mind completely under control, allows his senses to enjoy those objects that are necessary for the maintenance of life, but always preserves the evenness of his mind, whether the objects be pleasant or unpleasant. Thus he attains peace, serenity, and clear vision. This verse answers Arjuna's question: "How does he move?"

What does one attain through serenity?

प्रसादे सर्वदुःखानां हानिरस्योपजायते।
प्रसन्नचेतसो ह्याशु बुद्धिः पर्यवतिष्ठते॥ ६५॥

65. In that serenity there is an end of all sorrow; for the intelligence of the man of serene mind soon becomes steady.

An end of all sorrow—Sorrow is due to lack of discrimination between good and evil, true and false, which is noticed in the case of restless people.

Steady—Centred on the Self.

The man whose mind is serene and whose intelligence is steady has achieved his goal. Therefore, with a mind devoid of attachment and hate, the yogi should enjoy only those sense-objects that are indispensable for the preservation of his body,

Peace of mind alone leads to happiness.

नास्ति बुद्धिरयुक्तस्य न चायुक्तस्य भावना।
न चाभावयतः शान्तिरशान्तस्य कुतः सुखम्॥ ६६॥

66.. The man whose mind is not under his control has no Self-knowledge and no contemplation either. Without contemplation he can have no peace; and without peace, how can he have happiness?

Contemplation—On the nature of the Self.

True happiness is not in the thirst for objects but in the restraint of the senses from thirst for enjoyment. Thirst is misery indeed.

Why is the unsteady man incapable of Knowledge?

इन्द्रियाणां हि चरतां यन्मनोऽनुविधीयते।
तदस्य हरति प्रज्ञां वायुर्नावमिवाम्भसि॥ ६७॥

67. For even one of the roving senses, if the mind yields to it, carries away discrimination as a gale carries away a ship on the waters.

Roving senses—The senses wildly pursuing their objects.

Discrimination—The discrimination of the mind.

If a single uncontrolled sense can plunge a man into such a plight, the calamity of the man with all senses uncontrolled requires no underscoring. As a gale carries away a ship from her charted course and drives her astray, so the force of the uncontrolled sense carries away the aspirant's attention from Self-knowledge and turns it toward worldly objects.

Now the Lord concludes the topic of the subjugation of the senses:

तस्माद्यस्य महाबाहो निगृहीतानि सर्वशः।
इन्द्रियाणीन्द्रियार्थेभ्यस्तस्य प्रज्ञा प्रतिष्ठिता॥ ६८॥

68. Therefore, O mighty Arjuna, his wisdom is steady whose senses are completely restrained from their objects.

The man of steady wisdom can, at will, withdraw the senses from their objects and enter into communion with the Self.

या निशा सर्वभूतानां तस्यां जागर्ति संयमी।
यस्यां जाग्रति भूतानि सा निशा पश्यतो मुनेः॥ ६९॥

69. In that which is night to all beings, the man of self-control is awake; and where all beings are awake, there is night for the muni who sees.

To the ignorant the Supreme Reality is night. They see in It confusion and darkness. But the man of steady wisdom is fully awake with regard to Reality. Again, the manifold world of time and space is clear as day to the ignorant; but the man of wisdom sees in it the confusion of night.

Ignorance, or nescience, creates the idea of multiplicity and also of duty associated with means and ends. Knowledge removes the idea of multiplicity and also that of duty. Wherefore an ignorant person engages in the performance of duty with a view to attaining a result, and the wise never deviates. from Self-knowledge and does not yearn for anything as yet unattained.

The desireless person alone attains peace,

आपूर्यमाणमचलप्रतिष्ठं
समुद्रमापः प्रविशन्ति यद्वत्।
तद्वत्कामा यं प्रविशन्ति सर्वे
स शान्तिमाप्नोति न कामकामी॥ ७०॥

70. Not the desirer of desires attains peace, but he into whom all desires enter as the waters enter the ocean, which is full to the brim and grounded in stillness.

Waters from innumerable rivers enter the ocean; but this does not make the ocean overflow its bounds or change its nature, for it is based in stillness. Likewise, that man alone finds true peace in whom no agitation is created by the enjoyment of those objects with which he inevitably comes in contact during his life on earth. A man attains such a state through constant awareness of the unchangeable Reality that constitutes his innermost Self. He who looks outside for enjoyments never attains peace,

Because this is so,

विहाय कामान्यः सर्वान्पुमांश्चरति निःस्पृहः ।
निर्ममो निरहङ्कारः स शान्तिमधिगच्छति ॥७१॥

71. That man who lives completely free from desires, without longing, devoid of the sense of "I" and "mine," attains peace.

Lives—He lives only to work out his prārabdha karma, the action of his previous life that has produced his present body.

Desires—Even for the barest necessities of life.

Sense of "I" and "mine"—He is not egotistic about anything, not even about his scholarship and knowledge.

The verse refers to a man of complete renunciation, always aware of his identity with Brahman.

Devotion to Knowledge is extolled:

एषा ब्राह्मी स्थितिः पार्थ नैनां प्राप्य विमुह्यति ।
स्थित्वास्यामन्तकालेऽपि ब्रह्मनिर्वाणमृच्छति ॥७२॥

72. This is the Brāhmic state, O son of Pṛthā. Attaining it, one is no longer deluded. Being established therein even in the hour of death, one attains final liberation in Brahman.

Brāhmic state—The state of Brahman, Existence-Knowledge-Bliss Absolute.

No longer—A jñānī is never again deluded by the world.

Attaining the Knowledge of Brahman, even as late as the hour of death, one obtains final liberation. And what doubt can there be about the liberation of a man who practises the discipline of renunciation from an early age and dwells on Brahman throughout life?

ॐ तत्सदिति श्रीमद्भगवद्गीतासूपनिषत्सु
ब्रह्मविद्यायां योगशास्त्रे श्रीकृष्णार्जुनसंवादे
साङ्ख्ययोगो नाम द्वितीयोऽध्यायः ॥२॥

Thus in the Bhagavad Gītā, the Essence of the Upaniṣads, the Science of Brahman, the Scripture of Yoga, the Dialogue between Śrī Kṛṣṇa and Arjuna, ends the Second Chapter, entitled: THE WAY OF ULTIMATE REALITY

CHAPTER 3

THE WAY OF ACTION

[कर्मयोगः]

अर्जुन उवाच।

ज्यायसी चेत्कर्मणस्ते मता बुद्धिर्जनार्दन।
तत्किं कर्मणि घोरे मां नियोजयसि केशव॥ १॥

1. *Arjuna said:* If You hold, O Janārdana, that knowledge is superior to action, why, then, O Keśava, do You engage me in this terrible action?

Both the path of work and the path of knowledge and renunciation, for the purpose of attaining Self-knowledge, are described in the Gītā. In Chapter II, verses 55-72, Śrī Kṛṣṇa recommends to the jñānīs the path of renunciation. But in verse 47 He asks Arjuna to follow the path of action. He does not say, however, that Arjuna will experience the Supreme Bliss as the direct result of action. Arjuna's dilemma is this: How can the Lord first describe to him, a devout seeker of Bliss, the path of knowledge and renunciation, but then command him to an action attended by many obvious evils? How does one attain the Knowledge of Brahman? Along the path of action? Or along the path of renunciation? Or by some conjunction of the two? According to Śaṅkara the conclusion of the Bhagavad Gītā, and also of the Upaniṣads, is that Brahman can be directly realized only by the path of knowledge and renunciation, and not by any other means.

The second chapter gives a summary of the teaching of the Gītā: The aspirant for liberation must first practise motiveless action, surrendering the results to God. That will purify his heart. Next, he will practise discrimination, renunciation, and other disciplines, and give up worldly duties. Thus he will feel single-minded devotion to God. Next, this devotion will create a longing for the Knowledge of Reality, which destroys avidyā, or ignorance, which is compounded of the three guṇas. With the destruction of ignorance the aspirant will achieve cessation of birth and death in the relative world and thus ultimate liberation.

Arjuna feels confused by the Lord's praise of both the righteous war (II, 31-38) and the Knowledge of Brahman.

व्यामिश्रेणेव वाक्येन बुद्धिं मोहयसीव मे।
तदेकं वद निश्चित्य येन श्रेयोऽहमाप्नुयाम्॥ २॥

2. With these apparently contradictory words You seem to confuse my understanding. Therefore tell me definitely that one thing by which I shall reach the Highest Goal.

Seem to confuse—There is no confusion in the Lord's words; but to the dull understanding of Arjuna they seem confusing.

That one thing—If knowledge and action are intended for two distinct classes of aspirants and cannot be followed by one and the same person, then Arjuna asks Kṛṣṇa to teach him the one best suited to himself in accordance with the state and power of his understanding.

The Lord's reply is in conformity with the question.

श्रीभगवानुवाच।
लोकेऽस्मिन् द्विविधा निष्ठा पुरा प्रोक्ता मयानघ।
ज्ञानयोगेन साङ्ख्यानां कर्मयोगेन योगिनाम्॥ ३॥

3. *The Lord said:* Even of yore, O sinless one, a twofold devotion was taught by Me to the world: devotion to knowledge for the contemplative and devotion to work for the active.

Of yore—In the beginning of the created world. Even at the very beginning of the cycle of time, two classes of people, those with contemplative and those with active temperaments, were in existence.

Contemplative—As a result of meritorious action in previous lives, they are born, as it were, with a clear knowledge of the Self and the non-Self. They renounce the world even without embracing the householder's life and belong to that highest class of saṃnyāsīs known as paramahaṃsas, whose thoughts always dwell on Brahman. For those pure souls the path of knowledge is prescribed so that they may mature their knowledge of Brahman.

Active—Those who believe in external action as a means of self-unfoldment. Their understanding is still coloured. by the stain of duality. The performance of unselfish action purifies their souls and enables them to practise knowledge and contemplation.

According to Hindu philosophy the practice of a particular spiritual discipline is determined by the competence of the aspirant. Both the active and the contemplative have one goal, namely, the realization of Brahman. The path of action, however, does not lead directly to that realization.

An aspirant should perform his duties, determined by his birth and position in society, until he achieves purity of mind and becomes competent to follow the path of knowledge. There cannot be any knowledge of Brahman unless the mind is pure.

न कर्मणामनारम्भान्नैष्कर्म्यं पुरुषोऽश्नुते।
न च संन्यसनादेव सिद्धिं समधिगच्छति॥४॥

4. Not by merely abstaining from action does a man reach the state of actionlessness, nor by mere renunciation does he arrive at perfection.

Action—Different forms of worship, as well as other duties, through the performance of which a man purifies his mind.

Actionlessness—Perfection. Action, as it is generally understood, is the outcome of want and desire. A perfect man, on account of his Self-knowledge, is desireless and hence abstains from egotistic action.

Renunciation—Abandonment of action before fitness to pursue the path of knowledge has been achieved.

The performance of action is a way to freedom from activity. Through devotion to action one earns devotion to knowledge. Through unselfish action the seeker eliminates his selfish desires, and then attains the state of mind in which peace and the contemplation of Reality are enjoyed. As long as a man regards himself as a finite being he must work. But when he knows himself to be the infinite Spirit, he abstains from all egotistic activities.

Why does a person not attain perfection by mere renunciation unaccompanied by knowledge?

न हि कश्चित्क्षणमपि जातु तिष्ठत्यकर्मकृत्।
कार्यते ह्यवशः कर्म सर्वः प्रकृतिजैर्गुणैः॥५॥

5. Verily, no one can remain even for an instant without doing work. For, driven by the guṇas born of Prakṛti everyone is made to act, in spite of himself.

No one—The reference is to the unillumined, or ignorant, who are under the control of the guṇas.

Guṇas—These are sattva, rajas, and tamas. *See* note on II, 45.

In the case of an ignorant person all action is performed at the bidding of the guṇas. The guṇas belong to the non-Self, and an ignorant person cannot discriminate between the Self and the non-Self. A man of Knowledge, too, performs some action, perhaps for the preservation of his body. But he does not identify himself with Prakṛti or Nature. He is always conscious of his freedom from the guṇas. In his case the guṇas may perform their functions, but he remains completely unaffected.

An ignorant person must not neglect the duties enjoined upon him.

कर्मेन्द्रियाणि संयम्य य आस्ते मनसा स्मरन्।
इन्द्रियार्थान्विमूढात्मा मिथ्याचारः स उच्यते॥६॥

6. He who restrains his organs of action, but continues to dwell in his mind on the objects of the senses, deludes himself and is called a hypocrite.

Restrains etc.—In order to give himself or others an impression that he is meditating on God.

Organs of action—Hands, feet, vocal organ, and the organs of generation and evacuation.

True renunciation is not just the control of the organs of action or abstention from physical movement. It is the control of the mind and the organs of perception. It is the absence of longing for activity. An active mind and an actionless body do not indicate the life of saṃnyāsa. A person possessed of these has an impure mind and becomes sinful by embracing the monastic life.

यस्त्विन्द्रियाणि मनसा नियम्यारभतेऽर्जुन।
कर्मेन्द्रियैः कर्मयोगमसक्तः स विशिष्यते॥७॥

7. But he who restrains his senses with his mind and directs his organs of action to work, with no feeling of attachment—he, O Arjuna, is indeed superior.

He who restrains etc.—Refers to a karmayogi or saint; who is fit only for the path of action.

Senses—The five organs of perception or action.

Superior—Such a seeker will attain Knowledge through purification of the mind.

A true karmayogi engages in outer action but is inwardly detached from its result. It is not the action itself, but the greediness of the mind for the result, that strengthens our bondage to the world.

Wherefore,

नियतं कुरु कर्म त्वं कर्म ज्यायो ह्यकर्मणः।
शरीरयात्रापि च ते न प्रसिध्येदकर्मणः॥८॥

8. Do your allotted action; for action is superior to inaction. And even the bare maintenance of your body will not be possible if you remain inactive.

Allotted—The action allotted by the scriptures to different persons in accordance with their inherited tendencies.

A man conscious of his body and its demands must not remain inactive. But the case is quite different with a saṃnyāsī, who is free of body-consciousness.

Unselfish action does not create bondage.

यज्ञार्थात्कर्मणोऽन्यत्र लोकोऽयं कर्मबन्धनः।
तदर्थं कर्म कौन्तेय मुक्तसङ्गः समाचर॥९॥

9. The world becomes bound by action unless it be done for the sake of Sacrifice. Therefore, O son of Kuntī, give up attachment and do your work for the sake of the Lord.

Sacrifice—The Sanskrit word "yajña" means a religious. rite, a sacrifice, or worship; it also denotes any action performed with a spiritual motive. Further, the word means the Supreme Lord, in which sense it is used in this verse.

Work that is done with a view to pleasing the Lord and not from any personal motive does not bind the worker.

There is another reason for the enjoining of work upon those who cannot follow the path of knowledge:

सहयज्ञाः प्रजाः सृष्ट्वा पुरोवाच प्रजापतिः।
अनेन प्रसविष्यध्वमेष वोऽस्त्विष्टकामधुक्॥१०॥

10. The Prajāpati, in the beginning, created men together with sacrifice, and said: "By this shall you multiply. Let this be the Cow of Plenty and yield unto you the milk of your desires.

Prajāpati—The Creator, or Brahmā.

Sacrifice—In this verse the word means the sacrifices or religious rites mentioned in the ritualistic portion of the Vedas.

Men were created with a propensity for action, which is the means of self-expression and happiness in the lower stage of spiritual development. The performance of obligatory duties ensures welfare for all in the relative world.

How can welfare be achieved by sacrifice?

देवान्भावयतानेन ते देवा भावयन्तु वः ।
परस्परं भावयन्तः श्रेयः परमवाप्स्यथ ॥ ११ ॥

इष्टान्भोगान्हि वो देवा दास्यन्ते यज्ञभाविताः ।
तैर्दत्तानप्रदायैभ्यो यो भुङ्क्ते स्तेन एव सः ॥ १२ ॥

11-12. "With sacrifice shall you nourish the gods; and may the gods nourish you. Thus nourishing one another, you will obtain the Highest Good,

"The gods, nourished by sacrifice, will bestow on you the enjoyments you desire." He is verily a thief who enjoys the things that they give without offering to them anything in return.

Gods—The word in Sanskrit is "devas," literally, "shining ones." When a human being performs meritorious action on earth, he becomes a god after death and occupies a temporary position in heaven, where he is given charge of a cosmic process. Thus the Hindu scriptures describe the god of fire, the god of wind, the god of the ocean, and so on. *See* note on "Indra," IX, 20.

Highest Good—Knowledge of Brahman or happiness in heaven, depending on the motive of the aspirant. The sacrifice may be performed either for liberation or for worldly enjoyment. In the former case the sacrifice leads to purity of heart in this or in a subsequent life and ultimately conduces to the Knowledge of Brahman, whereas in the latter case it leads the sacrificer to heaven.

Enjoyments—Such as wife, children, wealth.

Thief—All householders owe debts to the gods, the ṛṣis, and the ancestors. The gods are those who control the cosmic processes. The ṛṣis are those who have given the culture to the race. The ancestors are those to whom man owes his body and life. The debts to these are repaid by sacrifice, by the study of scripture, and by the begetting of children. He who enjoys the pleasures of life without paying the above enumerated debts is indeed a thief.

In this relative world men and gods are interdependent. They are nourished by one another. Men offer oblations to the gods; the gods in return ensure men's welfare by sending rain and other gifts. Thus a chain of mutual obligation binds together all created beings."

Those who act in a spirit of sacrifice are superior persons.

यज्ञशिष्टाशिनः सन्तो मुच्यन्ते सर्वकिल्बिषैः ।
भुञ्जते ते त्वघं पापा ये पचन्त्यात्मकारणात् ॥ १३ ॥

13. Good men, who eat the remnant of the sacrifice, are freed from all sins; but wicked men, who cook food only for themselves, verily eat sin.

Remnant of the sacrifice—Food should first of all be offered to the gods and then enjoyed by men. In a broader sense, all action should be performed for the satisfaction of the Lord. Egotistic action is condemned.

All sins—Every householder commits inevitably the fivefold sin of killing, which results from the use of (1) the pestle and mortar, (2) the grinding-stone, (3) the oven, (4) the water-jar, and (5) the broom. He is absolved from the sins by the performance of the five obligatory duties known as yajña, or sacrifice. The five sacrifices are: devayajña (the offering of sacrifices to the gods), brahmayājña (the teaching and reciting of the scriptures), pitṛyajña (the offering of libations of water to the ancestors), nṛyajña (the feeding of the hungry), and bhutayajña (the feeding of the lower animals). The performance of these five daily sacrifices, or duties, spiritualizes life and establishes concord and harmony between the living and the dead, as well as between the superhuman, human, and subhuman worlds. The selfish life is transformed into an unselfish one. The individual becomes aware of the interdependence of all beings.

Action should be performed by those who are qualified for it; for it is action that sets the wheel of the cosmos going.

अन्नाद्भवन्ति भूतानि पर्जन्यादन्नसम्भवः ।
यज्ञाद्भवति पर्जन्यो यज्ञः कर्मसमुद्भवः ॥ १४ ॥

कर्म ब्रह्मोद्भवं विद्धि ब्रह्माक्षरसमुद्भवम्।
तस्मात्सर्वगतं ब्रह्म नित्यं यज्ञे प्रतिष्ठितम्॥ १५॥

14-15. From food all creatures are born; from rain food is produced; from sacrifice comes rain; sacrifice is born of action.

Know that action arises from the Vedas, and the Vedas from the Imperishable. Therefore the all-pervading Vedas ever rest in sacrifice.

Creatures—Reference to the physical bodies of created beings, which are produced from the seminal fluid and the ovum, the products of food.

Rain—"The offering thrown into the fire reaches the sun; from the sun comes rain; from rain, food; and from food, all creatures." (*Manu*, III, 76) The subtle principle into which sacrificial deeds are converted after they have been performed, and through which they later appear as fruit, is called "apūrva." The apūrva is the connecting link between the sacrifice and the fruit, the cause and the effect.

Action—The sacrifice prescribed in the Vedas, in which priests and sacrificer take part.

Imperishable—The Supreme Reality.

The all-pervading Vedas—As the breath comes out of a man, so the Vedas illumine all subjects and are the infinite store of knowledge. They deal with sacrifices and the modes of their performance.

The Supreme Reality is the source and basis of the Vedas, which prescribe for householders sacrifice or action. Therefore action should be performed.

The wheel of the cosmos has been set in motion by the Supreme Lord. Hence action is to be performed by all who are conscious of being parts of the relative world.

एवं प्रवर्तितं चक्रं नानुवर्तयतीह यः।
अघायुरिन्द्रियारामो मोघं पार्थ स जीवति॥ १६॥

16. Thus was the wheel set in motion; and he who does not follow it, but takes delight in the senses and lives in sin, O Pārtha lives in vain.

The wheel—It was set in motion by the Creator, Prajāpati, on the basis of the Vedas and the sacrifices.

Follow it—By studying the Vedas and performing the sacrifices therein enjoined.

Takes delight in the senses—Acts for the enjoyment of sense-pleasures and not for the gratification of the Lord,

The sense of this section (III, 4-16) is that the man ignorant of the Self should perform action for the purification of the mind. When the mind is purified, the aspirant becomes fit for Self-knowledge. A person still desirous of worldly ends may not refrain from action.

Karmayoga is not meant for knowers of the Self.

यस्त्वात्मरतिरेव स्यादात्मतृप्तश्च मानवः।
आत्मन्येव च सन्तुष्टस्तस्य कार्यं न विद्यते॥ १७॥

17. But verily, the man who rejoices in the Self and is satisfied with the Self and is content in the Self alone he has nothing for which he should work.

The man who rejoices etc.—Who has renounced all worldly attachment and is devoted to the Knowledge of the Self alone; a saṃnyāsī.

Rejoices in the Self—Not in the objects of the senses.

Is satisfied with the Self—Not with food and drink.

Is content in the Self—Not in the possession of external things.

A person endowed with Self-knowledge has no worldly duties to perform. According to the *Bṛhadāraṇyaka Upaniṣad,* the knowers of Brahman, endowed with Self-knowledge, renounce the desire for offspring, for wealth, and for the worlds; they lead a mendicant life, maintaining their bodies with only the barest necessaries. (III, v, 1)

Further,

नैव तस्य कृतेनार्थो नाकृतेनेह कश्चन।
न चास्य सर्वभूतेषु कश्चिदर्थव्यपाश्रयः॥ १८॥

18. He has no object to gain by what he does in this world, nor any to lose by what he leaves undone; nor is there anyone, among all beings, on whom he need depend for any object.

He—The man rejoicing in the Self.

Object to gain—He is not anxious for merit in order to enjoy happiness in heaven.

Any to lose—He is not afraid of demerit. Being totally devoid of ego, he is beyond the injunctions of the scriptures.

Anyone, among all beings—From the Creator, Brahmā, to a blade of grass. A man endowed with Self-realization does, not seek, the support of anyone in the relative world. Even the gods cannot injure him, he being the inmost Self of them also. Harm from higher cosmic powers is possible only before the attainment of Self-knowledge, because an unillumined, or ignorant, person sees multiplicity and considers himself to be separate from others. All fear comes from the perception of duality.

Since you have not yet attained Self-knowledge,

तस्मादसक्तः सततं कार्यं कर्म समाचर।
असक्तो ह्याचरन्कर्म परमाप्नोति पूरुषः॥ १९॥

19. Therefore always do without attachment the work you have to do; for a man who does his work without attachment attains the Supreme.

A seeker who does his duty for the gratification of God attains purity of mind and ultimately realizes the Highest Goal.

Wise men in the past acted in that manner.

कर्मणैव हि संसिद्धिमास्थिता जनकादयः।
लोकसङ्ग्रहमेवापि सम्पश्यन्कर्तुमर्हसि॥ २०॥

20. Verily, by action alone men like Janaka attained perfection. Further, you should perform work with a view to guiding people along the right path.

The scriptures mention kṣatriya sages who, in spite of their attainment of Knowledge, did not give up work. They attained purity of mind through the performance of duty and then realized Brahman. But their prārabdha karma made them continue their royal duties for the maintenance of the world order. Arjuna, too, should set an example of righteous living to the people by doing his kṣatriya duties.

How can a man guide people by performing his own duties?

यद्यदाचरति श्रेष्ठस्तत्तदेवेतरो जनः।
स यत्प्रमाणं कुरुते लोकस्तदनुवर्तते॥ २१॥

21. Whatever a great man does, that others follow; whatever he sets up as a standard, that the world follows.

Common people are more influenced by the living examples of great men than by the abstract teaching of the scriptures.

There is the example of the Lord Himself.

न मे पार्थास्ति कर्तव्यं त्रिषु लोकेषु किञ्चन।
नानवाप्तमवाप्तव्यं वर्त एव च कर्मणि॥२२॥

22. I have, O Pārtha no duty; there is nothing in the three worlds that I have not gained and nothing that I have to gain. Yet I continue to work.

Śrī Kṛṣṇa speaks of Himself as the Godhead. Though He transcends all claims of duty, yet He acts according to the scriptural injunctions to set an example to others.

Inactivity on the part of Kṛṣṇa would cause the ruin of all.

यदि ह्यहं न वर्तेयं जातु कर्मण्यतन्द्रितः।
मम वर्त्मानुवर्तन्ते मनुष्याः पार्थ सर्वशः॥२३॥

23. For should I not ever engage, unwearied, in action, O Pārtha men would in every way follow in My wake.

Follow in My wake—Because Śrī Kṛṣṇa is known to be the best ideal to follow.

What then would happen?

उत्सीदेयुरिमे लोका न कुर्यां कर्म चेदहम्।
सङ्करस्य च कर्ता स्यामुपहन्यामिमाः प्रजाः॥२४॥

24. If I should cease to work, these worlds would perish: I should cause the mixture of castes and destroy all these creatures.

Would perish—It is by action that the relative universe. is sustained.

Should Kṛṣṇa, the ideal man, desist from work, then people would not perform religious and moral actions. Social confusion would ensue. The Lord would thus bring about people's ruin instead of their welfare.

Therefore the man of Self-realization must work for the welfare of the world at large.

सक्ताः कर्मण्यविद्वांसो यथा कुर्वन्ति भारत।
कुर्याद्विद्वांस्तथासक्तश्चिकीर्षुर्लोकसङ्ग्रहम्॥२५॥

25. As the ignorant act, attached to their work, O Bhārata, so should an enlightened man act, but without attachment, in order that he may set people on the right path.

An ignorant person acts zealously for his personal happiness; but a wise man should act, with the same zeal, for the welfare of others.

The only incentive to action for a knower of the Self is the welfare of others.

न बुद्धिभेदं जनयेदज्ञानां कर्मसङ्गिनाम्।
जोषयेत्सर्वकर्माणि विद्वान्युक्तः समाचरन्॥ २६ ॥

26. Let no enlightened man unsettle the understanding of the ignorant, who are attached to action. He should engage them in action, himself performing it with devotion.

Unsettle—An ignorant person firmly believes that one should act to enjoy the result of work. The wise man should not unsettle this belief; otherwise the ignorant man would prematurely give up all work.

If the wise must act as the ignorant, then wherein lies the difference between them?

प्रकृतेः क्रियमाणानि गुणैः कर्माणि सर्वशः।
अहङ्कारविमूढात्मा कर्ताहमिति मन्यते॥ २७ ॥

27. All work is performed by the guṇas of Prakṛti. But he whose mind is deluded by egotism thinks, "I am the doer."

Guṇas of Prakṛti—The guṇas modify themselves into the outside world, the body, and the senses. These are the performers of all action. The Self looks on without participating in any way in the action done by the body and senses. An ignorant man, however, identifies the Self with the aggregate of the body and the senses, and thinks that the Self is the doer. Thus he ascribes to the Self all the characteristics that really belong to the guṇas.

For "guṇas" *See* note on II, 45.

But the enlightened man feels differently.

तत्त्ववित्तु महाबाहो गुणकर्मविभागयोः।
गुणा गुणेषु वर्तन्त इति मत्वा न सज्जते॥ २८ ॥

28. But, O mighty Arjuna, he who knows the truth about the guṇas and action, and what is distinct from them, holds himself unattached, perceiving that it is the guṇas that are occupied with the guṇas.

What is distinct from them—That is to say, the Self.

The enlightened man sees that the guṇas in the form of the senses are occupied with the guṇas in the form of the objects of sense, and that this constitutes man's action. So he always holds himself unattached, allowing the guṇas to perform their natural functions. The difference between an active enlightened man and an active ignorant man is that the former is beyond the influence of the guṇas, whereas the latter is controlled by them.

The topic under discussion is now concluded:

प्रकृतेर्गुणसम्मूढाः सज्जन्ते गुणकर्मसु।
तानकृत्स्नविदो मन्दान्कृत्स्नविन्न विचालयेत्॥ २९॥

29. Those who are deluded by the guṇas of Prakṛti attach themselves to the actions that those guṇas prompt. Nevertheless let no man who knows the whole unsettle the minds of the dull-witted, who know only a part.

Who knows the whole—The wise man, who through Self-knowledge knows everything.

Who know only a part—Those who do not see anything beyond the immediate effect of an action.

The wise should not confuse the ignorant, who are attached to the guṇas and action, by instructing them in Self-knowledge, which makes one give up worldly duties.

How should duties be regarded by those who seek liberation but are still attached to the guṇas?

मयि सर्वाणि कर्माणि संन्यस्याध्यात्मचेतसा।
निराशीर्निर्ममो भूत्वा युध्यस्व विगतज्वरः॥ ३०॥

30. Surrendering all action to Me, with mind intent on the Self, freeing yourself from longing and selfishness, fight—unperturbed by grief.

Me—Kṛṣṇa, the Divine Being, the Supreme Lord, the Omniscient, the Self of all.

Intent on the Self—Constantly remembering that one acts at the direction of the Lord, who is seated in one's heart as the Inner Guide.

The following is the result of the action described above:

ये मे मतमिदं नित्यमनुतिष्ठन्ति मानवाः।
श्रद्धावन्तोऽनसूयन्तो मुच्यन्ते तेऽपि कर्मभिः॥ ३१॥

31. Those who, full of faith, ever follow this teaching of Mine and do not carp at Me—they too are released from their works.

Faith—A mental attitude consisting primarily of sincerity. of purpose, humility, and reverence. *See* note on XVII, 3.

Do not carp at Me—Do not find fault with the Lord; do not feel that He has engaged the worker in a painful action.

They too—As well as the jñānīs.

Released from their works—Released from the merit and demerit that are the inevitable result of work.

The worker, too, sincerely surrendering the results of action to God and full of divine love, becomes free, like the jñānī, from the good and evil results of his action, and realizes Truth.

The evil effect that comes from disobeying the Lord's injunction:

ये त्वेतदभ्यसूयन्तो नानुतिष्ठन्ति मे मतम्।
सर्वज्ञानविमूढांस्तान्विद्धि नष्टानचेतसः ॥ ३२ ॥

32. But those who carp at My teaching and practise it not know that such senseless men, blind to all wisdom, are doomed to destruction.

Those who have no faith in the words of the Lord, as revealed through the scriptures and the words of a competent teacher, and maliciously refrain from the performance of their duties, cannot discriminate between right and wrong and ultimately come to ruin.

Why do some people neglect their duties, thus disobeying the Lord's injunction? It is because their lower nature proves too strong for them.

सदृशं चेष्टते स्वस्याः प्रकृतेर्ज्ञानवानपि।
प्रकृतिं यान्ति भूतानि निग्रहः किं करिष्यति ॥ ३३ ॥

33. Even the man of knowledge acts in accordance with his own nature. All beings follow their nature; what can restraint do?

Nature—A man's prakṛti, or nature, is formed by the impressions of the good and evil acts performed in a previous life; it manifests itself at the beginning of the present life. This nature is the mainspring of the man's action.

Restraint—Forcible repression of the senses.

If a man must follow his own nature, then where is the scope for personal exertion? If man's own efforts are futile, then scriptural injunctions, too, are futile.

इन्द्रियस्येन्द्रियस्यार्थे रागद्वेषौ व्यवस्थितौ।
तयोर्न वशमागच्छेत्तौ ह्यस्य परिपन्थिनौ ॥ ३४ ॥

34. The love and hatred that the senses feel for their objects are inevitable. But let no one come under their sway; for they are one's enemies.

Love and hatred—Love for the agreeable and hatred for the disagreeable.

Let no one come etc.—This is the injunction of the scriptures. Herein lies the field of man's efforts.

The senses have natural likes or dislikes for their objects, and men generally are influenced by them. But the seeker after Truth exercises his discrimination and subdues, at the, very outset, this strong attachment and aversion. Like a swift-moving river, the wild senses drag a man along to destruction; but man should exercise self-effort and jump into the boat of scriptural teachings and arrive safely at his destination. Man should exert himself to overcome his natural beastly propensities and follow the dictates of righteousness.

Under the misguidance of love and hatred, a man may mistake another's duty for his own. This generally happens when one's own duty becomes beset with suffering and pain.

श्रेयान्स्वधर्मो विगुणः परधर्मात्स्वनुष्ठितात्।
स्वधर्मे निधनं श्रेयः परधर्मो भयावहः ॥ ३५ ॥

35. Better is one's own dharma, though imperfectly performed, than the dharma of another well performed. Better is death in the doing of one's own dharma: the dharma of another is fraught with peril.

Arjuna's desire to desist from fighting, which is the duty of a kṣatriya, and to follow the peaceful and calm life of a hermit, is due to a natural instinct to shun the disagreeable and accept what is agreeable to the senses.

Arjuna asks for a clear statement regarding the source of evil.

अर्जुन उवाच।
अथ केन प्रयुक्तोऽयं पापं चरति पूरुषः।
अनिच्छन्नपि वार्ष्णेय बलादिव नियोजितः ॥ ३६ ॥

36. *Arjuna said:* But under what compulsion does a man commit sin, O Vārṣṇeya, in spite of himself and driven, as it were, by force?

Vārṣṇeya—*Lit.*, one belonging to the clan of the Vṛṣṇis; an epithet of Kṛṣṇa.

Man can discriminate between good and evil. He wants to do good; but he does evil, as though against his own wishes. He seems to be constrained by an outside force.

श्रीभगवानुवाच।

काम एष क्रोध एष रजोगुणसमुद्भवः।
महाशनो महापाप्मा विद्ध्येनमिह वैरिणम्॥ ३७॥

37. *The Lord said:* It is desire, it is wrath, which springs from rajas. Know that this is our enemy here, all devouring and the cause of all sin.

Desire—Desire alone is the enemy of the whole world, the cause of all evil.

Wrath—Desire, being obstructed, takes the form of wrath.

Springs from rajas—Rajas is the cause of evil and suffering. Therefore desire brings only suffering. Sattva overcomes rajas and keeps desire under control.

All-devouring—Desire is never satiated by the gratification of desire. One gets rid of desire only through the constant practice of detachment.

Cause of all sin—Man commits sin only at the bidding of desire.

How is desire our enemy?

धूमेनाव्रियते वह्निर्यथादर्शो मलेन च।
यथोल्बेनावृतो गर्भस्तथा तेनेदमावृतम्॥ ३८॥

38. As fire is concealed by smoke, as a mirror by dust, as an unborn babe by the womb, so is Knowledge concealed by ignorance.

The three illustrations refer to the different degrees to which desire in the form of ignorance envelops and conceals the inner Light in man.

आवृतं ज्ञानमेतेन ज्ञानिनो नित्यवैरिणा।
कामरूपेण कौन्तेय दुष्पूरेणानलेन च॥ ३९॥

39. Enveloped is Knowledge, O son of Kuntī, by the insatiable fire of desire, which is the constant foe of the wise.

Insatiable fire—"Desires can never be satiated by the gratification of desires. The more they are enjoyed, the more they grow, as fire by the pouring into it of butter." (*Mahābhārata*)

An ignorant person regards a desire as a friend when he is craving its fulfilment, but realizes it to be an enemy when he discovers that suffering alone is the after-effect of enjoyment. But a wise man, even before suffering the consequence of a desire, knows it to be an evil; he does not have to wait for the result. Hence desire is the constant enemy of the wise.

Kṛṣṇa points out the seat of desire, the fortress of the enemy, by the conquest of which the enemy is easily defeated.

इन्द्रियाणि मनो बुद्धिरस्याधिष्ठानमुच्यते।
एतैर्विमोहयत्येष ज्ञानमावृत्य देहिनम्॥४०॥

40. The senses, the mind, and the understanding are said to be its seat; through these it veils Knowledge and deludes the embodied soul,

Through these—Desire vitiates the senses, the mind, and the understanding veils Knowledge, and at last traps man in the net of delusion.

तस्मात्त्वमिन्द्रियाण्यादौ नियम्य भरतर्षभ।
पाप्मानं प्रजहि ह्येनं ज्ञानविज्ञाननाशनम्॥४१॥

41. Therefore, O lord of the Bhāratas, control your senses at the outset and slay this foul destroyer of Knowledge and Realization.

Knowledge and Realization—Knowledge of the Self is first learnt from the scriptures and the teacher. Then, through constant contemplation, it is transformed into Realization.

Where should one stand in order to cast off desires?

इन्द्रियाणि पराण्याहुरिन्द्रियेभ्यः परं मनः।
मनसस्तु परा बुद्धिर्यो बुद्धेः परतस्तु सः॥४२॥

एवं बुद्धेः परं बुद्ध्वा संस्तभ्यात्मानमात्मना।
जहि शत्रुं महाबाहो कामरूपं दुरासदम्॥४३॥

42-43. The senses are superior, they say; superior to the senses is the mind; superior to the mind is the understanding; superior to the understanding is He. Therefore know Him who is superior to the understanding, control the self by the Self, and destroy, O mighty Arjuna, the enemy, who comes in the guise of desire and is hard to overcome.

Superior—The senses are superior to the body. The body is gross and limited; the senses, comparatively speaking, are subtle and have a more extensive sphere of action.

Mind—Which consists of thoughts and desires and is of the nature of error and doubt. The mind is superior to the senses, for it directs their action.

Understanding—Which is characterized by determination and finality and is therefore superior to the mind.

He—The Self of man, the Dweller in the body, the Witness of the activities of the body, senses, mind, and understanding.

Control the self by the Self—By the Knowledge of the Higher Self one controls the lower self, that is to say, the mind.

ॐ तत्सदिति श्रीमद्भगवद्गीतासूपनिषत्सु
ब्रह्मविद्यायां योगशास्त्रे श्रीकृष्णार्जुनसंवादे
कर्मयोगो नाम तृतीयोऽध्यायः ॥ ३ ॥

Thus in the Bhagavad Gītā, the Essence of the Upaniṣads, the Science of Brahman, the Scripture of Yoga, the Dialogue between Śrī *Kṛṣṇa and Arjuna, ends the Third Chapter, entitled:* THE WAY OF ACTION

CHAPTER 4

THE WAY OF KNOWLEDGE

[ज्ञानकर्मसंन्यासयोगः]

श्रीभगवानुवाच।

इमं विवस्वते योगं प्रोक्तवानहमव्ययम्।
विवस्वान्मनवे प्राह मनुरिक्ष्वाकवेऽब्रवीत्॥ १॥

1. *The Lord said:* This eternal yoga I taught to Vivasvat; Vivasvat taught it to Manu; and Manu taught it to Ikṣvāku.

This eternal yoga—The yoga taught in the second and third chapters. The fruit of this yoga is liberation, which transcends time, space, and causality.

Vivasvat—The Sun-god.

Manu—The ancient law-giver of India.

Ikṣvāku—The ancestor of the kṣatriyas who trace their origin to the Sun-god.

In the beginning of the present cycle the Lord taught the eternal law regarding jñānayoga to the Sun-god, who transmitted it to the kṣatriyas, the rulers of the world. By this knowledge the kṣatriyas were strengthened. Only strong kṣatriya kings can protect the brāhmins who constitute the spiritual caste in Hindu society. When the military and the brāhmin castes are preserved, the social order is maintained. According to Hinduism the spiritual laws laid down in the Vedas are eternal. Through pure-souled ṛṣis they are revealed anew at the beginning of each cycle.

Jñānayoga, discussed in the second and third chapters, is based on renunciation and is attained through the performance of duty. Thus it comprehends both the life of activity (pravṛtti) and the life of retirement (nivṛtti) as taught in the Vedas. The path of knowledge has been described throughout the Gītā as leading directly to liberation. Therefore the Lord extols it by pointing out its antiquity.

एवं परम्पराप्राप्तमिमं राजर्षयो विदुः।
स कालेनेह महता योगो नष्टः परन्तप॥२॥

2. Thus handed down from one to another, it became known to the royal sages. But through long lapse of time, O destroyer of foes, this yoga has been lost to the world.

The teachings of this yoga were lost by falling into the hands of selfish and unrighteous people. It is the intention of Śrī Kṛṣṇa to revive it through the Gītā.

स एवायं मया तेऽद्य योगः प्रोक्तः पुरातनः।
भक्तोऽसि मे सखा चेति रहस्यं ह्येतदुत्तमम्॥३॥

3. The same ancient yoga I have told you today; for you are My devotee and friend, and it is a supreme secret.

Supreme secret—A secret that should be revealed only to those worthy of it.

Arjuna cannot understand how Śrī *Kṛṣṇa could have taught this yoga to Vivasvat, who was born much earlier than He.*

अर्जुन उवाच।
अपरं भवतो जन्म परं जन्म विवस्वतः।
कथमेतद्विजानीयां त्वमादौ प्रोक्तवानिति॥४॥

4. *Arjuna said:* Later was Your birth, and earlier the birth of Vivasvat. How, then, am I to understand that You taught him in the beginning?

The unenlightened Arjuna thinks Śrī Kṛṣṇa is an ordinary man and not the omnipotent and omniscient Lord. Kṛṣṇa wishes to remove this error.

श्रीभगवानुवाच।
बहूनि मे व्यतीतानि जन्मानि तव चार्जुन।
तान्यहं वेद सर्वाणि न त्वं वेत्थ परन्तप॥५॥

5. *The Lord said:* Many a birth have I passed through, O Arjuna, and so have you. I know them all, but you know them not, O scorcher of foes.

Śrī Kṛṣṇa knows the past, present, and future because He is the Lord Himself. He is unobstructed in His power of vision. But Arjuna, an ordinary mortal bound by ignorance, has only limited vision.

The Lord is untouched by dharma and adharma; therefore His birth was unlike that of an ordinary man.

अजोऽपि सन्नव्ययात्मा भूतानामीश्वरोऽपि सन्।
प्रकृतिं स्वामधिष्ठाय सम्भवाम्यात्ममायया॥ ६॥

6. Though I am unborn and eternal by nature, and though I am the Lord of all beings, yet, subjugating My Prakṛti I accept birth through My own māyā.

Eternal by nature—The Existence-Knowledge-Bliss Absolute, which forms the nature of the Lord, is eternal and changeless.

My Prakṛti—Māyā, which is made of the three guṇas, namely, sattva, rajas, and tamas, and deluded by which the embodied being does not recognize the Lord, who is his true Self. This māyā inheres in Brahman, but Brahman remains unaffected by it. It is like the poison of the cobra, which is in the cobra but cannot injure it.

Through My own māyā—It is through māyā that the Lord appears to be born. His embodiment is not real, as are the embodiments of other beings.

Actions, good and evil, produce the body in order that the embodied soul may experience their results. The soul assumes a body for such experience, and this is called birth. After the experience has been accomplished, the body is discarded, and that is called death. Therefore dharma and adharma are responsible for the birth of an embodied being. The embodiment of the Lord, on the other hand, cannot be due to dharma and adharma. He is not subject to the law of karma. He is the Lord of the universe and the Ruler of all laws, gross and subtle. The law of karma can affect only those who have egoistic and selfish motives. The Lord is free from ego. Therefore His embodiment as a human being is unlike the embodiment of other men. He assumes a human form, retaining His power over the inscrutable māyā by which other beings are bound. This māyā remains as a self-imposed limitation of the Lord as long as He chooses to dwell in a human body. On account of māyā He acts like a human being; but it does not affect His nature. After His mission in the world is over, He Himself withdraws māyā and regains His incorporeal nature. His activities in the world are for the purpose of setting an example to men. The embodiment of the Lord is only an appearance. A created being is under the control of māyā, but the Lord is the controller of māyā. The birth and death of the Lord depend on His own will; but the birth and death of an embodied being are due to the law of karma. This is the difference between an embodied being and the incarnate Lord.

When does the Lord assume a body?

यदा यदा हि धर्मस्य ग्लानिर्भवति भारत।
अभ्युत्थानमधर्मस्य तदात्मानं सृजाम्यहम्॥७॥

7. Whenever there is a decline of dharma, O Bhārata, and a rise of adharma, I incarnate Myself.

Dharma—*See* note on II, 7.

For what purpose?

परित्राणाय साधूनां विनाशाय च दुष्कृताम्।
धर्मसंस्थापनार्थाय सम्भवामि युगे युगे॥८॥

8. For the protection of the good, for the destruction of the wicked, and for the establishment of dharma, I am born in every age.

Destruction—The Lord is above love and hate. By destroying wickedness the Lord shows the way of liberation to the wicked.

In every age—The embodiment of the Lord is not confined to one particular age.

When righteousness is protected and wickedness destroyed, society lives according to dharma and affords opportunities to its members to lead a spiritual life.

What awaits the man who knows the true meaning of the Lord's embodiment and action in the world?

जन्म कर्म च मे दिव्यमेवं यो वेत्ति तत्त्वतः।
त्यक्त्वा देहं पुनर्जन्म नैति मामेति सोऽर्जुन॥९॥

9. Whoso knows, in the true light, My divine birth and action will not be born again when he leaves his body; he will attain Me, O Arjuna.

My divine birth—The Lord appears to be born, but in reality is beyond birth and death.

Action—The Lord is in reality beyond all action, though He appears to act for the cause of righteousness.

The man who knows the Lord's real nature as the Absolute Spirit, and also His embodiment in māyā, has realized the Ultimate Truth. Thus he transcends birth and death in the relative world and attains Brahman.

The path of liberation taught here by Kṛṣṇa is an ancient path.

वीतरागभयक्रोधा मन्मया मामुपाश्रिताः।
बहवो ज्ञानतपसा पूता मद्भावमागताः॥ १०॥

10. Freed from passion, fear, and anger, absorbed in Me, taking refuge in Me, and purified by the fire of Knowledge, many have become one with My Being.

The path of liberation taught here has been known and followed by seekers since the very beginning of creation and was not given to the world only by the Lord's Incarnation as Kṛṣṇa.

The Lord may be accused of partiality in that He bestows Self-knowledge on some and withholds it from others. The answer follows:

ये यथा मां प्रपद्यन्ते तांस्तथैव भजाम्यहम्।
मम वर्त्मानुवर्तन्ते मनुष्याः पार्थ सर्वशः॥ ११॥

11. In whatsoever way men approach Me, even so do I reward them; for it is My path, O Pārtha, that men follow in all things.

The Lord is not gracious to some and unkind to others. He is not open to the charge of granting liberation to some and withholding it from others. Different people seek the Lord with different motives. He rewards them all by granting their desires. But one cannot seek, at the same time, liberation and fulfilment of worldly desires. Wherefore the Lord bestows pleasures on those who seek pleasures; rewards unselfish men, who perform their prescribed duties and aim at liberation, by granting them discrimination; and rewards men of discrimination, who have renounced the world in pursuit of liberation, by granting them liberation: Likewise, the Lord rewards men in distress by rescuing them from their distress, and rewards seekers after wealth by giving them wealth. In whatever form a man worships the Lord, the Lord appears to him in that form. The various deities and cosmic forces, the angels, the Prophets, and the Incarnations are only different manifestations of the Lord Himself. If a man worship one of these for a definite purpose, he is worshipping the Lord Himself and the Lord fulfils that purpose. As there are innumerable ideals cherished by men, so there are innumerable forms of the Lord corresponding to those ideals. It is to Him alone that men offer worship under different names and forms, through different symbols and rites; likewise, from Him alone comes the fulfilment of all desires, whether they be for the enjoyment of worldly pleasures or for the realization of the Supreme Truth. As the Self within, He brings to fruition all wishes when the necessary conditions are fulfilled,

The following doubt arises: The Lord is free from love and hate. He is gracious to all creatures without distinction. He can fulfil every desire. Why do people not desire liberation and seek the Lord Himself? The answer follows:

काङ्क्षन्तः कर्मणां सिद्धिं यजन्त इह देवताः ।
क्षिप्रं हि मानुषे लोके सिद्धिर्भवति कर्मजा ॥ १२ ॥

12. Those who desire success in their works worship the gods here; for quickly, in this world of man, comes success from works.

People longing for worldly success worship minor gods or angels, who also are manifestations of the Lord. But on account of their selfish motives, their mode of worship is characterized by the attitude that the devotee and the god are two different beings. "He who, on the other hand, worships a separate god, thinking, 'He is separate from me and I am separate from him'—he knows not. He is to the gods as cattle are to men." (*Bṛhadāraṇyaka Upaniṣad*, I, iv, 10) Worldly success is quickly and easily attained, but not so Self-knowledge. Therefore people do not seek the latter.

Men are endowed with diverse temperaments and tendencies. All men are not born equal, because in them the preponderance of the different guṇas varies.

चातुर्वर्ण्यं मया सृष्टं गुणकर्मविभागशः ।
तस्य कर्तारमपि मां विद्ध्यकर्तारमव्ययम् ॥ १३ ॥

13. The four castes were created by Me according to the division of guṇas and karma. Though I am their Creator, yet know that I neither act nor change.

Four castes—These are the brāhmin, kṣatriya, vaiśya, and śūdra.

Division of guṇas and karma—The guṇas are sattva (goodness and harmony), rajas (foulness and activity), and tamas (darkness and inertia). The karma, or action, of a brāhmin, in whom sattva predominates, is characterized by control of the mind, control of the senses, austerity, etc. (XVIII, 42) The action of a kṣatriya, in whom rajas predominates and sattva is controlled by rajas, is characterized by heroism, high spirit, etc. (XVIII, 43) The action of a vaiśya, in whom rajas predominates and tamas is controlled by rajas, consists of agriculture, cattle-rearing, and trade. (XVIII, 44) The action of a śūdra, in whom tamas predominates and rajas is controlled by tamas, consists only of service. These four castes, determined by the division of guṇas and action, have been in existence among the Indo-Āryans since the very beginning of their society. Much later the hereditary caste-system was introduced, when the population increased enormously and other complexities of social life followed.

Though I am their Creator—The Lord is the Creator of the four castes only from the standpoint of māyā. Māyā is the immediate cause of everything that happens in the relative world. But since māyā has no existence independent of the Lord, He is said to be the Creator.

Neither act nor change—The Lord is not the agent, because He has no egoistic or selfish motive in the creation of the universe. For the same reason He remains unchanged by whatever happens in creation. It is selfish motives that bring about a change in the doer through the success or failure of his action,

The ignorant may speak of the Lord as the Creator, Preserver, and Destroyer of the universe, but in reality He is not so.

न मां कर्माणि लिम्पन्ति न मे कर्मफले स्पृहा।
इति मां योऽभिजानाति कर्मभिर्न स बध्यते॥ १४॥

14. Action does not defile Me; nor do I long for its fruit. He who knows Me thus is not bound by his action.

Does not defile Me—Because the Lord is totally free from egoism. Since He is unselfish, He is not reincarnated, like men, to reap the fruit of His action.

He who knows Me thus etc.—Anyone who knows his own inmost Self to be the Lord, unattached to action and its result, is not bound by action and will not be reborn in the world of māyā.

The Lord is described as the Creator, Preserver, and Destroyer of the universe only from the standpoint of māyā. But He Himself is absolutely unattached. He has not created the world through any special desire. How can He, in whom all desires find their fulfilment, be moved by a desire to create? The universe is the spontaneous movement of His nature, as the waves are of the ocean. It is the līlā, or sportive pleasure, of the Lord.

The seekers of Truth in ancient times worked in that spirit.

एवं ज्ञात्वा कृतं कर्म पूर्वैरपि मुमुक्षुभिः।
कुरु कर्मैव तस्मात्त्वं पूर्वैः पूर्वतरं कृतम्॥ १५॥

15. Men of old who sought liberation knew this and did their work. Therefore do your work as the ancients did in former times.

Men of old—King Janaka and others.

Knew this—That is to say, that the Self cannot have any desire for the fruit of action, nor can It be defiled by action.

Everyone conscious of his body must work. If he is ignorant, he should work for self-purification, and if he is wise and a knower of Truth, he should work to set an example to others. Śrī Kṛṣṇa expounds to Arjuna an ancient spiritual discipline.

The philosophy of action and inaction is extremely subtle.

किं कर्म किमकर्मेति कवयोऽप्यत्र मोहिताः।
तत्ते कर्म प्रवक्ष्यामि यज्ज्ञात्वा मोक्ष्यसेऽशुभात्॥ १६॥

16. Even the wise are perplexed as to what is action and what is inaction. Therefore I will tell you what action is, that you may know and be freed from evil.

Evil—The round of birth and death in māyā.

One must not oversimplify action and inaction by thinking that the former means the activity of the body, and the latter, its idleness.

कर्मणो ह्यपि बोद्धव्यं बोद्धव्यं च विकर्मणः।
अकर्मणश्च बोद्धव्यं गहना कर्मणो गतिः॥ १७॥

17. For verily, one has to understand what action really is, and likewise what forbidden action is, and also what inaction is. Hard to understand is the way of action.

Action—That which is prescribed by the scriptures and not merely approved by men.

Forbidden action—That which is forbidden by the scriptures.

Inaction—Renunciation of action.

Śrī Kṛṣṇa describes the true nature of action and inaction:

कर्मण्यकर्म यः पश्येदकर्मणि च कर्म यः।
स बुद्धिमान्मनुष्येषु स युक्तः कृत्स्नकर्मकृत्॥ १८॥

18. He who sees inaction in action, and action in inaction, he is wise among men, he is a yogi, and he has performed all action.

Inaction in action—It is only the ignorant that regard the Self as active. The yogi regards the Self as actionless even while he himself is engaged in action. Activity belongs to the body, the senses, and the mind. It is a function of the guṇas.

Action in inaction—The body, the senses, and the mind, regarded by the ignorant as actionless, are perceived by the yogi to be active. Hence he sees action in what the ignorant think to be inaction. Or the passage can mean: An ignorant person may strive hard to remain inactive because he regards work as the cause of suffering, and inaction as the way to knowledge. Such a person, though apparently inactive, is really active, since his mind is full of ideas. A wise man sees action in such inaction.

Performed all action—A wise person, devoid of the idea of agency, is really a free soul though he participates in action. Action does not bind him.

Action and inaction are not rightly understood; the one is mistaken for the other. Śrī Kṛṣṇa intends to remove this mistake. The real Self of man is actionless. Action pertains to the physical body, the senses, and the mind. But an unillumined, or ignorant, person falsely attributes action to the Self and says to himself, "*I* am the doer, *mine* is the action, by *me* will the fruit of action be reaped." Similarly, he falsely imputes to the Self the cessation of activity, which really pertains to the body and the senses, as also the happiness that results from such cessation; he says to himself: "I shall be quiet that I may be free from work and worry and be happy. I am quiet now; I am happy."

Through right knowledge a man sees inaction in action; he sees that action commonly associated with the Self really belongs to the body, and that the Self is actionless. Likewise, a man with right knowledge sees action in inaction; he knows that inaction is also a kind of action. Inaction is a correlative of action and pertains to the body. The Self is beyond action and inaction.

He who knows the meaning of action and inaction as expounded above is wise among men; he is a yogi. He does all action without being bound; he is free from the evil result of action. He has achieved everything.

The wisdom described in the foregoing verse is extolled:

यस्य सर्वे समारम्भाः कामसङ्कल्पवर्जिताः ।
ज्ञानाग्निदग्धकर्माणं तमाहुः पण्डितं बुधाः ॥ १९ ॥

19. He whose undertakings are all free from desires and self-will, and whose works are consumed in the fire of Knowledge—he, by the wise, is called a sage.

Free from desires and self-will—He has no egoistic purpose behind his action. If he is engaged in a worldly action, he performs it with a view to setting an example to men; if he has renounced the worldly life, he performs action only for the bare maintenance of his body.

Fire of Knowledge—The wisdom described in the foregoing verse is compared to a fire that consumes all good and evil deeds.

Even though a wise man may be seen engaging in action, his work is really no work.

त्यक्त्वा कर्मफलासङ्गं नित्यतृप्तो निराश्रयः ।
कर्मण्यभिप्रवृत्तोऽपि नैव किञ्चित्करोति सः ॥२०॥

20. Giving up attachment to the fruit of action, ever content, and dependent on none, though engaged in work, he does no work at all.

Ever content—Satisfied with the wisdom described in IV, 18.

Dependent on none—He has no desire to secure enjoyment in this life or hereafter.

Though engaged in work—Such a man may engage in work.

This is how a man of wisdom is described: He is always absorbed in the thought of God. He may engage in action that is necessary for the bare maintenance of his body. He might have been active before, but after his attainment of Knowledge he abandons action, since he finds no use for it. If he finds that for some reason or other he cannot give up action, he continues to work in order to set an example to the world. Or he may work in order to avoid offending the righteous men of society. Such a man, though engaged in action, is really not involved in it, since he never loses his consciousness of the actionless Self. His action is consumed in the fire of the knowledge described in IV, 18.

Śrī Kṛṣṇa speaks of the liberation of him who has realized his identity with Brahman, the innermost Self of all, who is free from the desire for enjoyment both here and hereafter, who therefore abstains from all action intended to secure objects of pleasure, who has renounced all action except what is necessary for the maintenance of his body, and who is steady in his devotion to Knowledge:

निराशीर्यतचित्तात्मा त्यक्तसर्वपरिग्रहः ।
शारीरं केवलं कर्म कुर्वन्नाप्नोति किल्बिषम् ॥ २१ ॥

21. Free from desire, with body and mind controlled, and surrendering all possessions, he incurs no sin through mere bodily activity.

Sin—This includes dharma, or merit, also. In the case of a man seeking the ultimate freedom, dharma, too, is an obstacle, like sin; for it creates bondage in the form of a result. Only he who is free from both dharma and adharma, merit and demerit, is liberated from saṃsāra, the round of birth and death in the relative world,

Bodily activity—Action necessary for the bare existence of the body, and that, too, without any attachment such as is implied in the words *"I* do." Since it is impossible for such a man to do any wrong, which may be called sin, he is not subject to rebirth in the relative world.

The import of the text seems to be that a knower of Brahman is always absorbed in his communion with the Absolute. Generally no outside activity is possible for him. Action for the bare maintenance of the body is done by him without any real identification with the body.

Things necessary for the maintenance of his body come to him without any effort on his part.

यदृच्छालाभसन्तुष्टो द्वन्द्वातीतो विमत्सरः ।
समः सिद्धावसिद्धौ च कृत्वापि न निबध्यते ॥ २२ ॥

22. Satisfied with what comes to him without any effort on his part, rising above the pairs of opposites, free from envy, and even-minded in success and failure, though acting, he is not bound.

Without any effort etc.—That is to say, unsolicited or by chance.

Even-minded—He remains calm whether or not he gets such things as might come to him without effort.

Though acting—Putting forth a minimum of action to secure the bare existence of the body.

Is not bound—Because he sees action in inaction, and inaction in action, knows that he does nothing at all, realizes that the guṇas act upon the guṇas, and is ever steady in the true Knowledge of the Self.

From the standpoint of the world such a man may appear to engage in action for the maintenance of his body, but from his own standpoint he is not the agent of the action. The egoistic motive of action has been consumed, in his case, in the fire of Knowledge.

There are some sages who begin life, on account of their prārabdha karma, as active men and then realize that the Self is the actionless Brahman. Though they are then entitled to give up works, yet for some reason they continue to be active as before. Such sages, too, are from their own standpoint inactive.

गतसङ्गस्य मुक्तस्य ज्ञानावस्थितचेतसः ।
यज्ञायाचरतः कर्म समग्रं प्रविलीयते ॥ २३ ॥

23. The works of a man whose attachment is gone, who is free, and whose mind is established in Knowledge, melt away entirely, being done as for a yajña.

Free—Free from the bondage imposed by both dharma and adharma.

Yajña—An action that is done with a view to pleasing the Lord, and not from any selfish motive. *See* note on "sacrifice," III, 9-10.

How is it that the action of such a man melts away without producing any result?

ब्रह्मार्पणं ब्रह्म हविर्ब्रह्माग्नौ ब्रह्मणा हुतम् ।
ब्रह्मैव तेन गन्तव्यं ब्रह्मकर्मसमाधिना ॥ २४ ॥

24. To him Brahman is the offering and Brahman is the oblation, and it is Brahman who offers the oblation in the fire of Brahman. Brahman alone is attained by him who thus sees Brahman in action.

Offering—The instrument by which the oblation is poured into the fire.

After attaining the Knowledge of Brahman, a man sees Brahman in everything. He sees Brahman in every part of the action: the instrument, the doer, the result, and the action itself. These have no existence apart from Brahman, just as the mirage has no existence apart from the desert. What appears to be water to the ignorant, is nothing but the desert. Likewise, what appears to the unenlightened as the instrument of action, the doer, and so on, is realized by one who is endowed with the Knowledge of Brahman as Brahman Itself. To him everything is Brahman.

Thus the action performed by the knower of Brahman to set an example to the world is in reality no action, since all the accessories of action are consumed, as it were, in the fire of Brahman. The Knowledge of Brahman removes all duality. Therefore action performed by a knower of Brahman melts away with its result and cannot bind its performer.

After describing the Knowledge Sacrifice, the Lord proceeds to enumerate other kinds of sacrifice in order to extol the former as the highest:

दैवमेवापरे यज्ञं योगिनः पर्युपासते।
ब्रह्माग्नावपरे यज्ञं यज्ञेनैवोपजुह्वति॥२५॥

25. Some yogis offer oblations to the devas alone, while others in the fire of Brahman offer the self by the self.

Yogis—Those who are devoted to action.

Devas—*Lit.*, shining ones. The word generally means deities such as the Rain-god and the Sun-god. *See* note on "Indra," IX, 20; also the glossary.

Others—Other knowers of Brahman.

Fire of Brahman—Brahman, described in the scriptures as Consciousness, Knowledge, and Bliss, and as the innermost Self of all. It is devoid of all limitations imposed by time, space, and causality.

The self—The self is in reality Brahman, but appears as the individual through association with the body, mind, intelligence, and senses.

To know the conditioned self as one with the unconditioned Brahman is to sacrifice the self in the fire of Brahman. This sacrifice is performed by those who have renounced all action and are devoted to the Knowledge of Brahman.

श्रोत्रादीनीन्द्रियाण्यन्ये संयमाग्निषु जुह्वति।
शब्दादीन्विषयानन्य इन्द्रियाग्निषु जुह्वति॥२६॥

26. Some offer oblations of hearing and the other senses in the fires of restraint; and some offer sound and other sensations in the fires of their, senses.

The yogis described in the first part of the text restrain the senses from their respective objects; those described in the second part direct the senses only to pure and unforbidden objects.

सर्वाणीन्द्रियकर्माणि प्राणकर्माणि चापरे।
आत्मसंयमयोगाग्नौ जुह्वति ज्ञानदीपिते॥२७॥

27. Some, again, offer all the actions of the senses and the functions of the prāṇa as oblations in the fire of self-control, kindled by knowledge.

Prāṇa—The vital breath, which sustains life in a physical body; the breath. In the books of yoga, prāṇa is described as having five modifications, according to its five different. functions. They are: prāṇa (the vital energy that controls breath), apāna (the vital energy that carries downward unassimilated food and drink), samāna (the vital energy that carries nutrition all over the body), vyāna (the vital energy that pervades the entire body), and udāna (the vital energy by which the contents of the stomach are ejected through the mouth). According to some writers on yoga, prāṇa and apāna mean, respectively, the in-going and the out-going breath.

Fire of self-control—Deep and one-pointed meditation.

In this case all the objects of the senses, as also all the actions of the body, together with the functions of the prāṇa, are dissolved in meditation, made one-pointed by discriminative wisdom.

द्रव्ययज्ञास्तपोयज्ञा योगयज्ञास्तथापरे।
स्वाध्यायज्ञानयज्ञाश्च यतयः संशितव्रताः ॥२८॥

28. Some, likewise, offer as oblations their wealth, austerity, and yoga; while others, of disciplined minds and severe vows, offer their scriptural study and knowledge.

Wealth—Giving away wealth to deserving persons.

Yoga—Comprises such practices as breath-control and the withdrawal of the mind from the objects of the world.

Knowledge—The understanding of the contents of the scriptures.

अपाने जुह्वति प्राणं प्राणेऽपानं तथापरे।
प्राणापानगती रुद्ध्वा प्राणायामपरायणाः ॥२९॥

29. Some, again, constantly practising the regulation of prāṇa, offer the oblation of prāṇa into apāna, and apāna into prāṇa, or stop the passage of both prāṇa and apāna. Yet others, restricting their food, offer their prāṇas in the prāṇas.

Prāṇa into apāna—Refers to a kind of breath-control called pūraka (filling in).

Apāna into prāṇa—Refers to a kind of breath-control called recaka (emptying).

Stop the passage etc.—A kind of breath-control known as kuṃbhaka.

Restricting their food—According to some teachers of yoga the student should fill half his stomach with food, one quarter with water, and leave one quarter free for the movement of air.

Offer their prāṇas etc.—Refers to a method of breath-control by which the aspirant controls a life-breath and sacrifices into it all the other life-breaths; these latter become, as it were, merged in the former. The different kinds of breath-control here referred to are described in rājayoga and haṭhayoga.

The result of the twelve sacrifices described above:

अपरे नियताहाराः प्राणान्प्राणेषु जुह्वति।
सर्वेऽप्येते यज्ञविदो यज्ञक्षपितकल्मषाः ॥ ३० ॥

यज्ञशिष्टामृतभुजो यान्ति ब्रह्म सनातनम्।
नायं लोकोऽस्त्ययज्ञस्य कुतोऽन्यः कुरुसत्तम ॥ ३१ ॥

30-31. All these know what sacrifice means, and by sacrifice are their sins consumed. Eating of the amṛta, the remnant of a sacrifice, they go to the Eternal Brahman. This world is not for him who makes no sacrifice, O best of the Kurus, much less the other.

Eternal Brahman—They realize the Eternal Brahman after attaining Knowledge through purification of the heart.

This world—The human world, where there is not much happiness.

The other—Heaven, which abounds in happiness.

The literal meaning of the text is that those who perform the sacrifices mentioned above and eat the food prescribed in the scriptures, in a prescribed manner, attain Brahman in course of time if they desire liberation. The food so eaten is called amṛta, or the elixir of immortality. The deeper meaning seems to be that all activities should be performed as a sacrifice, that is to say, in an unselfish spirit, surrendering the results to God. Action done in this spirit enables the doer to enjoy happiness on earth, if he still has any such lingering desire, or to attain Brahman, in due course, if he seeks liberation. But action performed in an egotistic spirit deprives one even of earthly happiness, not to speak of spiritual bliss.

एवं बहुविधा यज्ञा वितता ब्रह्मणो मुखे।
कर्मजान्विद्धि तान्सर्वानेवं ज्ञात्वा विमोक्ष्यसे ॥ ३२ ॥

32. Thus many kinds of sacrifice are strewn through the pages of the Vedas; know them all to be born of action, and you will be free.

The sacrifices described above do not touch the Ātman, or Self, which is actionless. By realizing that the Self is free from all action, one attains right knowledge and becomes free from the bondage of saṃsāra.

The Knowledge Sacrifice was described in IV, 24. Then other sacrifices were enumerated in 25-29. The latter enable the sacrificer to achieve human ends, whereas through Knowledge one realizes ultimate freedom. Hence the praise of the Knowledge Sacrifice.

श्रेयान्द्रव्यमयाद्यज्ञाज्ज्ञानयज्ञः परन्तप।
सर्वं कर्माखिलं पार्थ ज्ञाने परिसमाप्यते॥ ३३॥

33. The Knowledge Sacrifice is superior to all material sacrifices, O scorcher of foes; for all works, without exception, culminate in Knowledge.

Material sacrifices—Sacrifices performed with material objects produce only material results.

Culminate in Knowledge—The Knowledge of Brahman comprehends all action.

How does one gain that exalted Knowledge?

तद्विद्धि प्रणिपातेन परिप्रश्नेन सेवया।
उपदेक्ष्यन्ति ते ज्ञानं ज्ञानिनस्तत्त्वदर्शिनः॥ ३४॥

34. Learn it by prostration, by inquiry, and by service. The wise, who have seen the Truth, will teach you that Knowledge.

Prostration—The symbol of humility and reverence.

Inquiry—The disciple should ask the teacher about bondage and liberation and about ignorance and Knowledge.

Who have seen the Truth—Only the man who has realized the Truth is entitled to give spiritual instruction. Mere theoretical knowledge, however perfect, does not qualify one to be a spiritual teacher.

Humility, the spirit of inquiry, and personal service rendered to the teacher are the conditions of discipleship.

The result of Knowledge:

यज्ज्ञात्वा न पुनर्मोहमेवं यास्यसि पाण्डव।
येन भूतान्यशेषेण द्रक्ष्यस्यात्मन्यथो मयि॥ ३५॥

35. When you have known it, O Pāṇḍava you will not again fall into delusion; and through it you will see all beings in your Self and also in Me.

It—The Knowledge of Brahman.

Delusion—Relating to the death of Arjuna's friends and relatives assembled on the battle-field.

The Self and the Lord are identical. All beings, too, are identical with the immortal Self; through ignorance they appear as separate.

अपि चेदसि पापेभ्यः सर्वेभ्यः पापकृत्तमः।
सर्वं ज्ञानप्लवेनैव वृजिनं सन्तरिष्यसि॥३६॥

36. Even if you are the most sinful of sinners, yet by the raft of Knowledge alone will you be borne over all sin.

The worldly life, uninspired by Spirit, is of the nature of sin and is compared to a limitless ocean. But the knower of Truth crosses it by the help of the raft of Self-knowledge.

How does Knowledge destroy sin?

यथैधांसि समिद्धोऽग्निर्भस्मसात्कुरुतेऽर्जुन।
ज्ञानाग्निः सर्वकर्माणि भस्मसात्कुरुते तथा॥३७॥

37. As a fire, well kindled, reduces wood to ashes, so, O Arjuna, does the fire of Knowledge reduce all works to ashes.

Reduce all works to ashes—It renders them ineffective, so that they cannot bind the worker by producing results.

All works—There are three kinds of action: sañcita, āgāmi, and prārabdha. The sañcita karma is the vast store of accumulated actions done in the past, the fruits of which have not yet been reaped. The āgāmi karma is the action that will be performed by the individual in the future or the action performed by him in this life before his attainment of Knowledge. The prārabdha karma is the action that has begun to fructify, the fruit of which is being reaped in this life; it is a part of the sañcita karma inasmuch as this also is action done in the past. But the difference between the two is that whereas the sañcita karma is not yet operative, the prārabdha has already begun to bear fruit. The body lasts as long as the momentum given by the prārabdha karma remains. Knowledge destroys all karmas except the prārabdha karma; even a man of Knowledge must experience its result. But since he has realized the freedom and the blissful nature of the Soul, the prārabdha karma affects only his body; his mind is always absorbed in the consciousness of Brahman.

Therefore,

न हि ज्ञानेन सदृशं पवित्रमिह विद्यते।
तत्स्वयं योगसंसिद्धः कालेनात्मनि विन्दति॥३८॥

38. Verily, there exists no purifier on earth equal to Knowledge. A man who becomes perfect in yoga finds it within himself in course of time.

No purifier on earth—It is by Knowledge that sins are destroyed, as also ignorance, which is their cause.

Perfect in yoga—Through the performance of selfless duty and the practice of contemplation.

The surest means of acquiring Knowledge:

श्रद्धावाँल्लभते ज्ञानं तत्परः संयतेन्द्रियः।
ज्ञानं लब्ध्वा परां शान्तिमचिरेणाधिगच्छति॥३९॥

39. He who is full of faith and zeal and has subdued his senses obtains Knowledge; having obtained Knowledge, he soon attains the Supreme Peace.

Faith—In the teachings of the guru.

Zeal—Intense devotion to the means of obtaining Knowledge.

Subdued his senses—Mere external acts such as prostration, inquiry, and the rendering of personal service, as described in IV, 34, may be performed by an insincere person. But insincerity is impossible for a seeker who has practised the inner discipline described in this verse.

The Supreme Peace, or liberation, immediately follows the Knowledge of Brahman. No other intermediary discipline, such as the practice of yoga or the performance of specific duties, is necessary. An aspirant practises yoga or performs his duties prior to the attainment of Knowledge, for the purification of his mind.

One must not doubt the above instruction.

अज्ञश्चाश्रद्दधानश्च संशयात्मा विनश्यति।
नायं लोकोऽस्ति न परो न सुखं संशयात्मनः॥४०॥

40. But the man who is ignorant and without faith and always doubting goes to ruin. Not this world nor the world beyond nor happiness is for the doubting soul.

Ignorant—One who does not know the Self.

Always doubting—One who doubts his ability to attain Self-knowledge.

The man who is ignorant of the Self or without faith may easily enjoy material happiness on earth. But the doubting person is never happy. Owing to his sceptical disposition, he suspects people and things around him. He is doubtful concerning the world beyond.

योगसंन्यस्तकर्माणं ज्ञानसञ्छिन्नसंशयम्।
आत्मवन्तं न कर्माणि निबध्नन्ति धनञ्जय॥४१॥

41. Works do not bind the man, O Dhanañjaya, who relinquishes action through yoga, whose doubts are destroyed by Knowledge, and who is self-possessed.

Works—Works accomplished after the attainment of Knowledge. A man endowed with Self-knowledge realizes that action is the natural behaviour of the guṇas in the form of the senses toward the guṇas in the form of objects, and that the Self remains unaffected.

Do not bind—By producing good or bad results.

Who relinquishes action etc.—That is to say, he who surrenders the fruit of his action to the Lord and views alike success and failure.

Self-possessed—Ever watchful over his self.

तस्मादज्ञानसम्भूतं हृत्स्थं ज्ञानासिनात्मनः।
छित्त्वैनं संशयं योगमातिष्ठोत्तिष्ठ भारत॥४२॥

42. Therefore with the sword of Knowledge cut asunder this doubt about the Self, born of ignorance and residing in your heart, and devote yourself to yoga. Arise, O Bhārata!

The sword of Knowledge—The Knowledge by which one discriminates between the body and the Self and which consequently destroys grief and delusion.

Yoga—Karmayoga, which is a means of attaining right knowledge.

Arise—In order to fight. Fighting is the dharma of the kṣatriya Arjuna.

ॐ तत्सदिति श्रीमद्भगवद्गीतासूपनिषत्सु
ब्रह्मविद्यायां योगशास्त्रे श्रीकृष्णार्जुनसंवादे
ज्ञानकर्मसंन्यासयोगो नाम चतुर्थोऽध्यायः॥४॥

Thus in the Bhagavad Gītā, the Essence of the Upaniṣads, the Science of Brahman, the Scripture of Yoga, the Dialogue between Śrī Kṛṣṇa and Arjuna, ends the Fourth Chapter, entitled: THE WAY OF KNOWLEDGE.

CHAPTER 5

THE WAY OF RENUNCIATION

[संन्यासयोगः]

अर्जुन उवाच।

संन्यासं कर्मणां कृष्ण पुनर्योगं च शंससि।
यच्छ्रेय एतयोरेकं तन्मे ब्रूहि सुनिश्चितम्॥ १ ॥

1. *Arjuna said:* You praise, O Kṛṣṇa, the renunciation of works, and also yoga. Tell me for certain which of these two is the better.

Yoga—In this and the following verses the word means karmayoga, or the performance of selfless action as a yoga or spiritual discipline.

In IV, 18, 19, 21, 22, 24, 32, 37, and 41, the Lord has emphasized the renunciation of all works; and in IV, 42, He has asked Arjuna to engage in yoga, the performance of action. Now, these two injunctions are mutually opposed; they cannot be followed by the same individual at the same time. Arjuna wants to know which of the two, action or renunciation, would be conducive to his spiritual welfare.

श्रीभगवानुवाच।

संन्यासः कर्मयोगश्च निःश्रेयसकरावुभौ।
तयोस्तु कर्मसंन्यासात्कर्मयोगो विशिष्यते॥ २ ॥

2. *The Lord said:* Both renunciation and yoga lead to the Highest Good; but of the two, performance of action is superior to renunciation of action.

The performance of action is necessary for those aspirants who are conscious of multiplicity—the doer of the action, its accessories, and its results. Arjuna does not see the difference between the body and the Soul. He is grief-stricken at the thought of the death of his relatives. He is under the spell of ignorance. So Śrī Kṛṣṇa recommends for him the performance of action for the purification of his mind. The knowledge that is born in a pure heart gradually becomes mature through renunciation of action accompanied by the contemplation of Reality.

Why so? The answer follows:

ज्ञेयः स नित्यसंन्यासी यो न द्वेष्टि न काङ्क्षति।
निर्द्वन्द्वो हि महाबाहो सुखं बन्धात्प्रमुच्यते॥३॥

3. He who neither hates nor desires may be known as constantly practising renunciation; for, free from the pairs of opposites, O mighty Arjuna, he is easily freed from bondage.

He—A karmayogi, or performer of action.

Neither hates nor desires—Neither hates pain or objects causing pain, nor desires pleasure or objects causing pleasure. Either love or hate generally motivates all our worldly actions.

Practising renunciation—Even while performing action. he is like a saṃnyāsī, who formally renounces worldly duties.

The Lord contradicts the view that saṃnyāsa and karmayoga, meant for two different types of people, are opposed to each other and that they produce contrary results:

साङ्ख्ययोगौ पृथग्बालाः प्रवदन्ति न पण्डिताः।
एकमप्यास्थितः सम्यगुभयोर्विन्दते फलम्॥४॥

4. It is children, and not the wise, that speak of the path of knowledge and the path of action as distinct. He who is firmly set on one reaches the end of both.

Children—The ignorant.

Path of knowledge—The path of saṃnyāsa, the goal of which is the attainment of Self-knowledge through the renunciation of works.

Path of action—The discipline of this path is to maintain equanimity in success and failure.

End of both—That is to say, liberation through Self-knowledge. There is no difference so far as the ultimate result is concerned.

How can a man follow one path and obtain the result of both?

यत्साङ्ख्यैः प्राप्यते स्थानं तद्योगैरपि गम्यते।
एकं साङ्ख्यं च योगं च यः पश्यति स पश्यति॥५॥

5. The state reached by men of renunciation is reached by men of action too. He who sees that the way of renunciation and the way of action are one—he truly sees.

State—The state of liberation.

Men of renunciation—Saṃnyāsīs, who follow the path of knowledge.

Men of action—Those who perform action, surrendering the result to God. Through selfless action they attain purity of mind and thus qualify themselves for the path of knowledge.

One—Because both ultimately produce the same result, namely, liberation through Self-knowledge.

As a result of karmayoga followed in previous lives, the saṃnyāsīs are born with pure minds and entitled to the path of knowledge. The workers through selfless action will first. attain purity of mind and then be able to follow the path of knowledge leading to liberation.

The Lord, in V, 2, has declared that performance of action is superior to renunciation of action. In that verse both performance and renunciation of action are used in a mechanical sense. The mere performance of action, without the practice of equanimity as regards the result, is declared to be superior to the mere renunciation of action uninspired by knowledge, because the latter is the outcome of tamas. Real renunciation, based upon knowledge and known as sāṅkhya leads to liberation. Those who practise such renunciation are known as saṃnyāsīs or jñānīs. Action performed without any desire whatsoever for the result is known as yoga, and the performers of such action are known as yogis. They surrender the result of action to God and, being purified through action, become fit for knowledge, which leads to liberation.

If the aspirant after liberation must renounce action in the end, why should he not do so at once?

संन्यासस्तु महाबाहो दुःखमाप्तुमयोगतः।
योगयुक्तो मुनिर्ब्रह्म नचिरेणाधिगच्छति॥६॥

6. But renunciation of action, O mighty Arjuna, is hard to attain without performance of action; the sage, purified by devotion to action, quickly reaches Brahman.

Renunciation of action—Which is based upon knowledge and is resorted to by true saṃnyāsīs.

Hard to attain—One cannot be devoted to the path of knowledge without purity of mind.

Performance of action—In which the worker surrenders the result to God and does not seek it for himself.

Sage—The word "muni" in the text describes one who meditates on the Lord.

Brahman—The word is used here to denote renunciation (saṃnyāsa). "What is called nyāsa is Brahman; and Brahman is verily the Great." *(Taittirīya Upaniṣad.)*

A sage, purified by the performance of selfless action, soon attains Brahman, the true renunciation, in which state he devotes himself steadily to Self-knowledge. Hence, for the beginner, the performance of action is better than its renunciation, as declared by the Lord in V, 2.

Action generally creates bondage; how, then, can one devoted to action attain Brahman?

योगयुक्तो विशुद्धात्मा विजितात्मा जितेन्द्रियः।
सर्वभूतात्मभूतात्मा कुर्वन्नपि न लिप्यते॥७॥

7. He who is devoted to yoga and is pure in mind, who has conquered his body and subdued his senses, who has realized his Self as the Self of all beings—he is undefiled though he acts.

Devoted to yoga—Karmayoga, or selfless action.

All beings—All creatures from Brahmā to a blade of grass.

Undefiled—Not bound by action.

Though he acts—To set an example to others.

He is free from all taint of ego.

नैव किञ्चित्करोमीति युक्तो मन्येत तत्त्ववित्।
पश्यञ्शृण्वन्स्पृशञ्जिघ्रन्नश्नन्गच्छन्स्वपञ्श्वसन्॥८॥

प्रलपन्विसृजन्गृह्णन्नुन्मिषन्निमिषन्नपि।
इन्द्रियाणीन्द्रियार्थेषु वर्तन्त इति धारयन्॥९॥

8-9. "I do nothing at all," thinks the yogi, the knower of Truth; for in seeing, hearing, touching, smelling, and tasting; in walking, breathing, and sleeping;

In speaking, emitting, and seizing; in opening and closing the eyes, he is assured that it is only the senses. busied with their objects.

Yogi—The karmayogi, who is devoted to selfless action.

A man endowed with the Knowledge of the actionless Self sees inaction in action; for he realizes that in all works the senses occupy themselves with their objects and that the Self remains inactive. He may be said to have renounced action, for he sees no action as performed by himself.

But the man who has not yet attained Self-knowledge may also remain untainted by the result of his action.

ब्रह्मण्याधाय कर्माणि सङ्गं त्यक्त्वा करोति यः।
लिप्यते न स पापेन पद्मपत्रमिवाम्भसा॥ १०॥

10. He who works without attachment, resigning his actions to Brahman, is untainted by sin, as a lotus-leaf by water.

Resigning his actions etc.—He offers all his works to God. He works for God's sake, as a servant works for the sake of his master. He has no attachment to the result of action, even to mokṣa.

Lotus-leaf by water—Though a lotus-leaf remains in water, it is practically untouched by the water. When it is taken out of the water, no water clings to it.

The result of such action is the purification of the mind, and nothing else.

कायेन मनसा बुद्ध्या केवलैरिन्द्रियैरपि।
योगिनः कर्म कुर्वन्ति सङ्गं त्यक्त्वात्मशुद्धये॥ ११॥

11. Only with the body, the mind, the understanding, and the senses do the yogis act, without attachment, for the purification of the heart.

Only—Free from egotism and firmly established in the conviction: "I act only for the sake of the Lord and not for my personal benefit." The word "only," in the text, should be understood with the body, mind, and each instrument of action. Whatever instrument of action a yogi may use, he is free from egotism.

Yogis—The karmayogis, who perform selfless action.

How is it that the same action binds some and liberates others?

युक्तः कर्मफलं त्यक्त्वा शान्तिमाप्नोति नैष्ठिकीम्।
अयुक्तः कामकारेण फले सक्तो निबध्यते॥ १२॥

12. A selfless man who has renounced the fruit of his action attains peace, born of steadfastness. But the man who is not selfless and who is led by desire is attached to the fruit and therefore bound.

A selfless man—He who works for the sake of the Lord and not for his own benefit.

Attains peace etc.—Śaṅkara describes the following stages through which a selfless man attains peace: (1) purity of heart, (2) gaining of knowledge, (3) renunciation of action, (4) devotion to knowledge.

It has been said that the path of selfless action is superior to the path of renunciation for those who are not pure in heart; but the man of pure heart renounces action.

सर्वकर्माणि मनसा संन्यस्यास्ते सुखं वशी।
नवद्वारे पुरे देही नैव कुर्वन्न कारयन्॥ १३॥

13. The embodied soul who has subdued his senses, having renounced all actions with a discerning mind, dwells happily in the city of nine gates, neither working nor causing work to be done.

All actions—First, nitya, or obligatory, works, such as daily devotions, whose performance does not produce any merit, but whose non-performance produces demerit. Second, naimittika, or those works which should be performed on the occurrence of certain special events, such as the worship performed on the birth of a son: these are customary. Third, kāmya, works intended for securing special ends: these are optional. Fourth, niṣiddha, or action forbidden by the scriptures. He refrains from all these actions and lives only for the sake of exhausting the prārabdha karma, which has caused his present body.

Dwells happily—Established in Self-knowledge. He is happy because he has given up all action. He is calm and unworried, for he does not take interest in anything pertaining to the relative world.

City of nine gates—That is to say, the body, which has nine openings. These are the two eyes, the two nostrils, the two ears, the mouth, and the organs of generation and evacuation. In such a nine-gated city the embodied soul dwells, having renounced all action. Unlike the ignorant, he does. not identify himself with the body. After the exhaustion of the prārabdha karma his soul merges in Brahman.

Neither working etc.—Because he is totally free from the consciousness of "I," "me," or "mine." The Soul is always free from the idea of acting or causing action. Compare: "This Self is said to be... unchangeable" (II, 25); "This... Self neither acts nor is stained by action even while dwelling in the body" (XIII, 31); "It thinks *as it were* and moves *as it were*" (*Bṛhadāraṇyaka Upaniṣad*, IV, iii, 7).

Ideas of action and actor, etc., are due to māyā.

न कर्तृत्वं न कर्माणि लोकस्य सृजति प्रभुः।
न कर्मफलसंयोगं स्वभावस्तु प्रवर्तते॥ १४॥

14. Neither agency nor objects does the Supreme Spirit create for the world, nor does It bring about union with the fruit of action. It is Nature that does all this.

Agency—The Soul, being perfect by nature, does not of Itself urge anyone to action.

Objects—Objects of enjoyment.

Supreme Spirit—The Supreme Spirit residing in the body.

Union etc.—The union of the doer of an action with the fruit.

Nature—Prakṛti or māyā, whose essential character is inscrutable to the unenlightened mind.

The Soul of man, being one with Brahman, is perfect and filled with bliss. With It no desire or motive can be associated. Prakṛti or māyā, by mere proximity to the Soul, creates the illusory world, the idea of agency, and the fruit of action. The Soul comes under the apparent control of māyā and regards Itself as acting and enjoying the fruits of action. As long as the Soul remains identified with māyā, It is bound. But when It detaches Itself from māyā, It becomes free. Thus such ideas as those of duty, work, and the result belong to the relative world. They have no meaning whatever from the standpoint of the Supreme Lord.

नादत्ते कस्यचित्पापं न चैव सुकृतं विभुः।
अज्ञानेनावृतं ज्ञानं तेन मुह्यन्ति जन्तवः॥ १५॥

15. Nor does the all-pervading Spirit take on the sin or the merit of any. Knowledge is veiled in ignorance, and thereby mortals are deluded.

Any—Even of His devotees.

The Lord is all-perfect. He is of the nature of eternal Bliss and Love, which cannot be affected by the good and evil of the relative world. As there is neither day nor night from the standpoint of the sun, so there is neither virtue nor vice from the standpoint of the Lord, whose nature is Existence-Knowledge-Bliss Absolute. Through ignorance man separates himself from the Lord and comes under the spell of the ego. Thus he thinks of himself as the agent of various works, good or evil, and experiences pleasure and pain accordingly. The law of karma applies only to embodied beings in the relative world. When the aspirant becomes free from ignorance and realizes his identity with the Lord, he goes beyond virtue and vice and is not affected by the results of his actions.

The man of Knowledge is not deluded,

ज्ञानेन तु तदज्ञानं येषां नाशितमात्मनः ।
तेषामादित्यवज्ज्ञानं प्रकाशयति तत्परम् ॥ १६ ॥

16. But for those in whom this ignorance is destroyed by the Knowledge of the Self, that Knowledge, like the sun, reveals the Supreme.

Knowledge of the Self—The knowledge that discriminates between Self and non-Self.

As the sun destroys darkness and illumines all objects, so also discriminative knowledge dispels ignorance and reveals the Supreme Reality, which is the goal of knowledge.

The result of the Knowledge of God is described:

तद्बुद्धयस्तदात्मानस्तन्निष्ठास्तत्परायणाः ।
गच्छन्त्यपुनरावृत्तिं ज्ञाननिर्धूतकल्मषाः ॥ १७ ॥

17. Fixing their minds in Him, at one with Him, abiding in Him, realizing Him alone as the Supreme Goal, they reach a state from which there is no return, their sins having been destroyed by their Knowledge.

Abiding in Him—Renouncing all action and contemplating Him alone.

No return—The Soul of the illumined person does not return to the relative world to assume a physical body, since in his case virtue and vice, the cause of embodiment, are destroyed by the Knowledge of God. He does not come again under the sway of māyā.

Ignorance of God is sin, which is destroyed by Knowledge.

What is the characteristic of Knowledge?

विद्याविनयसम्पन्ने ब्राह्मणे गवि हस्तिनि।
शुनि चैव श्वपाके च पण्डिताः समदर्शिनः॥ १८॥

18. The wise see the same in all—whether it be a brāhmin endowed with learning and humility, or a cow or an elephant or a dog or an outcaste.

Humility—Which is the manifestation of inner serenity, the condition of a well disciplined soul.

Brahman alone is the indwelling Self of all. It makes no difference to Brahman whether It is reflected in a human or in an animal medium, as it makes no difference to the sun whether it is reflected in clean or dirty water, or in an ocean or a lake or a mud-puddle.

It may be objected that one who sees sameness in naturally diverse things cannot be wise. The answer follows:

इहैव तैर्जितः सर्गो येषां साम्ये स्थितं मनः।
निर्दोषं हि समं ब्रह्म तस्माद् ब्रह्मणि ते स्थिताः॥ १९॥

19. Those whose minds are thus set on sameness have even here overcome birth. Brahman is untainted and is the same in all; therefore in Brahman they rest.

Set on sameness—That is to say, who see the same pure Brahman in all beings.

Here—On this earth and in this very life.

Birth—A knower of Brahman, even before his death, cuts asunder the bondage that is responsible for a man's birth and death in the relative world; for he realizes his complete identity with Brahman, which is birthless and deathless.

Untainted—Though Brahman is the indwelling Self even of impure and defective bodies, yet It is uncontaminated by them.

The same in all—The same homogeneous Consciousness, called Brahman, is the innermost Reality of all, irrespective of the different bodies.

They rest—They are always aware of their identity with Brahman. The defects and blemishes of the body do not affect them.

The injunctions of the scriptures to avoid the wicked and honour the righteous are for beginners in spiritual life, who are conscious of duality.

The knower of Brahman is free from grief and rejoicing.

न प्रहृष्येत्प्रियं प्राप्य नोद्विजेत्प्राप्य चाप्रियम्।
स्थिरबुद्धिरसम्मूढो ब्रह्मविद् ब्रह्मणि स्थितः ॥२०॥

20. He who knows Brahman and is established in It, he who is undeluded and is steady of mind—he neither rejoices when experiencing what is pleasant, nor is distressed when experiencing what is unpleasant.

Steady of mind—He has the unwavering belief that the same perfect Brahman dwells in all bodies.

Neither rejoices etc.—He who identifies himself with the body rejoices or grieves on receiving what is pleasant or unpleasant. That does not happen to one who is aware of the identity of the Self and Brahman.

बाह्यस्पर्शेष्वसक्तात्मा विन्दत्यात्मनि यत्सुखम्।
स ब्रह्मयोगयुक्तात्मा सुखमक्षयमश्नुते॥२१॥

21. His heart being unattached to outer objects, he finds the joy that is in the Self; his heart being devoted to the contemplation of Brahman, he enjoys undying bliss.

The happiness from the enjoyment of outer objects is transitory; the Bliss of Brahman is eternal; therefore the former should be renounced in order to enjoy the latter. Through self-control a void is created in the heart; then this is filled with bliss through contemplation of Brahman.

The nature of happiness derived from contact with sense-objects:

ये हि संस्पर्शजा भोगा दुःखयोनय एव ते।
आद्यन्तवन्तः कौन्तेय न तेषु रमते बुधः ॥२२॥

22. For the enjoyments that arise from contact with objects are only sources of pain. They have a beginning and an end, O son of Kuntī, and the wise find no delight in them.

Sources of pain—All physical pain is traceable to sense-enjoyment. The same is true of sense-enjoyment in the other world. Pleasure derived from worldly objects cannot satisfy the soul's longing for happiness, as the water of a mirage cannot quench the thirst of a traveller in the desert.

A beginning and an end—The contact of one of the senses with its object marks the beginning of a pleasure, and their separation, the end. Thus sense-pleasure is only momentary.

Lust and anger are the two greatest enemies of the path to Bliss.

शक्नोतीहैव यः सोढुं प्राक्शरीरविमोक्षणात्।
कामक्रोधोद्भवं वेगं स युक्तः स सुखी नरः॥२३॥

23. He who is able to withstand the force of lust and anger even here before he quits the body—he is a yogi, he is a happy man.

The force of lust and anger—Kāma, or lust, is the longing one feels for a pleasurable object when one sees it, hears of it, or remembers it. Anger is due to the aversion one feels for a painful and disagreeable object when one sees it, hears of it, or remembers it; or one feels angry when one is obstructed in pursuit of a pleasurable object. Lust and anger create an agitation of mind accompanied by appropriate physical signs.

Before he quits the body—That is to say, up to the point of death. By thus marking death as the limit, the Lord teaches that one can never be sure of having eliminated anger and lust. Their causes are numerous; one should be on guard against them till the time of death. Or the clause may mean that a man should be as indifferent to the force of lust and anger, before death, as he is after death. A dead body does not react to anger and lust.

What kind of yogi attains Brahman?

योऽन्तःसुखोऽन्तरारामस्तथान्तर्ज्योतिरेव यः।
स योगी ब्रह्मनिर्वाणं ब्रह्मभूतोऽधिगच्छति॥२४॥

24. The yogi who is happy within, who rejoices within, and who is illumined within attains freedom in Brahman, himself becoming one with Brahman.

Within—In the Self.

Such a yogi, while still living in the body, enjoys absolute freedom because of his awareness of his identity with Brahman.

लभन्ते ब्रह्मनिर्वाणमृषयः क्षीणकल्मषाः।
छिन्नद्वैधा यतात्मानः सर्वभूतहिते रताः॥२५॥

25. With sins destroyed, doubts dispelled, senses controlled, and devoting themselves to the welfare of all beings, the sages attain freedom in Brahman.

Welfare of all beings—That is to say, never inflicting an injury on anyone by word, thought, or deed.

Sages—Men of right vision and total renunciation.

कामक्रोधवियुक्तानां यतीनां यतचेतसाम्।
अभितो ब्रह्मनिर्वाणं वर्तते विदितात्मनाम्॥ २६ ॥

26. Those who are free from lust and anger, who have subdued their minds and realized the Self—those saṃnyāsīs, both here and hereafter, attain freedom in Brahman.

Here and hereafter—They enjoy absolute freedom, whether dead or alive.

The realization of Brahman is briefly described:

स्पर्शान्कृत्वा बहिर्बाह्यांश्चक्षुश्चैवान्तरे भ्रुवोः।
प्राणापानौ समौ कृत्वा नासाभ्यन्तरचारिणौ॥ २७ ॥

यतेन्द्रियमनोबुद्धिर्मुनिर्मोक्षपरायणः।
विगतेच्छाभयक्रोधो यः सदा मुक्त एव सः॥ २८ ॥

27-28. Shutting out all external objects; fixing the gaze of his eyes between his brows; equalizing the outward and inward breaths moving in his nostrils; controlling his senses, mind, and understanding; being ever bent on liberation; ridding himself of desire, fear, and anger—such a man of contemplation is indeed always free.

Objects—Sound, touch, and other sense-objects.

Fixing the gaze etc.—When the eyes are half closed in meditation, the eye-balls remain motionless, and their gaze converges toward a point between the brows. On the other hand, when the eyes are fully open, they may stray to external objects, and when closed, the man may fall asleep.

Equalizing etc.—By the practice of prāṇāyāma, or breath-control.

Always free—He does not have to follow any other discipline for freedom.

What does a sage realize through meditation?

भोक्तारं यज्ञतपसां सर्वलोकमहेश्वरम्।
सुहृदं सर्वभूतानां ज्ञात्वा मां शान्तिमृच्छति॥ २९ ॥

29. And having known Me, who am the Dispenser of all sacrifices and austerities, the Great Lord of all worlds, the Friend of all beings, he attains Peace.

Me—The Lord, who is Nārāyaṇa Himself and who, in the form of Śrī Kṛṣṇa, is seated in Arjuna's chariot.

Dispenser—The Lord is the presiding Deity of sacrifices and the goal of austerities; He is the dispenser of the fruit of all actions.

Friend—The Lord is the doer of good to all beings.

ॐ तत्सदिति श्रीमद्भगवद्गीतासूपनिषत्सु
ब्रह्मविद्यायां योगशास्त्रे श्रीकृष्णार्जुनसंवादे
संन्यासयोगो नाम पञ्चमोऽध्यायः ॥५॥

Thus in the Bhagavad Gītā, the Essence of the Upaniṣads, the Science of Brahman, the Scripture of Yoga, the Dialogue between Śrī *Kṛṣṇa and Arjuna, ends the Fifth Chapter, entitled:* THE WAY OF RENUNCIATION

CHAPTER 6

THE WAY OF MEDITATION

[आत्मसंयमयोगः]

श्रीभगवानुवाच।

अनाश्रितः कर्मफलं कार्यं कर्म करोति यः।
स संन्यासी च योगी च न निरग्निर्न चाक्रियः॥ १॥

1. *The Lord said:* He who does the work he ought to do and does not seek its fruit—he is a saṃnyāsī and he is a yogi: not he who does no work and maintains no sacred fire.

The work he ought to do—Daily obligatory duties. An instance of such duties is the agnihotra, a sacrifice enjoined by the Vedas, requiring fire as an adjunct. According to the Hindu scriptures, householders must perform the daily obligatory duties.

Does not seek its fruit—He who is free from the desire for the fruit of action is not dependent thereon. He does not perform his obligatory duty with a motive, as a means of attaining some specific end.

Saṃnyāsī—He is to be regarded as a saṃnyāsī because he has renounced the fruit of action.

Yogi—He is to be regarded as a yogi because he has acquired steadfastness of mind by giving up the desire for the fruit of action.

Does no work—Mere renunciation of action, including what is conducive to the public welfare, such as digging wells or building roads, does not make a person a yogi.

Maintains no sacred fire—A saṃnyāsī gives up obligatory action in which fire is required as an accessory. Mere renunciation of such action does not make a man a saṃnyāsī.

He who performs his duty in the spirit described in the text is called a saṃnyāsī and a yogi only in a secondary sense. The Lord merely praises the householder who performs his duty giving up the desire for its fruit. Duty thus performed purifies his mind. Gradually he qualifies himself for the practice of meditation. Action is only an external aid to meditation and saṃnyāsa. A saṃnyāsī, absorbed in contemplation of Brahman, does not perform any obligatory action.

In what respect is karmayoga, or selfless action, to be considered the same as saṃnyāsa, or renunciation of action?

यं संन्यासमिति प्राहुर्योगं तं विद्धि पाण्डव।
न ह्यसंन्यस्तसङ्कल्पो योगी भवति कश्चन॥२॥

2. Know that what they call renunciation is the same as yoga, O Pāṇḍava for no one who has not renounced his desire can ever become a yogi.

They—Wise men, who are versed in the scriptures.

Renunciation—That is to say, saṃnyāsa, which consists in the abandonment of all action and its fruit.

Yoga—The performance of selfless action.

The same as yoga—There is a certain amount of similarity between karmayoga and pure saṃnyāsa, so far as the attitude of the agent is concerned. A real saṃnyāsī renounces all thought concerning action and its fruit; for thought causes desire, and desire impels one to action. A follower of karmayoga, too, renounces all thought of the fruit while he performs an action; for no one can be a yogi, a man of steadfastness, without renouncing such thought, since the thought of the result creates unsteadiness of mind.

Desire—Saṃkalpa, the untranslatable word of the text, is "the working of the imaging faculty, forming fancies, making plans and again brushing them aside, conceiving future results, starting afresh on a new line, leading to different issues, and so on and so forth. No one can be a karmayogi, or a devotee of action, who makes plans and wishes for the fruit of action."—Swāmī Swarūpānanda.

Saṃnyāsa and karmayoga are said to be the same because the Lord wants to extol the latter.

Selfless action leads its performer in due course to the yoga of meditation.

आरुरुक्षोर्मुनेर्योगं कर्म कारणमुच्यते।
योगारूढस्य तस्यैव शमः कारणमुच्यते॥३॥

3. For a sage who wants to attain yoga, action is said to be the means; but when he has attained yoga, serenity is said to be the means.

Action is said etc.—Through selfless action he purifies the mind. Then he acquires the desire and fitness for meditation.

Serenity—Abstinence from action. Through serenity he is gradually established in Truth.

The more a man abstains from action, the more free he is from trouble, the more his senses are controlled, and the more steady he feels in meditation. According to the *Mahābhārata*, the valuable treasures for a brāhmin are the feeling of oneness and evenness, truthfulness, refinement. steadiness, harmlessness, straightforwardness, and gradual withdrawal from all action.

When is a man said to have attained yoga?

यदा हि नेन्द्रियार्थेषु न कर्मस्वनुषज्जते।
सर्वसङ्कल्पसंन्यासी योगारूढस्तदोच्यते॥४॥

4. When a man has no attachment to the objects of the senses or to works, and when he has wholly renounced his will, he is said to have attained yoga.

Works—These include all works, whether obligatory, customary, or forbidden by the scriptures. Such works do not serve any purpose for the man who has attained yoga.

Will—It is the will that gives rise to the desire for objects in this world and the next. Renunciation of will denotes also the renunciation of desire and action. "O Desire, I know where your root lies. You are born of will (saṃkalpa). I shall not think of you, and you will cease to exist, with your root." (*Mahābhārata, Ś*āntiparva, 177-25)

Only through the attainment of yoga is the self raised from the many evils of worldliness.

उद्धरेदात्मनात्मानं नात्मानमवसादयेत्।
आत्मैव ह्यात्मनो बन्धुरात्मैव रिपुरात्मनः॥५॥

5. Let a man be lifted up by his own self; let him not lower himself; for he himself is his friend, and he himself is his enemy.

Be lifted up—From the perilous ocean of the world. The means is the attainment of yoga.

Is his friend—In the practice of yoga, a man's own self, endowed with discriminative knowledge, is the only friend. So-called friends and relatives are in reality the enemies of the aspirant; for, being objects of his affection and attachment, they create bondage.

The idea of friendship and enmity is explained:

बन्धुरात्मात्मनस्तस्य येनात्मैवात्मना जितः।
अनात्मनस्तु शत्रुत्वे वर्तेतात्मैव शत्रुवत्॥६॥

6. To him who has conquered himself by himself, his own self is a friend, but to him who has not conquered himself, his own self is hostile, like an external enemy.

He who is self—controlled, who has brought his body and mind under control, is his own friend. But in the case of a man who has no control over himself, his self injures him, like any external enemy.

How a man of self-control is his own friend is further explained:

जितात्मनः प्रशान्तस्य परमात्मा समाहितः।
शीतोष्णसुखदुःखेषु तथा मानापमानयोः॥७॥

7. He who has conquered himself and is serene in mind is constantly absorbed in the Supreme Self, alike in heat and cold, pleasure and pain, and honour and dishonour.

Himself—The self that is identified, through ignorance, with the aggregate of the body, senses, and so on.

Constantly absorbed—His own self has actually become one with the Supreme Self.

The highest characteristic of a yogi:

ज्ञानविज्ञानतृप्तात्मा कूटस्थो विजितेन्द्रियः।
युक्त इत्युच्यते योगी समलोष्टाश्मकाञ्चनः॥८॥

8. He is said to be a steadfast yogi whose heart, through knowledge and realization, is filled with satisfaction, who, having conquered his

senses, never vacillates, and to whom a clod, a stone, and gold are the same.

Knowledge—The knowledge of the teachings of the scriptures.

Realization—The experience of the teachings of the scriptures.

Filled with satisfaction—He seeks no satisfaction from any other quarter.

Never vacillates—In the presence of sense-objects. The illustration is given of an anvil, which remains unmoved though constantly struck by the hammer.

सुहृन्मित्रार्युदासीनमध्यस्थद्वेष्यबन्धुषु।
साधुष्वपि च पापेषु समबुद्धिर्विशिष्यते॥९॥

9. He who has equal regard for well-wishers, friends, and foes; for those who are related or indifferent to him; for the impartial and the malicious; and even for the righteous and the sinful—he stands supreme.

Equal regard—Free from attachment and aversion. He is not swayed in his opinion of a man by what the other is or does.

Well-wishers—Who do good to another person without expecting anything in return,

Friends—Who do good to another person out of natural love for him.

Indifferent—Who do not take sides with either of the contending parties.

Impartial—Who mean well by both the contending parties.

He stands supreme—He is the best among those who have attained yoga.

The directions for the practice of yoga:

योगी युञ्जीत सततमात्मानं रहसि स्थितः।
एकाकी यतचित्तात्मा निराशीरपरिग्रहः॥१०॥

10. A yogi should always try to concentrate his mind, retiring into solitude and living alone, having subdued his mind and body and got rid of his desires and possessions.

The words "solitude," "alone," and "got rid of his desires and possessions" indicate that the life of a saṃnyāsī is helpful for the practice of this yoga of meditation.

The Lord proceeds to describe particular modes of sitting, eating, and so forth, as aids to yoga:

शुचौ देशे प्रतिष्ठाप्य स्थिरमासनमात्मनः ।
नात्युच्छ्रितं नातिनीचं चैलाजिनकुशोत्तरम् ॥ ११ ॥

तत्रैकाग्रं मनः कृत्वा यतचित्तेन्द्रियक्रियः ।
उपविश्यासने युञ्ज्याद्योगमात्मविशुद्धये ॥ १२ ॥

11-12. In a clean spot having fixed his seat—a firm seat, neither too high nor too low—and having spread over it kuśa-grass, and then a deer skin, and then a cloth,

And sitting there, he should practise yoga for the purification of the self, restraining the activities of his mind and senses, and bringing his thoughts to a point.

The self—The mind.

The posture of the body:

समं कायशिरोग्रीवं धारयन्नचलं स्थिरः ।
सम्प्रेक्ष्य नासिकाग्रं स्वं दिशश्चानवलोकयन् ॥ १३ ॥

13. He should sit firm, holding his body, neck, and head erect and still, and gaze steadily at the tip of his nose, without looking around.

Gaze steadily etc.—This direction should not be taken in a literal sense; for in that case the mind would be fixed only on the tip of the nose and not on the Self. When the eyes are withdrawn from sense-objects, the mind becomes. steady and the eye-balls are still; the gaze is directed, *as it were*, to the tip of the nose. It will be taught later (VI, 25) that the mind should be made to dwell on the Self.

प्रशान्तात्मा विगतभीर्ब्रह्मचारिव्रते स्थितः ।
मनः संयम्य मच्चित्तो युक्त आसीत मत्परः ॥ १४ ॥

14. Completely serene and fearless, steadfast in the vow of a brahmacārī, disciplined in mind, and ever thinking on Me, he should sit in yoga, regarding Me as his Supreme Goal.

Brahmacārī—A religious student who lives with his teacher and observes the vows of celibacy and chastity and practises other spiritual disciplines.

Me—The Supreme Lord.

The fruit of yoga:

युञ्जन्नेवं सदात्मानं योगी नियतमानसः ।
शान्तिं निर्वाणपरमां मत्संस्थामधिगच्छति ॥ १५ ॥

15. Keeping himself ever steadfast in this manner, the yogi of subdued mind attains the Peace abiding in Me—the Peace that culminates in Nirvāṇa.

Nirvāṇa—Liberation characterized by freedom and bliss.

Regulations regarding the yogi's food and so forth:

नात्यश्नतस्तु योगोऽस्ति न चैकान्तमनश्नतः ।
न चातिस्वप्नशीलस्य जाग्रतो नैव चार्जुन ॥ १६ ॥

16. Yoga is not for him who eats too much nor for him who eats too little. It is not for him, O Arjuna, who sleeps too much nor for him who sleeps too little.

According to the books on yoga, a yogi should fill half his stomach with food, one quarter with water, and leave one quarter for the movement of air.

How can one succeed in yoga?

युक्ताहारविहारस्य युक्तचेष्टस्य कर्मसु ।
युक्तस्वप्नावबोधस्य योगो भवति दुःखहा ॥ १७ ॥

17. For him who is temperate in his food and recreation, temperate in his exertion at work, temperate in sleep and waking, yoga puts an end to all sorrows.

This and the preceding text resemble Buddha's teaching regarding the middle path.

When does a man attain yoga?

यदा विनियतं चित्तमात्मन्येवावतिष्ठते ।
निःस्पृहः सर्वकामेभ्यो युक्त इत्युच्यते तदा ॥ १८ ॥

18. When the well-controlled mind rests in the Self alone, free from longing for objects, then is one said to have attained yoga.

Objects—Seen or unseen, belonging to this world or the next.

An illustration is given:

यथा दीपो निवातस्थो नेङ्गते सोपमा स्मृता।
योगिनो यतचित्तस्य युञ्जतो योगमात्मनः ॥ १९ ॥

19. "As a lamp in a windless place does not flicker"—that is the figure used for the disciplined mind of a yogi practising concentration on the Self.

Windless place—A place sheltered from the wind.

Used—By those who are versed in yoga.

Yoga is a unique state of Self-realization.

यत्रोपरमते चित्तं निरुद्धं योगसेवया।
यत्र चैवात्मनात्मानं पश्यन्नात्मनि तुष्यति ॥ २० ॥

सुखमात्यन्तिकं यत्तद् बुद्धिग्राह्यमतीन्द्रियम्।
वेत्ति यत्र न चैवायं स्थितश्चलति तत्त्वतः ॥ २१ ॥

यं लब्ध्वा चापरं लाभं मन्यते नाधिकं ततः।
यस्मिन्स्थितो न दुःखेन गुरुणापि विचाल्यते ॥ २२ ॥

तं विद्याद् दुःखसंयोगवियोगं योगसंज्ञितम्।
स निश्चयेन योक्तव्यो योगोऽनिर्विण्णचेतसा ॥ २३ ॥

20-23. That in which the mind, restrained by the practice of concentration, rests quiescent; that in which, seeing the Self through the self, one rejoices in one's own Self;

That in which one knows the boundless joy beyond the reach of the senses and grasped only by the understanding; that in which being established, one never departs from Reality;

That on gaining which one thinks there is no greater gain, and wherein established one is not moved even by the heaviest of sorrows—

Let that be known as yoga, which is severance from the contact of pain. It is to be practised with perseverance and with an undaunted mind.

Seeing the Self through the self—Seeing the supreme Intelligence and the all-resplendent Light by the self, that is to say, by the mind purified through the practice of contemplation.

Beyond the reach of the senses—That is to say, not caused by any sense-object.

By the understanding—Direct and immediate knowledge gained without the instrumentality of the senses. In deep meditation the senses do not function; they are resolved into their cause, the mind. And when the mind becomes steady and cognition alone functions, then the indescribable Self is realized.

Heaviest of sorrows—Even including the pain caused by a sword or other sharp weapon.

Severance from the contact of pain—In the state of yoga one does not feel even a trace of pain, which also includes material happiness inseparable from pain.

Undaunted mind—There should be no relaxation of effort even though there is no quick result and the practice appears difficult.

The supreme discipline regarding yoga:

सङ्कल्पप्रभवान्कामांस्त्यक्त्वा सर्वानशेषतः।
मनसैवेन्द्रियग्रामं विनियम्य समन्ततः ॥२४॥

शनैः शनैरुपरमेद् बुद्ध्या धृतिगृहीतया।
आत्मसंस्थं मनः कृत्वा न किञ्चिदपि चिन्तयेत्॥२५॥

24-25. Renouncing entirely all the desires born of the will, drawing back the senses from every direction by strength of mind, let a man little by little attain tranquility with the help of the buddhi armed with fortitude. Once the mind is established in the Self, he should think of nothing else.

By strength of mind—Endowed with discrimination.

Established in the Self—When the aspirant is convinced that the Self is everything and that nothing else exists besides It.

What should one do if the mind becomes restless under the influence of rajas?

यतो यतो निश्चरति मनश्चञ्चलमस्थिरम्।
ततस्ततो नियम्यैतदात्मन्येव वशं नयेत्॥२६॥

26. Let him withdraw the fickle and unquiet mind from whatever causes it to wander away, and restore it to the control of the Self alone.

Fickle and unquiet—Fickleness and restlessness are the natural characteristics of the mind in its impure state.

Whatever causes it etc.—Sound, smell, and other objects are responsible for the mind's wandering away.

The means of bringing under control the restless mind are the realization of the illusoriness of sense-objects and the cultivation of indifference to them. Through the practice of discrimination and detachment the mind gradually attains inner peace.

The result of the yoga of meditation:

प्रशान्तमनसं ह्येनं योगिनं सुखमुत्तमम्।
उपैति शान्तरजसं ब्रह्मभूतमकल्मषम्॥२७॥

27. Supreme Bliss comes to the yogi whose mind is completely tranquil and whose passions are quieted, who is free from stain and who has become one with Brahman.

Passions—All passions, including delusion and attachment.

Free from stain—Unaffected by the illusion of dharma and adharma.

One with Brahman—A jīvanmukta, liberated while living in a body.

The purpose of yoga is achieved.

युञ्जन्नेवं सदात्मानं योगी विगतकल्मषः।
सुखेन ब्रह्मसंस्पर्शमत्यन्तं सुखमश्नुते॥२८॥

28. Thus making his self ever steadfast, the yogi, freed from sins, easily enjoys the touch of Brahman, which is exceeding bliss.

The bliss that is derived from contact with Brahman is infinite.

The result of the realization of oneness with Brahman:

सर्वभूतस्थमात्मानं सर्वभूतानि चात्मनि।
ईक्षते योगयुक्तात्मा सर्वत्र समदर्शनः॥२९॥

29. With the heart concentrated by yoga, viewing all things with equal regard, he beholds himself in all beings and all beings in himself.

Viewing all things etc.—Seeing the same Spirit dwelling in all objects.

He sees the identity of Ātman, the inmost Reality of himself, and Brahman, the inmost Reality of the universe.

यो मां पश्यति सर्वत्र सर्वं च मयि पश्यति।
तस्याहं न प्रणश्यामि स च मे न प्रणश्यति॥३०॥

30. He who sees Me everywhere and sees everything in Me, to him I am never lost, nor is he ever lost to Me.

After realizing his unity with Brahman, the yogi never loses his awareness of It. The Self of the yogi and the Self of Brahman have become one.

The result of this Knowledge is mokṣa, or liberation.

सर्वभूतस्थितं यो मां भजत्येकत्वमास्थितः।
सर्वथा वर्तमानोऽपि स योगी मयि वर्तते॥३१॥

31. He who, having been established in oneness, worships Me dwelling in all beings—that yogi, in whatever way he leads his life, lives in Me.

In all beings—The Lord dwells in all beings as their inmost Self, irrespective of their outer forms.

The yogi who sees the Lord in all beings and worships Him through all beings has attained liberation. No matter how he lives and acts, he is always free. He is no longer under the control of scriptural injunctions.

The best among the yogis is he who is compassionate to all beings.

आत्मौपम्येन सर्वत्र समं पश्यति योऽर्जुन।
सुखं वा यदि वा दुःखं स योगी परमो मतः॥३२॥

32. Him I hold to be the supreme yogi, O Arjuna, who looks on the pleasure and pain of all beings as he looks on them in himself.

This verse is the golden rule of Hinduism. The highest yogi sees that whatever is pleasant to him is pleasant to all others, including subhuman beings, and that whatever is painful to him is painful to all others. Therefore he cannot cause pain to any. He leads a life of complete non-violence. The highest yogi is he who is devoted to right knowledge and who, in action, is harmless to all.

Arjuna thinks that such a state of yoga is hard to attain. He asks Kṛṣṇa the method of its realization:

अर्जुन उवाच।

योऽयं योगस्त्वया प्रोक्तः साम्येन मधुसूदन।
एतस्याहं न पश्यामि चञ्चलत्वात्स्थितिं स्थिराम्॥ ३३॥

33. *Arjuna said:* This yoga, which You, O Madhusūdana, have declared to be characterized by evenness—I do not see how it can long endure, because of the restlessness of the mind.

Evenness—The mind, free from torpidity and restlessness, becomes one with the Self.

चञ्चलं हि मनः कृष्ण प्रमाथि बलवद् दृढम्।
तस्याहं निग्रहं मन्ये वायोरिव सुदुष्करम्॥ ३४॥

34. For the mind, O Kṛṣṇa, is restless, turbulent, powerful, and obstinate. To control it is as hard, it seems to me, as to control the wind.

Kṛṣṇa—The word is derived from the root "kṛṣ," which mean "to scrape." Kṛṣṇa is so called because He scrapes or draws away all sins from His devotees.

Turbulent—It agitates the body and senses and brings them under the control of objects.

Powerful—The mind cannot be easily subdued by reasoning.

The Lord indicates the way to control the mind:

श्रीभगवानुवाच।

असंशयं महाबाहो मनो दुर्निग्रहं चलम्।
अभ्यासेन तु कौन्तेय वैराग्येण च गृह्यते॥ ३५॥

35. *The Lord said:* Doubtless, O mighty Arjuna, the mind is restless and hard to control; but by practice and by detachment, O son of Kuntī, it can be restrained.

Practice—The effort of the mind toward calmness. Practice becomes firmly grounded when it is followed for a long time, and unremittingly, with devotion. The end is easily achieved with the help of austerity, continence, discrimination, and faith. The aspirant must not lose courage in the face of repeated failures.

Detachment—Freedom from thirst for any pleasure seen. or heard of. It is acquired through a constant perception of evil in all sensuous happiness, either of this life or hereafter.

Who can succeed in yoga?

असंयतात्मना योगो दुष्प्राप इति मे मतिः।
वश्यात्मना तु यतता शक्योऽवाप्तुमुपायतः॥३६॥

36. Yoga is hard to attain, I think, by a man who cannot control himself; but it can be attained by him who has controlled himself and who strives by right means.

Who has controlled himself—By means of constant practice and detachment,

Yoga is the science of religion. The test of its validity lies in one's seeing results through actual experimentation. Hence the teachers of yoga emphasize self-control and other disciplines.

While practising yoga, a man renounces all worldly endeavours. He also gives up those meritorious actions that bring happiness in heaven. But suppose he slips from the path and dies without attaining Knowledge. Arjuna is afraid that such a man is lost both to yoga and to the world.

अर्जुन उवाच।
अयतिः श्रद्धयोपेतो योगाच्चलितमानसः।
अप्राप्य योगसंसिद्धिं कां गतिं कृष्ण गच्छति॥३७॥

37. *Arjuna said:* A man who is endowed with faith, but not with steadfastness, and whose mind has wandered away from yoga—what end does he gain, O Kṛṣṇa, having failed to obtain perfection in yoga?

Faith—In the efficacy of yoga.

Has wandered away from yoga—Before his death. During the last moments of his life he is unable to commune with the Self through yoga.

Does he attain neither heaven nor liberation?

कच्चिन्नोभयविभ्रष्टश्छिन्नाभ्रमिव नश्यति।
अप्रतिष्ठो महाबाहो विमूढो ब्रह्मणः पथि॥३८॥

38. Fallen from both, unsupported, and bewildered in the way leading to Brahman, does he not, O mighty Kṛṣṇa, perish like a riven cloud?

Both—Both the path of worldly success and the path of yoga.

Unsupported—Without support either in material enjoyment or in yoga.

Riven cloud—A patch of cloud that has detached itself from a big cloud in order to reach a second big cloud, but, unable to reach its destination, drifts and ultimately disappears.

Only Kṛṣṇa, the omniscient Lord, can remove such a doubt.

एतन्मे संशयं कृष्ण छेत्तुमर्हस्यशेषतः।
त्वदन्यः संशयस्यास्य छेत्ता न ह्युपपद्यते॥ ३९॥

39. You should completely dispel, O Kṛṣṇa, this doubt of mine; for no one but You can destroy such a doubt.

The reassurance of the Lord regarding His devotees:

श्रीभगवानुवाच।
पार्थ नैवेह नामुत्र विनाशस्तस्य विद्यते।
न हि कल्याणकृत्कश्चिद् दुर्गतिं तात गच्छति॥ ४०॥

40. *The Lord said:* O Pārtha there is no destruction for him either in this world or the next: no evil, My son, befalls a man who does good.

No destruction—A yogi who falls from the path will not have a lower birth in his next life.

My son—A disciple is looked upon as a son.

A man who does good—That is to say, who strives for Self-realization.

What, then, will happen to him?

प्राप्य पुण्यकृतां लोकानुषित्वा शाश्वतीः समाः।
शुचीनां श्रीमतां गेहे योगभ्रष्टोऽभिजायते॥ ४१॥

41. The man who has fallen away from yoga goes to the worlds of the righteous. Having lived there for unnumbered years, he is reborn in the home of the pure and the prosperous.

The worlds of the righteous—The worlds inhabited by those pious souls who have performed great religious sacrifices while living on this earth.

Unnumbered years—As long as the merit of his past spiritual life remains.

Pure—Whose conduct is governed by religion.

अथवा योगिनामेव कुले भवति धीमताम्।
एतद्धि दुर्लभतरं लोके जन्म यदीदृशम्॥४२॥

42. Or he is born in a family of yogis rich in wisdom. Verily, such a birth is hard to gain in this world.

A family of yogis etc.—Poor in material resources but rich in wisdom.

Hard to gain—A birth in a family of wise yogis is more difficult to obtain than the one mentioned in the preceding text.

The reward mentioned in the preceding text is enjoyed by a yogi of lesser merit.

तत्र तं बुद्धिसंयोगं लभते पौर्वदेहिकम्।
यतते च ततो भूयः संसिद्धौ कुरुनन्दन॥४३॥

43. There he comes in touch with the knowledge acquired in his former body, O son of the Kurus, and strives still further for perfection.

Knowledge—The spiritual knowledge he attained in his previous life, which accompanies him, as subconscious impressions, in this life.

Whatever progress a man makes in the path of yoga he retains. He again starts from there when the next opportunity comes.

पूर्वाभ्यासेन तेनैव ह्रियते ह्यवशोऽपि सः।
जिज्ञासुरपि योगस्य शब्दब्रह्मातिवर्तते॥४४॥

44. By that former practice alone he is led on in spite of himself. Even he who merely wishes to know of yoga rises superior to the performer of Vedic rites.

Former practice—The practice in his former life.

Is led on in spite of himself—He may be unaware of the spiritual tendencies from his previous life, or he may be averse to leading a spiritual life owing to the interference of past unfavourable karma; but this ignorance and aversion are swept away by the force of good tendencies of his former life, and he is borne on to the goal of Self-realization in spite of himself.

Rises superior—The realization of a man who merely inquires about Self-knowledge transcends the results of the sacrifices and other rituals extolled in the Vedas. Therefore what doubt can there be of the ultimate liberation of the aspirant who practises yoga with steady devotion?

प्रयत्नाद्यतमानस्तु योगी संशुद्धकिल्बिषः।
अनेकजन्मसंसिद्धस्ततो याति परां गतिम्॥ ४५॥

45. A yogi, striving diligently, is purified of all sins, and, becoming perfect through many births, reaches the Supreme Goal.

Striving diligently—In every succeeding birth he adds a little more to his knowledge of yoga.

Becoming perfect etc.—Little by little acquiring, through many births, the knowledge of Reality, he ultimately attains perfection.

तपस्विभ्योऽधिको योगी ज्ञानिभ्योऽपि मतोऽधिकः।
कर्मिभ्यश्चाधिको योगी तस्माद्योगी भवार्जुन॥ ४६॥

46. The yogi is greater than men of austerities, greater than men of knowledge, greater than men of action. Therefore be a yogi, O Arjuna.

Austerities—Mortification of the flesh, and the penances prescribed for the expiation of sin.

Knowledge—Of the teachings of the scriptures.

Action—Fire-sacrifice and other rituals enjoined in the Vedas; also philanthropic activities.

Through austerities, study, Vedic rituals, and philanthropic action, one attains purity of heart and then follows the path of Self-knowledge. But the practice of yoga enables one to arrive directly at the Supreme Goal.

योगिनामपि सर्वेषां मद्गतेनान्तरात्मना।
श्रद्धावान्भजते यो मां स मे युक्ततमो मतः॥ ४७॥

47. And of all yogis, the one who worships Me with faith, his inmost self abiding in Me—him do I hold to be the most closely united with Me in yoga.

There are yogis who worship lesser deities. There are, again, those who are devoted to various austere practices in order to attain self-control. Śrī Kṛṣṇa here extols the yogi who loves God with all his heart and soul. Love of God is the easiest and best form of yoga. The sixth chapter ends with a note of emphasis on the path of bhakti (devotion).

ॐ तत्सदिति श्रीमद्भगवद्गीतासूपनिषत्सु
ब्रह्मविद्यायां योगशास्त्रे श्रीकृष्णार्जुनसंवादे
आत्मसंयमयोगो नाम षष्ठोऽध्यायः॥ ६॥

Thus in the Bhagavad Gītā, the Essence of the Upaniṣads, the Science of Brahman, the Scripture of Yoga, the Dialogue between Śrī Kṛṣṇa and Arjuna, ends the Sixth Chapter, entitled: THE WAY OF MEDITATION

CHAPTER 7

THE WAY OF REALIZATION

[ज्ञानविज्ञानयोगः]

श्रीभगवानुवाच।

मय्यासक्तमनाः पार्थ योगं युञ्जन्मदाश्रयः।
असंशयं समग्रं मां यथा ज्ञास्यसि तच्छृणु॥ १॥

1. *The Lord said:* Hear, O Pārtha how, with your mind attached to Me, and taking refuge in Me, and practising yoga, you will without any doubt know Me in full.

With your mind attached to Me—A man performs a Vedic sacrifice, practises austerities, or makes a gift, in order to obtain a worldly end. But a yogi's mind is attached to the. Lord alone. So he sets aside all other disciplines and worships the Lord with complete concentration.

Taking refuge in Me—The Lord alone is the whole basis of the yogi's being and the goal of his action.

Practising yoga—Being united with the Lord in contemplation.

In full—The six attributes generally associated with the Lord are infinite Greatness, Strength, Power, Grace, Knowledge, and Detachment.

Śrī Kṛṣṇa ended the sixth chapter by describing the supreme yogi as one who, with his inmost self abiding in Him, adores the Lord. Arjuna will now be taught the nature of the Lord Himself, who is the object of the yogi's unwavering devotion.

The Knowledge of the Lord is extolled:

ज्ञानं तेऽहं सविज्ञानमिदं वक्ष्याम्यशेषतः ।
यज्ज्ञात्वा नेह भूयोऽन्यज्ज्ञातव्यमवशिष्यते ॥ २ ॥

2. I shall teach you in full both knowledge and experience, which being known, nothing more remains here for you to know.

Knowledge and experience—The awareness that the Lord exists and that He is the inmost Spirit of all is knowledge. One acquires this knowledge through study of the scriptures and reasoning about their contents. But to realize the Lord in oneself and in all beings and to act according to that realization is experience, vijñāna. To give an illustration: To know that one can obtain fire from wood is knowledge; but to kindle wood and cook one's meal on the fire and be nourished by that meal is experience, vijñāna. The Knowledge of God, in Hindu philosophy, is inseparable from experience.

Nothing more remains etc.—The implication is that the Lord is everything; therefore when He is fully known everything is known. The Lord, as Satcidānanda (Existence-Knowledge-Bliss Absolute), forms the real essence of all objects; names and forms are illusory superimpositions.

This integral knowledge of the Lord is a rare and difficult thing.

मनुष्याणां सहस्रेषु कश्चिद्यतति सिद्धये ।
यततामपि सिद्धानां कश्चिन्मां वेत्ति तत्त्वतः ॥ ३ ॥

3. Among thousands of men, one, here and there, strives for perfection; and of those who strive and succeed, one, perchance, knows Me in truth.

In truth—The Being of the Lord and His diverse manifestations are indeed incomprehensible to the human mind. He is the Impersonal Reality, the Personal God, and many other things besides.

According to the Hindu scriptures, only a soul born in a human body is able to realize the Lord. Subhuman beings and superhuman beings (such as gods and angels) only experience the results of the actions performed by them as human beings in previous births. The consciousness that acts as instinct in subhuman beings manifests itself as reason in man. Of all living beings on earth, man alone can inquire about his self and its relationship with the Lord. Among innumerable human beings, only a few, comparatively speaking, develop a desire for such an inquiry. Among those who show such desire, only a few, again, know the means of attaining knowledge and strive after it. Again, among those who strive, only a fortunate few succeed in acquiring the true knowledge of the Lord. Hence the knowledge of God is rare on this earth.

Śrī Kṛṣṇa describes the nature of the Lord:

भूमिरापोऽनलो वायुः खं मनो बुद्धिरेव च।
अहङ्कार इतीयं मे भिन्ना प्रकृतिरष्टधा॥४॥

4. Earth, water, fire, air, ether, mind, reason, and ego: such is the eightfold division of My Nature.

This eightfold division is taken from Sāṅkhya philosophy. Mind (manas), referred to in the text, stands for ahaṅkāra, or I-consciousness, of Sāṅkhya philosophy; reason (buddhi), for mahat (cosmic mind), which is the cause of ahaṅkāra; and ego (ahaṅkāra), for avyakta, or the unmanifest (the seed state of the manifest universe). These eight—the five elements, I-consciousness, mahat, and the unmanifest—constitute the Prakṛti or Nature, of Sāṅkhya philosophy. The elements are of two kinds: subtle or rudimentary, and gross. Each of the subtle elements is endowed with a property of its own. Ether (ākāśa) has the property of producing sound; air (vāyu), the property of producing touch; fire (agni), the property of producing visibility; water (ap), the property of producing flavour; and earth (bhūmi), the property of producing smell. These are the five ways in which a man, through his five sense-organs, becomes aware of Nature, or matter. Hence the Hindu philosophers have divided matter into five elements. Manas (the inner organ that creates doubt), buddhi (the inner organ that decides), and I-consciousness also belong to the realm of matter, or Prakṛti. The gross elements are formed by a peculiar combination of the subtle elements, in which one half of each of the subtle elements combines with one eighth of the remaining four elements. Thus gross ether = $\frac{1}{2}$ subtle ether + $\frac{1}{8}$ air + $\frac{1}{8}$ fire+ $\frac{1}{8}$ water + $\frac{1}{8}$ earth. From ether is produced air. From air, containing the element of ether, is produced fire. From fire, containing the elements of ether and air, is produced water. From water, containing the elements of ether, air, and fire, is produced earth. Earth contains, besides its own subtle element, something of the four preceding entities. Since air springs from ether, it has the properties of both sound and touch. Each of the succeeding elements possesses, besides its own property, the properties of the preceding elements. Earth, for example, has the properties of smell (which is its own), flavour, visibility, touch, and sound.

The other category of Sāṅkhya philosophy, besides Prakṛti, or Nature, is Puruṣa, or Soul. Sāṅkhya philosophy believes in a multiplicity of souls. Each living being has its own soul. According to the Non-dualistic Vedānta, Brahman is the only Reality. Under the influence of Its own māyā, Brahman appears as the different elements, gross and subtle, which supply the material cause of the universe and its created beings.

The manifestation of the Lord described above is of the nature of matter and therefore inferior, impure, and harmful. It constitutes the bondage of saṃsāra. There is a higher manifestation of the Lord, which is now revealed:

अपरेयमितस्त्वन्यां प्रकृतिं विद्धि मे पराम्।
जीवभूतां महाबाहो ययेदं धार्यते जगत्॥५॥

5. This is My lower nature. But, different from it, know, O mighty Arjuna, My higher nature—the Indwelling Spirit by which the universe is sustained.

According to the Upaniṣad, the Lord created the different forms and then entered them as their living souls. Insentient matter is sustained by the living Spirit. Contemplating matter, the soul becomes entangled in the world; contemplating the Spirit, it attains liberation. Hence the Spirit-form of the Lord is superior to His matter-form.

The omniscient Lord, through His two natures, is the cause of the entire universe.

एतद्योनीनि भूतानि सर्वाणीत्युपधारय।
अहं कृत्स्नस्य जगतः प्रभवः प्रलयस्तथा॥६॥

6. Know that these two form the womb of all beings. I am the origin of the entire universe and also its dissolution.

These two—The lower and the higher nature, or Prakṛti.

The womb—That is to say, the cause. The lower nature manifests itself as the material body, and the higher nature as the living soul, the experiencer.

I am the origin etc.—At the time of evolution names, forms, and life arise from Prakṛti and at the time of involution they go back into it. But Prakṛti independent of the Lord, cannot create. It is His instrument of creation, preservation, and dissolution. Hence the Lord is the Ultimate Cause of the universe.

Therefore,

मत्तः परतरं नान्यत्किञ्चिदस्ति धनञ्जय।
मयि सर्वमिदं प्रोतं सूत्रे मणिगणा इव॥७॥

7. There exists nothing whatever higher than I am, O Dhanañjaya. All is strung on Me as a row of gems on a thread.

There exists nothing etc.—There exists no other cause of the universe except the Lord.

All—The universe and the created beings.

Row of gems etc.—The Lord is the support of the universe, as the string is of the gems on a necklace. Without the string the gems will lie scattered; without the Lord, the planets, stars, and all else will be dispersed. The Lord, manifesting Himself through the physical and moral laws, sustains the relative world. He is also the Unity that underlies the diversity of names and forms.

The Lord is also the essence of the universe.

रसोऽहमप्सु कौन्तेय प्रभास्मि शशिसूर्ययोः।
प्रणवः सर्ववेदेषु शब्दः खे पौरुषं नृषु॥८॥

8. I am the savour of waters, O son of Kuntī, the radiance of the sun and moon; I am the syllable Om in all the Vedas, the sound in ether, the manliness in man.

Savour—This is the essence of water. *See* note on VII, 4.

Om—Om is the most sacred word of the Vedas and may be compared to the Word referred to by St. John in the opening of the Fourth Gospel: "In the beginning was the Word, and the Word was with God, and the Word was God." According to Hindu philosophy, the whole of this universe has both name and form (nāmarūpa) as the prerequisite of its manifestation. The form is its outer crust, of which the name or idea is the inner essence or kernel. The name is inseparable from a word or sound. The universe perceived by the five senses is the form, behind which stands the eternal, inexpressible *sphoṭa*, or Word, or Logos. This eternal *sphoṭa,* the essential, beginningless material of all ideas or names, is the power through which the Lord creates the universe; nay, the Lord first becomes conditioned as the *sphoṭa* by His own māyā, and then evolves Himself as the more concrete sense-perceived universe. The symbol of the *sphoṭa* is Om, also written *Aum*. Since the word is inseparable from the idea, Om and the eternal *sphoṭa* are inseparable.

Therefore the eternal Om is the mother or source of all names and forms and hence the holiest of all holy words. There may be other words to denote the eternal and inexpressible *sphoṭa*; but the Hindus contend that Om is a unique word and uniquely apposite. The *sphoṭa* is the material or foundation of all sounds or words, which are inseparable from names or ideas; yet it is not any definite, fully formed word. That is to say, if all the peculiarities that distinguish one word from another be removed, then what remains will be the *sphoṭa,* or Om. Therefore Om is called the Nāda-Brahman, or Sound-Brahman. The three letters, *a, u*, and *m,* pronounced in combination as Om, are the generalized symbol of all possible sounds. *A* is the root sound, the key, pronounced without the tongue's touching any part of the palate. It is the least differentiated of all sounds. Again, all articulate sounds are produced in the space between the root of the tongue and the lips—the throat sound is *a*, and *m* is the last sound. *U* represents the rolling forward of the impulse that begins at the root of the tongue and ends at the lips. If properly pronounced, Om will represent the whole gamut of sound—production; and no other word can do this. Therefore Om is the fittest symbol of the *sphoṭa,* the Logos, the Word "which was at the beginning." As the *sphoṭa,* being the finer aspect of the manifested universe, is nearer to the Lord and is indeed the first manifestation of His divine wisdom, Om is the true symbol of God.[1] It is the symbol of both the Personal God (in His aspect of Creator, Preserver, and Destroyer) and Impersonal Reality. *A, u,* and *m* represent creation, preservation, and destruction respectively. The elongated, undifferentiated, gong-like sound that comes at the end of the utterance of Om is the symbol of Impersonal and Transcendental Reality. This symbol Om was not created by any human reasoning, but was revealed to pure-souled mystics when, in meditation, their minds were attuned to the Highest. *See* note on XVII, 23.

Sound in ether—Ether, or ākāśa, is the first element to be evolved from Brahman at the time of creation. The property of the rudimentary ākāśa is sound. Therefore it is the essence of ākāśa.

Manliness in man—It is manliness that is the essential quality of a man.

The Lord exists in all beings as their essential quality. That which is real and essential in water is the Lord; and this is true of all objects and beings.

पुण्यो गन्धः पृथिव्यां च तेजश्चास्मि विभावसौ।
जीवनं सर्वभूतेषु तपश्चास्मि तपस्विषु॥९॥

9. I am the sweet fragrance in earth and the brightness in fire. In all beings I am the life, and I am the austerity in ascetics.

---

1 This interpretation of Om is taken from Bhakti—Yoga by Swami Vivekananda.

Sweet fragrance in earth—The property of rudimentary earth is fragrance, which is sweet and agreeable before it combines with the other elements.

Brightness in fire—This is the essence of fire, by which it reveals all objects or heats them or burns them or illumines them.

In all beings etc.—The Lord is the Life without which no being can live or exist.

Austerity in ascetics—The power by which the ascetics endure all opposites, such as heat and cold, love and hate, pleasure and pain.

बीजं मां सर्वभूतानां विद्धि पार्थ सनातनम्।
बुद्धिर्बुद्धिमतामस्मि तेजस्तेजस्विनामहम्॥ १०॥

10. Know Me, O son of Pṛthā, to be the Eternal Seed of all things that exist; I am the intelligence of the intelligent and the daring of the brave.

Eternal Seed—Unlike an ordinary seed, which dies after bringing forth its sprout, the Lord, the Eternal Seed of all beings, still exists though the universe in course of time disappears.

Intelligence—The discriminative faculty of the mind.

बलं बलवतां चाहं कामरागविवर्जितम्।
धर्माविरुद्धो भूतेषु कामोऽस्मि भरतर्षभ॥ ११॥

11. I am the strength of the strong, free from longing and attachment. I am, O lord of the Bhāratas, the desire in all beings that is not contrary to dharma.

Strength of the strong—The strength that is free from longing and attachment and that sustains a man's body and mind in his effort to do his duties. It is not the strength that creates thirst in a worldly person to enjoy sensuous pleasures.

Longing—Kāma: thirst for objects not present to the senses.

Attachment—Rāga: love for the objects presented to the senses, in spite of the knowledge of their illusoriness.

Desire—For instance, the desire for as much of food and drink as is necessary for the sustenance of the body. Or the word may mean the desire for legitimate offspring.

ये चैव सात्त्विका भावा राजसास्तामसाश्च ये।
मत्त एवेति तान्विद्धि न त्वहं तेषु ते मयि॥ १२॥

12. And whatever things there be—of the nature of sattva, rajas, and tamas—know they are all from Me alone. I am not, however, in them; they are in Me.

Things—These include the different states of mind.

Sattva, rajas, or tamas—*See* note on "guṇas," II, 45.

I am not etc.—These guṇas constitute Prakṛti or Nature, which is the inferior manifestation of the Lord. Therefore the Lord is their ultimate cause. But the Lord is not, as in the case of worldly men, under the control of the guṇas. The guṇas, on the contrary, are subject to Him.

The universe and all its beings are in the Lord, but the Lord is not in them. The universe is only an appearance superimposed by illusion (māyā) on the Lord. It is like a mirage in the desert. From the standpoint of the onlooker, the illusory water exists in the desert; but the desert does not depend upon or exist in the mirage. Likewise the universe, apparently superimposed on the Lord, exists in the Lord, but the Lord is not in the universe. None of the properties of the universe touches the Lord, just as the water of the mirage cannot soak a single grain of the desert sand.

The world does not know the Lord, who by nature is eternal, pure, intelligent, and free; who is the Self of all beings; and who, through His grace, redeems all creatures from the unending chain of birth and death, caused by māyā.

त्रिभिर्गुणमयैर्भावैरेभिः सर्वमिदं जगत्।
मोहितं नाभिजानाति मामेभ्यः परमव्ययम्॥ १३॥

13. Deluded by these threefold guṇas constituting Nature, this whole world fails to recognize Me, who am above the guṇas and immutable.

Deluded etc.—All beings are deluded by love, hatred, attachment, and the other characteristics of the guṇas.

Recognize Me—Though the Lord is the inmost Self of all beings and the object of direct and immediate perception. Above the guṇas—The Lord, in His purest essence, is untouched by the guṇas, which belong only to His Prakṛti.

Immutable—Not subject to birth, death, or any other changes.

How can one overcome the inscrutable māyā of the Lord?

दैवी ह्येषा गुणमयी मम माया दुरत्यया।
मामेव ये प्रपद्यन्ते मायामेतां तरन्ति ते॥ १४॥

14. Verily, this divine māyā of Mine, consisting of the guṇas, is hard to overcome. But those who take refuge in Me alone, shall cross over this māyā.

Divine—Inscrutable to human reason.

Hard to overcome—By self-effort if unaided by divine grace.

Take refuge in Me alone—Abandoning all dharmas, or duties, become devoted to God alone, who is the Lord of māyā and the inmost Self of every being. If a man's hands. are firmly tied by a strong rope, he cannot free himself by his own efforts; someone else must remove his bonds. Likewise, an aspirant cannot get rid of māyā by his own efforts; for all his thinking, discrimination, and other activities pertain to the domain of māyā. The Lord cannot be realized by yoga, karma, discrimination, or any other means except His grace. Spiritual disciplines, with their background of I-consciousness, only convince the seeker of their futility as means to realize the Lord. Then the seeker practises complete self-surrender, which elicits the divine grace. The purpose of spiritual practices is the realization that the Lord cannot be attained through them. The divine māyā appears insurmountable to the egotist, but it is easily overcome by the humble devotee of the Lord. An elephant that challenges a swift river is swept away by its strong current, but an insignificant minnow, approaching it with humility, goes up the rushing stream.

Shall cross over etc.—Shall be liberated from the bondage of māyā.

Māyā, a concept of Vedānta philosophy, explains the relative universe. According to the Non-dualistic Vedānta, Brahman is the only Reality. It alone exists. Its nature is Existence-Knowledge-Bliss Absolute. It is birthless, deathless, eternal, and immortal. Brahman is beyond cause and effect. Hence, from the standpoint of Brahman, there is neither creation of the universe nor preservation nor destruction. But from the relative standpoint the *fact* of creation cannot be denied, though the *act* of creation cannot be proved. Vedānta, in order to interpret the universe, makes use of the concept of māyā, which is generally translated as "illusion," "ignorance," "nescience," and so on. Through ignorance we superimpose the characteristics of one object upon another, though the superimposed characteristics do not in any way change the substratum. Illusions such as seeing a snake in a rope, a mirage in the desert, and silver in seashells are often cited by the Vedāntists to prove this. As long as the perceiver is under the influence of illusion, the snake, the mirage, and the silver appear to be real. But they do not in any way affect the real nature of the rope, the desert, and the shells. Likewise, through illusion, or māyā, Brahman appears as the universe. The ideas of time, space, causality, name, and form are superimposed upon the Pure Consciousness. But they do not alter the nature of Brahman. This power of creating illusion is inherent in Brahman Itself and is unknown and unknowable to the human mind, which itself is a product of māyā. One cannot inquire into the cause of a dream as long as one is dreaming.

The following are some of the characteristics of māyā: It is something positive, though intangible; it cannot be described as either being or non-being. It is positive because it is the source of the manifold universe. It is not of the nature of existence or being, because it does not exist when Truth is realized. Again, it is not non-existent or non-being (like the son of a barren woman), for it produces the illusion of the relative world.

Māyā is intangible: it cannot be grasped by reason, for reasoning itself is in māyā. To try to prove māyā by reasoning is like trying to see darkness by means of darkness. Again, māyā cannot be proved by Knowledge, for when Knowledge is awakened there remains no trace of māyā. Hence it will remain for ever inscrutable to the human mind.

Māyā consists of the three guṇas: sattva, rajas, and tamas. They constitute māyā and are present in everything that exists in Nature.

Māyā is beginningless, for the very conception of time is due to māyā. But it has an end. The Knowledge of Brahman ends it.

Under the influence of māyā the Self, which is the same. as the immortal Brahman, regards Itself as an embodied being and experiences the suffering and misery of the world. With the help of māyā, but retaining control of it, Brahman appears as an Avatar, or Incarnation, in order to subdue. the power of iniquity and establish righteousness. The goal of spiritual discipline is to get rid of māyā and realize one's divine nature.

If through the worship of the Lord one gets rid of māyā, why do not all worship Him?

न मां दुष्कृतिनो मूढाः प्रपद्यन्ते नराधमाः ।
माययापहृतज्ञाना आसुरं भावमाश्रिताः ॥ १५ ॥

15. Evil-doers and the deluded and the vilest among men, deprived of knowledge by māyā and following the way of the asuras, do not worship Me.

Way of the asuras—The conduct of the demons; that is to say, cruelty, untruth, and the like. The traits of the asuras, or demoniacal person, are described in the sixteenth chapter of the Gītā.

It must not be thought that the Lord has created some persons with evil tendencies in order to punish them. He is impartial—without any attachment or hatred for any created being. Only those whose sins, the result of their own evil action, have been destroyed feel His attraction. As a magnet exercises uniform attraction, He attracts all beings to Him. When the dirt of wickedness covering our soul is washed away by the tears of divine love, we become united with the Lord. Every soul will eventually realize God.

Only fortunate souls worship God.

चतुर्विधा भजन्ते मां जनाः सुकृतिनोऽर्जुन।
आर्तो जिज्ञासुरर्थार्थी ज्ञानी च भरतर्षभ॥ १६ ॥

16. Four types of virtuous men worship Me, O Arjuna: the man in distress, the man seeking knowledge, the man seeking enjoyment, and, O best of the Bhāratas, the man endowed with wisdom.

Virtuous men—Anyone seeking the Lord, whatever his motive, is a fortunate and righteous soul.

The man seeking knowledge—Wishing to learn Self-knowledge, or the Knowledge of God.

Enjoyment—Both here and hereafter.

The man endowed with wisdom—One who has renounced all desires born of māyā.

Not all people in distress or seeking knowledge and enjoyment worship the Lord. Only the fortunate among them take refuge in Him for the fulfilment of their desires.

Among the four types described above, the man of wisdom is the best.

तेषां ज्ञानी नित्ययुक्त एकभक्तिर्विशिष्यते।
प्रियो हि ज्ञानिनोऽत्यर्थमहं स च मम प्रियः॥ १७ ॥

17. Of these, the wise man, ever steadfast and devoted to the One alone, is the best. For supremely dear am I to the man of wisdom, and he is dear to Me.

Devoted to the One—The jñānī sees no one except the Lord Himself as the object of devotion. Since he does not identify himself with the body, ego, and the rest, he does not experience any mental distraction; so his devotion to the Lord is one-pointed and unswerving.

Supremely dear am I etc.—The wise man knows the Lord to be his very Self. Therefore the Lord is very dear to him. It is well known that everyone loves the self most dearly. The Lord, too, considers the wise man to be His very Self and therefore His beloved.

Are the three others likewise dear to the Lord?

उदाराः सर्व एवैते ज्ञानी त्वात्मैव मे मतम्।
आस्थितः स हि युक्तात्मा मामेवानुत्तमां गतिम्॥ १८॥

18. Noble indeed are they all; but the man endowed with wisdom I deem to be My very Self. For, steadfast in mind, he remains fixed in Me alone as the Supreme Goal.

Noble indeed etc.—The three others, who have motives behind their worship, are also dear to the Lord. The Lord always loves His devotees, whether their devotion to Him is selfish or unselfish.

My very Self—The Lord is the indwelling Self of all; but the jñānī alone is aware of it.

Compared to unbelievers, the devotees who worship the Lord for selfish purposes are noble, for their minds are directed to Him. But those who love the Lord alone as the Supreme Goal and whose love is untainted by any selfish desire are the best of devotees.

Rare indeed is the man endowed with divine wisdom.

बहूनां जन्मनामन्ते ज्ञानवान्मां प्रपद्यते।
वासुदेवः सर्वमिति स महात्मा सुदुर्लभः॥ १९॥

19. At the end of many births the man of wisdom seeks refuge in Me, realizing that Vāsudeva is all. Rare indeed is such a high-souled person.

At the end etc.—After many lives spent in spiritual discipline one attains maturity of knowledge and obtains the direct vision of the Lord.

Vāsudeva—An epithet of the Lord, who is also the inmost Self of all beings.

All—The whole universe with its sentient and insentient beings.

Why do all not realize that the Lord alone is everything?

कामैस्तैस्तैर्हृतज्ञानाः प्रपद्यन्तेऽन्यदेवताः।
तं तं नियममास्थाय प्रकृत्या नियताः स्वया॥ २०॥

20. But those whose discrimination has been led astray by various desires resort to other deities, following diverse rituals, constrained by their own natures.

Various desires—For offspring, wealth, heaven, the defeat of enemies, and so on.

Other deities—Imperfect forms of the Lord, which correspond to their selfish desires.

Diverse rituals—Rites peculiar to the worship of such minor deities.

Own natures—Tendencies acquired in previous lives. On account of these tendencies they see the highest good in a petty ideal.

The Lord helps those, too, who worship other deities.

यो यो यां यां तनुं भक्तः श्रद्धयार्चितुमिच्छति।
तस्य तस्याचलां श्रद्धां तामेव विदधाम्यहम्॥ २१॥

21. Whatever may be the form a devotee seeks to worship with faith—in that form alone I make his faith unwavering.

Form—All deities are only minor forms of the all-pervading Supreme Lord.

Faith—Faith alone brings success in worship.

The deepening of the devotee's faith in every form of worship comes only from the Lord. Through this intense faith the devotee obtains the result of his worship, even though he has set before himself a limited goal. It is the Lord alone who bestows the fruit of worship.

स तया श्रद्धया युक्तस्तस्याराधनमीहते।
लभते च ततः कामान्मयैव विहितान्हि तान्॥ २२॥

22. Possessed of that faith, he worships that form and from it attains his desires, which are, in reality, granted by Me alone.

Faith—Deepened by the grace of the Lord on account of the devotee's earnestness.

Granted by Me alone—The Supreme and Omniscient Lord alone knows the precise relationship between an action and its fruit. He is the dispenser of the fruit of action.

Different are the results of the worship of the minor deities and the worship of the Supreme Lord.

अन्तवत्तु फलं तेषां तद्भवत्यल्पमेधसाम्।
देवान्देवयजो यान्ति मद्भक्ता यान्ति मामपि॥ २३॥

23. But finite is the result gained by these men of small minds. Those who worship the deities go to the deities; those who worship Me come to Me.

Finite is the result etc.—Any enjoyment in the world of time and space comes to an end.

Men of small minds—Because they take a petty object as the Supreme Goal.

Deities—The deities are the manifestations of the Lord in the relative world.

Come to Me—Realize the transcendental and eternal aspect of the Spirit.

The same exertion is needed for the worship either of the Lord or of the minor deities; but the results are totally different. Yet men, deluded by transitory desires, do not seek the Lord Himself, who is the source of all peace, happiness, and knowledge.

If the worship of the Lord and of the minor deities require the same exertion but produce totally different results, why do seekers neglect the Lord and worship the deities?

अव्यक्तं व्यक्तिमापन्नं मन्यन्ते मामबुद्धयः।
परं भावमजानन्तो ममाव्ययमनुत्तमम्॥ २४॥

24. Not knowing My supreme Nature, immutable and transcendent, foolish men think that I, the Unmanifest, am endowed with a manifest form.

The ignorant think that the Lord, too, like an ordinary mortal, comes down from the unmanifested state and assumes a body, impelled by His past karma. This belief is due to their ignorance of His real Nature, which is unchanging and ever luminous. Thus disregarding the Lord, the foolish worship the minor deities for the fulfilment of their selfish desires.

What is the cause of this ignorance?

नाहं प्रकाशः सर्वस्य योगमायासमावृतः।
मूढोऽयं नाभिजानाति लोको मामजमव्ययम्॥ २५॥

25. Veiled by My māyā born of the guṇas, I am not revealed to all. This deluded world knows Me not as the unborn and eternal.

Māyā—Māyā, which conceals the real nature of the Lord, belongs to the Lord Himself. Keeping this māyā under His Control, the Supreme Lord appears as Kṛṣṇa and the other Incarnations. *See* pp. 265-267.

All embodiments are due to māyā. Ordinary mortals are under the control of māyā; therefore they cannot know their true divine nature. But in the case of the Incarnation, the all-powerful māyā is under His control; therefore He is never unaware of His own nature. Ignorant persons do not recognize an Incarnation of God, on account of the veil of māyā, but regard Him as an ordinary man.

Māyā, which limits the knowledge of men, cannot obstruct the Lord's knowledge.

वेदाहं समतीतानि वर्तमानानि चार्जुन।
भविष्याणि च भूतानि मां तु वेद न कश्चन॥२६॥

26. I, O Arjuna, know the beings that are of the past, that are of the present, and that are to come; but Me no one knows.

I know—Because māyā is under the control of the Lord.

What is the obstacle to their knowledge, by which mortals are deluded and remain ignorant of the Lord?

इच्छाद्वेषसमुत्थेन द्वन्द्वमोहेन भारत।
सर्वभूतानि सम्मोहं सर्गे यान्ति परन्तप॥२७॥

27. All beings, from their very birth, O Bhārata, are deluded by the spell of the pairs of opposites arising from desire and aversion.

Pairs of opposites—*See* note on II, 45.

Those who are deluded by the passions of love and hate and the other pairs of opposites cannot even acquire a proper knowledge of the outer world. That the knowledge of the inmost Self is impossible for them goes without saying. Being under the spell of illusion from their birth, ignorant men do not know that the Lord is their Self.

Who are the fortunate souls free from the pairs of opposites and devoted to the worship of the Lord?

येषां त्वन्तगतं पापं जनानां पुण्यकर्मणाम्।
ते द्वन्द्वमोहनिर्मुक्ता भजन्ते मां दृढव्रताः॥२८॥

28. But the men of virtuous deeds, whose sin is ended, are free from the delusion of the pairs and worship Me with firm resolve.

Virtuous deeds—Which purify the mind.

Firm resolve—Seekers endowed with a pure mind are firm in their conviction that the Lord alone is real; they renounce everything else and devote themselves to the worship of the Lord.

Through the virtuous deeds of many lives one's sins are destroyed and the delusion of duality gradually disappears. As the mind becomes purer, one acquires concentration, firmness of resolve, and love of the Lord.

Through worshipping Me they acquire knowledge and attain the goal of life.

जरामरणमोक्षाय मामाश्रित्य यतन्ति ये।
ते ब्रह्म तद्विदुः कृत्स्नमध्यात्मं कर्म चाखिलम्॥२९॥

29. Those who take refuge in Me to gain release from old age and death—they will come to know Brahman, they will come to know all about the individual soul, and all about action as well.

Take refuge in Me—Devoted only to the Lord, whose nature is immortal.

Release from old age etc.—That is to say, liberation from relative existence. Their worship is not motivated by any earthly desire.

Individual soul—The Divinity that is the reality underlying the individual soul.

साधिभूताधिदैवं मां साधियज्ञं च ये विदुः।
प्रयाणकालेऽपि च मां ते विदुर्युक्तचेतसः॥३०॥

30. Those who know Me as the One that underlies all the elements, as the One that underlies all the gods, and as the One that sustains all the sacrifices, will, with steadfast mind, know Me even in the hour of death.

Their consciousness of the Lord will remain undiminished even in the hour of death. The practice of the knowledge of God throughout life enables one to remember Him in the hour of death. If one gives up the body with the knowledge of God, one attains liberation.

ॐ तत्सदिति श्रीमद्भगवद्गीतासूपनिषत्सु
ब्रह्मविद्यायां योगशास्त्रे श्रीकृष्णार्जुनसंवादे
ज्ञानविज्ञानयोगो नाम सप्तमोऽध्यायः॥७॥

Thus in the Bhagavad Gītā, the Essence of the Upaniṣads, the Science of Brahman, the Scripture of Yoga, the Dialogue between Śrī *Kṛṣṇa and Arjuna, ends the Seventh Chapter, entitled:* THE WAY OF REALIZATION

CHAPTER 8

THE WAY TO THE IMPERISHABLE BRAHMAN

[अक्षरब्रह्मयोगः]

अर्जुन उवाच।

किं तद् ब्रह्म किमध्यात्मं किं कर्म पुरुषोत्तम।
अधिभूतं च किं प्रोक्तमधिदैवं किमुच्यते॥ १॥

अधियज्ञः कथं कोऽत्र देहेऽस्मिन्मधुसूदन।
प्रयाणकाले च कथं ज्ञेयोऽसि नियतात्मभिः॥ २॥

1-2. *Arjuna said:* What is Brahman? What is the individual soul? And what is action, O Supreme Person? What is it that is said to underlie all the elements?

And what is it that is said to underlie all the gods? And who, O Madhusūdana, sustains all the sacrifices here in the body? And in what way? And how, again, are You to be known at the time of death by those who have practised self-control?

Arjuna seeks the explanation of certain terms used by Kṛṣṇa at the end of the seventh chapter.

श्रीभगवानुवाच।

अक्षरं ब्रह्म परमं स्वभावोऽध्यात्ममुच्यते।
भूतभावोद्भवकरो विसर्गः कर्मसंज्ञितः॥ ३॥

3. *The Lord said:* Brahman is the Imperishable, the Supreme. Dwelling in each body, Brahman is called the individual soul. The offering of the oblation, which brings into existence all beings and supports them, is called action.

Brahman—Compare: "At the command of this Imperishable, O Gārgi, heaven and earth are held in their proper places." *(Bṛhadāraṇyaka Upaniṣad*, III, viii, 9)

Dwelling in each body—The Supreme Brahman alone. exists in every individual body as the Pratyagātman, the Ego, the inmost Self, and is known as the Adhyātma. As the culmination of the spiritual discipline, this inmost Self is realized as one with Brahman.

Individual soul—The word used in the text is "Adhyātma."

The offering etc.—According to the Vedas, the offering of oblations to the gods brings about the births of all creatures: the oblations cause rain, and the rain causes food, and food causes created beings. The offering of oblations in sacrifice is called karma, or action.

अधिभूतं क्षरो भावः पुरुषश्चाधिदैवतम्।
अधियज्ञोऽहमेवात्र देहे देहभृतां वर॥४॥

4. That which underlies all the elements is the perishable entity; and that which underlies all the gods is the Puruṣa, the Cosmic Spirit. And He who sustains all the sacrifices is Myself, here in the body, O best of men.

That which underlies all the elements—It comprises all material objects, everything that comes into existence. The word used in the text is "adhibhūta."

That which underlies all the gods—The word used in the text is "adhidaivata."

Puruṣa—*Lit.*, That by which everything is filled, or That which lies in the body. It is the Cosmic Spirit (Hiraṇyagarbha), or Universal Soul, that manifests Itself as the controlling Deity of the sun and also as the consciousness. that functions through the eyes and other sense-organs.

He who sustains etc.—The Vedas describe Viṣṇu as the presiding Deity of all sacrifices, as the dispenser of their fruits, and also as identified with them. Śrī Kṛṣṇa is an Incarnation of Viṣṇu. As the Inner Controller

(Antaryāmī) of the body, He is the presiding Deity directing the various physical functions, which are described as acts of sacrifice. Though He rests in the body, yet He is not attached to it and is completely different from the senses. The word used in the text is "adhiyajña."

अन्तकाले च मामेव स्मरन्मुक्त्वा कलेवरम्।
यः प्रयाति स मद्भावं याति नास्त्यत्र संशयः ॥५॥

5. And whoso, at the time of death, leaves his body remembering Me alone and goes forth—he attains My Being; concerning this there is no doubt.

Me—That is to say, the Lord, who is the inmost Self of all beings.

The thought at the time of death determines the future of the soul.

यं यं वापि स्मरन्भावं त्यजत्यन्ते कलेवरम्।
तं तमेवैति कौन्तेय सदा तद्भावभावितः ॥६॥

6. For whatever object a man thinks of at the final moment, when he leaves his body—that alone does he attain, O son of Kuntī, being ever absorbed in the thought thereof.

Object—Any particular deity or any other object.

The Hindu scriptures lay great stress on the thought and the state of mind at the time of death as determining the future of the soul. Thought is endowed with a self-creative power. Our inner being changes into that of which we insistently think with faith and devotion. We become that on which we keep our minds fixed and to which we constantly aspire. The ever recurring thought of a lifetime, whether good or bad, presents itself vividly at the time of death. We cannot get rid of it, as the sleeping man cannot get rid of his dream. Since the character of the body next to be attained is determined by what a man thinks intensely at the time of death, he should always think of God if he wants to attain Him after leaving the body. This idea of the Gītā is not analogous to the indulgences and facilities of popular religion. The absolution and last unction of the priest does not make death edifying and spiritual after an unedifying and profane life. Even while the priest performs his rites, the dying man may be cherishing in his mind the thought in which he has indulged all through life.

Because the thought of a life—time is remembered at the time of death,

तस्मात्सर्वेषु कालेषु मामनुस्मर युध्य च।
मय्यर्पितमनोबुद्धिर्मामेवैष्यस्यसंशयः ॥७॥

7. Therefore, at all times, constantly remember Me and fight. With your mind and understanding absorbed in Me, you will surely come to Me.

Fight—For the purification of the mind. The mind is purified when a man performs his own dharma, regarding himself as an instrument of God. Only a pure mind can constantly remember God. Arjuna is a kṣatriya. His duty is to fight to uphold righteousness.

Constant practice is the effective discipline for the realization of the Lord.

अभ्यासयोगयुक्तेन चेतसा नान्यगामिना।
परमं पुरुषं दिव्यं याति पार्थानुचिन्तयन्॥८॥

8. Engaged in the yoga of constant practice and not allowing the mind to wander away to anything else, he who meditates on the supreme, resplendent Puruṣa reaches Him, O son of Pṛthā.

Practice—Consisting in the uninterrupted repetition of one and the same idea, with reference to the Lord as the sole object of meditation. Such practice, by which one's heart and soul are given to the Lord alone, is known as yoga.

Meditates—Following the instruction of the teacher and the scriptures.

Resplendent Puruṣa—The presiding Deity of the solar orb, who is the manifestation of the Absolute as the Cosmic Spirit. He is also known as the Saguṇa Brahman.

What sort of Puruṣa does a yogi realize?

कविं पुराणमनुशासितार-
मणोरणीयंसमनुस्मरेद्यः।
सर्वस्य धातारमचिन्त्यरूप-
मादित्यवर्णं तमसः परस्तात्॥९॥

प्रयाणकाले मनसाऽचलेन
भक्त्या युक्तो योगबलेन चैव।
भ्रुवोर्मध्ये प्राणमावेश्य सम्यक्
स तं परं पुरुषमुपैति दिव्यम्॥१०॥

9-10. He who, at the time of passing away, steady in mind, filled with love, and armed with the strength of yoga, well fixes his prāṇa between his brows and meditates on the omniscient and primal Being, the Ruler, the Dispenser of all, who is subtler than an atom, whose form is beyond comprehension, and who, like the glorious sun, is beyond all darkness—he who thus meditates reaches the resplendent Supreme Person.

Armed with the strength of yoga—This is attained as a result of the constant practice of samādhi.

Well fixes etc.—A kind of prāṇāyāma, or breath-control, described in the books on yoga.

Dispenser of all—Who allots to all living beings actions. and their results in all their variety.

Glorious sun—He is glorious with the splendour of His eternal Intelligence.

Darkness—Māyā, or delusion.

The goal described here is Brahmaloka, the Abode of the Saguṇa Brahman, or Brahman with attributes. This Abode is the highest manifestation of Brahman in the relative plane. Subsequently, at the end of the cycle, the dwellers in Brahmaloka attain complete liberation.

Meditation on the Supreme Person through Om is described in verses 11-13:

यदक्षरं वेदविदो वदन्ति
विशन्ति यद्यतयो वीतरागाः।
यदिच्छन्तो ब्रह्मचर्यं चरन्ति
तत्ते पदं सङ्ग्रहेण प्रवक्ष्ये ॥ ११ ॥

11. I will now briefly describe to you that state which those who know the Vedas call the Imperishable, and into which enter the saṃnyāsīs, self-controlled and freed from attachment, and in desire for which seekers lead the life of continence.

Imperishable—Devoid of all attributes. "This verily is That, the Imperishable, O Gārgī, which the brahmanas declare as not gross, not subtle." (*Bṛhadāraṇyaka Upaniṣad*, III, viii, 8)

Continence—The reference is to the religious students known as brahmacārīs, who live with their teacher, observing the vows of continence and celibacy and practising other spiritual disciplines.

The language of this verse is taken from the *Kaṭha Upaniṣad,* I, ii, 15.

सर्वद्वाराणि संयम्य मनो हृदि निरुध्य च।
मूर्ध्न्याधायात्मनः प्राणमास्थितो योगधारणाम्॥ १२॥

ओमित्येकाक्षरं ब्रह्म व्याहरन्मामनुस्मरन्।
यः प्रयाति त्यजन्देहं स याति परमां गतिम्॥ १३॥

12-13. He who closes all the doors of the senses, confines the mind within the heart, draws the prāṇa into the head, and engages in the practice of yoga, uttering Om, the single syllable denoting Brahman, and meditates on Me—he who so departs, leaving the body, attains the Supreme Goal.

Confines the mind etc.—Concentrating the thought in the lotus of the heart, which is the seat of the Lord.

Draws the prāṇa etc.—By the practice of yoga.

Om—*See* note on VII, 8.

Leaving the body—The established yogic way of giving up the body.

Supreme Goal—The soul of the yogi goes to Brahmaloka.

Om has been declared in various verses of the Upaniṣads to be the symbol of both the Supreme Brahman and the Brahman with attributes. By meditating on Om the aspirant. enjoys bliss in Brahmaloka and subsequently attains liberation in the Supreme Brahman. The dwellers in Brahmaloka are not subject to birth and death. Brahmā, a manifestation of Brahman in time and space, is the presiding Deity of Brahmaloka. He is the Creator God of Hindu mythology, Viṣṇu and Śiva being the Protector God and the Destroyer God respectively. (Regarding Brahmaloka, *See* note on VIII, 16.)

What kind of yogi easily attains the Lord?

अनन्यचेताः सततं यो मां स्मरति नित्यशः।
तस्याहं सुलभः पार्थ नित्ययुक्तस्य योगिनः॥ १४॥

14. I am easy of access to that ever steadfast yogi who, O Pārtha constantly meditates on Me and gives no thought to anything else.

Therefore it is the duty of all men to contemplate the Lord without interruption.

What does the easy accessibility of the Lord do for a man?

मामुपेत्य पुनर्जन्म दुःखालयमशाश्वतम्।
नाप्नुवन्ति महात्मानः संसिद्धिं परमां गताः॥ १५॥

15. Having come to Me, these high-souled men are no more subject to rebirth, which is transitory and the abode of pain; for they have reached the highest perfection.

Abode of pain—Pain of all kinds is inevitable in a human body.

Those who die without realizing the Lord come back again to earth. Life on earth, in spite of many moments of illusory happiness, is intrinsically painful. On account of their intense love of God, the devotees do not experience suffering on earth, and after death they attain Him.

From all planes in the relative universe people come back to the life on earth.

आब्रह्मभुवनाल्लोकाः पुनरावर्तिनोऽर्जुन।
मामुपेत्य तु कौन्तेय पुनर्जन्म न विद्यते॥ १६॥

16. The dwellers in all the worlds, from the realm of Brahmā downward, are subject to rebirth, O Arjuna; but for those who reach Me, O son of Kuntī, there is no further return to embodiment.

All the worlds—Because these worlds belong to the relative universe. They exist in time and space and are subject to the law of causation. They are impermanent.

Brahmaloka is the highest plane of existence in the relative universe. Its inhabitants enjoy intense happiness, which is their reward for leading a spiritual life on earth. But after the exhaustion of their meritorious deeds through enjoyment, some of the dwellers in Brahmaloka, like those of other planes, return to the earth for rebirth. There is, however, one class of devotees who do not come back from Brahmaloka. They are those fortunate souls who do not cherish any worldly desire, but who, for some reason, have not attained supreme liberation in the human body. After death they follow the path of light and arrive in Brahmaloka. There they remain absorbed in contemplation of Brahman and attain final liberation at the end of the cycle, when the entire relative universe, with Brahmā, merges in Brahman.

Complete liberation, attended by the cessation of birth and death, is possible only for a man who has realized his identity with Brahman. All other worlds, whether subhuman or superhuman, are places of enjoyment where men, departing from this earth, experience the fruit of their action.

One can directly attain liberation through love of God alone, without having to wait for the dissolution of the universe.

People return to the earth from all planes, including Brahmaloka, on account of their being limited by time.

सहस्रयुगपर्यन्तमहर्यद्‌ ब्रह्मणो विदुः।
रात्रिं युगसहस्रान्तां तेऽहोरात्रविदो जनाः॥ १७॥

17. Those who know that the day of Brahmā lasts a thousand aeons, and that the night of Brahmā lasts a thousand aeons again, are indeed the people who know day and night.

Brahmā—The first manifestation of the Absolute in time and space; also known as Prajāpati and Virāj.

Are indeed etc.—Those who calculate day and night by the rising and setting of the sun have only a partial understanding of day and night.

According to Hindu mythology the world period is divided into four yugas (cycles or aeons): Satya, Tretā, Dwāpara, and Kali. The cycle of Satya abounds in virtue, vice being practically non-existent. But with each succeeding age virtue diminishes and vice increases. The cycle of Kali is the reverse of Satya. The Satya Yuga endures for 1,728,000 years, the Tretā for 1,296,000 years, the Dwāpara for 864,000 years, and the Kali for 432,000 years. These four cycles, rotating a thousand times, make one day of Brahmā, and the same number of years one night. Fifteen such days make one fortnight of Brahmā, two fortnights one month, and twelve months one year. After living for one hundred years, Brahmā dies. Brahmā, too, like all other entities of the relative world, is impermanent and under the control of māyā. The longevity of Brahmā seems endless and fantastic from a man's restricted viewpoint, but it is momentary from the standpoint of the timeless and eternal Reality. The happiness associated with Brahmā, or the highest manifestation of Reality in the relative universe, is also momentary. The yogis, through their spiritual insight, see innumerable Brahmās arising and disappearing, like bubbles, in the Ocean of the Great Cause. Thus they do not feel any attachment even to the happiness of the highest heaven, how much less to that of earth.

What happens during Brahmā's day and night?

अव्यक्ताद्‌ व्यक्तयः सर्वाः प्रभवन्त्यहरागमे।
रात्र्यागमे प्रलीयन्ते तत्रैवाव्यक्तसंज्ञके॥ १८॥

18. At the approach of the day all manifest objects come forth from the unmanifested, and at the approach of the night they merge again into that which is called the unmanifested.

Approach of the day—When Brahmā awakes.

All manifest objects—Both animate and inanimate.

Unmanifested—The sleep state of Brahmā.

Approach of the night—When Brahmā goes to sleep.

There is an eternal cycle of alternating periods of cosmic manifestation and non-manifestation, each period called respectively a day and a night of the Creator, Brahmā, each of equal length in time, the long aeon of His waking, which endures for a thousand ages, the long aeon of His sleep, for another thousand silent ages. At the coming of the day all manifestations are born out of the unmanifest; at the coming of the night all disappear into the unmanifest. The text describes the evolution and involution of the universe according to Hindu philosophy. Every period of evolution is preceded by one of involution. The process is eternal in the relative world. But the chain can be destroyed by the Knowledge of Brahman. Hinduism does not believe in a creation preceded by the condition of absolute non-existence.

It may be contended that a man appearing at the beginning of a cycle reaps the fruit of action he has not done, or that a man of the previous cycle does not reap the fruit of action he has done. The following verse shows that individuality is not destroyed by the mere process of involution. The law of karma operates whether the universe is in a state of evolution or involution.

भूतग्रामः स एवायं भूत्वा भूत्वा प्रलीयते।
रात्र्यागमेऽवशः पार्थ प्रभवत्यहरागमे॥ १९॥

19. The same multitude of beings, coming forth again and again, merge, in spite of themselves, O Pārtha, at the approach of the night, and remanifest themselves at the approach of the day.

The same multitude etc.—Comprising the moving and the non-moving who existed in the preceding cycle or age, and who did not attain liberation.

Coming forth again and again etc.—Repeatedly they come forth and dissolve by the effect of their own karma.

In spite of themselves—The law of karma is inexorable.

In this world of māyā, all beings lead, as it were, a merry-go-round existence. There is no freedom as long as one is caught in the wheel of karma. The *Ṛg Veda* says that the sun, the moon, and the different worlds of the preceding cycle repeat themselves in the succeeding one. Therefore one should cultivate detachment and free oneself from māyā.

After describing the impermanence of the different worlds, Śrī Kṛṣṇa speaks of the eternal nature of the Supreme Lord.

परस्तस्मात्तु भावोऽन्योऽव्यक्तोऽव्यक्तात्सनातनः।
यः स सर्वेषु भूतेषु नश्यत्सु न विनश्यति॥२०॥

20. But beyond this unmanifested there is yet another Unmanifested Eternal Being, who does not perish when all beings perish.

This unmanifested—The seed state of the whole multitude of created beings; the night of Brahmā.

Another—Of altogether different kind. It is supra-cosmic and beyond avidyā.

Unmanifested—Because imperceptible to the senses.

Eternal Being—The Imperishable Brahman.

Who does not perish—Because It is beyond time, space, and causality.

All beings—From Brahmā downwards.

अव्यक्तोऽक्षर इत्युक्तस्तमाहुः परमां गतिम्।
यं प्राप्य न निवर्तन्ते तद्धाम परमं मम॥२१॥

21. This Unmanifested is called the Imperishable; It is said to be the Ultimate Goal, from which those who reach It never come back. That is My Supreme Abode.

Never come back—To the relative existence. The knower of Brahman never again falls under the spell of māyā, or ignorance.

Supreme Abode—The relative universe is the inferior manifestation of Brahman.

The Ultimate Goal referred to in the text does not indicate any state or condition, but the Imperishable Brahman Itself, Existence-Knowledge-Bliss Absolute.

The means of attaining that Supreme Abode:

पुरुषः स परः पार्थ भक्त्या लभ्यस्त्वनन्यया।
यस्यान्तःस्थानि भूतानि येन सर्वमिदं ततम्॥२२॥

22. That Supreme Puruṣa, in whom all beings abide and by whom the entire universe is pervaded, can be attained, O Pārtha by whole-souled devotion directed to Him alone.

Puruṣa—Brahman is called Puruṣa, Person, because It dwells in every body *(pura),* or because It is full.

In whom all beings abide—Because He is the ultimate cause. The effect is included in the cause.

The entire universe is pervaded—The Lord pervades the whole universe like the fragrance pervading sandal-wood.

Whole-souled devotion etc.—Bhakti, or love of the Lord, is the same as knowledge of Him. It proceeds from the realization that nothing exists except the Lord.

The two paths that the yogis follow after death:

यत्र काले त्वनावृत्तिमावृत्तिं चैव योगिनः।
प्रयाता यान्ति तं कालं वक्ष्यामि भरतर्षभ॥२३॥

23. Now I will tell you, O greatest of the Bhāratas, the time in which the yogis depart never to return, and also the time in which they depart to return.

Yogis—Those who are engaged in meditation. This also includes the ritualists, who perform the sacrifices and other actions prescribed in the Vedas.

To return—To be reborn.

Verses 23—26 in the eighth chapter refer to the two paths. described by the ancient Vedantic mystics. They are known as the devayāna, or path of the gods, and the pitṛyāna, or path of the fathers. Souls departing from this world follow these paths according to their merit. The path of the gods is associated with fire, light, day-time, the bright fortnight of the lunar month, and the northern solstice. The path of the fathers is associated with smoke, night, the dark fortnight of the lunar month, and the southern solstice. The path of the gods leads the departing souls to Brahmaloka, whence they do not come back to the earth for rebirth. They attain final freedom after the end of the cycle. The path of the fathers leads the departing souls to Candraloka, or the sphere of the moon, where they enjoy great happiness on account of the meritorious action performed by them on earth. After reaping the fruit, they come back to earth for rebirth to satisfy their unfulfilled desires. These paths have been dealt with in the Upaniṣads, prominently in the *Chāndogya* Upaniṣad, V, x, 1-4, and also in the *Brahma-sūtras,* IV, ii, 18-21.

The path of non-return:

अग्निर्ज्योतिरहः शुक्लः षण्मासा उत्तरायणम्।
तत्र प्रयाता गच्छन्ति ब्रह्म ब्रह्मविदो जनाः॥२४॥

24. Fire, light, day-time, the bright half of the moon, and the six months of the northward passage of the sun—taking this path, the knowers of Brahman go to Brahman.

Fire, light, etc.—According to Śaṅkarācārya each of the steps mentioned in the list means its presiding deity. Thus "fire" means the deity presiding over fire. According to the belief of the Vedic times every physical object, such as the sun, moon, and so on, is controlled by a deity who is a lower manifestation of the Supreme Brahman.

Knowers of Brahman—Here "Brahman" refers to the Saguṇa Brahman, or Brahman with attributes. It is distinguished from the Supreme Brahman, or Nirguṇa Brahman, that is to say, Brahman without any attribute.

Go to Brahman—That is to say, in course of time, after the completion of the cycle. The aspirants who have attained Self-knowledge obtain immediate liberation. For them neither return nor non-return has any meaning. They transcend time, space, and causality.

The text describes the "northern path." It is also known as the path of the gods, or the path of light, by which Brahmaloka is attained by yogis who worship Brahman through the symbol Om—as referred to in verses 8-13 of this chapter. The *Chāndogya Upaniṣad* (IV, xv, 5) thus describes the path of the gods:

"Now, such a one—whether his after-death rites are performed or not—goes to light, from light to day, from day to the bright half of the month, from the bright half of the month to the six months during which the sun rises northward, from the months to the year, from the year to the sun, from the sun to the moon, from the moon to the lightning. Then he meets a person who is not a human being. This person carries the soul to Brahman. This is the divine path, the path of Brahman. Those proceeding by this path do not return to the whirl of humanity."

The path of return:

धूमो रात्रिस्तथा कृष्णः षण्मासा दक्षिणायनम्।
तत्र चान्द्रमसं ज्योतिर्योगी प्राप्य निवर्तते ॥ २५ ॥

25. Smoke, night, the dark half of the moon, and the six months of the southward passage of the sun—taking this path, the yogi reaches the lunar path and thence returns.

Smoke, night, etc.—As in the previous verse, "smoke," "night," and so on denote the deities controlling these objects.

Yogi—Ritualists and those who perform philanthropic actions, desiring a reward.

Returns—To this earth after their enjoyment in the lunar sphere is over. This enjoyment is the result of their action on earth.

The Hindu scriptures often speak of the four courses that men may follow after death. These are determined by one's thought and action while on earth. First, the yogis who lead an extremely righteous life, meditate on Brahman, and follow the various disciplines of yoga, repair, after death, to Brahmaloka (roughly corresponding to the heaven of the Christians) and from there, in due course, attain salvation, known as kramamukti, or gradual emancipation. Second, the ritualists and the philanthropists, who cherish a desire for the fruit of their devotion and charity, repair, after death, to Candraloka, or the lunar sphere. After enjoying there immense happiness as the fruit of their meritorious action, they come back to earth, since they still cherish desires for worldly happiness. These are called gods or deities in Hinduism. Third, those who perform actions forbidden by religion assume, after death, subhuman bodies and dwell in what is generally known as hell. After expiating their evil actions, they are reborn on earth. Fourth, the persons who perform extremely vile actions spend many births as such insignificant beings as mosquitos and fleas.

The relative value of a created being depends on the degree of consciousness manifested by it. The consciousness manifested by the dweller in Brahmaloka is very high, and the consciousness manifested by the insects is very low. The man endowed with Self-knowledge attains liberation in this very life. His soul does not go to any sphere, for he has realized its identity with the all-pervading Consciousness. Different courses after death have been pointed out by the Hindu scriptures in order to warn people against neglecting Self-knowledge and to exhort them to realize Brahman, which alone is the source of eternal peace and happiness. According to the Hindu scriptures, all living beings, without any exception whatsoever, will attain Self-knowledge and liberation.

शुक्लकृष्णे गती ह्येते जगतः शाश्वते मते।
एकया यात्यनावृत्तिमन्ययावर्तते पुनः ॥२६॥

26. These two paths—the bright and the dark—are deemed to be the world's eternal paths. Following the one, a man does not come back, and following the other, he is reborn.

Bright—Because it is reached by means of knowledge and its course is marked throughout by bright objects.

Dark—Because avidyā, or ignorance, makes one follow it, and also because the path is marked throughout by smoke and other dark things.

Eternal—Because saṃsāra, or the universe, is eternal from the relative point of view.

Swami Vivekananda has an interesting theory of the universe and its various planes or spheres. All these spheres are products of matter and energy, or what Sāṅkhya philosophy calls ākāśa and prāṇa, in varying degrees. The lowest or most condensed is the solar sphere, consisting of the visible universe, in which prāṇa appears as physical force and ākāśa as sense-perceived matter. The next is the lunar sphere, which surrounds the solar sphere. This is not the moon at all, but the habitation of the gods. In this sphere prāṇa appears as the psychic forces and ākāśa as the tanmātras, or fine, rudimentary elements. Beyond this is the electric sphere, that is to say, a condition in which prāṇa is almost inseparable from ākāśa; there one can hardly tell whether electricity is force or matter. Next is Brahmaloka, where prāṇa and ākāśa do not exist as separate entities; both are merged in the mind-stuff, the primal energy. In the absence of prāṇa and ākāśa, the jīva, or individual soul, contemplates the whole universe as the sum total of the cosmic mind. This appears as a puruṣa, an abstract universal soul, yet not the Absolute, for still there is multiplicity. From this sphere the jīva subsequently finds his way to Unity, which is the end and goal of his earthly evolution.

According to the Non-dualistic Vedānta these spheres are only visions that arise in succession before the Soul, which Itself neither comes nor goes. The sense-perceived world in which a man lives is a similar vision. At the time of dissolution these visions gradually disappear, the gross merging in the fine. The purpose of the Hindu philosophers in treating of cosmology is to awaken in man's heart a spirit of detachment from the relative universe.

The experience of happiness in different planes or spheres after death is transitory. The dwellers in those planes come back to earth and commence again their life of pain and suffering. Even the most fortunate dwellers in Brahmaloka must wait a long time before they attain complete liberation. On the other hand, Self-knowledge, which can be attained by every human being, confers upon its possessor liberation in this very life. He does not have to wait for a future time to taste the bliss of immortality. This attainment of liberation through Self-knowledge, while living in a physical body, is the goal of human life. The Hindu scriptures treat of the various cycles and planes and spheres, and also of the various courses open to the soul after death, in order to spur men to strive for Self-knowledge and the attainment of liberation here on earth.

The results of following the two paths:

नैते सृती पार्थ जानन्योगी मुह्यति कश्चन।
तस्मात्सर्वेषु कालेषु योगयुक्तो भवार्जुन॥२७॥

27. No yogi who understands these two paths is ever deluded. Therefore, O Arjuna, at all times be steadfast in yoga.

The wise yogi knows that, of the two paths, the one leads to saṃsāra and the other to mokṣa, or liberation. Therefore he rejects the former and takes up the latter.

The glory of yoga:

वेदेषु यज्ञेषु तपःसु चैव
दानेषु यत्पुण्यफलं प्रदिष्टम्।
अत्येति तत्सर्वमिदं विदित्वा
योगी परं स्थानमुपैति चाद्यम्॥२८॥

28. The yogi who knows this transcends all the rewards laid down for the study of the Vedas, for sacrifices, for austerities, for making gifts: he reaches the Supreme, Primal Abode.

This—The answers to the seven questions of Arjuna, given in the eighth chapter of the Gītā. One must not merely understand, but also follow, the teachings implied in the answers.

ॐ तत्सदिति श्रीमद्भगवद्गीतासूपनिषत्सु
ब्रह्मविद्यायां योगशास्त्रे श्रीकृष्णार्जुनसंवादे
अक्षरब्रह्मयोगो नामाष्टमोऽध्यायः॥८॥

Thus in the Bhagavad Gītā, the Essence of the Upaniṣads, the Science of Brahman, the Scripture of Yoga, the Dialogue between Śrī *Kṛṣṇa and Arjuna, ends the Eighth Chapter, entitled:* THE WAY TO THE IMPERISHABLE BRAHMAN

CHAPTER 9

THE WAY OF THE SOVEREIGN WISDOM AND SOVEREIGN MYSTERY

[राजविद्याराजगुह्ययोगः]

श्रीभगवानुवाच।

इदं तु ते गुह्यतमं प्रवक्ष्याम्यनसूयवे।
ज्ञानं विज्ञानसहितं यज्ज्ञात्वा मोक्ष्यसेऽशुभात्॥ १॥

1. *The Lord said:* To you, O Arjuna, who do not carp, I will propound this, the greatest mystery of knowledge combined with realization, by understanding which you will be released from evil.

This—The Knowledge of Brahman, indicated by such scriptural passages as: "Vāsudeva is all," "All this is the Self," "One without a second." This Knowledge is the direct means of attaining liberation.

Greatest mystery—Dharma is a mystery; greater is the mystery of the self dwelling in the body; and the greatest mystery is the knowledge of the identity of the individual self and the Supreme Self.

Evil—The bondage of the world.

The eighth chapter of the Gītā has dealt with emancipation by stages through the process of meditation. But this indirect way is not the only means of emancipation. The direct way is described in the ninth chapter.

In praise of this knowledge:

प्रत्यक्षावगमं धर्म्यं सुसुखं कर्तुमव्ययम् ॥ २ ॥
अश्रद्दधानाः पुरुषा धर्मस्यास्य परन्तप ।

2. It is the sovereign science, the sovereign mystery, and the supreme purifier. It is perceived by direct experience, it accords with dharma, it is easy to practise, and it is imperishable.

Sovereign science—Because of its majesty. Indeed, the science of Brahman is the most profound of all sciences.

Supreme purifier—As a lamp, when lighted in a room, instantly destroys the accumulated darkness of ages, so the Knowledge of Brahman, when realized in the heart, reduces to ashes, root and all, the accumulated karma of all the past lives.

Perceived by direct experience—The Bliss of Brahman is as directly perceived as the feeling of pleasure and pain.

Accords with dharma—An object endowed with many delectable qualities may be opposed to dharma; but such is not the case with the Knowledge of Brahman.

Easy to practise—Easily acquired when taught by a qualified teacher.

Imperishable—Generally it is seen that an action which requires little trouble and is easily accomplished produces an insignificant result. But the Knowledge of Brahman, though easily acquired, is quite the contrary. The Bliss of Brahman is eternal.

Therefore the Knowledge of Brahman should be pursued by all desiring real peace and happiness.

On account of their lack of faith, worldly beings do not pursue the Knowledge of Brahman.

राजविद्या राजगुह्यं पवित्रमिदमुत्तमम् ।
अप्राप्य मां निवर्तन्ते मृत्युसंसारवर्त्मनि ॥ ३ ॥

3. Men without faith in this dharma do not attain Me, O dreaded Arjuna, but return to the path of the world fraught with death.

Without faith etc.—Who regard the physical body as the Self and do not believe in the indestructibility and immortality of the soul.

Faith, or an unswerving conviction of the existence of God, the soul, and immortality, is the prerequisite of spiritual life.

Śrī Kṛṣṇa formulates the sovereign wisdom:

मया ततमिदं सर्वं जगदव्यक्तमूर्तिना।
मत्स्थानि सर्वभूतानि न चाहं तेष्ववस्थितः ॥४॥

4. By Me, in My unmanifested form, are all things in this universe pervaded. All beings exist in Me, but I do not exist in them.

Me The Supreme Lord and the Ultimate Cause of all. My unmanifested form—Consciousness, or Ātman, which is imperceptible to the senses.

All things in this universe—From the highest Brahmā, or the Cosmic Spirit, to a blade of grass.

Pervaded—Nothing can exist unless the Lord, or Existence-Knowledge-Bliss Absolute, forms its substratum. It is said in the Upaniṣads that the Lord, after creating objects, entered them as their indwelling Consciousness.

All beings exist in Me—Beings may be likened to a piece of cloth, and the Lord to the thread comprising its warp and woof. The cloth cannot exist without the warp and woof.

I do not exist in them—Because Brahman is incorporeal and hence unconnected with any object.

The two forms of the Lord, the manifested and the unmanifested, have been described in the seventh chapter of the Gītā (VII, 4-5). The illusory and unreal world appears to be real and tangible on account of the reality of the Lord forming its substratum. No change can be perceived without the background of changelessness. The illusion of a mirage is not seen without the background of the desert. The continuity in a moving picture cannot be perceived without the background of the unmoving screen; it is the fixed screen that makes the separate and disjoined pictures appear as a continuous story. Likewise, the presence of the Lord as the immutable Consciousness creates the appearance of continuity and history in an ever changing, illusory universe. If He, as Existence, did not form the basis of the universe, nothing would be perceived to exist. Therefore all existent entities are pervaded by the Lord's existence, which itself is imperceptible to the senses. A thing devoid of inner reality cannot exist or be an object of experience. The Lord is the inner reality of everything. The reality of the Lord makes real everything in the world. But the reality of the Lord does not depend upon the world. He always exists, whether the universe of name and form exists or not. The Lord is incorporeal and therefore has no real contact with the material world. He cannot be contained in any object. He is self-existent and self-luminous. Only a fraction of His majesty illumines the sun, the moon, and the universe; but He Himself, in His purest essence, is transcendental.

न च मत्स्थानि भूतानि पश्य मे योगमैश्वरम्।
भूतभृन्न च भूतस्थो ममात्मा भूतभावनः॥५॥

5. And yet the beings do not dwell in Me—behold, that is My divine mystery. My Spirit, which is the support of all beings and the source of all things, does not dwell in them.

Do not dwell in Me—Because the Self is not attached to anything. "Devoid of attachment, He never enters into relationship with anything." (*Bṛhadāraṇyaka Upaniṣad*, III, ix, 26)

Divine mystery—The Lord is all-pervasive and yet free from contact with any object.

Support of all beings—As their inmost reality and essence.

Source of all things—Only from the relative standpoint. In reality the Lord is not the cause of anything, for nothing exists besides Him.

Does not dwell in them—Because the Lord is unconnected with any object on account of His incorporeal nature.

The infinite Lord cannot be contained in a finite universe. But why cannot the universe and its beings dwell in Him? The Lord, in reality, is neither the container nor the contained. In Him there is not the slightest trace of duality. In His purest essence He is above the law of cause and effect. In the final realization, the object and the subject become one; the whole universe merges in the Lord. In that state the Lord remains as One without a second, a homogeneous concentration of Consciousness. The concepts of container and contained, cause and effect, apply to the realm of manifestation, or māyā. Even though the Lord manifests, through māyā, the tangible relative universe, and appears to be its cause and support, yet He is always One and without a second, transcendental, incorporeal, and unattached. This is His eternal mystery.

An illustration of the idea contained in the two preceding verses:

यथाकाशस्थितो नित्यं वायुः सर्वत्रगो महान्।
तथा सर्वाणि भूतानि मत्स्थानीत्युपधारय॥६॥

6. As the mighty wind blowing everywhere ever rests in the ākāśa, know that in the same manner all beings rest in Me.

Rests in the ākāśa—Without affecting the ākāśa in any way, because ākāśa is unattached to the wind.

Ākāśa—Ethereal space.

All beings rest in Me—Without affecting the Lord in any way. Good and evil, pain and pleasure, and the other traits of this great universe do not touch the Lord, because from His standpoint they are illusory, and also because He is entirely spiritual in nature. He can never be touched by anything happening in time and space. As a light cannot be affected by the good or evil deed done with its help, so the soul, which in its essence is one with the Lord, cannot be affected by the good and evil action of the body and mind.

Though the Lord is incorporeal and unattached, His māyā is the cause of the creation and dissolution of all beings.

सर्वभूतानि कौन्तेय प्रकृतिं यान्ति मामिकाम्।
कल्पक्षये पुनस्तानि कल्पादौ विसृजाम्यहम्॥७॥

7. At the end of a cycle all beings, O son of Kuntī, enter into My Prakṛti and at the beginning of a cycle I generate them again.

My Prakṛti—The inferior mode of the Lord, consisting of sattva, rajas, and tamas in their undifferentiated state.

Generate—Bring them forth, or manifest them, at the time of the next evolution.

The whole process of creation, preservation, and destruction is due to the Lord's māyā. He is unaffected by it. Vedānta philosophy recognizes the *fact* of creation (from the standpoint of māyā), but not the *act* of creation. The Lord, devoid of ego and motive, does not create. Creation implies unsatisfied desires. But as long as one is subject to māyā, one cannot deny the fact of creation. It is like our dreams. A dream cannot be denied as a fact as long as we dream. But, actually, we never become what we see in dreams. Māyā, or the inferior nature of the Lord, projects out of itself all the names and forms at the time of creation. Consciousness, or the higher nature of the Lord, endows them with life. At the end of the cycle the names and forms of the manifested universe go back into the seed state and remain merged in Prakṛti and Prakṛti itself remains in a state of equilibrium of the three guṇas. When the balance is lost, creation takes place. This process of creation and destruction is without beginning. Better terms to express creation and destruction, in agreement with the Hindu view, are manifestation or evolution, and mergence or involution. The Lord in His pure essence remains unaffected by the activities of His māyā, though the insentient māyā is actuated by His proximity. (For "māyā," *See* note on VII, 14.)

Śrī Kṛṣṇa anticipates the question: How does the Lord, who is immutable and detached, create the world?

प्रकृतिं स्वामवष्टभ्य विसृजामि पुनः पुनः।
भूतग्राममिमं कृत्स्नमवशं प्रकृतेर्वशात्॥८॥

8. Controlling My own Prakṛti I send forth, again and again, all this multitude of beings, helpless under the sway of māyā.

Controlling My own Prakṛti—The Lord, with the help of Prakṛti manifests the universe. Because of His very proximity, insentient Nature acts. He is only a witness. Māyā, or Prakṛti is under His control. But the jīva, or created being, is under the control of māyā.

Send forth—Living beings come out from Prakṛti which has gone to sleep at the end of the previous cycle. Dissolution, or the state in which the three guṇas remain in perfect balance, is called the sleep of Prakṛti

Helpless etc.—The beings who, at the end of the previous cycle, merged in Prakṛti are still under the influence of māyā, or ignorance. As Prakṛti becomes active at the beginning of the next cycle, the beings also assume appropriate births according to their past karma.

The Lord, in His purest essence, is unattached. He does not create; for creation serves no purpose of His. In this universe, which is conjured up by māyā, all beings are governed by the law of karma. Since the creation is falsely superimposed upon the Lord, therefore what is perceived to be the universe existing in time and space is, from the standpoint of Reality, nothing but the Lord Himself. In the illusion of a rope appearing as a snake, the falsely perceived snake. is, in reality, nothing but the rope.

It may be objected that the Lord, because He is responsible for the manifestation of diverse beings of unequal condition, is guilty of partiality and therefore subject to dharma and adharma arising from the creation. The answer follows:

न च मां तानि कर्माणि निबध्नन्ति धनञ्जय।
उदासीनवदासीनमसक्तं तेषु कर्मसु॥९॥

9. And these acts, O Dhanañjaya, do not bind Me; for I remain unattached to them, as one unconcerned.

These acts—Relating to the unequal creation of diverse beings.

Unattached to them—Because the Lord is conscious of the immutability of the Self. He is unconcerned about the fruit of action. It is attachment to the fruit that binds. He is unconcerned, because He is totally devoid of the feeling "I do."

The creation belongs to the realm of māyā; the Lord is beyond māyā. There is no contact or relationship between the Lord and creation, as there is no contact between the desert and a mirage. He is totally free from any desire, purpose, motive, or agency so far as the creation is concerned.

A man devoid of egotism and attachment, like the Lord, is free from the binding effect of action. Anyone working as the Lord works enjoys unimpaired freedom. Otherwise he remains bound by his action, like a silk-worm in its cocoon.

There is an apparent contradiction in the two statements of the Lord that He generates all beings (IX, 7) *and that He is unconcerned about creation* (IX, 9). *It is thus resolved:*

मयाध्यक्षेण प्रकृतिः सूयते सचराचरम्।
हेतुनानेन कौन्तेय जगद्विपरिवर्तते॥ १०॥

10. Prakṛti under My guidance, gives birth to all things, moving and unmoving; and because of this, O son of Kuntī, the world revolves.

Prakṛti—Māyā, consisting of the three guṇas.

Under My guidance—The Lord acting as the unconcerned witness.

Because of this etc.—All objects, moving and unmoving, wheel round and round because of the proximity of the Lord as Consciousness. All the activities in the world, expressed in such terms as "I shall enjoy," "I see," "I feel," "I shall gain," "I shall learn," and so on, are possible only because of consciousness. These ideas arise in consciousness. There is no other conscious being in the universe except the all-pervading Lord. Therefore the whole universe revolves in its course on account of the proximity of the Lord. Prakṛti or insentient Nature, cannot perform any conscious action.

It is absurd to ask the purpose of creation. The enjoyment of the Lord surely cannot be the purpose; for He is devoid of desire and does not enjoy. He is Pure Consciousness and a disinterested witness. And there is no other enjoyer; for there is no other consciousness; none but a conscious being is capable of enjoyment. The question regarding the purpose of creation cannot be asked if one remembers that creation is māyā, or an illusion.

The position of the Lord with reference to creation is explained in verses 7-9 by a method that gradually trains the student to grasp a subtle point. The Lord begins by stating that He projects all beings at the beginning of evolution: Prakṛti is only an instrument in His hands. Next, He says He is not affected by that act, since He sits by as one neutral, perfectly unattached. Lastly, the Lord leads up to the final truth that really He does nothing and that Prakṛti animated by His proximity, produces the universe. It is His light that lights up Prakṛti and makes it live and act. That is the only relationship between the Lord and His Prakṛti

The ignorant disregard the Lord, who is of the nature of eternity, purity, knowledge, and freedom, and who is the inmost Self of all beings.

अवजानन्ति मां मूढा मानुषीं तनुमाश्रितम्।
परं भावमजानन्तो मम भूतमहेश्वरम्॥११॥

11. Fools disregard Me when I assume a human form; for they are unaware of My higher nature as the Supreme Lord of all beings.

Disregard Me—As an ordinary human being.

From time to time the Lord assumes a human form so that men may attain a godly nature. In that state the Lord acts outwardly like a human being, though always remaining in full possession of the knowledge that He is unattached to any material thing and that He is the very Self of all beings. The deluded only see Him acting as a man and therefore disregard Him, as an ordinary human being.

Śrī Kṛṣṇa pities the ignorant, who worship other gods and not the Lord:

मोघाशा मोघकर्माणो मोघज्ञाना विचेतसः।
राक्षसीमासुरीं चैव प्रकृतिं मोहिनीं श्रिताः॥१२॥

12. Being of the deceitful nature of fiends and demons, they cherish vain hopes, perform vain actions, pursue vain knowledge, and are devoid of judgement.

Fiends and demons—The word "rākṣa" in the text denotes a fiend who indulges in deeds of cruelty, and the word "asura," a demon who is full of lust, passion, and pride.

Vain hopes—Because they expect that the worship of deities other than the Lord will bring them quick results in the form of material power and prosperity.

Vain actions—Their performance of sacrifices and observance of rituals are futile because they disregard the Lord, who dwells in them as their inmost Spirit.

Vain knowledge—Because they take delight in useless polemics.

Śrī Kṛṣṇa implies that if a man observes the rituals of religion, cherishes ambition, and cultivates scholarship, but denies the Lord, he does not derive any benefit from his labour.

The aspirants who cherish love for the Lord are extolled:

महात्मानस्तु मां पार्थ दैवीं प्रकृतिमाश्रिताः।
भजन्त्यनन्यमनसो ज्ञात्वा भूतादिमव्ययम्॥ १३॥

13. But the great-souled men, O Pārtha who are endowed with the divine nature, worship Me with undisturbed minds, knowing that I am immutable and the origin of all beings.

Divine nature—Such as possession of faith and control of the mind, senses, and body.

All beings—Living creatures and inanimate elements.

Adoration of the Lord through love:

सततं कीर्तयन्तो मां यतन्तश्च दृढव्रताः।
नमस्यन्तश्च मां भक्त्या नित्ययुक्ता उपासते॥ १४॥

14. Ever glorifying Me, always striving with self-control, remaining firm in their vows, bowing before Me, they worship Me with love and unwavering steadiness.

Glorifying Me—With appropriate chants and hymns.

Bowing before Me—Before sacred images and holy men, because the manifestation of the Lord is very vivid in them.

Different modes of worship through the path of knowledge:

ज्ञानयज्ञेन चाप्यन्ये यजन्तो मामुपासते।
एकत्वेन पृथक्त्वेन बहुधा विश्वतोमुखम्॥ १५॥

15. Others, again, offer the oblation of knowledge and worship Me either as one with them or as distinct from them; and still others in various ways worship Me, whose form is the whole universe.

Oblation of knowledge—The knowledge of the Lord is itself a sacrifice (yajña).

As one with them—The non-dualistic view.

Distinct from them—The dualistic view: The Lord exists in the forms of various deities; or the worshipper is different from the Lord, His servant.

Various ways—As various divinities, such as the sun, the wind, Brahmā, or Rudra.

The Lord is the inmost Self of everything; therefore all diverse forms of worship are in essence His worship.

अहं क्रतुरहं यज्ञः स्वधाहमहमौषधम्।
मन्त्रोऽहमहमेवाज्यमहमग्निरहं हुतम्॥ १६ ॥

16. I am the sacrifice, I am the worship, I am the oblation to the manes, and I am cereal. I am the hymn, I am the melted butter, I am the fire, and I am the offering.

Sacrifice—The word "kratu" in the text denotes a class of Vedic rites.

Worship—The word "yajña" in the text denotes the worship enjoined in the smṛti.

Cereal—Eaten by all living beings.

Hymn—With which oblations are offered to the manes and the gods.

Fire—Into which the oblation is made.

Through the symbol of a sacrifice the Lord suggests that He alone forms all the accessories of worship and also the act and the result of worship.

Furthermore,

पिताहमस्य जगतो माता धाता पितामहः।
वेद्यं पवित्रमोङ्कार ऋक्साम यजुरेव च॥ १७॥

17. I am the Father of this universe, the Mother, the Sustainer, and the Grandsire. I am the knowable, the purifier, and the syllable Om. I am also the Ṛk, the Sāman, and the Yajus.

Father—The efficient cause.

Mother—The material cause.

Sustainer—The dispenser of the fruits of action to different beings according to their merit. The Lord sustains the universe through the law of karma, which is the law of causality operating on the moral plane.

Grandsire—The subtle is the cause of the gross. The Lord is the cause of the subtle. He is the cause of both the manifest and the unmanifest. Hence, He is called the Grandsire.

Knowable—By knowing the Lord one knows everything in the world; for He is the inmost essence of all.

Purifier—The heart becomes pure through knowledge of God.

Om—The means of attaining the Knowledge of Brahman.

The Ṛk etc.—That is to say, the essence of the Vedas.

Furthermore,

गतिर्भर्ता प्रभुः साक्षी निवासः शरणं सुहृत्।
प्रभवः प्रलयः स्थानं निधानं बीजमव्ययम्॥ १८॥

18. I am the Goal and the Support; the Lord and the Witness; the Abode, the Refuge, and the Friend. I am the origin and the dissolution; the ground, the storehouse, and the Imperishable Seed.

Goal—To be attained by men in the form of heavenly happiness or of supreme liberation.

Witness—Of what is done and left undone by living beings. Nothing can be hidden from the Lord, who is omniscient and omnipresent.

Abode—In Him we all live, move, and have our being. Ground—The substratum of the universe—both in its gross and in its subtle form.

Imperishable Seed—The Lord is the seed of the universe. and its living beings. As the universe is eternal, so the Lord is the imperishable seed. Or, unlike an ordinary seed, the Lord is the eternal seed; for He exists even when the universe is dissolved.

And also,

तपाम्यहमहं वर्षं निगृह्णाम्युत्सृजामि च।
अमृतं चैव मृत्युश्च सदसच्चाहमर्जुन॥ १९॥

19. I give heat; I hold back and send forth rain. I am immortality, O Arjuna, and also death. I am being and I am non-being.

Heat—As the sun.

Hold back—During the dry season.

Send forth—During the rainy season.

Immortality—Enjoyed by the gods. It is relative immortality.

Death—Of mortals on earth.

Being—The manifested universe, the effect.

Non-being—The unmanifested, the cause.

The words "being" and "non-being" are used in the sense of the manifested and the unmanifested. The unmanifested, or "non-being," is the cause of the manifested, or "being." The word "non-being" is not used in the text in the sense of "non-existence."

The devotees regard the Lord in various ways and follow different methods of worship.

That those who do not worship the Lord for liberation are caught in the wheel of birth and death is stated in the following two verses:

त्रैविद्या मां सोमपाः पूतपापा
यज्ञैरिष्ट्वा स्वर्गतिं प्रार्थयन्ते।
ते पुण्यमासाद्य सुरेन्द्रलोक-
मश्नन्ति दिव्यान्दिवि देवभोगान्॥ २०॥

20. Those who know the three Vedas and drink the soma-juice and are purified from sin worship Me with sacrifices and pray for passage to heaven. They reach the holy world of Indra and enjoy in heaven the celestial pleasures of the gods.

Those who know etc.—Who perform the sacrifices mentioned in the three Vedas, namely, the Ṛk, the Sāman, and the Yajus.

Drink the soma-juice—What is left after the oblation is made. The reference is to a Vedic injunction.

Me—Not as the Lord, but in the forms of Indra, Vasu, and other deities who fulfil the worldly ambitions of their devotees.

Passage to heaven—The highest goal of these devotees. is enjoyment in heaven.

Indra—The lord of the gods. The gods of Hindu mythology denote positions in heaven that men enjoy after death as the fruits of their meritorious action performed on earth with a view to obtaining happiness. A man becomes Indra if he performs a hundred sacrifices.

ते तं भुक्त्वा स्वर्गलोकं विशालं
क्षीणे पुण्ये मर्त्यलोकं विशन्ति।
एवं त्रयीधर्ममनुप्रपन्ना
गतागतं कामकामा लभन्ते॥२१॥

21. Having enjoyed the vast heavenly world, they come back to the world of mortals when their merit is exhausted. Thus abiding by the injunctions of the three Vedas and desiring desires, they are subject to death and rebirth.

Injunctions of the three Vedas—The rituals and sacrifices enjoined in the Vedas.

Subject to death and rebirth—They do not attain liberation from the ever turning wheel of birth and death.

But people free from desires and endowed with right knowledge attain the Supreme Goal of life.

अनन्याश्चिन्तयन्तो मां ये जनाः पर्युपासते।
तेषां नित्याभियुक्तानां योगक्षेमं वहाम्यहम्॥२२॥

22. Those persons who worship Me, meditating on their identity with Me and ever devoted to Me—to them I carry what they lack and for them I preserve what they already have.

Meditating on their identity with Me—They totally lose their individuality in the Lord and look upon Him as their own Self. Or the word "ananyaḥ" in the text may mean "without any other [thought]." In that case the translation should be: Those persons who worship Me, never harbouring any other thought, etc.

I carry—Because the Lord considers the jñānī to be His very Self and most dear to Him. *See* VII, 17-18.

The Lord promises complete protection to those who love Him with all their body, heart, and soul. A devotee, totally absorbed in the Lord, may forget his own safety and security, but the Lord never forgets him. All men, no doubt, receive from the Lord what they need; but as long as *they themselves* think of their own welfare, they must earn it by their own effort. But *the Lord Himself* carries the necessaries of life to those who, lost in the thought of Him, cannot take care of themselves.

All the deities are, no doubt, different forms of the Lord Himself. To worship them is to worship Him. Why, then, should their worshippers be deprived of liberation? Śrī Kṛṣṇa explains that their worship is tainted with ignorance:

येऽप्यन्यदेवता भक्ता यजन्ते श्रद्धयान्विताः।
तेऽपि मामेव कौन्तेय यजन्त्यविधिपूर्वकम्॥ २३॥

23. Even those devotees who, endowed with faith, worship other gods, worship Me alone, O son of Kuntī, though in a wrong way.

Other gods—Indra and others. The motive behind the worship is the attainment of power and enjoyment.

Wrong way—Because they do not seek liberation. They are steeped in ignorance. Hence, they come back to the world to satisfy their unfulfilled desires.

The wrong method of worship:

अहं हि सर्वयज्ञानां भोक्ता च प्रभुरेव च।
न तु मामभिजानन्ति तत्त्वेनातश्च्यवन्ति ते॥ २४॥

24. For I alone am the Enjoyer and the Lord of all sacrifices. But these men do not know Me in reality; hence they fall.

The oblations in sacrifices may be offered to minor gods. But the Lord is the Self and the inmost Consciousness of the gods also; hence He is the real Master and Enjoyer of all sacrifices. Ignorant devotees offer their worship to the gods and attain an appropriate heaven; but after the enjoyment of the fruit of their devotion, they return to the mortal world.

Every act of worship produces its own result. No worship is futile.

यान्ति देवव्रता देवान्पितॄन्यान्ति पितृव्रताः।
भूतानि यान्ति भूतेज्या यान्ति मद्याजिनोऽपि माम्॥ २५॥

25. Those who worship the gods go to the gods, those who worship the manes go to the manes, those who worship the spirits go to the spirits, and those who worship Me come to Me.

Spirits—A class of beings lower than the gods but higher than men.

Me—The Imperishable Lord, of the nature of Supreme Bliss.

The same effort is needed for all forms of worship, but the results are quite different. People do not worship the Lord on account of their ignorance and therefore cannot enjoy imperishable happiness.

Not only does single-minded devotion to the Lord lead to an imperishable result, but it is also very simple and easy to achieve.

पत्रं पुष्पं फलं तोयं यो मे भक्त्या प्रयच्छति।
तदहं भक्त्युपहृतमश्नामि प्रयतात्मनः ॥ २६ ॥

26. Whosoever offers Me, with devotion, a leaf, a flower, a fruit, or water—that I accept, the pious offering of the pure in heart.

The minor gods demand sacrifices entailing much effort and wealth, and the reward they give is transitory. But the Lord, endowed with infinite powers and splendours, asks only love from His devotees and in return rewards them with imperishable happiness.

Because this is so, therefore,

यत्करोषि यदश्नासि यज्जुहोषि ददासि यत्।
यत्तपस्यसि कौन्तेय तत्कुरुष्व मदर्पणम् ॥ २७ ॥

27. Whatever you do, whatever you eat, whatever you offer in sacrifice, whatever you give away, and whatever you practise in the form of austerities, O son of Kuntī—do it as an offering to Me.

No outward worship is necessary to please the Lord. Every action of man may be transformed into worship if the Lord is constantly kept in mind. Since the One and the manifold are two manifestations of the same Reality, one can adore God through both work and meditation. If an action is not egocentric it becomes an act of worship.

The result of such worship:

शुभाशुभफलैरेवं मोक्ष्यसे कर्मबन्धनैः।
संन्यासयोगयुक्तात्मा विमुक्तो मामुपैष्यसि ॥ २८ ॥

28. Thus shall you be free from the bondage of actions, which bear good or evil results. With your mind firmly set on the yoga of renunciation, you shall become free and come to Me.

Thus—By surrendering the fruits of all actions to the Lord.

Yoga of renunciation—The offering of all works to the Lord constitutes the yoga of renunciation. The followers of this yoga perform their duties but do not seek the result of their action. Therefore this method combines both yoga (karmayoga) and saṃnyāsa (renunciation).

You shall become free etc.—Even while living in the body you will be free from the bondage of action and after death you will attain final liberation in Me.

Is the Lord endowed with love and hatred? Does He bestow His grace on His devotees alone and not on others?

समोऽहं सर्वभूतेषु न मे द्वेष्योऽस्ति न प्रियः।
ये भजन्ति तु मां भक्त्या मयि ते तेषु चाप्यहम्॥२९॥

29. I am the same toward all beings; to Me there is none hateful or dear. But those who worship Me with devotion—they are in Me, and I too am in them.

The nature of the Lord may be compared to fire, which gives heat to all. Those who are near the fire feel the heat, and those who are away do not feel it. Or His nature may be compared to the wind, which blows for all boats on the water. Those sails that are in good condition can take advantage of the wind, but the sails with holes fail to do so. The Lord is impartial to all.

Those who love the Lord and perform their duties in a selfless manner become pure in heart. The pure in heart dwell in the Lord. Thus they feel His grace. But this is not due to any particular attachment on His part. The Lord, too, dwells in them; that is to say, His presence is felt in them and not in the hearts of sinners. But it does not mean that the Lord hates sinners. As the sun's light, though falling on everything, is reflected in a clean mirror, so the glory of the Lord is visible only in those persons from whose minds all dirt has been removed by spiritual discipline.

The glory of devotion to the Lord:

अपि चेत्सुदुराचारो भजते मामनन्यभाक्।
साधुरेव स मन्तव्यः सम्यग्व्यवसितो हि सः॥३०॥

30. Even the most sinful man, if he worships Me with unswerving devotion, must be regarded as righteous; for he has formed the right resolution.

Right resolution—To give up the evil ways of life. If a man believes that devotion to the Lord is the way to liberation and acts accordingly, then he is said to have made a noble resolution.

Forgetfulness of the Lord constitutes sin, and remembrance of Him is sanctity. The darkness of accumulated sins is instantaneously removed by the Light of God.

He abandons evil ways and by dint of right resolution becomes a saint.

क्षिप्रं भवति धर्मात्मा शश्वच्छान्तिं निगच्छति।
कौन्तेय प्रतिजानीहि न मे भक्तः प्रणश्यति॥३१॥

31. He soon becomes righteous and attains eternal peace. Proclaim it boldly, O son of Kuntī, that My devotee never perishes.

My devotee—He whose inmost soul has been given to the Lord.

Ordinary spiritual disciplines, unless well practised, do not produce perfect results. But sincere love of God brings imperishable peace to the devotee.

Love of God redeems even those who are otherwise disqualified for Vedic salvation.

मां हि पार्थ व्यपाश्रित्य येऽपि स्युः पापयोनयः।
स्त्रियो वैश्यास्तथा शूद्रास्तेऽपि यान्ति परां गतिम्॥ ३२॥

32. For those who take refuge in Me, O Pārtha though they be of sinful birth—women, vaiśyas, and śūdras—even they attain the Supreme Goal.

The vaiśyas are engaged in agriculture and trade; women and śūdras are debarred from the study of the Vedas. Therefore all these classes of people remain outside the Vedic scheme of salvation. The statement regarding vaiśyas, śūdras, and women refers to an ancient Indian religious tradition. In many places the Gītā raises a voice of protest against certain narrow injunctions of the Vedas.

Śrī Kṛṣṇa spurs Arjuna to the realization of the Lord:

किं पुनर्ब्राह्मणाः पुण्या भक्ता राजर्षयस्तथा।
अनित्यमसुखं लोकमिमं प्राप्य भजस्व माम्॥ ३३॥

33. How much more, then, if they be holy brāhmins or royal seers devoted to God! Having come into this transitory, joyless world, worship Me.

Holy—Of pure birth.

Royal seers—Kings who have attained saintliness. Arjuna belongs to this class.

Human birth is conducive to the practice of spiritual discipline. But it is not easy to be born in a human body. The world is transitory and its happiness unreal. Therefore every man should direct his whole attention to the realization of the Lord, which alone brings imperishable happiness. The aim of human life is the attainment of jīvanmukti, or liberation in this very life.

How should one worship the Lord?

मन्मना भव मद्भक्तो मद्याजी मां नमस्कुरु।
मामेवैष्यसि युक्त्वैवमात्मानं मत्परायणः ॥ ३४ ॥

34. Fix your mind on Me, be devoted to Me, sacrifice to Me, bow down to Me. Having thus disciplined yourself, and regarding Me as the Supreme Goal, you will come to Me.

As the rivers, following their different courses, ultimately merge in the ocean and give up their names and forms, so the devotees, losing their names and forms, become one with the Supreme Reality.

ॐ तत्सदिति श्रीमद्भगवद्गीतासूपनिषत्सु
ब्रह्मविद्यायां योगशास्त्रे श्रीकृष्णार्जुनसंवादे
राजविद्याराजगुह्ययोगो नाम नवमोऽध्यायः ॥ ९ ॥

Thus in the Bhagavad Gītā, the Essence of the Upaniṣads, the Science of Brahman, the Scripture of Yoga, the Dialogue between Śrī *Kṛṣṇa and Arjuna, ends the Ninth Chapter, entitled:* THE WAY OF THE SOVEREIGN WISDOM AND SOVEREIGN MYSTERY

CHAPTER 10

THE DIVINE MANIFESTATIONS

[विभूतियोगः]

श्रीभगवानुवाच।

भूय एव महाबाहो शृणु मे परमं वचः।
यत्तेऽहं प्रीयमाणाय वक्ष्यामि हितकाम्यया॥१॥

1. *The Lord said:* Once more, O mighty Arjuna, listen to My supreme word, which I, from a desire for your welfare, will impart to you, to your great delight.

Supreme word—Revealing the supreme truth.

Some of the glories of the divine manifestations have been touched on in the seventh and ninth chapters. These, as also the essential nature of the Lord, are now described in detail in the tenth chapter.

The manifestations of the Lord are a mystery. Therefore Śrī Kṛṣṇa, out of compassion for Arjuna, intends to describe them.

न मे विदुः सुरगणाः प्रभवं न महर्षयः।
अहमादिर्हि देवानां महर्षीणां च सर्वशः॥२॥

2. Neither the hosts of gods nor the great sages know My origin; for, in all respects, I am the source of the gods and the sages.

Origin—The word "prabhavaṃ" in the text may also mean "lordly power.'

In all respects—The Lord is both the efficient cause of the gods and the inspirer of their wisdom and intelligence.

The Lord is without a cause. He is changeless and immutable. Yet He manifests His glories in the universe in various ways. The mystery of these manifestations is not known even to the gods and sages, much less to ordinary mortals. Human reasoning cannot know His nature, He reveals Himself, out of His infinite compassion, in the pure hearts of His devotees.

The result of the knowledge of the Lord:

यो मामजमनादिं च वेत्ति लोकमहेश्वरम्।
असम्मूढः स मर्त्येषु सर्वपापैः प्रमुच्यते॥ ३॥

3. He who knows that I am unborn and without a beginning, and also that I am the Supreme Lord of the worlds—he, undeluded among mortals, is freed from all sins.

Unborn—The Lord is the cause of the gods and the great sages and everything that exists. He is unborn.

Supreme Lord—He is transcendental, untouched by ignorance or its effect, the universe.

All sins—Committed consciously or unconsciously.

Ignorance of the Lord is the cause of sin. When a man does not know that he, in reality, is the pure Brahman, then he conjures up the vision of the universe with its opposites. He becomes conscious of good and evil, dharma and adharma. He participates in the activities of the world. The awareness of multiplicity impels him to hatred for disagreeable things and creates attachment to the agreeable. But the knowledge of the Lord as his inmost Self, untouched by relativity, destroys ignorance and its effect. Thus he is freed from all sins. The penances prescribed by religion do not destroy the cause of sin, which is ignorance; hence they cannot liberate the bound soul, Knowledge of the Lord, alone, gives liberation.

बुद्धिर्ज्ञानमसम्मोहः क्षमा सत्यं दमः शमः।
सुखं दुःखं भवोऽभावो भयं चाभयमेव च॥ ४॥

अहिंसा समता तुष्टिस्तपो दानं यशोऽयशः।
भवन्ति भावा भूतानां मत्त एव पृथग्विधाः॥ ५॥

4-5. Intelligence, knowledge, non-delusion, forbearance, truth, self-control and calmness, pleasure and pain, birth and death, fear and fearlessness;

Non-injury, equanimity, contentment, austerity, charity, fame and obloquy—these different attributes of beings arise from Me alone.

Intelligence—A power of the mind by which a man understands subtle objects.

Knowledge—By which one knows the distinction between the Self and other objects.

Non-delusion—Discrimination in action whenever a particular situation arises.

Forbearance—Tranquility of mind when abused or assaulted.

Truth—Giving utterance to one's own actual experience. of things, as heard or seen, with a view to conveying it correctly to another person.

Self-control—The withdrawal of the external senses, such as sight, hearing, etc., from their respective objects. Calmness—Tranquility of the mind, or inner sense.

Non-injury—To any living being.

Contentment—Satisfaction with what one already possesses.

Charity—Sharing one's own things with others as far as one's means permit.

The Lord, alone, is the cause and basis of the universe and all its beings. Created beings are endowed with different attributes according to their karma. The law of karma functions in the relative world through the power of the Lord.

महर्षयः सप्त पूर्वे चत्वारो मनवस्तथा।
मद्भावा मानसा जाता येषां लोक इमाः प्रजाः ॥ ६ ॥

6. The seven great sages and the four Manus of ancient times, endowed with My power, were born of My mind; and from them have sprung all the creatures in the world.

Endowed with My power—Because their thoughts were directed exclusively to the Lord.

Born of My mind—They were produced from the thought of the Lord.

According to the theory of creation given in the Purāṇas, or Hindu mythology, Brahman associated with māyā generated the universe. The first manifestation of Brahman in time and space is known as Hiraṇyagarbha, Prāṇa, or Sūtrātmā. Literally, these terms mean the "Golden Egg," "Life," and the "Cosmic Soul," or Ātman, which pervades the universe as a thread runs through a garland. Hiraṇyagarbha produced from its mind the first four created beings, namely Sanaka, Sanandana, Sanātana, and Sanatkumāra. It intended them to participate in the creation. However, endowed from their very birth with self—control, detachment, and the spirit of austerity, they went straightway to the forest and devoted themselves to meditation. Then Hiraṇyagarbha produced seven sages and four Manus, all from its mind, and ordered them to people the world with animate and inanimate beings. Having been created with a little worldly instinct, they carried out the command of their creator. The seven great ṛṣis, or sages, were the original teachers of spiritual wisdom. The Manus were the rulers of the world and were endowed with lordly powers. Because their thoughts were directed to the Lord, the sages and the Manus were endowed with wisdom and power. The present inhabitants of the world, according to Hindu mythology, have descended from these primeval personages and inherited their wisdom.

The result of knowing these glories of the Lord:

एतां विभूतिं योगं च मम यो वेत्ति तत्त्वतः।
सोऽविकम्पेन योगेन युज्यते नात्र संशयः ॥७॥

7. He who knows in truth this glory and power of Mine acquires unshakable devotion; of this there is no doubt.

Glory—The vast extent of the Lord's being. The knowledge of the Lord is infinite.

Power—The omniscience of the Lord, as also His ability to achieve mighty things. The power and wisdom of the ṛṣis and the Manus, referred to in the previous verse, is only a fraction of the Lord's infinite power and wisdom.

Unshakable devotion—This devotion is often compared to the anvil in a blacksmith's shop. In spite of repeated hammer-blows the anvil remains unshaken. Likewise, the true devotee of the Lord remains unshaken in his love of God in spite of the occasional doubts inevitable in spiritual life. Such devotion leads to the Knowledge of the Absolute.

The nature of this unshakable devotion:

अहं सर्वस्य प्रभवो मत्तः सर्वं प्रवर्तते।
इति मत्वा भजन्ते मां बुधा भावसमन्विताः ॥८॥

8. I am the origin of all; from Me all things evolve. The wise know this and worship Me with all their heart.

The Supreme Brahman, manifested in the relative world as the Lord Kṛṣṇa, is the Source and the Ultimate Cause of the whole universe. The moral and physical laws controlling and sustaining the activities in the universe are manifestations of His glory and power. He is the inner Regulator of all beings; hence He alone controls the universe in all its changes, including creation and destruction, action, results, and experiences. In short, He is the power behind the evolution of the cosmos. The universe without the Lord is empty and non-existent, like a mirage without the desert, or a dream without a dreaming mind. Thus realizing the emptiness of the world by itself and knowing the Lord as the Self of all, the Cause of all, the Omniscient Master of all, the wise set themselves to the task of knowing Him alone. The more they know Him, the more they love Him with all their heart. Through love and knowledge, earnestness and reverence, they gradually attain Self-knowledge.

Worship of the Lord through love:

मच्चित्ता मद्गतप्राणा बोधयन्तः परस्परम्।
कथयन्तश्च मां नित्यं तुष्यन्ति च रमन्ति च॥९॥

9. With their thought fixed on Me, with their life absorbed in Me, enlightening one another about Me, and always conversing about Me, they derive satisfaction and delight.

Life—The word "prāṇa" in the text may also mean the

senses.

Enlightening one another etc.—By means of reason and scriptural passages.

Satisfaction—Due to the cessation of all thirst for worldly objects. According to the *Mahābhārata*, all the happiness derived from worldly objects and all the bliss enjoyed in heaven are not worth a sixteenth part of what comes from the cessation of desires.

The Lord Himself, through His grace, gives right knowledge to those who worship Him with love.

तेषां सततयुक्तानां भजतां प्रीतिपूर्वकम्।
ददामि बुद्धियोगं तं येन मामुपयान्ति ते॥१०॥

10. On those who are ever devoted to Me and worship Me with love, I bestow the yoga of understanding, by which they come to Me.

With love—Not for any selfish purpose of their own, but out of love for the Lord.

Yoga of understanding—The word "buddhi-yoga" in the text refers to a superior and exalted condition of the mind produced by meditation on the Lord, by which the aspirant realizes the real nature of the Lord, free from all limitation.

The realization of the Lord is possible only through His grace, which He bestows on those who worship Him with whole-souled love. As a result of His grace their hearts become pure, and, being pure in heart, they see God. Men can never know the true essence of the Lord through their worldly minds or their power of reasoning. The attainment of true understanding, by which the Lord can be known and which comes through His grace alone, is the purpose of all spiritual endeavour and discipline.

Why does the Lord give right understanding to His devotees?

तेषामेवानुकम्पार्थमहमज्ञानजं तमः ।
नाशयाम्यात्मभावस्थो ज्ञानदीपेन भास्वता ॥ ११ ॥

11. Solely out of compassion for them, I, dwelling in their hearts, dispel with the shining lamp of wisdom the darkness born of ignorance.

Solely out of compassion etc.—The Lord is ever solicitous for the liberation of created beings.

Dwelling in their hearts—The Lord manifests Himself through man's intelligence.

Dispel... the darkness—This darkness comprises both the beginningless nescience and the illusory perceptions. resulting from that nescience. Nescience, or avidyā, cannot be destroyed by any phenomenal knowledge, since the latter itself belongs to nescience. Only the Light of the Lord can destroy it. The Divine Light shines through the buddhi, or understanding, and it is this illumined buddhi that dispels the nescience and illusory knowledge.

Lamp of wisdom—Characterized by discrimination; fed with the oil of contentment due to divine love; fanned by the wind of earnest meditation on the Lord; furnished with the wick of right intention purified by the cultivation of piety, chastity, and the other virtues; held in the chamber of the heart devoid of worldliness; placed in the sheltered recess of the mind withdrawn from sense-objects and untainted by attachment and aversion; shining with the light of right knowledge generated by incessant practice of concentration and meditation.—Śaṅkarācārya.

Born of ignorance—The beginningless avidyā and also the illusory knowledge caused by avidyā. Avidyā, or māyā, functions in two ways: first, it conceals the light of the Lord, and second, it manifests the illusory world.

No amount of worldly knowledge can destroy the darkness of man's heart. Worldly knowledge itself is a manifestation of nescience, as dreams are the result of unconsciousness, by which the sleeping man is overcome. It is the Lord who, manifesting Himself through man's consciousness, removes the darkness of his mind. The intelligence, illumined by the Light of the Lord, reveals the Lord. The purpose of spiritual discipline is to purify the mind so that the Lord, the indwelling Soul, may manifest Himself through it. The pure in heart, eager for the Light, always receive the Light through the Lord's grace.

Arjuna desires to know in detail the Lord's glories, which have been briefly described by Kṛṣṇa.

अर्जुन उवाच।

परं ब्रह्म परं धाम पवित्रं परमं भवान्।
पुरुषं शाश्वतं दिव्यमादिदेवमजं विभुम्॥ १२॥

आहुस्त्वामृषयः सर्वे देवर्षिर्नारदस्तथा।
असितो देवलो व्यासः स्वयं चैव ब्रवीषि मे॥ १३॥

12-13. *Arjuna said:* You are the Supreme Brahman, the Supreme Abode, the Supreme Holiness. All the sages have declared You to be the eternal, self-luminous Person, the first of the gods, unborn and all-pervading; likewise have the divine sages Nārada, Asita, Devala, and Vyāsa proclaimed. So, too, have You said unto me.

सर्वमेतदृतं मन्ये यन्मां वदसि केशव।
न हि ते भगवन्व्यक्तिं विदुर्देवा न दानवाः॥ १४॥

14. I hold as true all that You have said to me, O Keśava. Verily, neither the gods nor the demons, O Lord, know Your manifestations.

Neither the gods nor the demons etc.—Arjuna refers to the various Incarnations of the Lord, in the past, for the protection of the gods and the destruction of the demons. Neither the gods nor the demons, at that time, were aware of the Lord's glories, though they witnessed them with their own eyes. The Lord remains for ever inscrutable to the worldly-minded.

Lord—The word "Bhagavan" in the text signifies One in whom ever exist in their fullness all powers, all dharma, all glory, all success, all renunciation, and all freedom. The word also refers to Him who knows the origin, the dissolution, and the future of all beings, and the nature of knowledge and ignorance.

स्वयमेवात्मनात्मानं वेत्थ त्वं पुरुषोत्तम।
भूतभावन भूतेश देवदेव जगत्पते॥ १५॥

15. You alone know Yourself through Yourself, O Supreme Person, O Creator of all beings, O Lord of all beings, O God of gods, O Ruler of the world.

Know Yourself—Since the Lord is endowed with unsurpassed wisdom, sovereignty, and other divine attributes, none else knows all the manifestations of the Lord, much less His unconditioned and transcendent nature.

Through Yourself—Without any outside help.

Supreme Person—Beyond māyā and the three guṇas.

You alone know Your own manifestations; not even the gods understand them.

वक्तुमर्हस्यशेषेण दिव्या ह्यात्मविभूतयः।
याभिर्विभूतिभिर्लोकानिमांस्त्वं व्याप्य तिष्ठसि॥ १६॥

16. You should indeed tell me, in full, of Your divine powers, whereby You pervade all the worlds and abide in them.

You should indeed tell me—Since the Lord's nature is unknown and unknowable to others.

Arjuna has come to realize that the whole creation is nothing but the manifestation of the Lord's powers, and no one but the Lord Himself knows their mystery. So he desires to learn about those powers from the Lord Himself.

कथं विद्यामहं योगिंस्त्वां सदा परिचिन्तयन्।
केषु केषु च भावेषु चिन्त्योऽसि भगवन्मया॥ १७॥

17. How may I know You, O Yogi, by constant meditation? In what various things, O Lord, are You to be contemplated by me?

How may I know You etc.—Arjuna realizes his own dull understanding. He asks Śrī Kṛṣṇa in what manner he should meditate constantly on the

Lord so that his intelligence may be purified and he may know the Lord's unconditioned being.

Yogi—The Lord is addressed as a yogi because He is endowed with infinite powers and glories.

The whole universe is the manifestation of the Lord's glory. All objects reflect His glory. He is the reality immanent in all things. But some objects, high in evolution and endowed with more power and wisdom, reflect the Lord's glory more than others. Though all objects reflect light, yet it is seen more in a mirror than in a piece of wood. It is easy for devotees to meditate on God through those objects in which His glory is most manifest. Hence Kṛṣṇa will presently describe some of the prominent manifestations of the Lord in the universe.

विस्तरेणात्मनो योगं विभूतिं च जनार्दन।
भूयः कथय तृप्तिर्हि शृण्वतो नास्ति मेऽमृतम्॥ १८॥

18. Tell me once more, in detail, O Janārdana, of Your yoga-powers and glories; for I am never filled with hearing Your ambrosial words.

Janārdana—An epithet by which Kṛṣṇa is called when He is thought of as fulfilling man's prayers for prosperity and liberation.

श्रीभगवानुवाच।
हन्त ते कथयिष्यामि दिव्या ह्यात्मविभूतयः।
प्राधान्यतः कुरुश्रेष्ठ नास्त्यन्तो विस्तरस्य मे॥ १९॥

19. *The Lord said:* I will tell you now of My divine attributes, O best of the Kurus—only of those that are pre-eminent; for there is no limit to My extent.

Those that are pre-eminent—So that Arjuna may most readily see the power of the Lord.

God is infinite and His manifestation is infinite. He manifests Himself in the universe through innumerable forms. Each form is a symbol of an attribute of the Lord. The true seer finds each finite form carrying in it its own revelation of the infinite.

The foremost manifestation of the Lord:

अहमात्मा गुडाकेश सर्वभूताशयस्थितः।
अहमादिश्च मध्यं च भूतानामन्त एव च॥ २०॥

20. I am the Self, O Guḍākeśa, seated in the hearts of all creatures. I am the beginning, the middle, and the end of all beings.

Self—The Lord should be thought of as the inmost Self of all creatures.

Guḍākeśa—*Lit*., conqueror of sleep; an epithet of Arjuna.

Beginning etc.—All beings have come from the Lord, they are sustained by Him, and in the end they all merge in Him.

If one is unable to meditate on the Lord as the Self, then one should think of Him in the things mentioned below; for He is the essence of all things.

आदित्यानामहं विष्णुर्ज्योतिषां रविरंशुमान्।
मरीचिर्मरुतामस्मि नक्षत्राणामहं शशी॥२१॥

21. Of the Ādityas I am Viṣṇu; of lights I am the radiant sun. I am Marīci of the Maruts, and among the orbs of night I am the moon.

Ādityas—A group of twelve deities.

Maruts—The winds.

Śrī Kṛṣṇa enumerates, in this and the following verses, the various beings—gods, superhuman and human and subhuman creatures, angels, etc.—and points out that the chief and the head of each class is a special manifestation of the Godhead.

वेदानां सामवेदोऽस्मि देवानामस्मि वासवः।
इन्द्रियाणां मनश्चास्मि भूतानामस्मि चेतना॥२२॥

22. Of the Vedas I am the Sāman; of the gods I am Indra. Of the senses I am the mind, and in living beings I am intelligence.

Vedas—The sacred scriptures of the Hindus.

Sāman—The Sāma-Veda is noted for its rhythm and melody.

Mind—Through the mind the sense-organs receive the impressions of objects and react upon them. According to Hindu psychology there are eleven senses: five senses of perception, five organs of action, and the mind.

Intelligence—Through intelligence, or discriminative consciousness, manifesting itself in the aggregate of the body and senses, a man becomes conscious of himself and the outside world.

रुद्राणां शङ्करश्चास्मि वित्तेशो यक्षरक्षसाम्।
वसूनां पावकश्चास्मि मेरुः शिखरिणामहम्॥२३॥

23. Of the Rudras I am Śiva; of the Yakṣas and Rākṣasas I am Kuvera. Of the Vasus I am fire, and of mountains I am Meru.

Rudras—A group of gods, eleven in number, supposed to be collateral manifestations of Siva, who is their leader.

Yakṣas and Rākṣasas—A class of demigods.

Kuvera—The lord of wealth.

Vasus—A class of deities, usually eight in number.

Meru—Abounding in gold and other treasures.

पुरोधसां च मुख्यं मां विद्धि पार्थ बृहस्पतिम्।
सेनानीनामहं स्कन्दः सरसामस्मि सागरः ॥२४॥

24. Of priests, O Pārtha know Me to be the chief, Bṛhaspati. Of generals I am Skanda; of reservoirs of water I am the ocean.

Bṛhaspati—The high priest of Indra, king of heaven.

Skanda—The commander-in-chief of the armies in heaven.

महर्षीणां भृगुरहं गिरामस्म्येकमक्षरम्।
यज्ञानां जपयज्ञोऽस्मि स्थावराणां हिमालयः ॥२५॥

25. Of the great ṛṣis I am Bhṛgu, and of words I am the monosyllable "Om." Of sacrifices I am the sacrifice of japa; of immovable things I am the Himalaya.

Bhṛgu—Noted for his power and realization. According to Hindu mythology the Lord Himself bears on His chest Bhṛgu's foot-print.

Om—The most effective symbol of the Lord in both His personal and His impersonal aspect.

Japa—Repetition of the Lord's name. Various sacrifices have been prescribed for the spiritual progress of the aspirant. Most of them require the slaughter of animals or costly ingredients. But repetition of the Lord's name is the simplest and most effective way to attain Him.

अश्वत्थः सर्ववृक्षाणां देवर्षीणां च नारदः।
गन्धर्वाणां चित्ररथः सिद्धानां कपिलो मुनिः ॥२६॥

26. Of all trees I am the aśvattha, and of the devarṣis I am Nārada. Of the Gandharvas I am Citraratha, and of the perfected ones I am the sage Kapila.

Aśvattha—The holy fig tree.

Devarṣis —Who are, at the same time, gods and ṛṣis, or seers of mantras.

Gandharvas—A class of demigods regarded as the singers or musicians of the gods.

Perfected ones—Those who from their very birth are endowed with a high degree of righteousness, knowledge, detachment, and lordship.

उच्चैःश्रवसमश्वानां विद्धि माममृतोद्भवम्।
ऐरावतं गजेन्द्राणां नराणां च नराधिपम्॥ २७॥

27. Of horses know Me to be Uccais-śravas, born of the amṛta; of lordly elephants I am Airāvata, and of men I am the monarch.

Uccais-śravas—The name of the kingly horse that came out of the ocean when, according to Hindu mythology, it was churned for the amṛta, or elixir of immortality.

Airāvata—This royal elephant had the same origin as Uccais-śravas. Both horse and elephant were given to Indra, the king of the gods.

आयुधानामहं वज्रं धेनूनामस्मि कामधुक्।
प्रजनश्चास्मि कन्दर्पः सर्पाणामस्मि वासुकिः॥ २८॥

28. Of weapons I am the thunderbolt; of cows I am Kāmadhuk. I am Kandarpa, the cause of offspring, and of serpents I am Vāsuki.

Thunderbolt—The weapon belonging to Indra. The sage Dadhīci gave his own bones to make this powerful missile. Kāmadhuk—The famous cow of the sage Vaśiṣṭha, which fulfilled all desires. Or it may mean any cow that yields abundant milk.

Kandarpa—The name of the Hindu god of love. Through his influence man and woman seek each other's company.

Cause of offspring—The implication is that the sexual relation is justified only for begetting children and not simply for physical enjoyment.

Vāsuki—The mythical king of the serpents.

अनन्तश्चास्मि नागानां वरुणो यादसामहम्।
पितॄणामर्यमा चास्मि यमः संयमतामहम्॥ २९॥

29. Of the Nāgas I am Ananta; of the dwellers in water I am Varuṇa. Of the Pitṛs I am Aryamā, and of those that practise self-control I am Yama.

Nāgas—A class of snakes.

Dwellers in water—The deities that control lakes, seas, oceans, etc.

Pitṛs—Departed ancestors.

Yama—The king of death, who decides the fate of the departed souls and rewards or punishes them. He is endowed with great self-control so that he may not be swayed by personal preferences.

प्रह्लादश्चास्मि दैत्यानां कालः कलयतामहम्।
मृगाणां च मृगेन्द्रोऽहं वैनतेयश्च पक्षिणाम्॥ ३०॥

30. Of the Daityas I am Prahlāda, and of measurers I am Time. Of beasts I am the lion, and of birds I am Garuḍa.

Daityas—*Lit.*, the offspring of Diti. The word generally signifies the demons, who challenge the power of good.

Prahlāda—Who was endowed with great love of God and other spiritual attributes.

Time—Which is without beginning and end in the relative world and is the ultimate measurer of all things.

Garuḍa—The carrier of the Lord Viṣṇu.

पवनः पवतामस्मि रामः शस्त्रभृतामहम्।
झषाणां मकरश्चास्मि स्रोतसामस्मि जाह्नवी॥ ३१॥

31. Of purifiers I am the wind; of warriors I am Rāma. Of fishes I am the shark, and of rivers I am the Ganges.

Rāma—The great hero of the *Rāmāyaṇa.*

सर्गाणामादिरन्तश्च मध्यं चैवाहमर्जुन।
अध्यात्मविद्या विद्यानां वादः प्रवदतामहम्॥ ३२॥

32. Of created things I am the beginning and the end and also the middle, O Arjuna. Of all sciences I am the Science of the Self, and in disputation I am reason.

The Science of the Self—Because it is the basis of all other sciences, and also because it leads men to liberation.

अक्षराणामकारोऽस्मि द्वन्द्वः सामासिकस्य च।
अहमेवाक्षयः कालो धाताहं विश्वतोमुखः॥ ३३॥

33. Of letters I am the letter A, and of compound words I am the Dvanda. I Myself am inexhaustible Time, and I am the Dispenser facing everywhere.

The letter A—It is the first of letters, and all sounds are based on the A sound. In Sanskrit it is pronounced as *o* in r*o*d.

Compound words—Sanskrit grammar lays down rules for joining two or more words into a compound word, in which the meaning of the component parts may be fully or partly retained. The peculiarity of the Dvanda compound is that it keeps intact the meanings of its component parts.

Time—The word here signifies the moment. As a unit of time, one moment follows another in never ending succession.

Dispenser—The gods also give the fruits of action to their devotees; but these fruits belong to the realm of the finite. The Lord, however, bestows on His devotee the supreme fruit of liberation.

Facing everywhere—It is the Lord alone whom we see on all sides. Through all mouths He eats, through all eyes He sees, through all cars He hears, and through all minds. He thinks.

मृत्युः सर्वहरश्चाहमुद्भवश्च भविष्यताम्।
कीर्तिः श्रीर्वाक्क नारीणां स्मृतिर्मेधा धृतिः क्षमा ॥ ३४ ॥

34. I am all-seizing Death. I am the prosperity of those who are to be prosperous, and of female powers I am Glory, Fortune, Speech, Memory, Intelligence, Constancy, and Forbearance.

All-seizing Death—As the loss of life is death, so also is the loss of fortune. The Lord's power is more manifest in the former, since that form of death is the stronger of the two. Or the Lord is called all-seizing Death because at the time of the cosmic dissolution everything merges in Him.

Female powers—Glory, Fortune, etc. are the seven most exalted female deities.

बृहत्साम तथा साम्नां गायत्री छन्दसामहम्।
मासानां मार्गशीर्षोऽहमृतूनां कुसुमाकरः ॥ ३५ ॥

35. Of the Sāman hymns I am the Bṛhat-Sāman, and of metres I am the Gāyatrī. Of months I am Mārgaśirṣa, and of seasons I am the flowery spring.

Bṛhat-Sāman—Which contains the hymns to Indra and formulates the science of liberation.

Gāyatrī—A Vedic metre of twenty-four syllables; also the name of a sacred Vedic verse repeated daily by every brāhmin at the time of his regular devotions.

Mārgaśirṣa—In ancient times the Hindu calendar began with this month, which includes part of November and of December.

द्यूतं छलयतामस्मि तेजस्तेजस्विनामहम्।
जयोऽस्मि व्यवसायोऽस्मि सत्त्वं सत्त्ववतामहम्॥ ३६ ॥

36. I am the gambling of cheats; I am the vigour of the strong. I am victory; I am effort; I am the quality of sattva in the good.

Gambling of cheats—Such as dice-play, card-play, etc. Through these means cunning people cheat others. Every manifestation of power, glory, success, or intelligence comes from the Lord Himself. It may be distorted if the medium of manifestation is wicked or unrighteous.

Quality of sattva—Of the three guṇas, sattva denotes goodness, serenity, harmony, and so on.

वृष्णीनां वासुदेवोऽस्मि पाण्डवानां धनञ्जयः।
मुनीनामप्यहं व्यासः कवीनामुशना कविः॥ ३७॥

37. Of the Yādavas I am Vāsudeva and of the Pāṇḍavas I am Arjuna. Of the sages I am Vyāsa, and of seers I am Uśanas the seer.

Yādavas—The race of Kṛṣṇa.

Vāsudeva—Kṛṣṇa, whose father's name was Vāsudeva Pāṇḍavas—The five sons of Pāṇḍu: Yudhiṣṭhira, Bhīma, Arjuna, Nakula, and Sahadeva.

Sages—Philosophers and thinkers.

Vyāsa—The compiler of the Vedas.

Seers—Inspired poets, who see Truth through their power of intuition.

दण्डो दमयतामस्मि नीतिरस्मि जिगीषताम्।
मौनं चैवास्मि गुह्यानां ज्ञानं ज्ञानवतामहम्॥ ३८॥

38. I am the rod of those that chastise and the statesmanship of those that conquer. Of secret things I am silence, and of the wise I am the wisdom.

Chastise—That is to say, the wicked.

Statesmanship—Which is the most effective way of conquering an enemy. The Hindu law-givers recommend four methods of dealing with an enemy, namely, appeasement, coercion, internal division, and statesmanship, according to the situation.

The Lord summarizes His glories:

यच्चापि सर्वभूतानां बीजं तदहमर्जुन।
न तदस्ति विना यत्स्यान्मया भूतं चराचरम्॥ ३९॥

39. And that which is the seed of all beings—that am I, O Arjuna. There is no being, whether moving or unmoving, that can exist without Me.

Can exist without Me—The Lord is Existence-Knowledge-Bliss Absolute. Anything that is without the Lord is void. He alone pervades all.

नान्तोऽस्ति मम दिव्यानां विभूतीनां परन्तप।
एष तूद्देशतः प्रोक्तो विभूतेर्विस्तरो मया॥ ४०॥

40. There is no end of My divine manifestations, O dreaded Arjuna. This is but a partial statement by Me of the multiplicity of My attributes.

There is no end etc.—As the Lord is infinite, His manifestations are infinite in number.

यद्यद्विभूतिमत्सत्त्वं श्रीमदूर्जितमेव वा।
तत्तदेवावगच्छ त्वं मम तेजोंऽशसम्भवम्॥ ४१॥

41. Whatever glorious or beautiful or mighty being exists anywhere, know that it has sprung from but a spark of My splendour.

अथवा बहुनैतेन किं ज्ञातेन तवार्जुन।
विष्टभ्याहमिदं कृत्स्नमेकांशेन स्थितो जगत्॥ ४२॥

42. But what need is there of your acquiring this detailed knowledge, O Arjuna? With a single fragment of Myself I stand supporting the whole universe.

One can never fully know the Lord through His manifestations in time and space. It is enough to know that the whole universe represents only a particle of the Lord's glory. He transcends the universe. "All beings form His foot." (*Taittirīya Āraṇyaka.)*

ॐ तत्सदिति श्रीमद्भगवद्गीतासूपनिषत्सु
ब्रह्मविद्यायां योगशास्त्रे श्रीकृष्णार्जुनसंवादे
विभूतियोगो नाम दशमोऽध्यायः ॥ १० ॥

Thus in the Bhagavad Gītā, the Essence of the Upaniṣads, the Science of Brahman, the Scripture of Yoga, the Dialogue between Śrī *Kṛṣṇa and Arjuna, ends the Tenth Chapter, entitled:* THE DIVINE MANIFESTATIONS

CHAPTER 11

THE VISION OF THE UNIVERSAL FORM

[विश्वरूपदर्शनयोगः]

अर्जुन उवाच।

मदनुग्रहाय परमं गुह्यमध्यात्मसंज्ञितम्।
यत्त्वयोक्तं वचस्तेन मोहोऽयं विगतो मम॥१॥

1. *Arjuna said:* Out of compassion for me You have spoken words of ultimate profundity concerning the Self, and they have dispelled my delusion.

My delusion—Arjuna is deluded to think he will be responsible for the slaying of his relatives on the battlefield, forgetting that the Lord alone is the doer, and man only His instrument.

The tenth chapter ended with a declaration of the Lord that He supports the whole universe by a single fragment of His being. Arjuna is now desirous of seeing with his own eyes the form of the Lord that sustains the world system.

भवाप्ययौ हि भूतानां श्रुतौ विस्तरशो मया।
त्वत्तः कमलपत्राक्ष माहात्म्यमपि चाव्ययम्॥२॥

2. I have learnt from You at length, O lotus-eyed Kṛṣṇa, of the origin and dissolution of beings, and also of Your inexhaustible greatness.

Origin and dissolution etc.—The Lord Himself is the origin and dissolution of beings.

Inexhaustible greatness—The infinite and ineffable greatness of the Lord consists in the fact that He remains unchanging, impartial, unagitated, detached, and indifferent. although He is the Creator of the universe, the guide and controller of all beings, the cause of their participating in good and evil actions, and the giver of their rewards and punishments.

एवमेतद्यथात्थ त्वमात्मानं परमेश्वर।
द्रष्टुमिच्छामि ते रूपमैश्वरं पुरुषोत्तम॥३॥

3. As You have declared Yourself to be, O Supreme Lord—even so it is. Yet do I desire to see Your Īśvara-form, O Supreme Puruṣa.

Īśvara-form—The divine form as possessed of omnipotence, omnipresence, infinite wisdom, infinite strength, infinite virtue, and infinite splendour.

Arjuna evinces humility:

मन्यसे यदि तच्छक्यं मया द्रष्टुमिति प्रभो।
योगेश्वर ततो मे त्वं दर्शयात्मानमव्ययम्॥४॥

4. If, O Lord, You think me able to behold it, then, O Master of yogis, reveal to me Your immutable Self.

श्रीभगवानुवाच।
पश्य मे पार्थ रूपाणि शतशोऽथ सहस्रशः।
नानाविधानि दिव्यानि नानावर्णाकृतीनि च॥५॥

5. *The Lord said:* Behold My forms, O Pārtha by the hundreds and the thousands—manifold and divine, various in shape and hue.

पश्यादित्यान्वसून्रुद्रानश्विनौ मरुतस्तथा।
बहून्यदृष्टपूर्वाणि पश्याश्चर्याणि भारत॥६॥

6. Behold the Ādityas and the Vasus and the Rudras and the twin Aświns and the Maruts; behold, O Bhārata, many wonders that no one has ever seen before.

इहैकस्थं जगत्कृत्स्नं पश्याद्य सचराचरम्।
मम देहे गुडाकेश यच्चान्यद् द्रष्टुमिच्छसि॥७॥

7. Behold here today, O Guḍākeśa, the whole universe, of the moving and the unmoving, and whatever else you desire to see, all concentrated in My body.

Today—It takes an ordinary mortal millions of births to grasp the universe in its entirety. And the Lord reveals to Arjuna's eyes the entire panorama.

Whatever else you desire to see—Future events such as the ultimate outcome of the battle, about which Arjuna has been in doubt. The past, present, and future—nay, time itself—exist only in a fragment of the Lord.

All concentrated in My body—Related and unified in the Lord.

Śrī Kṛṣṇa is about to reveal to Arjuna the most staggering vision: the vision of the One in the many, the many in the One, the vision that shows that all are the One. This vision alone explains and justifies the apparent contradictions of the relative world and reconciles the antinomies of justice and mercy, fate and free will, suffering and divine love. It reveals all that was, is, and shall be. It relates and unifies the diversity of the world. Seeing God in all and all in God, man overcomes all doubt and perplexity and submits to the divine will. Thus even the most terrible thing in the world loses its terror and even the most hateful thing becomes a mode of the Lord's manifestation. The man blessed with this vision accepts the world with an all-embracing joy and great courage and goes forward with sure steps to discharge his appointed task. He sees all things *in one view*, and not in a divided, partial, and bewildered fashion.

न तु मां शक्यसे द्रष्टुमनेनैव स्वचक्षुषा।
दिव्यं ददामि ते चक्षुः पश्य मे योगमैश्वरम्॥८॥

8. But with these eyes of yours you cannot see Me. I give you a divine eye; behold, now, My sovereign yoga-power.

Eyes of yours—The human eye can see only outward appearances of things and their manifold forms.

Divine eye—Which alone can see the Godhead, the unity that underlies all appearances.

सञ्जय उवाच।
एवमुक्त्वा ततो राजन्महायोगेश्वरो हरिः।
दर्शयामास पार्थाय परमं रूपमैश्वरम्॥९॥

9. *Sañjaya said:* Having spoken thus, O King, Hari, the great Lord of Yoga, revealed to Arjuna His supreme form as Īśvara:

King—Refers to Dhṛtarāṣṭra Sañjaya is his reporter of the events on the battle-field.

अनेकवक्त्रनयनमनेकाद्भुतदर्शनम्।
अनेकदिव्याभरणं दिव्यानेकोद्यतायुधम्॥ १०॥

दिव्यमाल्याम्बरधरं दिव्यगन्धानुलेपनम्।
सर्वाश्चर्यमयं देवमनन्तं विश्वतोमुखम्॥ ११॥

10-11. With many faces and eyes, presenting many wondrous sights, bedecked with many celestial ornaments, armed with many divine uplifted weapons; wearing celestial garlands and vestments, anointed with divine perfumes, all-wonderful, resplendent, boundless, and with faces on all sides.

दिवि सूर्यसहस्रस्य भवेद्युगपदुत्थिता।
यदि भाः सदृशी सा स्याद्भासस्तस्य महात्मनः॥ १२॥

12. If the radiance of a thousand suns were to burst forth at once in the sky, that would be like the splendour of the Mighty One.

तत्रैकस्थं जगत्कृत्स्नं प्रविभक्तमनेकधा।
अपश्यद्देवदेवस्य शरीरे पाण्डवस्तदा॥ १३॥

13. There, in the person of the God of gods, Arjuna beheld the whole universe, with its manifold divisions, all gathered together in one.

With its manifold divisions—Gods, demigods, manes, men, and so on.

The multitudinously divided universe is unified in the person of the Lord.

ततः स विस्मयाविष्टो हृष्टरोमा धनञ्जयः।
प्रणम्य शिरसा देवं कृताञ्जलिरभाषत॥ १४॥

14. Then, overcome with wonder, his hair standing on end, Arjuna bowed his head to the Lord, joined his palms in salutation, and thus addressed Him:

अर्जुन उवाच।
पश्यामि देवांस्तव देव देहे
सर्वांस्तथा भूतविशेषसङ्घान्।

ब्रह्माणमीशं कमलासनस्थ-
मृषींश्च सर्वानुरगांश्च दिव्यान्॥ १५॥

15. *Arjuna said:* In Thy body, O Lord, I behold all the gods and all the diverse hosts of beings—the Lord Brahmā, seated on the lotus, and all the ṛṣis and the celestial serpents.

अनेकबाहूदरवक्त्रनेत्रं
पश्यामि त्वां सर्वतोऽनन्तरूपम्।
नान्तं न मध्यं न पुनस्तवादिं
पश्यामि विश्वेश्वर विश्वरूप॥ १६॥

16. I behold Thee with myriads of arms and bellies, with myriads of faces and eyes; I behold Thee, infinite in form, on every side, but I see not Thy end nor Thy middle nor Thy beginning, O Lord of the universe, O Universal Form!

किरीटिनं गदिनं चक्रिणं च
तेजोराशिं सर्वतो दीप्तिमन्तम्।
पश्यामि त्वां दुर्निरीक्ष्यं समन्ताद्
दीप्तानलार्कद्युतिमप्रमेयम्॥ १७॥

17. I behold Thee on all sides glowing like a mass of radiance, with Thy diadem and mace and discus, blazing everywhere like burning fire and the burning sun, hard to look at, and passing all measure.

Arjuna can endure this dazzling vision because he is endowed with the divine eye. Ordinary consciousness is blasted by such radiance.

त्वमक्षरं परमं वेदितव्यं
त्वमस्य विश्वस्य परं निधानम्।
त्वमव्ययः शाश्वतधर्मगोप्ता
सनातनस्त्वं पुरुषो मतो मे॥ १८॥

18. Thou art the Imperishable, the Supreme Being to be realized; Thou art the Supreme Support of the universe; Thou art the undying Guardian of the Eternal Dharma; Thou art, in my belief, the Primal Being.

This great vision reveals also the terrific image of the Destroyer:

अनादिमध्यान्तमनन्तवीर्य-
मनन्तबाहुं शशिसूर्यनेत्रम्।

पश्यामि त्वां दीप्तहुताशवक्त्रं
स्वतेजसा विश्वमिदं तपन्तम्॥ १९ ॥

19. I behold Thee as one without beginning, middle, or end; with infinite arms and immeasurable strength; with the sun and moon as Thine eyes; with Thy face shining like a blazing fire; and burning with Thy radiance the whole universe.

द्यावापृथिव्योरिदमन्तरं हि
व्याप्तं त्वयैकेन दिशश्च सर्वाः।
दृष्ट्वाद्भुतं रूपमुग्रं तवेदं
लोकत्रयं प्रव्यथितं महात्मन्॥ २० ॥

20. By Thee alone are filled all the space between heaven and earth, and all the quarters of the sky. O Mighty One, the three worlds behold Thy marvellous and appalling form and tremble with fear.

अमी हि त्वां सुरसङ्घा विशन्ति
केचिद्भीताः प्राञ्जलयो गृणन्ति।
स्वस्तीत्युक्त्वा महर्षिसिद्धसङ्घाः
स्तुवन्ति त्वां स्तुतिभिः पुष्कलाभिः ॥ २१ ॥

21. Into Thee enter these hosts of gods, and some in fear extol Thee with folded hands. And bands of Ṛṣis and Siddhas exclaim, "May there be peace!" and praise Thee with splendid hymns.

Siddhas—Semi-divine beings of great purity and holiness, endowed with supernatural powers.

Exclaim etc.—In order to ward off the imminent destruction of the world.

रुद्रादित्या वसवो ये च साध्या
विश्वेऽश्विनौ मरुतश्चोष्मपाश्च।
गन्धर्वयक्षासुरसिद्धसङ्घा
वीक्षन्ते त्वां विस्मिताश्चैव सर्वे॥ २२ ॥

22. The Rudras, Ādityas, Vasus, and Sādhyas; the Viśwas, Aświns, Maruts, and Uṣmapās; and the hosts of Gandharvas, Yakṣas, Asuras, and Siddhas—all behold Thee and are amazed.

Uṣmapās—The manes.

रूपं महत्ते बहुवक्त्रनेत्रं
महाबाहो बहुबाहूरुपादम्।
बहूदरं बहुदंष्ट्राकरालं
दृष्ट्वा लोकाः प्रव्यथितास्तथाहम्॥ २३॥

23. Beholding Thy great form, O Mighty Lord, with myriads of mouths and eyes, with myriads of arms and thighs and feet, with myriads of bellies, and with myriads of terrible tusks—the worlds are affrighted, and so am I.

The Universal Form of the Lord reveals to Arjuna the terrible, as well as the beautiful, aspect of the creation; both are necessary to complete the picture. The Lord manifests Himself in the relative world through both good and evil, pain and pleasure, life and death, and the other pairs of opposites; whereas, in His inmost essence, He can be described only as Peace and Blessedness.

The cause of Arjuna's terror:

नभःस्पृशं दीप्तमनेकवर्णं
व्यात्ताननं दीप्तविशालनेत्रम्।
दृष्ट्वा हि त्वां प्रव्यथितान्तरात्मा
धृतिं न विन्दामि शमं च विष्णो॥ २४॥

24. When I look upon Thy blazing form reaching to the skies and shining in many colours, when I see Thee with Thy mouths opened wide and Thy great eyes glowing bright, my inmost soul trembles in fear, and I find neither courage nor peace, O Viṣṇu!

Viṣṇu—An epithet of the Godhead, because of Its all-pervasive nature.

दंष्ट्राकरालानि च ते मुखानि
दृष्ट्वैव कालानलसन्निभानि।
दिशो न जाने न लभे च शर्म
प्रसीद देवेश जगन्निवास॥ २५॥

25. When I behold Thy mouths, striking terror with their tusks, like Time's all—consuming fire, I am disoriented and find no peace. Be gracious, O Lord of the gods, O Abode of the universe!

Time's all-consuming fire—The fire that consumes the world at the time of cosmic dissolution.

अमी च त्वां धृतराष्ट्रस्य पुत्राः
सर्वे सहैवावनिपालसङ्घैः ।
भीष्मो द्रोणः सूतपुत्रस्तथासौ
सहास्मदीयैरपि योधमुख्यैः ॥ २६ ॥

वक्त्राणि ते त्वरमाणा विशन्ति
दंष्ट्राकरालानि भयानकानि ।
केचिद्विलग्ना दशनान्तरेषु
सन्दृश्यन्ते चूर्णितैरुत्तमाङ्गैः ॥ २७ ॥

26-27. All these sons of Dhṛtarāṣṭra together with the hosts of monarchs, and Bhīṣma Droṇa, and Karṇa, and the warrior chiefs of our side as well, enter precipitately Thy tusked and terrible mouths, frightful to behold. Some are seen caught between Thy teeth, their heads crushed to powder.

Arjuna has had doubts concerning the ultimate outcome of the war. Now he has a prevision of the holocaust that will take place on the battle-field, in which the leaders of both sides will be destroyed; he further realizes that his party will be victorious. The inexorable law of the cosmos, emanating from the Godhead, will accomplish all this, using Arjuna merely as an instrument.

यथा नदीनां बहवोऽम्बुवेगाः
समुद्रमेवाभिमुखा द्रवन्ति ।
तथा तवामी नरलोकवीरा
विशन्ति वक्त्राण्यभिविज्वलन्ति ॥ २८ ॥

28. As the many torrents of the rivers rush toward the ocean, so do the heroes of the mortal world rush into Thy fiercely flaming mouths.

यथा प्रदीप्तं ज्वलनं पतङ्गा
विशन्ति नाशाय समृद्धवेगाः ।
तथैव नाशाय विशन्ति लोका-
स्तवापि वक्त्राणि समृद्धवेगाः ॥ २९ ॥

29. As moths rush swiftly into a blazing fire to perish there, even so do these creatures swiftly rush into Thy mouths to their own destruction.

Neither Arjuna nor anyone else can stop the Lord's will. Men's efforts and reasons are helpless before the march of events already accomplished by the Godhead.

लेलिह्यसे ग्रसमानः समन्ताल्-
लोकान्समग्रान्वदनैर्ज्वलद्भिः।
तेजोभिरापूर्य जगत्समग्रं
भासस्तवोग्राः प्रतपन्ति विष्णो॥ ३०॥

30. Thou lickest Thy lips, devouring all the worlds on every side with Thy flaming mouths. Thy fiery rays fill the whole universe with their radiance and scorch it, O Viṣṇu!

Thou lickest Thy lips—The Lord is enjoying this destruction with evident delight.

If men's destiny and the divine will conspire together to scorch the earth with the fire of destruction, the effort of the individual to stop it cannot be anything but useless.

Arjuna's soul is troubled; he finds no peace. In pain he cries out:

आख्याहि मे को भवानुग्ररूपो
नमोऽस्तु ते देववर प्रसीद।
विज्ञातुमिच्छामि भवन्तमाद्यं
न हि प्रजानामि तव प्रवृत्तिम्॥ ३१॥

31. Tell me who Thou art that wearest this frightful form. Salutations to Thee, O God Supreme! Have mercy. I desire to know Thee, who art the Primal One; for I do not understand Thy purpose.

Thy purpose—In willing this holocaust.

Kṛṣṇa has been Arjuna's life-long friend and companion. In the twinkling of an eye He has transformed Himself into the Supreme Godhead, a part of whose Universal Form manifests the horror of destruction. Arjuna, frightened and bewildered, begs to be enlightened as to the real nature of the Lord.

श्रीभगवानुवाच।
कालोऽस्मि लोकक्षयकृत्प्रवृद्धो
लोकान्समाहर्तुमिह प्रवृत्तः।
ऋतेऽपि त्वां न भविष्यन्ति सर्वे
येऽवस्थिताः प्रत्यनीकेषु योधाः॥ ३२॥

32. *The Lord said:* I am mighty, world-destroying Time, now engaged here in slaying these men. Even without you, all these warriors standing arrayed in the opposing armies shall not live.

Time—A manifestation of the Godhead. Time absorbs into the womb of oblivion all names and forms.

In slaying these men—The Lord in the fullness of time. destroys the old structures in order to build up a new, mighty, and splendid kingdom. Destruction is always a simultaneous or alternate element that keeps pace with creation, and it is by destroying and renewing that the Lord carries on His long work of preservation. In the relative world destruction is the first condition of progress. Individually, the man who does not destroy his lower self cannot rise to a greater existence. On a larger scale, the nation or community or race that shrinks too long from destroying and replacing its outworn forms of life is itself destroyed, and out of its debris other nations, communities, and races are formed.

Even without you—The abstention or non-intervention or protest of the individual cannot prevent the fulfilment of the divine will; rather, by the lacuna, it increases confusion.

Kālī or Rudra, the Destroyer God, as well as Brahmā, the Creator God, are both manifestations of the Godhead in the relative world. The one is incomplete, helpless, nay, illusory, without the other. The weak mind of man, desiring fair and comforting truths or pleasant fables, robs Reality of one of Its aspects and thus deludes itself with a half-truth. To ignore the stern and destructive aspect of Reality is to miss the full significance of divine love and peace and calmness and eternity. To put the responsibility for all that seems to be terrible or destructive on the shoulders of a semi-omnipotent Devil, or to explain the apparent evil as part of Nature, or to throw the burden of it all on man and his sins, are clumsy, if convenient, devices. The Gītā teaches us to see Reality as a whole. God the bountiful and prodigal Creator and Preserver is also God the Destroyer and Devourer.

तस्मात्त्वमुत्तिष्ठ यशो लभस्व
जित्वा शत्रून् भुङ्क्ष्व राज्यं समृद्धम्।
मयैवैते निहताः पूर्वमेव
निमित्तमात्रं भव सव्यसाचिन्॥ ३३ ॥

33. Therefore stand up and win glory; conquer your enemies and enjoy an opulent kingdom. By Me and none other have they already been slain; be an instrument only, O Arjuna.

Arjuna—The word used in the text is "Savyasācin," an epithet given to Arjuna on account of his dexterity in shooting arrows with his left hand as well as his right.

The Lord, as all-devouring Time, has already killed the warriors. None can stay the hand of the divine will. Śrī Kṛṣṇa reminds Arjuna that the latter has been appointed by the Lord as His human instrument in this struggle, which none can prevent and which will vindicate the power of righteousness by destroying the force of evil. Let Arjuna's will be one with the will of God. Let him cooperate with God in fulfilling a supreme purpose. The reward that is promised is also determined by the divine will. Arjuna has been chosen for the grand prize on account of his good karma in the past.

द्रोणं च भीष्मं च जयद्रथं च
कर्णं तथान्यानपि योधवीरान्।
मया हतांस्त्वं जहि मा व्यथिष्ठा
युध्यस्व जेतासि रणे सपत्नान्॥ ३४॥

34. Kill Droṇa and Bhīṣma and Jayadratha and Karṇa, and the other great warriors as well, who have already been killed by Me. Be not distressed by fear. Fight, and you shall conquer your foes in the battle.

Who have already been killed by Me—That is to say, in the foreordaining mind of the Lord. Arjuna was afraid of incurring sin by killing his elders, teachers, or relatives. Now he is made to realize that he is only an instrument in the hands of God, who alone is responsible for all actions. The consciousness of the divine agency and its consistent application in all works release man from responsibility.

Be not distressed by fear—Droṇa, Bhīṣma and the others mentioned in the text are great warriors. Droṇa has in his possession many celestial weapons. Bhīṣma by a divine boon, does not have to die until he likes. As to Jayadratha, his father had received a boon that whoever would cause his son's head to drop on the earth would lose his own head too. Karṇa is armed with a divine weapon that makes him invincible. There is a lurking fear, in Arjuna's mind, of their invincibility. The Lord, with His words of reassurance, encourages Arjuna to do his duty with a fearless heart.

You shall conquer etc.—Because such is the divine will. Arjuna is not permitted to take credit for his victory.

सञ्जय उवाच।

एतच्छ्रुत्वा वचनं केशवस्य
कृताञ्जलिर्वेपमानः किरीटी।
नमस्कृत्वा भूय एवाह कृष्णं
सगद्गदं भीतभीतः प्रणम्य॥ ३५॥

35. *Sañjaya said:* Having heard these words of Kṛṣṇa, Arjuna trembled, folded his hands in adoration, and bowed down. Overwhelmed with fear, he saluted Kṛṣṇa and then addressed Him again, with faltering voice.

Trembled—His trembling, fear, faltering voice, and so on, show that Arjuna is shaken with emotion. The Universal Form of the Lord, emphasizing destruction, strikes terror into his heart, and the encouragement of the Lord fills him with gratitude.

As the reader may remember, the two sides on the battlefield are represented by the hundred sons of Dhṛtarāṣṭra and the five sons of Pāṇḍu. Since Dhṛtarāṣṭra is blind, Sañjaya acts as his reporter.

Sañjaya's words are very significant. He hopes that King Dhṛtarāṣṭra will clearly foresee the inevitable destruction of his sons and thus, in despair, bring about peace by fulfilling the just demands of Yudhiṣṭhira and his brothers. But Dhṛtarāṣṭra is blind both physically and spiritually. Destiny must be fulfilled.

अर्जुन उवाच।

स्थाने हृषीकेश तव प्रकीर्त्या
जगत्प्रहृष्यत्यनुरज्यते च।
रक्षांसि भीतानि दिशो द्रवन्ति
सर्वे नमस्यन्ति च सिद्धसङ्घाः॥ ३६॥

36. *Arjuna said:* It is right, O Hṛṣīkeśa, that the world rejoices and delights in glorifying Thee; the Rākṣasas flee on all sides in terror, and the hosts of Siddhas all bow to Thee in adoration.

The world rejoices—Because there lies behind the terrifying form the reassuring, fearless, and delightful Being of the Lord. He always protects the righteous.

Flee on all sides etc.—Because the power of evil and darkness cannot stand the force of good and light, which is the nature of the Lord.

Siddhas—Perfected souls.

For the following reason, also, the Lord is the object of delight:

कस्माच्च ते न नमेरन्महात्मन्
गरीयसे ब्रह्मणोऽप्यादिकर्त्रे।
अनन्त देवेश जगन्निवास
त्वमक्षरं सदसत्तत्परं यत्॥ ३७॥

37. And why should they not bow down to Thee, O Mighty Being, greater than all, since Thou art the Primal Cause even of Brahmā? O Infinite One, Lord of gods, Abode of the universe, Thou art the Imperishable, Being and non-being, and that which is the Supreme.

Brahmā—The Creator God, who is only one aspect of His Trinity, the other two aspects being Viṣṇu (the Preserver God) and Śiva (the Destroyer God).

Primal Cause etc.—There are evolution and involution of the Trinity, but the Godhead is eternal and immutable.

Being and non-being—Existence and non-existence, relatively speaking, are the two conditions of the Spirit's manifestation.

The Supreme—That which lies beyond Being and nonbeing and is their basis. A timeless eternity is the characteristic of the Absolute, of which time is only a manifestation in māyā.

त्वमादिदेवः पुरुषः पुराण-
स्त्वमस्य विश्वस्य परं निधानम्।
वेत्तासि वेद्यं च परं च धाम
त्वया ततं विश्वमनन्तरूप॥ ३८॥

38. Thou art the first of gods, the ancient Soul; Thou art the supreme Resting—place of the universe; Thou art the Knower and That which is to be known and the Ultimate Goal. And by Thee is the world pervaded, O Thou of infinite form.

First of gods—Because of His being the Creator of the universe.

Ancient Soul—He is called Puruṣa, or Soul, because He lies in each body. He is ancient because He is the manifester of time.

Supreme Resting-place etc.—At the time of the great dissolution the universe rests in Him.

Knower—Of everything great and small.

By Thee is the world pervaded—The illusory world is seen because the Lord forms its unchanging substratum. As, in the illusion of a rope appearing as a snake, the rope pervades the snake, so also, in the illusion of the Lord appearing as the universe, the Lord pervades the universe.

The Lord is the inmost essence of all the gods.

वायुर्यमोऽग्निर्वरुणः शशाङ्कः
प्रजापतिस्त्वं प्रपितामहश्च।
नमो नमस्तेऽस्तु सहस्रकृत्वः
पुनश्च भूयोऽपि नमो नमस्ते॥३९॥

39. Thou art Wind and Death and Fire and Moon and the Lord of Water. Thou art Prajāpati and the Great-grandsire. Salutations, salutations to Thee a thousand times, and again and yet again salutations, salutations to Thee!

Prajāpati—One of the first created beings, whose offspring are the men and women of the world.

Great-grandsire—The father of Brahmā, who is the grandfather of men.

Arjuna's emotions are greatly aroused. He repeats his salutations:

नमः पुरस्तादथ पृष्ठतस्ते
नमोऽस्तु ते सर्वत एव सर्व।
अनन्तवीर्यामितविक्रमस्त्वं
सर्वं समाप्नोषि ततोऽसि सर्वः॥४०॥

40. Salutations to Thee before, salutations to Thee behind, salutations to Thee on every side, O All! Infinite in might and immeasurable in strength, Thou pervadest all and therefore Thou art all.

On every side—Since the Lord is present everywhere.

But the Supreme Being has been living with Arjuna as his friend and companion without being recognized as the Godhead. Arjuna has treated Him as a man and overlooked His divinity; so he now asks His forgiveness:

सखेति मत्वा प्रसभं यदुक्तं
हे कृष्ण हे यादव हे सखेति।
अजानता महिमानं तवेदं
मया प्रमादात्प्रणयेन वापि॥४१॥

यच्चावहासार्थमसत्कृतोऽसि
विहारशय्यासनभोजनेषु।
एकोऽथवाप्यच्युत तत्समक्षं
तत्क्षामये त्वामहमप्रमेयम्॥४२॥

41-42. Whatever I have rashly said from inadvertence or love, addressing Thee as "O Kṛṣṇa," "O Yādava," or "O Friend," regarding Thee merely as a friend, unaware of Thy greatness; and in whatever other ways I may have shown disrespect to Thee while playing or resting, while sitting or eating, while alone, O Eternal Lord, or in the presence of others—all that I implore Thee, O Immeasurable, to forgive.

Thy greatness—The Universal Form.

पितासि लोकस्य चराचरस्य
त्वमस्य पूज्यश्च गुरुर्गरीयान्।
न त्वत्समोऽस्त्यभ्यधिकः कुतोऽन्यो
लोकत्रयेऽप्यप्रतिमप्रभाव॥४३॥

43. Thou art the Father of the world—of all that move and all that do not move. Thou art the object of its worship, its most venerable Teacher. There is no one equal to Thee; how then, in the three worlds, could there be another superior to Thee, O Thou of incomparable might?

तस्मात्प्रणम्य प्रणिधाय कायं
प्रसादये त्वामहमीशमीड्यम्।
पितेव पुत्रस्य सखेव सख्युः
प्रियः प्रियायार्हसि देव सोढुम्॥४४॥

44. Therefore I bow down and prostrate my body before Thee, the adorable Lord, and seek Thy grace. Bear with me, O Lord, as a father with a son, as a friend with a friend, as a lover with his beloved.

अदृष्टपूर्वं हृषितोऽस्मि दृष्ट्वा
भयेन च प्रव्यथितं मनो मे।
तदेव मे दर्शय देव रूपं
प्रसीद देवेश जगन्निवास॥४५॥

किरीटिनं गदिनं चक्रहस्तं
इच्छामि त्वां द्रष्टुमहं तथैव।
तेनैव रूपेण चतुर्भुजेन
सहस्रबाहो भव विश्वमूर्ते॥४६॥

45-46. I rejoice that I have seen what was never seen before; but my mind is also troubled with fear. Show me that other form of Thine. Be gracious, O Lord of gods, O Abode of the universe. I would see Thee as before, with Thy crown and Thy mace and the discus in Thy hand. Assume again Thy four-armed shape, O Thou of a thousand arms and of endless. shapes.

Thy four-armed shape—Śrī Kṛṣṇa is none other than the Lord Viṣṇu. His divine form has four arms, holding a conch, a discus, a mace, and a lotus. That form He now and then reveals to His devotees. Arjuna always cherishes it in his heart, though Kṛṣṇa moves in the world as an ordinary mortal with two arms.

The Universal Form of the Lord, embodying the gods, the demons, and the different forces of Nature, and also revealing the terror of destruction, is, for the ordinary mind, overwhelming, appalling, incommunicable. The reason may seek the vastness, omnipresence, omnipotence, and completeness of the Godhead, but the heart wants a tender manifestation that is capable of loving and being loved in return. Therefore the Lord assumes, for the sake of His devotees, a humanized form. It is this mediating aspect—Nārāyaṇa, the God-man—that reassures and soothes the hungry soul of the devotee. It makes the Lord close, intimate, visible, and living. The devotee establishes with this humanized symbol a tender, human relationship and regards it as Father, Mother, Friend, Companion, or Beloved. At the wish of the devotee the Lord withdraws the human form and reveals to him His impersonal and universal aspect.

To allay Arjuna's fear Śrī Kṛṣṇa assumes His usual form and consoles him:

श्रीभगवानुवाच।
मया प्रसन्नेन तवार्जुनेदं
रूपं परं दर्शितमात्मयोगात्।
तेजोमयं विश्वमनन्तमाद्यं
यन्मे त्वदन्येन न दृष्टपूर्वम्॥४७॥

47. *The Lord said:* By My grace, through My own yoga-power, O Arjuna, I have shown you this supreme form, resplendent, universal, infinite, and primeval, which none but you has ever seen.

My grace—Because Arjuna is the beloved devotee of Kṛṣṇa. The revelation of the Lord depends on His grace alone; man cannot force it by his own efforts.

Yoga-power—The lordly power inherent in the Godhead.

Arjuna must consider himself highly blessed for having seen the Universal Form.

न वेदयज्ञाध्ययनैर्न दानै-
र्न च क्रियाभिर्न तपोभिरुग्रैः।
एवंरूपः शक्य अहं नृलोके
द्रष्टुं त्वदन्येन कुरुप्रवीर॥४८॥

48. Neither by the study of the Vedas and sacrifices, nor by gifts, nor by rituals, nor by severe penances, is this form of Mine to be seen in the world of men by anyone but you, O chief of the Kurus.

By human endeavour through knowledge, austerities, sacrifice, and self-denial one can see a particular aspect of the Godhead. But Arjuna has seen the Lord in His Universal Form, reconciling all the aspects of divinity at one and the same time and in one and the same vision. In an ineffable oneness are revealed all the facets of the Godhead—spirit and matter, being and becoming, creation and destruction, infinite and finite, space and time, past and future. This vision is vouchsafed only to the devotee who adores the Lord with single-minded, all-consuming, and unswerving love.

मा ते व्यथा मा च विमूढभावो
दृष्ट्वा रूपं घोरमीदृङ्ममेदम्।
व्यपेतभीः प्रीतमनाः पुनस्त्वं
तदेव मे रूपमिदं प्रपश्य॥४९॥

49. Be not afraid, be not bewildered, on seeing this terrific form of Mine. Free from fear and glad at heart, behold again My other form.

My other form—Which is so dear to Arjuna. This form of the Lord has four arms.

सञ्जय उवाच।
इत्यर्जुनं वासुदेवस्तथोक्त्वा
स्वकं रूपं दर्शयामास भूयः।

आश्वासयामास च भीतमेनं
भूत्वा पुनः सौम्यवपुर्महात्मा ॥५०॥

50. *Sañjaya said:* Having thus addressed Arjuna, Vāsudeva revealed to him His own form. The Great One assumed a graceful shape again and comforted the terrified Pāṇḍava

Graceful shape—The human shape that Arjuna cherishes in his heart.

अर्जुन उवाच।
दृष्ट्वेदं मानुषं रूपं तव सौम्यं जनार्दन।
इदानीमस्मि संवृत्तः सचेताः प्रकृतिं गतः ॥५१॥

51. *Arjuna said:* Looking at this gentle form of Yours, O Janārdana, I now feel composed in mind; I am myself again.

The bhaktas, or lovers of God, do not like to dwell on His impersonal and transcendental form. As long as they live in a human body, they desire to worship a Personal God through love.

श्रीभगवानुवाच।
सुदुर्दर्शमिदं रूपं दृष्टवानसि यन्मम।
देवा अप्यस्य रूपस्य नित्यं दर्शनकाङ्क्षिणः ॥५२॥

52. *The Lord said:* It is very hard to see this form of Mine, which you have seen. Even the gods are ever eager to see this form.

The gods may desire to see the Universal Form of the Lord, but they cannot see it. According to the Hindu religion, the gods pass their time in the heavenly realm enjoying intense and refined material pleasures. In order to experience the boon of liberation they have to be born again on earth as men.

नाहं वेदैर्न तपसा न दानेन न चेज्यया।
शक्य एवंविधो द्रष्टुं दृष्टवानसि मां यथा ॥५३॥

53. Neither by the Vedas, nor by penances, nor by alms-giving, nor yet by sacrifice, am I to be seen in the form in which you have now beheld Me.

How can one see the Lord's Universal Form?

भक्त्या त्वनन्यया शक्य अहमेवंविधोऽर्जुन।
ज्ञातुं द्रष्टुं च तत्त्वेन प्रवेष्टुं च परन्तप ॥५४॥

54. But by devotion to Me alone may I be known in this form, O Arjuna, realized truly, and entered into, O dreaded prince.

Devotion to Me alone—Love that seeks nothing but the Lord and that makes the devotee see the Lord alone through all the senses. Such unswerving love removes all distinctions between the devotee and the Lord and enables the former, if he desires, to enjoy the Knowledge of Brahman.

May I be known etc.—As declared in the scriptures.

Realized truly—By means of direct and immediate perception.

Entered into—The devotee attains final liberation in the Lord after giving up the body.

The essential teaching of the Gītā, which leads to the highest bliss, is now summed up:

मत्कर्मकृन्मत्परमो मद्भक्तः सङ्गवर्जितः ।
निर्वैरः सर्वभूतेषु यः स मामेति पाण्डव ॥५५॥

55. He who does My work and looks on Me as the Supreme Goal, who is devoted to Me, who is without attachment and without hatred for any creature—he comes to Me, O Pāṇḍava

Does My work—That is to say, dedicates all works to the Lord and seeks no reward for himself.

Without attachment—To relatives, wealth, and so on, though he may have to live in their midst.

Without hatred—Even for those who may do him harm.

Comes to Me—Uninterruptedly enjoys the Lord as long as he lives and afterwards becomes one with Him.

ॐ तत्सदिति श्रीमद्भगवद्गीतासूपनिषत्सु
ब्रह्मविद्यायां योगशास्त्रे श्रीकृष्णार्जुनसंवादे
विश्वरूपदर्शनयोगो नामैकादशोऽध्यायः ॥११॥

Thus in the Bhagavad Gītā, the Essence of the Upaniṣads, the Science of Brahman, the Scripture of Yoga, the Dialogue between Śrī Kṛṣṇa and Arjuna, ends the Eleventh Chapter, entitled: THE VISION OF THE UNIVERSAL FORM

CHAPTER 12

THE WAY OF DIVINE LOVE

[भक्तियोगः]

अर्जुन उवाच।

एवं सततयुक्ता ये भक्तास्त्वां पर्युपासते।
ये चाप्यक्षरमव्यक्तं तेषां के योगवित्तमाः ॥ १ ॥

1. *Arjuna said:* Those devotees who, ever steadfast, worship You after this fashion, and those others who worship the Imperishable and Unmanifest—which of these have greater knowledge of yoga?

Ever steadfast—Always united with the Lord through actions performed for the Lord's sake. These devotees have the Lord alone for their support. They constantly meditate on His manifested Universal Form and work as His instruments, surrendering the results to Him.

After this fashion—Referring to the last verse of the preceding chapter (XI, 55).

Those others etc.—Referring to the saṃnyasis, who renounce all desires and actions in order to realize their oneness with Brahman.

Worship—The word is used here in the sense of meditation or contemplation. It is obvious that worship implying a subject and object cannot be applied to the aspirant seeking the Knowledge of Brahman.

Unmanifest—Inapprehensible by the senses, since Brahman is devoid of all upādhis, or limiting adjuncts.

Aspirants can meditate on the Godhead in two ways. The devotees of the Impersonal Brahman regard It as the incomprehensible, indefinable, formless, relationless, actionless, featureless, attributeless, and transcendental Absolute. The devotees of the Personal God regard the Godhead as the Lord of the universe, the Supreme Person, the Creator, Preserver, and Destroyer, the omniscient and omnipresent Lord, endowed with the Universal Form and possessed of the great powers of yoga. The Absolute never puts on any form, abstains from all action, enters into no relation with the universe, and is eternally silent and immutable; but the Personal God is our Lord and Master, the Source and Origin of all beings, immanent in all things, manifest in both nature and living beings as their inmost Self. Both these aspects of the Godhead have been described by Kṛṣṇa in the Gītā, though with an emphasis on the Impersonal aspect in Chapters Two through Ten. The eleventh chapter deals with the Universal Form of the Godhead and ends with an exhortation to Arjuna to worship It as the Lord of the universe. Now Arjuna asks which of the two methods of worship is better: meditation on the Impersonal or worship of the Lord through work and love.

श्रीभगवानुवाच।

मय्यावेश्य मनो ये मां नित्ययुक्ता उपासते।
श्रद्धया परयोपेताः ते मे युक्ततमा मताः ॥२॥

2. *The Lord said:* Those who have fixed their minds on Me, and who, ever steadfast and endowed with supreme faith, worship Me—them do I hold to be perfect in yoga.

Me—The Universal Form, which reveals the Godhead as the Supreme Lord of the universe.

Ever steadfast—As described in the last verse of the eleventh chapter.

Supreme faith—By which one sees God in all beings and also in the Absolute.

Worship Me—As the omniscient Lord, free from attachment, aversion, and other evil passions.

Them do I hold etc.—Because they pass their days and nights in the uninterrupted thought of the Lord.

No real contrast is meant between the worshippers of the Personal God and the Impersonal Brahman, as will be explained later on.

Are not the others, then, perfect in yoga? The Lord says that there cannot be any question of their realization of the Godhead:

ये त्वक्षरमनिर्देश्यमव्यक्तं पर्युपासते।
सर्वत्रगमचिन्त्यञ्च कूटस्थमचलन्ध्रुवम्॥३॥

सन्नियम्येन्द्रियग्रामं सर्वत्र समबुद्धयः।
ते प्राप्नुवन्ति मामेव सर्वभूतहिते रताः॥४॥

3-4. And those who have completely controlled their senses and are of even mind under all conditions and thus worship the Imperishable, the Ineffable, the Unmanifest, the Omnipresent, the Incomprehensible, the Immutable, the Unchanging, the Eternal—they, devoted to the welfare of all beings, attain Me alone, and none else.

Those Referring to the all-renouncing saṃnyāsīs.

Under all conditions—Whether they meet with agreeable or disagreeable conditions, because they see the Lord in everything.

Worship—That is to say, meditate on Brahman, in accordance with the instructions of the scriptures and the teacher, and dwell uninterruptedly in the current of that one thought. An apt illustration is the unbroken stream of oil when it is poured from one vessel to another.

Immutable—The word "Kūṭastha" in the text means He who dwells in māyā as its Witness, Substratum, and Lord.

Attain Me alone etc.—It needs no emphasizing that the devotees of the Impersonal realize the Godhead alone. It is not necessary to reiterate that they are perfect yogis, since they are one with the Lord Himself. "The man endowed with wisdom I deem to be My very Self." (VII, 18)

But the path of the Personal God is easier for the majority of men.

क्लेशोऽधिकतरस्तेषामव्यक्तासक्तचेतसाम्।
अव्यक्ता हि गतिर्दुःखं देहवद्भिरवाप्यते॥५॥

5. The task of those whose minds are set on the Unmanifest is more difficult; for the ideal of the Unmanifest is hard to attain for those who are embodied.

Unmanifest—The indefinable and incomprehensible Absolute.

Is more difficult—Those who seek the Absolute follow a more difficult discipline than the worshippers of the Personal God. The former must practise utmost self-control, renounce the world outwardly and inwardly, wipe out all human emotion and desire, and still the mind in the contemplation of the Absolute. The worshippers of the Personal God have a tangible Ideal of the Lord, to whom they can direct their emotion and love.

Those who are embodied—Those who are conscious of their bodies and attached to them.

Obviously no contrast is meant between the followers of the attributeless Absolute and the worshippers of the Personal God, since both attain the same goal. The path of the Absolute is more difficult; for it requires the complete abandonment of all attachment to the body. The followers of the other path regard their bodies as instruments of God and perform their duties dedicating the results to Him. A devotee conscious of his body and ego cannot easily fix his mind on the Absolute. The more a man realizes himself to be incorporeal Spirit, the easier it becomes for him to think of the Lord as Spirit and Consciousness.

There are two classes of spiritual seekers. Some like to retain their egos, which have been purified by the love and knowledge of God, establish a relationship with the Lord, and enjoy communion with Him through meditation, worship, and service of His devotees. They regard the world and all beings as manifestations of the Lord. They follow the path of affirmation. There are others, however, who desire completely to merge their egos in the Absolute. They follow the steep path of renunciation and denial. Their spiritual discipline culminates in their absorption in what is known as nirvikalpa samādhi, a transcendental experience in which the individual soul becomes one with Brahman. It is said in the Hindu scriptures that, in the case of an ordinary mortal, after that all-annihilating experience the body drops off like a dead leaf. But a few special souls, such as an Incarnation of God and His intimate disciples, can return to the relative plane of consciousness after the attainment of nirvikalpa samādhi and live in the world for the fulfilment of a divine mission. While dealing with the world they feel the presence of an "ego," which is, however, unlike an ordinary ego, because it has been purged of worldliness by the Knowledge of God. Through this "pure ego" they establish an intimate relationship with the Lord and enjoy the company of His devotees. But whenever they want, they can merge themselves in the Absolute. They live in the borderland between the Relative and the Absolute. Looking up, they realize the featureless and attributeless Brahman, and looking down, they see the universe of name and form filled with the essence of the Lord.

Both classes of aspirants, the worshippers of the Personal God and the devotees of the Absolute, transcend the sorrow and suffering of the relative world and enjoy the bliss of communion with the Godhead.

Different kinds of liberation are described in the Hindu scriptures. One is called *sājujya mukti*, a state of liberation. in which the individual soul becomes totally unified with the Godhead, no trace of individuality being left. This liberation is sought by the jñānī, the follower of the path of knowledge. In the following kinds of liberation the individuality of the soul is retained though it is completely purged of its earthly nature. Attaining *sālokya mukti*, the devotee dwells eternally in the highest heaven with the Lord. In *sāmīpya mukti*, the devotee always enjoys the nearness of the Lord, his Beloved. Realizing *sārṣṭi mukti*, the devotee attains equality with the Lord in power and all the divine attributes. The dualists seek one of these three forms of liberation. Peace, blessedness, joy, immortality, absence of worldliness, and freedom from relativity characterize all the forms of liberation.

The worshippers of the Universal Form easily attain perfection through the Lord's grace.

ये तु सर्वाणि कर्माणि मयि संन्यस्य मत्पराः।
अनन्येनैव योगेन मां ध्यायन्त उपासते॥ ६॥

तेषामहं समुद्धर्ता मृत्युसंसारसागरात्।
भवामि नचिरात्पार्थ मय्यावेशितचेतसाम्॥ ७॥

6-7. But those who consecrate all their actions to Me, regarding Me as the Supreme Goal, and who worship Me, meditating on Me with single-minded concentration—to them, whose minds are thus absorbed in Me, verily I become ere long, O Pārtha the Saviour from the death-fraught ocean of the world.

Me—The Lord of the universe.

Single-minded concentration—Because to them the Lord alone is real and the world illusory.

Death-fraught—Life in the world is only another phase of death.

Ocean of the world—It is as hard to cross the world as it is to cross the ocean.

The disciplines of the followers of the Absolute consist in discrimination and renunciation, and also in learning the Truth from the teacher and the scriptures, and reasoning, and contemplation. The devotees of the Universal Form worship the Lord with love, dedicate all actions to Him, and meditate on Him with unswerving devotion. These latter, through the Lord's grace, very soon attain liberation from the suffering and death of mortal life,

Therefore,

मय्येव मन आधत्स्व मयि बुद्धिं निवेशय।
निवसिष्यसि मय्येव अत ऊर्ध्वं न संशयः॥८॥

8. Fix your mind on Me alone, rest your thought on Me alone, and in Me alone you will live hereafter. Of this there is no doubt.

Mind—The internal organ of knowledge that thinks about the pros and cons of a matter.

Me—The Lord in His Universal Form.

Thought—The word in the text is "buddhi," which means the determinative faculty, by which doubt created by the mind is destroyed and a decision arrived at.

Hereafter After the death of the body. If a devotee, while alive, thinks of the Lord alone with all his heart and soul, he attains Him after death.

The Lord suggests a simple discipline for those who cannot follow the hard path:

अथ चित्तं समाधातुं न शक्नोषि मयि स्थिरम्।
अभ्यासयोगेन ततो मामिच्छाप्तुं धनञ्जय॥९॥

9. If you are unable to fix your mind steadily on Me, O Dhanañjaya, then seek to reach Me by the yoga of constant practice.

The yoga of constant practice—Practice consists in withdrawing the thought from all objects and fixing it, again and again, on one ideal. The "yoga of constant practice" means the steadfastness of mind acquired by such practice.

If a devotee finds it impossible to fix his mind on the Universal Form, he is asked to worship a tangible symbol, such as an image of God, and meditate on it in his heart, and thus through repeated practice acquire a steadiness of thought that can be directed to the Lord.

अभ्यासेऽप्यसमर्थोऽसि मत्कर्मपरमो भव।
मदर्थमपि कर्माणि कुर्वन्सिद्धिमवाप्स्यसि॥१०॥

10. If you are incapable of constant practice, then devote yourself to My service. For even by rendering service to Me you will attain perfection.

My service—Such external forms of worship as repeating the name and the glories of the Lord, listening to His glories sung by others, observing fasts and other austerities, showing reverence to His images, and offering the Lord flowers, food, perfume, and so on; or the service of the Lord may mean any action that is done for His sake only. Through such service purity of mind is attained, which is followed by steadiness, knowledge of the Lord, and realization of Him.

अथैतदप्यशक्तोऽसि कर्तुं मद्योगमाश्रितः।
सर्वकर्मफलत्यागं ततः कुरु यतात्मवान्॥ ११॥

11. If you are unable to do even this, then be self-controlled, surrender the fruit of all action, and take refuge in Me.

Be self-controlled—Control the lower self, or the ego, which craves the fruit of action.

Surrender the fruit etc.—If the devotee does not seek the fruit of action, his mind remains free to remember the Lord.

The practice of indifference to the fruit of action and its surrender to the Lord set the devotee on the spiritual path.

The yoga of desireless action is extolled:

श्रेयो हि ज्ञानमभ्यासाज्ज्ञानाद्ध्यानं विशिष्यते।
ध्यानात्कर्मफलत्यागस्त्यागाच्छान्तिरनन्तरम्॥ १२॥

12. Knowledge is better than practice, and meditation is better than knowledge. Renunciation of the fruit of action is better than meditation; peace immediately follows such renunciation.

Knowledge—Of the truth behind things.

Practice The act of listening to the teachings of the scriptures with a view to obtaining knowledge; or the word may mean the practice of meditation with a firm resolve. Knowledge is better than mere practice that is not accompanied with discrimination.

Meditation is better etc.—Meditation based on knowledge is superior to mere knowledge.

Renunciation of the fruit etc.—When a devotee, practising self-control and seeking refuge in the Lord, renounces the fruit of action, he immediately attains inner calm and peace. For one tranquil in heart the cessation of ignorance comes without delay.

The abandonment of the fruit of action, taught as a means to Divine Bliss, applies to an ignorant person who, unable to follow the paths recommended before, engages in work. This abandonment is extolled in the text because the path of action is intended to be taught here. The renunciation of desires brings peace immediately to the ignorant person engaged in work, and also to the enlightened aspirant who is steadily devoted to meditation. Therefore the renunciation of desires is a common factor in the attainment of peace both for the ignorant and for the enlightened, and hence is extolled by Śrī Kṛṣṇa.

Two methods of worship have been discussed: the worship of the Universal Form and the worship of the immutable Absolute. The former, meant for the beginner, emphasizes action for the Lord's sake and presupposes a distinction between the Lord and the individual soul. The Lord is the deliverer of these worshippers. The other method of worship is meant for the jñānīs, who do not see any distinction between the Lord and the individual soul. They do not depend on any external being for their liberation, since they realize that the whole universe lies in the Self. These two paths of worship are different, though in the long run they bring the same result of liberation to their respective followers. Behind the immutable Absolute and the Universal Form lies the same Godhead. The following verses describe the attributes of the worshippers of the Absolute through which they directly attain immortality. Only the all-renouncing saṃnyāsīs can practise these virtues in full.

अद्वेष्टा सर्वभूतानां मैत्रः करुण एव च।
निर्ममो निरहङ्कारः समदुःखसुखः क्षमी॥१३॥

सन्तुष्टः सततं योगी यतात्मा दृढनिश्चयः।
मय्यर्पितमनोबुद्धिर्यो मद्भक्तः स मे प्रियः॥१४॥

13-14. He who never hates any being and is friendly and compassionate to all, who is free from the feelings of "I" and "mine" and even—minded in pain and pleasure, who is forbearing, ever content, and steady in contemplation, who is self-controlled and possessed of firm conviction, and who has consecrated his mind and understanding to Me—dear to Me is the one who is thus devoted to Me.

Never hates any being—Even those who cause him pain; for he regards all creatures as himself.

Friendly and compassionate to all—He, a saṃnyāsī, has given assurance of fearlessness to all. In his heart a universal love dwells, and from it a universal compassion flows.

Even-minded etc.—Pain and pleasure do not cause in him hatred and attachment.

Ever content—He is satisfied, whether he obtains the means of bodily sustenance or not.

Firm conviction—Regarding the essential nature of the Self.

He is a soul of peace with whom all are at peace.

यस्मान्नोद्विजते लोको लोकान्नोद्विजते च यः।
हर्षामर्षभयोद्वेगैर्मुक्तो यः स च मे प्रियः॥१५॥

15. He by whom the world is not afflicted and whom the world cannot afflict, he who is free from joy and anger, fear and anxiety—he is dear to Me.

Who is free etc.—Because he is detached from his constantly agitated lower nature, he is free from its waves of joy, fear, anxiety, anger, and desire, and is the embodiment of calm.

अनपेक्षः शुचिर्दक्ष उदासीनो गतव्यथः।
सर्वारम्भपरित्यागी यो मद्भक्तः स मे प्रियः॥१६॥

16. He who is free from dependence, who is pure and prompt, unconcerned and untroubled, and who has renounced all undertakings—dear to Me is the man who is thus devoted to Me.

Dependence—Upon the body, the senses, objects, and their mutual connections.

Pure—Both outwardly and inwardly. Outward purity is obtained through washing, and inward purity through self-control. Patanjali states that an aspirant desirous of attaining inner purity should show friendship toward the happy, mercy toward the unhappy, gladness toward the good, and indifference toward the evil.

Prompt—Able to decide rightly and instantly about matters demanding immediate action. The word may also mean vigilant.

Unconcerned—Impartial even in the affairs of a friend.

All undertakings—Calculated to secure objects of desire, whether of this world or the next; all egotistic and personal initiative. A devotee lets the divine will flow through him undeflected by his own desires and preferences; and yet for that very reason he is swift and skillful in all actions. The divine will and intelligence working through him enable him to accomplish all actions rightly and promptly.

यो न हृष्यति न द्वेष्टि न शोचति न काङ्क्षति।
शुभाशुभपरित्यागी भक्तिमान्यः स मे प्रियः ॥ १७॥

17. He who rejoices not and hates not, who grieves not and desires not, who has renounced both good and evil and is full of devotion—he is dear to Me.

Rejoices not—On attaining what is desirable.

Hates not—The undesirable.

Grieves not—On parting with a beloved object.

Desires not—The unattained.

Renounced both good and evil—Because a devotee regards all things coming from God as good.

The Lord stresses sameness, desirelessness, and freedom from the claims of the lower egotistic nature as the foundation of spiritual life:

समः शत्रौ च मित्रे च तथा मानापमानयोः।
शीतोष्णसुखदुःखेषु समः सङ्गविवर्जितः ॥ १८॥

तुल्यनिन्दास्तुतिर्मौनी सन्तुष्टो येन केनचित्।
अनिकेतः स्थिरमतिर्भक्तिमान्मे प्रियो नरः ॥ १९॥

18-19. He who is alike to foe and friend, unaltered in honour and dishonour; who is the same in cold and heat, in pleasure and pain; who is free from attachment, who is unchanged by praise and blame; who is silent, content with whatever he has, homeless, firm of mind, and full of devotion—that man is dear to Me.

Alike to foe and friend etc.—It is a man's attachment to worldly things that fosters the idea of enmity, friendship, etc.

The same in cold and heat etc.—These pairs affect worldly persons alone.

Content with whatever he has—Content with the bare means of sustenance.

The enumeration of the virtues of a saṃnyāsī is concluded:

ये तु धर्म्यामृतमिदं यथोक्तं पर्युपासते।
श्रद्दधाना मत्परमा भक्तास्तेऽतीव मे प्रियाः ॥२०॥

20. Exceedingly dear to Me are they who regard Me as the Supreme Goal and, endowed with faith and devotion, follow this Immortal Dharma.

This Immortal Dharma—The law of life that confers upon its follower the boon of Immortality, and that has been described above, beginning with XII, 13.

Since he who practises the virtues described in XII, 13, and the following verses is exceedingly dear to the Lord, they should be cherished by all seekers of liberation and all those who desire to enjoy the supreme Blessedness.

ॐ तत्सदिति श्रीमद्भगवद्गीतासूपनिषत्सु
ब्रह्मविद्यायां योगशास्त्रे श्रीकृष्णार्जुनसंवादे
भक्तियोगो नाम द्वादशोऽध्यायः ॥१२॥

Thus in the Bhagavad Gītā, the Essence of the Upaniṣads, the Science of Brahman, the Scripture of Yoga, the Dialogue between Śrī *Kṛṣṇa and Arjuna, ends the Twelfth Chapter, entitled:* THE WAY OF DIVINE LOVE

Chapter 13

THE DISCRIMINATION BETWEEN MATTER AND SPIRIT

[क्षेत्रक्षेत्रज्ञविभागयोगः]

अर्जुन उवाच।

प्रकृतिं पुरुषं चैव क्षेत्रं क्षेत्रज्ञमेव च।
एतद्वेदितुमिच्छामि ज्ञानं ज्ञेयं च केशव॥१॥

1. *Arjuna said:* Prakṛti and Puruṣa, the Field and the Knower of the Field, knowledge and that which is to be known—all this, O Keśava, I desire to learn.

This verse is omitted in many editions of the Gītā.

All material bodies, sense-organs, and sense-objects are made of Prakṛti—Nature, or matter. The aggregate of the body and the senses serves a twofold purpose for living beings: enjoyment of sense-objects and attainment of liberation. This aggregate is now described:

श्रीभगवानुवाच।

इदं शरीरं कौन्तेय क्षेत्रमित्यभिधीयते।
एतद्यो वेत्ति तं प्राहुः क्षेत्रज्ञ इति तद्विदः॥२॥

2. *The Lord said:* This body, O son of Kuntī, is called the Field, and he who knows it is called the Knower of the Field by those who describe them.

Body—To be described in verses 5 and 6 of this chapter.

Field—The word in the text is "kṣetra," which signifies both "body" and "matter." The body is called "field" because the fruits of action are reaped in it as in a field, or because it is subject to decay,

Knows it—As distinct from the Self, or Spirit.

Knower of the Field—The word in the text is "Kṣetrajña," which means the individual soul, which is, in reality, one with the Supreme Soul.

In the seventh chapter Śrī Kṛṣṇa described the two prakṛtis of the Lord. The inferior prakṛti, or matter, consists of three guṇas and is divided into eight parts; it entangles the Spirit in the world. The three guṇas are sattva, rajas, and tamas. The superior prakṛti is the individualized soul (jīva), who is the Knower of the Field and, in reality, one with the Lord Himself. Through these two prakṛtis the Supreme Lord creates, sustains, and ultimately dissolves the universe. The thirteenth chapter proposes to describe the two prakṛtis—the Field and the Knower of the Field—in order to determine finally the nature of the Supreme Lord Himself.

क्षेत्रज्ञं चापि मां विद्धि सर्वक्षेत्रेषु भारत।
क्षेत्रक्षेत्रज्ञयोर्ज्ञानं यत्तज्ज्ञानं मतं मम॥३॥

3. And know that I am the Knower in all Fields, O Bhārata; and only the knowledge of the Field and its Knower do I regard as true knowledge.

I—The Supreme Lord.

Knowledge of the Field and its Knower—Knowledge of matter and Spirit.

We see innumerable living beings, ranging from the highest Cosmic Person, or Brahmā, to the meanest worm, dwelling in numberless bodies or "fields." They are the knowers of their respective bodies. These living beings perform various actions, good or bad, and experience their results. They are subject to bondage; through spiritual discipline they ultimately attain liberation. But according to Vedānta the individualized soul is really one with the Supreme Lord. Through ignorance the Supreme Lord, birthless and deathless, becomes associated with the manifold upādhis, or limitations, of bodies. From the standpoint of knowledge, the Knower of the Field is the Supreme Lord and not the *saṃsārī*, or individualized soul, entangled in the world. Though the Supreme Lord, as the Knower of the Field, dwells in all bodies, yet He is not affected by the traits of these bodies, such as birth, growth, decay, death, and so on; for the idea of His being associated with the body is due to ignorance. Not a single grain of sand in the desert is made wet by all the waters of the mirage one sees there through ignorance. The terms "bondage" and "liberation" cannot be ascribed to the Lord, though it is He alone who dwells in the body. They are used with reference to the individual soul, who is created by ignorance and falsely called the Master, or Knower, of the Field, the body.

The salient points of the topics to be discussed:

तत्क्षेत्रं यच्च यादृक्च यद्विकारि यतश्च यत्।
स च यो यत्प्रभावश्च तत्समासेन मे शृणु॥४॥

4. Hear briefly from Me what the Field is, what its nature is, what its modifications are, whence it comes, who its Knower is, and what His powers are.

Inspired and intuitive knowledge, as also reason and philosophy, have described the nature of Spirit and matter.

ऋषिभिर्बहुधा गीतं छन्दोभिर्विविधैः पृथक्।
ब्रह्मसूत्रपदैश्चैव हेतुमद्भिर्विनिश्चितैः॥५॥

5. All this has been sung by sages in many and different ways, in various distinctive hymns, and also in well reasoned and convincing passages indicative of Brahman.

In many and different ways—In various treatises on yoga.

Hymns—Of the Vedas.

The Field is described:

महाभूतान्यहङ्कारो बुद्धिरव्यक्तमेव च।
इन्द्रियाणि दशैकं च पञ्च चेन्द्रियगोचराः॥६॥

इच्छा द्वेषः सुखं दुःखं सङ्घातश्चेतना धृतिः।
एतत्क्षेत्रं समासेन सविकारमुदाहृतम्॥७॥

6-7. The great elements, I-consciousness, understanding, and the unmanifested; the ten senses, the mind, the five objects of the senses;

Desire, hatred, pleasure, pain, the aggregate, intelligence, and fortitude—this, briefly stated, is the Field together with its modifications.

Great elements—The five bhūtas—ether, air, fire, water, and earth—in their subtle form as originally evolved. They pervade all the modifications of matter. *See* note on VII, 4.

I-consciousness—The cause of the five elements.

Understanding—The word "buddhi" in the text is defined as the determining faculty. It is the cause of I-consciousness.

Unmanifested—The word in the text is "avyakta." It is the energy, or śakti, of the Lord, spoken of in VII, 14.

Ten senses—Five organs of perception and five organs of action. The former consist of ears, eyes, nose, tongue, and skin. The latter consist of hands, feet, vocal organ, and the organs of evacuation and generation.

Mind—The inner organ, whose functions are doubt and volition.

Five objects of the senses—Sound and the rest. They comprise the five gross elements.

Desire—This is a property of the antaḥkaraṇa, the inner Sense-organ.

Hatred, pleasure, pain—These belong to the category of matter because they are objects of knowledge.

Aggregate—The combination of the body and the senses.

Intelligence—A mental state that manifests itself in the aggregate. It is a reflection of Ātman, or Consciousness, and is material in nature, for it is knowable. One is aware of the presence or absence of intelligence.

Fortitude—A state of mind by which the depressed body and mind are upheld. It is also material in nature, for it is an object of knowledge. One is conscious of its presence or absence. According to Vedānta the knower, or subject, is Spirit, and the object of knowledge is matter.

The five great elements, I-consciousness (ahaṅkāra), understanding (buddhi), and the unmanifested (avyakta) are known as Prakṛti or Nature, with its eightfold division.

The categories beginning with the great elements and ending in the five objects of the senses comprise the twenty-four cosmic principles of Sāṅkhya philosophy.

The categories beginning with desire and ending in fortitude are described by Vaiśeṣika philosophy as the attributes of Ātman. But according to Vedānta they are the attributes. of matter.

Matter, or the Field, referred to in the first verse of this chapter as the body, is thus described with all its modifications.

It will be said presently that through a knowledge of the powers of the Knower of the Field, or the Supreme Lord, immortality is attained. Aspirants must cultivate certain virtues in order to be qualified for the knowledge of the Lord, who alone is the object of knowledge. These virtues, described below, are designated as knowledge because they are the means of attaining Knowledge.

अमानित्वमदम्भित्वमहिंसा क्षान्तिरार्जवम्।
आचार्योपासनं शौचं स्थैर्यमात्मविनिग्रहः॥८॥

इन्द्रियार्थेषु वैराग्यमनहङ्कार एव च।
जन्ममृत्युजराव्याधिदुःखदोषानुदर्शनम्॥९॥

असक्तिरनभिष्वङ्गः पुत्रदारगृहादिषु।
नित्यं च समचित्तत्वमिष्टानिष्टोपपत्तिषु॥१०॥

मयि चानन्ययोगेन भक्तिरव्यभिचारिणी।
विविक्तदेशसेवित्वमरतिर्जनसंसदि॥११॥
अध्यात्मज्ञाननित्यत्वं तत्त्वज्ञानार्थदर्शनम्।
एतज्ज्ञानमिति प्रोक्तमज्ञानं यदतोऽन्यथा॥१२॥

8-12. Humility, modesty, non-violence, forbearance, and uprightness; service to the teacher, purity, steadfastness, and self-control;

Dispassion toward sense-objects, absence of ego, perception of the evil of birth, death, old age, sickness, and pain;

Non-attachment, non-identification of self with children, wife, home, and the rest, unvarying evenness of mind in the midst of agreeable and disagreeable events;

Unswerving devotion to Me through constant meditation on non-separation, resorting to solitude, aversion to the society of men;

Constancy in the knowledge of the Self, and an insight into the object of the knowledge of Truth—this is declared to be knowledge, and all that is contrary to it is ignorance,

Forbearance—Not being affected when injured by others.

Teacher—Who teaches the means of attaining liberation.

Dispassion toward sense-objects—Toward objects seen or heard of.

Old age—The evil of old age consists in the decay of intelligence, power, and strength.

Pain—Whether arising from factors inherent in oneself or caused by an external agent or produced by supernatural forces. From the perception of the evil of pain in birth, death, and the rest, arises indifference to physical pleasures. Then the senses are directed toward the inmost Self for a glimpse of the Divine Light. The perception of the evil of pain in birth, death, and so on, is spoken of as knowledge because such perception leads to the Knowledge of Reality. According to the materialistic point of view, life in the world, in spite of its many dark shadows, is worth while; but according to the spiritual point of view, life as we lead it in the world is a sorry thing, though it brings us many illusory and transient joys.

Non-identification of self etc.—An intense attachment to son, wife, and so on, makes one feel happy or miserable when they are happy or miserable.

Unvarying evenness of mind etc.—Due to the consciousness that the Self, dwelling within, is impervious to the shocks of external events.

Meditation on non-separation—A steady, unwavering meditation on the Lord with the idea that there is no being higher and therefore He is our sole Refuge.

Solitude—A wood, the sand—bank of a river, or a temple is generally helpful for the practice of meditation.

Society of men—Unenlightened and undisciplined worldly people.

Constancy in the knowledge of the Self—To meditate on transient phenomena is to accept mortality. The soul, a victim of appearance, misses its divine nature and goes on whirling about in the cycle of births and deaths of its bodies.

Insight into the object etc.—The end of knowledge is mokṣa, the cessation of mortal existence; it is the attainment of immortality.

All that is contrary etc.—Such as pride, hypocrisy, cruelty, impatience, insincerity, and the like. All this is ignorance and therefore should be avoided as tending to the perpetuation of saṃsāra.

What is it that is realized through the knowledge described above?

ज्ञेयं यत्तत्प्रवक्ष्यामि यज्ज्ञात्वामृतमश्नुते।
अनादिमत्परं ब्रह्म न सत्तन्नासदुच्यते॥ १३॥

13. I will now describe that which ought to be known, through the knowing of which one attains Immortality. It is the Supreme Brahman,

which is without beginning and is said to be neither being nor non-being.

It is stated in the text that Brahman cannot be described as "being" or "non-being." Sat, or "being," is used with reference to an object that can be proved to exist by words or the senses. An object the existence of which cannot be proved by words or the senses is "asat," or "non-being." Thus a pot can be an object of consciousness accompanied with the idea of existence (when it stands before a man), or an object of consciousness accompanied with the idea of nonexistence (when it is removed). Brahman is beyond the reach of the senses. It cannot be, like a pot, an object of consciousness accompanied with the idea of either existence or non-existence, and therefore It is said to be neither "being" nor "non-being." Brahman can be known through the evidence of the scriptures, which is based on the direct and intuitive experience of the seer.

Brahman cannot be denoted by such a word as "sat," or "being"; for a word employed to denote a thing signifies the thing as associated with a certain *genus* (such as cow or horse), a certain *quality* (such as *black* or *white)*, a certain *act* (such as to *cook* or *to teach*), or a certain *mode of relation* (such as *landlord* or *cattleman*). Brahman is inexpressible by words because It belongs to no genus and because It is devoid of action, qualities, and relations.

Brahman, being inaccessible to word or thought, might be regarded as asat, or non-being. To prevent this mistake the Lord proceeds to declare Its reality as manifested through the upādhis, the senses of living beings. Brahman exists as the inmost Self of all, as the source of all activities of the senses, as the source whence arises our consciousness of existence with reference to all illusory objects in the relative world, and as the Lord of the universe. There must be a self-conscious principle behind the activities of insentient objects such as the body and senses.

सर्वतः पाणिपादं तत्सर्वतोऽक्षिशिरोमुखम्।
सर्वतः श्रुतिमल्लोके सर्वमावृत्य तिष्ठति॥ १४॥

14. Its hands and feet are everywhere; Its eyes, heads, and faces are everywhere; Its ears are everywhere; Its existence envelops all.

Its existence envelops all—Brahman pervades all beings as existence and consciousness.

That Brahman exists is indicated by the activity of the sense—organs; for there must be consciousness behind their functioning. The sense-organs act in virtue of the mere presence of Brahman, or consciousness. Matter, or the Field (kṣetra)—consisting of body, sense-organs, and so on—is the upādhi, or limiting adjunct, of Brahman, or the Knower of the Field. The manifold, falsely imagined in Brahman, or Spirit, owing to the variety of the upādhis, is illusory. Hands, feet, and so on, are ascribed to Brahman in a figurative sense. Through them Its existence is indicated. Brahman is taught by the method of superimposition and negation; that is to say, upādhis are falsely superimposed upon It and then negated through the process of discrimination, revealing Pure Consciousness.

It must not be supposed that Brahman is really endowed with the upādhis, or limitations, of body, sense-organs, and the rest. They are merely superimposed upon It.

सर्वेन्द्रियगुणाभासं सर्वेन्द्रियविवर्जितम्।
असक्तं सर्वभृच्चैव निर्गुणं गुणभोक्तृ च॥ १५॥

15. It shines through the functions of all the senses, and yet It is devoid of senses. It is unattached, and yet It sustains all. It is devoid of guṇas, and yet It enjoys them.

It shines through the functions etc.—The term "senses," which comprises the organs of both perception and action, includes as well the mind and intelligence (buddhi), which also form upādhis of Brahman. Brahman manifests Itself through the upādhis of the outer and inner senses, that is to say, through their functions, viz., determination, purposes, thoughts, hearing, speech, and the like. Brahman functions, *as it were*, through the functions of all the senses. This functioning of Brahman is an appearance. It does not actually function when the senses function. "Though without hands and feet, yet It moves swiftly and It grasps. It sees without the eye. It hears without the ear." (*Śvetāśvatara Upaniṣad*, III, 19)

It is unattached—Because Brahman is incorporeal.

It sustains all—Brahman permeates all objects as "sat," Existence. No object can be imagined to exist without "Existence." Even an illusion must have a basis for its existence. A mirage cannot exist without the basis of the desert. Hence Brahman sustains all illusory objects.

It is devoid of guṇas etc.—The guṇas belong to Prakṛti or matter. Brahman is free from them. Yet the experience of the guṇas, in the form of sound and other objects, by the soul is possible because it is animated by consciousness, which is the very nature of Brahman. Therefore the existence of Brahman is indicated from the experience of objects by the individualized soul. That Brahman enjoys the guṇas is used in a figurative sense.

Further,

बहिरन्तश्च भूतानामचरं चरमेव च।
सूक्ष्मत्वात्तदविज्ञेयं दूरस्थं चान्तिके च तत्॥ १६ ॥

16. It is without and within all beings. It is unmoving and also moving. It is incomprehensible because It is subtle. It is far away, and yet It is near.

Without and within—It is both the external body and the inmost Self. As gold forms the, outside and inside of a gold ornament, or as water forms the outside and inside of a wave, so Brahman pervades the inside and outside of the macrocosm and the microcosm.

Unmoving and also moving—The moving and unmoving objects form the upādhis of Brahman. Just as a rope may appear as a snake, so Brahman appears as both moving and unmoving bodies.

Subtle—Beyond the reach of the senses.

Far away—To the unenlightened, who imagine It to be millions of miles away and unknowable even through the efforts of billions of years.

It is near—To the enlightened, for they realize It to be the inmost Self of all.

Brahman is the one Spirit in all and the Cause of the universe.

अविभक्तं च भूतेषु विभक्तमिव च स्थितम्।
भूतभर्तृ च तज्ज्ञेयं ग्रसिष्णु प्रभविष्णु च॥ १७ ॥

17. It is indivisible, and yet It is, as it were, divided among beings. That Knowable Brahman is the Sustainer of all beings, and also their Devourer and Generator.

It is indivisible, and yet It is etc.—An instance of this is ākāśa, or space, which, though indivisible, appears to be divided according to its association with various upādhis, such as a jar, a pot, or a pitcher. Thus one speaks of the space inside a jar or the space inside a pot. Sky-scrapers also seem to divide the indivisible sky. Though Brahman is one and indivisible, yet It appears to be different in different bodies.

Knowable—A reference to verse 12.

Sustainer—During the period when the universe is sustained.

Devourer—At the time of dissolution.

Generator—At the time of creation, or manifestation.

The illusion of a snake is produced by the presence of a rope; the snake is seen to exist because the rope is there; and it ultimately merges in the rope when the real nature of the object is known. So also all the beings of the universe come from Brahman at the time of creation, are sustained by It at the time of preservation, and merge in It at the time of destruction. As in the case of the illusion of the snake in the rope all that is real is the rope, so in this illusory universe all that is real is Brahman.

An objection may be raised that Brahman is darkness, inasmuch as It is not perceived though existing everywhere. It is not so. Brahman is the Illuminer of all.

ज्योतिषामपि तज्ज्योतिस्तमसः परमुच्यते ।
ज्ञानं ज्ञेयं ज्ञानगम्यं हृदि सर्वस्य विष्ठितम् ॥ १८ ॥

18. The Light even of lights, It is said to be beyond darkness. As knowledge, the object of knowledge, and the goal of knowledge, It is set firm in the hearts of all.

The Light even of lights—The existence of Brahman can be recognized as the Light illumining the sun, moon, and so on, and also the mind, reason (buddhi), and the rest. "That Light illumined by which the sun shines." (*Taittirīya Brāhmaṇa.*) "By Its light all this shines." (Śvetāśvatara *Upaniṣad*, VI, 14)

Beyond darkness—Uncontaminated by ajñāna, or nescience.

Goal of knowledge—When Brahman is realized, It forms the fruit of knowledge.

Set firm in the hearts of all—These three (knowledge, the object of knowledge, and the goal of knowledge) are implanted pre—eminently in the heart of every living being. There alone they are clearly manifested. Brahman is within everyone; It is not merely in heaven.

The topic is concluded:

इति क्षेत्रं तथा ज्ञानं ज्ञेयं चोक्तं समासतः ।
मद्भक्त एतद्विज्ञाय मद्भावायोपपद्यते ॥ १९ ॥

19. Thus briefly have been set forth the Field and also knowledge and the object of knowledge. My devotee who understands this becomes worthy of My state.

Field—Described in verses 5-6.

Knowledge—Described in verses 7-11.

Object of knowledge—Described in verses 12-17.

My devotee—Who regards the Supreme Lord as the soul of everything and who knows that all that one sees or hears or touches is the Lord.

My state—The ultimate liberation.

One who understands the Field, knowledge, and the object of knowledge knows the whole doctrine of the Vedas and the Gītā.

The two prakṛtis of the Lord, the superior and the inferior, have been described in the seventh chapter. It has also been said that all created beings are born of them. (VII, 6) *This subject is further elucidated:*

प्रकृतिं पुरुषं चैव विद्ध्यनादी उभावपि।
विकारांश्च गुणांश्चैव विद्धि प्रकृतिसम्भवान्॥२०॥

20. Know that Prakṛti and Puruṣa are both without beginning; and know, too, that all forms and guṇas are born of Prakṛti

Prakṛti—Inert Nature, or matter.

Puruṣa—Soul, or Spirit, as opposed to matter.

Without beginning—Prakṛti and Puruṣa are the two aspects, or natures, of Īśvara, the Lord. As the Lord is without beginning, so His natures, too, are without beginning. His very Lordship consists in His possessing these two natures, Prakṛti and Puruṣa, by which He creates, preserves, and dissolves the universe.

Forms—From intelligence (buddhi) down to the gross body.

Guṇas—Sattva, rajas, and tamas, which manifest themselves in the form of pleasure, pain, delusion, and so on.

Are born of Prakṛti—Prakṛti is māyā, the śakti, or power, of the Lord. It is the cause of the manifestation of the relative universe. Since Prakṛti or māyā, is the eternal source of all forms and guṇas, Brahman remains ever changeless and immutable.

The functions of Prakṛti and Puruṣa:

कार्यकारणकर्तृत्वे हेतुः प्रकृतिरुच्यते।
पुरुषः सुखदुःखानां भोक्तृत्वे हेतुरुच्यते॥२१॥

21. Prakṛti is said to be the cause of the generation of the body and the organs, and Puruṣa is said to be the cause of the experience of pleasure and pain.

Cause—Because Prakṛti is the material from which the body and the organs are produced. Kapila and other philosophers hold this opinion.

Body—The five elements out of which the body is made, and the five sense-objects, are included under the term "body," or "kārya," used in the text.

Organs—These are thirteen, namely, the five organs of perception, the five organs of action, the mind, intelligence (buddhi), and I-consciousness (ahaṅkāra). Pleasure, pain, delusion, and the rest, which are born of the three guṇas of Prakṛti are included under the term "organs" (karaṇa), since they cannot exist independently of the sense-organs.

Puruṣa—It is synonymous with jīva (the individualized soul), Kṣetrajña (the Knower of the Field), and bhoktā (the enjoyer). Obviously the Puruṣa does not here signify the Paramātman, or Highest Self. It is here an intelligent principle and a conditioned being.

Puruṣa and Prakṛti are stated to be the cause of saṃsāra, or phenomenal existence. Prakṛti transforms itself into body and senses, as also into pleasure, pain, and so on, and Puruṣa experiences pleasure and pain. This conjunction between Puruṣa and Prakṛti—due to ignorance—makes relative life possible. Even though the Puruṣa, the Soul, identifies Himself with the body and appears to experience pleasure and pain, yet in reality He remains unchanging. It is this apparent experience which constitutes His illusory world, or saṃsāra, and which makes Him a saṃsārī, or phenomenal being.

How does the birthless and immutable Ātman experience pleasure and pain?

पुरुषः प्रकृतिस्थो हि भुङ्क्ते प्रकृतिजान्गुणान्।
कारणं गुणसङ्गोऽस्य सदसद्योनिजन्मसु॥ २२॥

22. Puruṣa, embodied in Prakṛti experiences the guṇas born of Prakṛti It is attachment to these guṇas that is the cause of His birth in good and evil wombs.

Puruṣa, embodied in Prakṛti—It is due to avidyā, ignorance, that the Puruṣa identifies Himself with the body and senses, which are the transformations of Prakṛti

Experiences the guṇas—The guṇas manifest themselves. as pleasure, pain, and delusion. On account of identification with Prakṛti the Puruṣa thinks He is happy, miserable, deluded, wise, and so on.

It is attachment etc.—Identification with pleasure, pain, and delusion is responsible for the Puruṣa's birth in good and evil bodies.

Good and evil wombs—Good wombs are those of gods and the like; evil wombs are those of lower animals.

Avidyā, or ignorance, and kāma, or attachment to the guṇas, together constitute the cause of saṃsāra, or relative existence. The aspirant seeking liberation should avoid them both. Ignorance is to be removed by knowledge, the knowledge of the Field and the Knower of the Field as imparted in the beginning of the chapter. Attachment is to be destroyed by cultivating vairagya, or dispassion. To renounce the illusory world is the injunction of the Gītā.

Puruṣa is entangled in the world on account of His ignorance. But this entanglement is only apparent and not real. His real nature is described:

उपद्रष्टानुमन्ता च भर्ता भोक्ता महेश्वरः ।
परमात्मेति चाप्युक्तो देहेऽस्मिन्पुरुषः परः ॥ २३ ॥

23. The Supreme Spirit in the body is said to be the one who is the Witness and the Approver, the Supporter and the Enjoyer, and who is the Sovereign Lord and the Highest Self.

Witness—The word "upadraṣṭā" in the text technically signifies an expert in a sacrificial act, who sits by the side. of the priests and the sacrificer but does not take an active part in the sacrifice. He merely witnesses what is right or wrong in the actions of the sacrificer and the priests.

Approver—The Self expresses approbation or satisfaction concerning the actions of the body, senses, mind, and the rest. Being a witness, It does not stand in the way of the body and senses engaged in their respective activities.

Supporter—The Self is called the Supporter because the body, senses, mind, and the rest, reflect Its intelligence and thus perform activities to serve the purpose of the individualized self.

Enjoyer—The Self is called the Enjoyer for the following reason: It is of the nature of eternal Intelligence. All the different states of mind—characterized by pleasure, pain, or delusion become manifest on account of the intelligence of the Self.

Sovereign Lord—As one with the universe and independent of everything.

Highest Self—It is called the highest because It is superior to body, senses, mind, and all material adjuncts. The topic will be further discussed in XV, 17.

The result of Self-knowledge:

य एवं वेत्ति पुरुषं प्रकृतिं च गुणैः सह।
सर्वथा वर्तमानोऽपि न स भूयोऽभिजायते॥२४॥

24. He who thus knows Puruṣa and Prakṛti along with the guṇas, is not born again, howsoever he may comport himself.

Thus knows Puruṣa—As his very Self and as the basic Reality underlying all manifestations, such as the universal or the individual soul,

And Prakṛti—As indefinable and beginningless nescience, which is destroyed by the Knowledge of the Self.

Is not born again—The absence of Self-knowledge is the cause of embodiment.

Howsoever he may etc.—Whether he is engaged in prescribed duties or in those forbidden by law. If liberation is possible for such a person, then it goes without saying that one who stands firm in the path of duty obtains liberation if he has also been endowed with Self-knowledge.

Different paths lead to Self-knowledge. However arrived at, this Knowledge carries us beyond death to Immortality.

ध्यानेनात्मनि पश्यन्ति केचिदात्मानमात्मना।
अन्ये साङ्ख्येन योगेन कर्मयोगेन चापरे॥२५॥

25. Some by meditation perceive the Self in themselves through the mind, some by devotion to knowledge, and some by devotion to work.

By meditation etc.—This path is followed by the highest class of aspirants. Meditation is defined as withdrawing the hearing, seeing, and the functioning of the other senses into the mind away from sound, form, and other objects; next withdrawing the mind into the inmost Intelligence; and then contemplating the Intelligence with undeviating concentration. Meditation is continuous thinking, and the mind of one absorbed in it, like an unbroken stream of flowing oil, dwells on the ideal uninterruptedly. Through meditation the yogi beholds the Self, the inmost Intelligence, in the self, the buddhi, by the self, or mind, refined and made one-pointed by contemplation and self-control.

Devotion to knowledge—The word "sāṅkhya in the text denotes knowledge attained through philosophical discrimination between the Self and Nature. The yogis devoted to the path of knowledge realize that Ātman is distinct from Nature and its three guṇas and is the detached Witness of their actions.

Devotion to work—Which consists in performing action. for the satisfaction of the Lord alone. Through such unselfish action the mind becomes pure and the aspirant ultimately attains Knowledge.

The paths of meditation, knowledge, and work are prescribed for the three classes of aspirants, namely, the superior, mediocre, and inferior.

The path of liberation for those aspirants who are of very low understanding:

अन्ये त्वेवमजानन्तः श्रुत्वान्येभ्य उपासते।
तेऽपि चातितरन्त्येव मृत्युं श्रुतिपरायणाः ॥ २६ ॥

26. And there are yet some who do not know It by these means. They hear of It from others and worship. They too pass beyond death through their devotion to what they have heard.

It—The Self.

From others—From teachers or holy men, who tell them the method of meditation.

Worship—In full faith.

Death—Life in the world is inseparable from death.

They are ignorant and for the attainment of liberation depend entirely on the authority of others' instructions. They too succeed.

It has been stated that the knowledge of the identity of the individual soul and the Lord leads to liberation. The reason is stated:

यावत्सञ्जायते किञ्चित्सत्त्वं स्थावरजङ्गमम्।
क्षेत्रक्षेत्रज्ञसंयोगात्तद्विद्धि भरतर्षभ ॥ २७ ॥

27. Whatever is born—whether animate or inanimate—know, O Bhārata prince, that it is through union of the Field and the Knower of the Field.

Union—What is the nature of this union between the Field and the Knower of the Field, matter and Spirit, body and Soul? Matter and Spirit are entirely opposed to each other in nature; Spirit is incorporeal. Hence the union between them is not like the union between two material objects. Vedānta philosophy describes the relationship between matter and Spirit, or object and Subject, by the term "adhyāsa," which means "false superimposition of one thing upon another." The attributes of matter are superimposed upon Spirit and *vice versa*. This superimposition is due to māyā, or absence of discrimination. It is like the illusion of a snake in a rope, or a mirage in the desert. In such illusions the attributes of the snake or the mirage are superimposed upon the rope and the desert. This unreal relationship, created by ignorance, conjures up before our vision the manifold of the relative world.

Now a description is given of right knowledge, which destroys ignorance, the cause of embodiment, and enables one to attain liberation:

समं सर्वेषु भूतेषु तिष्ठन्तं परमेश्वरम्।
विनश्यत्स्वविनश्यन्तं यः पश्यति स पश्यति॥२८॥

28. He who sees the Supreme Lord abiding alike in all beings, and not perishing when they perish—verily he alone sees.

Abiding alike—As Sat, or Reality.

All beings—From the highest deity to a grain of sand. The same Divine Spirit dwells in all. The material form is only a mask. The difference between one object and another, from the relative standpoint, lies in the degree of manifestation of the Spirit. In a saint this Spirit is highly manifested, and in a lowly object It is hidden.

The result of right knowledge:

समं पश्यन्हि सर्वत्र समवस्थितमीश्वरम्।
न हिनस्त्यात्मनात्मानं ततो याति परां गतिम्॥२९॥

29. Because he sees the Lord present alike everywhere, he does not injure Self by self, and thus he reaches the supreme state.

An ignorant person does not see the Self in others and, owing to false knowledge, regards the non-Self (such as body and mind) as the Self. Identifying the true Self with the body, he engages in good and evil actions and is born again and again to reap their results. Thus through ignorance he repeatedly injures his Self by identifying it with a new body. Through right knowledge he sees the Self as detached from the body and thus attains supreme liberation.

How can the one Lord abide alike in all beings, since they, endowed with different qualities, act in different ways?

प्रकृत्यैव च कर्माणि क्रियमाणानि सर्वशः।
यः पश्यति तथात्मानमकर्तारं स पश्यति॥३०॥

30. He who sees that all actions are done only by Prakṛti and that the Self is actionless—verily, he alone sees.

Prakṛti—The māyā, or śakti, or power, of the Lord, transformed into body, senses, and so on.

Realization of the unity of existence leads to the attainment of Brahman.

यदा भूतपृथग्भावमेकस्थमनुपश्यति।
तत एव च विस्तारं ब्रह्म सम्पद्यते तदा॥३१॥

31. When he sees that the manifold nature of beings is centred in the One and that all evolution is from that One alone, he becomes one with Brahman.

Manifold nature of beings etc.—All the various classes of beings abide in Brahman, or the Self. This is the realization of the essential unity of the universe and the Self.

All evolution is from that etc.—Compare: "From the Self is life, from the Self is desire, from the Self is love, from the Self is ākāśa, from the Self is light, from the Self are the waters, from the Self is manifestation and disappearance, from the Self is the soul." (*Chāndogya Upaniṣad,* VII, xxvi, 1)

Becomes one with Brahman—He realizes the all-pervading nature of the Self because the cause of all limitation has been destroyed by the knowledge of unity with Brahman.

This verse refutes the view of Sāṅkhya philosophy that Nature, or Prakṛti and its manifestations are quite distinct. from Puruṣa, or Spirit, and that Prakṛti exists independent. of Puruṣa.

If the Supreme Lord is the self of all embodied beings, how can He be unaffected by their physical traits?

अनादित्वान्निर्गुणत्वात्परमात्मायमव्ययः।
शरीरस्थोऽपि कौन्तेय न करोति न लिप्यते॥३२॥

32. Having no beginning and possessing no guṇas, this supreme and imperishable Self, O son of Kuntī, neither acts nor is stained by action even while dwelling in the body.

Having no beginning—Being without any cause.

Imperishable—Because It is without parts and qualities.

Stained by action—That is to say, affected by the fruit of action. This is due to the fact that the Lord is not the doer of action.

If the Spirit dwelling in the body does not act and is not tainted by the result of action, then, it may be asked, who is the agent of the action and the reaper of its fruit? There is no embodied self distinct from the Supreme Lord, and the Supreme Lord is actionless. The answer is: It is Prakṛti that acts. (V, 14) Through illusion arises the idea of the action, the doer, and the result of action. No action really exists in the Supreme Lord. From the standpoint of Reality there exists neither good nor evil. When the knowledge of the unity of the Lord and the universe is veiled by ignorance, there arises the idea of the pairs of opposites, and also the idea of action characterized by agency, instrument, and result.

An illustration:

यथा सर्वगतं सौक्ष्म्यादाकाशं नोपलिप्यते।
सर्वत्रावस्थितो देहे तथात्मा नोपलिप्यते॥ ३३॥

33. As the ākāśa that pervades all things is not stained, because of its subtlety, even so the Self dwelling in the body everywhere is not stained.

The ākāśa, or ether, is so subtle that it pervades all things without obstruction and is not affected by the good or evil qualities of the objects it pervades. Likewise, the Supreme Self, dwelling in the bodies of gods and angels, men and animals, plants and stones, is not affected by their natural qualities.

The illuminer is not affected by the objects It illumines.

यथा प्रकाशयत्येकः कृत्स्नं लोकमिमं रविः।
क्षेत्रं क्षेत्री तथा कृत्स्नं प्रकाशयति भारत॥ ३४॥

34. As the one sun illumines the whole world, so does He who dwells in the body, O Bhārata, illumine the whole body.

By the illustration of the sun it is shown that, like the sun, the Self is one and unsoiled, that is to say, untouched by the traits of those It illumines.

The chapter is concluded:

क्षेत्रक्षेत्रज्ञयोरेवमन्तरं ज्ञानचक्षुषा।
भूतप्रकृतिमोक्षं च ये विदुर्यान्ति ते परम्॥ ३५॥

35. They who perceive with the eye of wisdom this distinction between the Field and the Knower of the Field, and also the deliverance from Prakṛti the cause of all beings—they attain the Supreme.

Eye of wisdom—Self-knowledge,

Prakṛti—Avidyā, or ignorance, which is the material cause of all beings.

The means of deliverance from ignorance are meditation, renunciation, and other spiritual disciplines.

ॐ तत्सदिति श्रीमद्भगवद्गीतासूपनिषत्सु
ब्रह्मविद्यायां योगशास्त्रे श्रीकृष्णार्जुनसंवादे
क्षेत्रक्षेत्रज्ञविभागयोगो नाम त्रयोदशोऽध्यायः॥ १३॥

Thus in the Bhagavad Gītā, the Essence of the Upaniṣads, the Science of Brahman, the Scripture of Yoga, the Dialogue between Śrī *Kṛṣṇa and Arjuna, ends the Thirteenth Chapter, entitled:* THE DISCRIMINATION BETWEEN MATTER AND SPIRIT

CHAPTER 14

THE DISCRIMINATION OF THE THREE GUṆAS

[गुणत्रयविभागयोगः]

श्रीभगवानुवाच।

परं भूयः प्रवक्ष्यामि ज्ञानानां ज्ञानमुत्तमम्।
यज्ज्ञात्वा मुनयः सर्वे परां सिद्धिमितो गताः ॥ १ ॥

1. *The Lord said:* Once more I will expound that Supreme Knowledge, the most exalted of all forms of knowledge, by gaining which all the sages have attained highest perfection after passing from this world.

From this world—From the bondage of the body.

The connexion with the preceding chapter is this: It has been stated that matter and Spirit—both dependent on the Lord—are the cause of the universe. The soul, on account of its attachment to the guṇas, is born in various bodies, good or bad. The fourteenth chapter deals with the guṇas.

इदं ज्ञानमुपाश्रित्य मम साधर्म्यमागताः।
सर्गेऽपि नोपजायन्ते प्रलये न व्यथन्ति च ॥ २ ॥

2. They who, having devoted themselves to this Knowledge, have partaken of My nature, are not born at the time of creation, nor are they troubled at the time of dissolution.

Creation—The appearance of a new cycle.

Dissolution—The end of a cycle, when names and forms merge in Prakṛti It is a temporary pause followed by a new evolution. All the bound souls go into a sleep state during the dissolution and are born in new bodies during the new creation according to their past action.

The union of matter and Spirit, under the control of the Supreme Lord, causes the birth of all beings. The view of Sāṅkhya philosophy that they can create independently of the Lord is refuted.

मम योनिर्महद् ब्रह्म तस्मिन्गर्भं दधाम्यहम्।
सम्भवः सर्वभूतानां ततो भवति भारत॥३॥

3. The Great Nature is My womb; in that I place the germ, and thence are born all beings, O Bharata.

Great Nature—The Great Nature, or Prakṛti or māyā ("Brahma" in the text), is an aspect of the Lord and inheres in Him.

Germ—The seed that impregnates the Great Nature and gives rise to Hiraṇyagarbha, the Golden Egg, which in turn produces all beings. During the period of dissolution the soul (Kṣetrajña), still under the influence of nescience, remains merged in Prakṛti At the time of the next creation the Lord endows the soul with a reflection of His Intelligence and unites it with an appropriate body determined by its past karma.

The Lord is the Father and Mother of the universe. Matter and Spirit are His two aspects and inhere in Him. As the Over-soul, He casts the seed; as the Mother, the Nature-soul, He receives it. From the embryo thus formed, from Hiraṇyagarbha, are produced all created beings.

Not only at the beginning of a cycle does the Lord unite matter and Spirit in order to cause the birth of created beings, but of every birth that takes place on earth He is the ultimate cause.

सर्वयोनिषु कौन्तेय मूर्तयः सम्भवन्ति याः।
तासां ब्रह्म महद्योनिरहं बीजप्रदः पिता॥४॥

4. Whatever form is produced, O son of Kuntī, in any womb, the Great Nature is its womb, and I am the seed-giving Father.

Whatever form—Pertaining to gods, angels, men, animals, birds, or trees.

Created beings are produced from the union of Puruṣa and Prakṛti by the power of the Lord. The Soul, or Spirit, becomes entangled in the world by its contact with the body, or matter.

सत्त्वं रजस्तम इति गुणाः प्रकृतिसम्भवाः।
निबध्नन्ति महाबाहो देहे देहिनमव्ययम्॥५॥

5. The guṇas—sattva, rajas, and tamas—which are born of Prakṛti bind fast in the body the immortal, embodied soul, O mighty Arjuna.

Guṇas—*See* note on II, 45.

Bind fast—The bondage of the soul is not real; for the soul, in reality, is ever free.

Embodied soul—He who dwells in the body and appears to be identified with it.

The nature of sattva and the way it binds:

तत्र सत्त्वं निर्मलत्वात्प्रकाशकमनामयम्।
सुखसङ्गेन बध्नाति ज्ञानसङ्गेन चानघ॥६॥

6. Of these, sattva, being stainless, is luminous and healthful. It binds, O sinless Arjuna, by creating attachment to happiness and attachment to knowledge.

Stainless—Because through sattva one can destroy the deluding power of māyā.

Luminous—On account of its purity, sattva is the perfect mirror to reflect spiritual bliss.

Healthful—Of the nature of peace and serenity.

A man under the influence of sattva becomes attached to happiness and knowledge and says, "I am happy; I have attained knowledge." Happiness and knowledge are attributes of mind, which is a form of matter. They belong to the category of the object and pertain to the kṣetra. (XIII, 6) The Self, which is of the nature of freedom and totally unattached, becomes bound by identification with matter. This is how sattva binds a soul to the world.

The nature of rajas and how it binds:

रजो रागात्मकं विद्धि तृष्णासङ्गसमुद्भवम्।
तन्निबध्नाति कौन्तेय कर्मसङ्गेन देहिनम्॥७॥

7. Know that rajas is the essence of passion and the cause of thirst and attachment. It binds fast the embodied soul, O son of Kuntī, by attachment to action.

The essence of passion—Like a dye, it stains the stainless. soul and makes it appear permeated with desires.

Action—Productive of visible and invisible results. It is thirst and attachment that impel a worldly person to action. Thirst is directed to an object not yet attained, and attachment, to what has already been attained.

Though the Self is actionless, yet rajas makes It feel, "I am the doer."

The nature of tamas and how it binds:

तमस्त्वज्ञानजं विद्धि मोहनं सर्वदेहिनाम्।
प्रमादालस्यनिद्राभिस्तन्निबध्नाति भारत॥८॥

8. And know further that tamas is born of ignorance and that it deludes all embodied creatures. It binds fast, O Bhārata, by inadvertence, indolence, and sleep.

Ignorance—The veiling power of māyā. The other power of māyā is the projecting power, which functions mainly through rajas. Māyā is armed with these two powers.

Under the influence of tamas one becomes inattentive, slothful, and inert.

The respective functions of the three guṇas:

सत्त्वं सुखे सञ्जयति रजः कर्मणि भारत।
ज्ञानमावृत्य तु तमः प्रमादे सञ्जयत्युत॥९॥

9. Sattva binds one to happiness, and rajas to action, O Bharata; whereas tamas veils knowledge and binds one to inadvertence.

Through the influence of sattva man feels happy in spite of the presence of grief and suffering; through the influence of rajas man is impelled to action in spite of his being happy; through the influence of tamas man is deprived of the power of discrimination and neglects his imperative duties.

How do the guṇas function in an individual?

रजस्तमश्चाभिभूय सत्त्वं भवति भारत।
रजः सत्त्वं तमश्चैव तमः सत्त्वं रजस्तथा॥१०॥

10. Sattva asserts itself by prevailing over rajas and tamas, O Bhārata; rajas asserts itself by prevailing over sattva and tamas; and tamas asserts itself by prevailing over sattva and rajas.

When one of the guṇas prevails over the other two, it produces its own effect. Thus sattva produces knowledge and happiness, rajas causes attachment and impels one to action, and tamas veils discrimination and causes inertia and inadvertence.

What is the characteristic mark by which to know that sattva is predominant?

सर्वद्वारेषु देहेऽस्मिन्प्रकाश उपजायते।
ज्ञानं यदा तदा विद्याद्विवृद्धं सत्त्वमित्युत॥ ११॥

11. When the light of knowledge shines through all the gateways of the body, then it may be known that sattva has prevailed.

Gateways—That is to say, the senses, which are, for the soul, the gateways of perception.

The cultivation of sattva is, no doubt, the highest virtue in the relative world. But it must not be mistaken for liberation, or the Highest Good, which consists in transcending all the guṇas. If too much cherished, sattva soon degenerates into rajas and tamas, which are always present, in however small proportion, along with sattva.

The characteristic marks of predominant rajas:

लोभः प्रवृत्तिरारम्भः कर्मणामशमः स्पृहा।
रजस्येतानि जायन्ते विवृद्धे भरतर्षभ॥ १२॥

12. Greed, activity, enterprise, unrest, longing—these arise, O lord of the Bhāratas, when rajas prevails.

The characteristic marks of predominant tamas:

अप्रकाशोऽप्रवृत्तिश्च प्रमादो मोह एव च।
तमस्येतानि जायन्ते विवृद्धे कुरुनन्दन॥ १३॥

13. Darkness, indolence, inadvertence, delusion—all these arise, O descendant of Kuru, when tamas prevails.

Darkness—Absence of discrimination.

Life after death is influenced by the guṇas.

यदा सत्त्वे प्रवृद्धे तु प्रलयं याति देहभृत्।
तदोत्तमविदां लोकानमलान्प्रतिपद्यते॥ १४॥

14. If the embodied soul meets with death when sattva prevails, it goes to the spotless realms of those who know the Highest.

Spotless realms—The exalted heavens where tamas and rajas can never assert themselves.

Who know the Highest—Who worship such deities as Hiraṇyagarbha and Brahmā.

रजसि प्रलयं गत्वा कर्मसङ्गिषु जायते।
तथा प्रलीनस्तमसि मूढयोनिषु जायते॥ १५॥

15. If the embodied soul meets with death when rajas prevails, it is born among those who are attached to action; and if it meets with death when tamas prevails, it is born in the wombs of creatures devoid of reason.

Those who are attached to action—That is to say, men.

Creatures devoid of reason—Beasts and the like.

A summary of the preceding verses:

कर्मणः सुकृतस्याहुः सात्त्विकं निर्मलं फलम्।
रजसस्तु फलं दुःखमज्ञानं तमसः फलम्॥ १६॥

16. The fruit of a good action is said to be good and clean; the fruit of rajas is pain; and the fruit of tamas is ignorance,

Good action—An action characterized by sattva.

The happiness that accrues from sattva is a reflection of the Bliss of Brahman.

The functions of the guṇas are summed up:

सत्त्वात्सञ्जायते ज्ञानं रजसो लोभ एव च।
प्रमादमोहौ तमसो भवतोऽज्ञानमेव च॥ १७॥

17. From sattva springs knowledge, and from rajas, greed; from tamas spring inadvertence, delusion, and ignorance.

From sattva springs knowledge—It is for this reason that the fruit of action influenced by sattva is characterized by happiness. This knowledge is only a means to the attainment of Self-knowledge.

From rajas, greed—It is for this reason that the fruit of action influenced by rajas bears pain.

ऊर्ध्वं गच्छन्ति सत्त्वस्था मध्ये तिष्ठन्ति राजसाः।
जघन्यगुणवृत्तिस्था अधो गच्छन्ति तामसाः ॥ १८ ॥

18. Those who are established in sattva go upward; those who are moved by rajas remain in the middle; and those who are steeped in tamas, being weighted by the tendencies of the lowest guṇa, go downward.

Upward—Into the realms of higher beings.

In the middle—Among men.

Tendencies of the lowest guṇa—Such as inertia, indolence, and so on.

Downward—To the level of beasts.

Through different births the Spirit experiences pleasure, pain, and delusion on account of Its attachment to the three guṇas. Liberation is possible only through right knowledge, which is now taught:

नान्यं गुणेभ्यः कर्तारं यदा द्रष्टानुपश्यति।
गुणेभ्यश्च परं वेत्ति मद्भावं सोऽधिगच्छति ॥ १९ ॥

19. When a man of insight beholds no agent other than the guṇas, and also knows Him who is beyond the guṇas, he attains My being.

No agent other than the guṇas—It is the guṇas that transform themselves into bodies, senses, and sense-objects. The agent, the instrument, and the result of action are only modifications of the guṇas and belong to Prakṛti

Him—The Lord, who dwells in man as his inmost Self. He is the Witness of the guṇas and their functions.

Attains My being—Then his identity with Brahman becomes manifest.

The result of detachment from the guṇas is the attainment of Immortality.

गुणानेतानतीत्य त्रीन्देही देहसमुद्भवान्।
जन्ममृत्युजरादुःखैर्विमुक्तोऽमृतमश्नुते ॥ २० ॥

20. When the embodied soul has risen above the three guṇas of which its body is made, it gains deliverance from birth, death, old age, and pain and becomes immortal.

Has risen above—That is to say, while living in the body.

Gains deliverance—Even before giving up the body.

अर्जुन उवाच।

कैर्लिङ्गैस्त्रीन्गुणानेतानतीतो भवति प्रभो।
किमाचारः कथं चैतांस्त्रीन्गुणानतिवर्तते॥२१॥

21. *Arjuna said*: What are the marks, O Lord, of the man who has risen above the three guṇas? What is his conduct? And how does he rise above the guṇas?

श्रीभगवानुवाच।

प्रकाशं च प्रवृत्तिं च मोहमेव च पाण्डव।
न द्वेष्टि सम्प्रवृत्तानि न निवृत्तानि काङ्क्षति॥२२॥

उदासीनवदासीनो गुणैर्यो न विचाल्यते।
गुणा वर्तन्त इत्येवं योऽवतिष्ठति नेङ्गते॥२३॥

समदुःखसुखः स्वस्थः समलोष्टाश्मकाञ्चनः।
तुल्यप्रियाप्रियो धीरस्तुल्यनिन्दात्मसंस्तुतिः॥२४॥

मानापमानयोस्तुल्यस्तुल्यो मित्रारिपक्षयोः।
सर्वारम्भपरित्यागी गुणातीतः स उच्यते॥२५॥

22-25. *The Lord said:* He who hates not light, activity, and delusion when they are present, nor longs for them, O Pāṇḍava when they are absent;

He who, sitting like one unconcerned, is unmoved by the guṇas, who remains firm and never wavers, knowing that the guṇas alone are active;

He who dwells in the Self and regards alike pleasure and pain, who looks on a clod, a stone, and a piece of gold as of equal worth, who remains the same amidst agreeable and disagreeable things, who is a man of wisdom, and who sees no difference between praise and blame;

He who is the same in honour and dishonour, the same to friend and foe, and who has renounced all undertakings—such a man is said to have risen above the guṇas.

Light—The effect of sattva.

Activity—The effect of rajas.

Delusion—The effect of tamas.

He who hates not light etc.—The man of right knowledge does not hate the effects of the three guṇas when they clearly present themselves as objects of consciousness, nor does he long for them when they have disappeared. This answers Arjuna's first question. These are marks that others cannot perceive; they can be perceived only by the individual in whom they appear. No man can perceive the hatred or desire that presents itself to another man's consciousness.

The guṇas alone are active—Since the guṇas transform themselves into body, senses, and objects, all actions are only the functioning of the guṇas. The Self is the detached Witness.

Has renounced all undertakings—He initiates no action, but leaves all works to be done by the guṇas.

These attributes, described in XIV, 22-25, have to be acquired by special effort prior to the attainment of Self-knowledge. The aspirant for Self-knowledge should therefore cultivate these virtues, as they are the means of attaining it. But on the birth of Self-knowledge, when the aspirant has become a jīvanmukta, liberated while still living in the human body, all the virtues mentioned here form part and parcel of his nature and serve as marks of liberation, which he can perceive for himself.

How does one pass beyond the three guṇas?

मां च योऽव्यभिचारेण भक्तियोगेन सेवते।
स गुणान्समतीत्यैतान्ब्रह्मभूयाय कल्पते॥ २६॥

26. And he who worships Me with the yoga of undeviating love rises above the guṇas and becomes fit to be one with Brahman.

Me—The Lord, who dwells in the hearts of all as their inmost Self.

Love—Which is based on the knowledge of the Lord.

To be one with Brahman—That is to say, he is ready for liberation.

Why?

ब्रह्मणो हि प्रतिष्ठाहममृतस्याव्ययस्य च।
शाश्वतस्य च धर्मस्य सुखस्यैकान्तिकस्य च॥ २७॥

27. For I am the Abode of Brahman, the Immortal and the Immutable, and of the Eternal Dharma, and of Absolute Bliss.

I—The inmost Self, in whom Brahman, the Supreme Self, abides.

Dharma—Law and righteousness.

ॐ तत्सदिति श्रीमद्भगवद्गीतासूपनिषत्सु
ब्रह्मविद्यायां योगशास्त्रे श्रीकृष्णार्जुनसंवादे
गुणत्रयविभागयोगो नाम चतुर्दशोऽध्यायः ॥ १४ ॥

Thus in the Bhagavad Gītā, the Essence of the Upaniṣads, the Science of Brahman, the Scripture of Yoga, the Dialogue between Śrī Kṛṣṇa and Arjuna, ends the Fourteenth Chapter, entitled: THE DISCRIMINATION OF THE THREE GUNAS

Chapter 15

THE WAY TO THE SUPREME SELF

[पुरुषोत्तमयोगः]

श्रीभगवानुवाच।

ऊर्ध्वमूलमधःशाखमश्वत्थं प्राहुरव्ययम्।
छन्दांसि यस्य पर्णानि यस्तं वेद स वेदवित्॥ १ ॥

1. *The Lord said:* They speak of an imperishable Aśvattha Tree with its root above and branches below. Its leaves are the Vedas, and he who knows it knows the Vedas.

They—The scriptures.

Imperishable—The Tree of saṃsāra, or cosmic existence, rests on a continuous series of births and deaths without beginning or end. This Tree cannot be cut down except by the knowledge and experience of man's identity with Brahman.

Aśvattha—*Lit.*, that which does not endure till the next day. The phenomenal world is compared to the aśvattha tree on account of its changing nature.

Root above—In an ordinary tree the tap—root extends downward; but in the Tree of the World the tap—root is above. This root is Brahman with māyā (Saguṇa Brahman), since the Immutable Absolute (Nirguṇa Brahman) is beyond the category of causality. The root is described as "above" because

Brahman with māyā is very subtle and very great, and is supreme over all things.

Branches—The mahat (cosmic mind), ahaṅkāra (I-consciousness), tanmātras (the five subtle elements), and the other cosmic principles are its branches, extending downward. As the branches go downward they become grosser.

Its leaves are the Vedas—Just as the leaves protect a tree, so the Vedas (especially the sacrificial portion) serve to protect the Tree of the World by formulating its dharma (meritorious action) and adharma (the opposite of dharma), with their causes and fruits, and also showing the way to prosperity and well—being in the relative world. The knowledge of the Vedas gives men a knowledge of the gods, of the principles and powers of the cosmos; the fruits of this knowledge are enjoyment and lordship on earth, in heaven, and in the world between.

He who knows it etc.—Because nothing else remains to be known beyond the Tree of the World and its root, Brahman.

The fourteenth chapter ended with the note that to worship the Lord with undeviating love leads to liberation. But such love is not possible without detachment from the world. So the Lord begins the present discourse with a description of the World Tree in order to create in the aspirant an intense dispassion leading to love and knowledge of the Supreme Lord.

Now follows another figurative description of the different parts of the World Tree:

अधश्चोर्ध्वं प्रसृतास्तस्य शाखा
गुणप्रवृद्धा विषयप्रवालाः ।
अधश्च मूलान्यनुसन्ततानि
कर्मानुबन्धीनि मनुष्यलोके ॥ २ ॥

2. Above and below spread its branches, nourished by the guṇas. Sense—objects are its buds; and its clustering roots spread downward in the world of men, giving rise to action.

Above—Up to the world of Brahmā, the highest heaven.

Below—To the human and subhuman planes.

Guṇas—The three guṇas form the material basis of the branches.

Sense-objects are its buds—Sound, form, and the other objects are the buddings of its foliage.

Roots—These are the secondary roots; the tap—root has been mentioned in the preceding verse. These roots are the latent impressions, attachment, aversion, and so on, which are both the cause and the effect of good and evil deeds. They bind one fast to actions, both good and evil, and perpetuate the Tree of the World. After exhausting the effects of meritorious action in the higher or lower worlds—as gods or as animals—the souls return to the world of men for new actions, to be determined by their past works.

In the world of men—These secondary roots extend particularly in the world of men. On this earth alone can souls perform action that bears fresh results, whereas as gods or animals they reap the fruit of what they did as human beings. Since the relative world is sustained by men's actions, the roots of the Cosmic Tree are said to spread especially in the world of men.

न रूपमस्येह तथोपलभ्यते
नान्तो न चादिर्न च सम्प्रतिष्ठा।
अश्वत्थमेनं सुविरूढमूलं
असङ्गशस्त्रेण दृढेन छित्त्वा॥३॥

ततः पदं तत्परिमार्गितव्यं
यस्मिन्गता न निवर्तन्ति भूयः।
तमेव चाद्यं पुरुषं प्रपद्ये।
यतः प्रवृत्तिः प्रसृता पुराणी॥४॥

3-4. Its true form is not comprehended here, nor its end, nor its origin, nor even its existence. Having cut down this firm-rooted Aśvattha with the strong axe of detachment, one should pray, "I take refuge in that Primal Being from whom has streamed forth this eternal activity," and seek that Goal from which they who have reached it never return.

True form—As described above. The relative world is very much like a dream or a mirage or a magic city produced by the juggler's art. It appears and disappears constantly.

End—In the absence of right knowledge the relative. universe has no end, inasmuch as ignorance, latent desires, and works, by their action and reaction, keep it perpetually going. The only way to put an end to it is to resort to renunciation through the practice of detachment.

Existence—The nature of the universe as we perceive it.

Strong—Strengthened by a resolute bent of mind toward the Supreme Self, and sharpened again and again on the whetstone of true discrimination.

Detachment—From children, wealth, and the heavenly world. It is nivṛtti, the cessation of the original urge to action, that leads to liberation, the consummation of birth in the relative world.

From whom has streamed forth—Brahman, or the Absolute, is the ultimate source from which has been projected the illusory Tree of the Universe, just as an illusory object is created by a magician.

Eternal activity—The never ceasing current of evolution, that is to say, the phenomenal world.

Disciplines for the attainment of the Goal:

निर्मानमोहा जितसङ्गदोषा
अध्यात्मनित्या विनिवृत्तकामाः।
द्वन्द्वैर्विमुक्ताः सुखदुःखसंज्ञै-
र्गच्छन्त्यमूढाः पदमव्ययं तत्॥५॥

5. Free from pride and delusion, having conquered the evil of attachment, ever devoted to the Supreme Self, with desires completely stilled, liberated from the pairs of opposites known as pleasure and pain, the undeluded reach that Immutable Goal.

These are the characteristics of a true saṃnyāsī.

That Goal is designated:

न तद्भासयते सूर्यो न शशाङ्को न पावकः।
यद्गत्वा न निवर्तन्ते तद्धाम परमं मम॥६॥

6. It the sun illumines not, nor the moon, nor fire. It is My Supreme Abode, and they who reach it never return.

Never return—For embodiment in the relative universe. Those who have not realized the Lord are born again and again under the compulsion of the law of karma. The enlightened soul is under no compulsion to return to mortal life.

It appears that at the time of cosmic dissolution or of deep sleep the soul forgets its individuality and its phenomenal nature and becomes one with Existence. Who, then, is the jīva, or individualized soul? This is explained in the following five verses:

ममैवांशो जीवलोके जीवभूतः सनातनः।
मनःषष्ठानीन्द्रियाणि प्रकृतिस्थानि कर्षति॥७॥

7. An eternal portion of Myself, having become a living soul in a world of living beings, draws to itself the five senses, with the mind for the sixth, which abide in Prakṛti

Myself—The Supreme Lord.

Having become—Through māyā, or ignorance.

A living soul—The phenomenal being, or jīva.

Draws to itself—While returning from deep sleep or from the state of cosmic dissolution to the plane of name and form.

The jīva, or individualized soul, is that aspect of the Supreme Lord which manifests itself in everyone as the doer and the enjoyer, being limited by upādhis, or conditions, set up by avidyā, or ignorance. But in reality, both the jīva and the Supreme Lord are the same. The individualized soul is like the sun reflected in water; the reflected sun is only a portion of the real sun. On the removal of the water, the reflected sun returns to the original sun and remains one with it. The sun is the Supreme Lord, and the water is the mind, created by nescience. Or the individualized soul is like the ākāśa (space or ether) in a jar, which is a portion of the infinite ākāśa; the ākāśa limited by the jar becomes one with the infinite ākāśa on the destruction of the jar, which was the cause of limitation. Afterwards it cannot again be separated from the infinite ākāśa. This explains the statement "from which they who have reached it never return."

According to this description of the jīva, each soul is in reality divine, however partial the actual manifestation of Divinity may be in its physical environment. It is much greater than its present appearance, and its goal is to transcend material limitations. In reality, the Infinite cannot have any parts. The appearance of the individualized living soul is due to avidyā.

At the time of cosmic dissolution or of deep sleep, the individualized soul, no doubt, remains merged in Prakṛti or the Nature of the Lord; but this Prakṛti is tainted by ignorance, or māyā; it is not the pure essence of the Lord. Therefore the soul returns from Prakṛti to the world of the manifold at the time of a new evolution or of waking. And at that time it brings with it the mind and the senses, which also have merged in Prakṛti for the enjoyment of the world. But the soul that merges in Brahman after the attainment of Self-knowledge does not come back to mortal life.

शरीरं यदवाप्नोति यच्चाप्युत्क्रामतीश्वरः।
गृहीत्वैतानि संयाति वायुर्गन्धानिवाशयात्॥८॥

8. When the lord acquires a body, and when he leaves it, he takes these with him and goes on his way, as the wind carries away the scents from their places.

The lord—Of the aggregate of body and senses; that is to say, the individualized soul, jīva, mentioned above.

Acquires a body—To reap the results of his past action.

These—The sense-organs and mind.

Places—The flowers.

After death the gross physical body is destroyed by cremation or burial; but the subtle body, which includes the mind and senses, accompanies the soul as the smell of flowers 'accompanies the wind. When the soul is reborn, it enters the new body with the senses and mind and uses them to enjoy the world and its objects.

The sense-organs are described:

श्रोत्रं चक्षुः स्पर्शनं च रसनं घ्राणमेव च।
अधिष्ठाय मनश्चायं विषयानुपसेवते॥९॥

9. Presiding over the ear and the eye, the organs of touch, taste, and smell, and also over the mind, he experiences sense-objects.

The transmigrating soul is only visible to men of wisdom.

उत्क्रामन्तं स्थितं वापि भुञ्जानं वा गुणान्वितम्।
विमूढा नानुपश्यन्ति पश्यन्ति ज्ञानचक्षुषः॥१०॥

10. The deluded do not perceive him when he departs from the body or dwells in it, when he experiences objects or is united with the guṇas; but they who have the eye of wisdom perceive him.

Deluded—Because their minds are attracted by the enjoyment of objects seen and unseen.

Do not perceive him—Though the self is nearest to everyone and can most easily be perceived.

United with the guṇas—That is to say, when the soul experiences pleasure, pain, and delusion, through which the three guṇas manifest themselves.

Eye of wisdom—The knowledge acquired from the study of the scriptures aided by reflection and reason.

No Self-knowledge is possible without yoga.

यतन्तो योगिनश्चैनं पश्यन्त्यात्मन्यवस्थितम्।
यतन्तोऽप्यकृतात्मानो नैनं पश्यन्त्यचेतसः ॥ ११ ॥

11. Those who strive, armed with yoga, behold him dwelling within themselves; but the undisciplined and the thoughtless do not perceive him, though they strive.

Yoga—Balance and poise acquired through concentration and self-control.

Undisciplined—Whose minds are not purified by austerity and self-control.

Thoughtless—Who have not abandoned their evil ways and whose pride has not been subdued.

Mere study of the scriptures, even aided by reason and reflection, will not be of much avail to those whose minds are impure and who cannot discriminate between the Real and the unreal.

The next four verses describe the immanence of the Lord as the all-illumining Light, as the all-sustaining Life, as the nourishing factor in all living organisms, and as the Self in the hearts of all:

यदादित्यगतं तेजो जगद्भासयतेऽखिलम्।
यच्चन्द्रमसि यच्चाग्नौ तत्तेजो विद्धि मामकम्॥ १२ ॥

12. The light that is in the sun and illumines the whole universe, the light that is in the moon and is likewise in fire—know that light to be Mine.

गामाविश्य च भूतानि धारयाम्यहमोजसा।
पुष्णामि चौषधीः सर्वाः सोमो भूत्वा रसात्मकः ॥ १३ ॥

13. Entering the earth, I sustain all beings by My energy, and becoming the sapid moon, I nourish all herbs.

Entering the earth—The earth is firmly held by energy, which is a manifestation of the Lord's power.

Moon—It is the sap that gives savour to cereals. The moon ("soma" in the text) is the repository of all sap and imparts it to plants through the dew. The planting of wheat or rice seedlings in moonlight is a custom followed in many parts of the world.

अहं वैश्वानरो भूत्वा प्राणिनां देहमाश्रितः।
प्राणापानसमायुक्तः पचाम्यन्नं चतुर्विधम्॥ १४॥

14. As the fire Vaiśvānara I enter into the bodies of all living creatures, and mingling with the upward and downward breaths, I digest the four kinds of food.

The fire Vaiśvānara—The fire abiding in the stomach, by which food is digested.

Upward and downward breaths—Prāṇa and apāna.

Four kinds of food—Those that are eaten by mastication or sucking or licking or direct swallowing.

सर्वस्य चाहं हृदि सन्निविष्टो
मत्तः स्मृतिर्ज्ञानमपोहनञ्च।
वेदैश्च सर्वैरहमेव वेद्यो
वेदान्तकृद्वेदविदेव चाहम्॥ १५॥

15. And I am seated in the hearts of all; from Me are memory and knowledge, and their loss as well. It is I alone who am to be known through all the Vedas; I am indeed the Author of Vedānta and the Knower of the Vedas.

Hearts of all—As the inner Onlooker, I witness all that is good and evil in their hearts.

From Me are memory etc.—It is through the inner Consciousness that one becomes conscious of the experiences of one's past births (memory) and knows of things transcending the ordinary limits of time and space (knowledge). Through evil actions this inner Consciousness is obscured and one suffers loss of memory and knowledge.

The Author of Vedānta—It is the Lord who keeps the teachings of Vedānta alive through a succession of teachers.

In the foregoing four verses have been described the glories of the Lord as manifested through superior upādhis, or conditions, such as the sun, the moon, and so on. In the following verses is stated the true nature of the Lord, pure, unlimited, and untainted by perishable or imperishable upādhis:

द्वाविमौ पुरुषौ लोके क्षरश्चाक्षर एव च।
क्षरः सर्वाणि भूतानि कूटस्थोऽक्षर उच्यते॥ १६॥

16. There are two beings in the world: the Perishable and the Imperishable. The Perishable comprises all creatures, and the Imperishable is said to be the Unchanging.

Two beings—Two categories, described in the text as "Puruṣas" because they are the upādhis, or limiting conditions, of the Puruṣa, or Supreme Spirit.

The Perishable—Which comprises all changing forms.

The Imperishable—The māyā-śakti, or power of the Lord, which deludes all. It is the germ of all perishable beings and manifests itself through various forms of illusion. Saṃsāra, from the relative standpoint, is endless; hence its seed is also imperishable. Saṃsāra is destroyed only by the Knowledge of Brahman. Or the word "Imperishable" may mean the conscious Enjoyer in everyone, who remains unchanged through all the experiences of man.

Quite distinct from the Perishable and the Imperishable, and untainted by the evils of either, is the Supreme Lord, eternal, pure, and free.

उत्तमः पुरुषस्त्वन्यः परमात्मेत्युदाहृतः ।
यो लोकत्रयमाविश्य बिभर्त्यव्यय ईश्वरः ॥ १७ ॥

17. But there is another Being, the Highest, called the Supreme Self, who, as the Immutable, pervades and sustains the three worlds.

Another—Distinct from the two described in the previous verse.

Supreme Self—He is called Puruṣottama, or the Supreme Self, because He is higher than the body, mind, and the rest, and because He is the inmost Consciousness in all bodies.

Pervades—By His vital energy, or sentiency.

Sustains—By His mere presence as Sat, or Existence.

The Lord Himself is the Supreme Self.

यस्मात्क्षरमतीतोऽहमक्षरादपि चोत्तमः ।
अतोऽस्मि लोके वेदे च प्रथितः पुरुषोत्तमः ॥ १८ ॥

18. As I surpass the Perishable and as I am higher even than the Imperishable, I am extolled in the world and in the Vedas as the Supreme Self.

The Perishable—The illusory Tree of the World, described at the beginning of the chapter.

The Imperishable—Which constitutes the seed of that Tree.

The words "Perishable" and "Imperishable" may also mean the physical body and the conscious creature. The latter is under the control of the Supreme Self.

The result of the Knowledge of the Self as described above:

यो मामेवमसम्मूढो जानाति पुरुषोत्तमम्।
स सर्वविद्भजति मां सर्वभावेन भारत॥ १९॥

19. He who, undeluded, knows Me thus as the Supreme Self—he knows all, O Bhārata, and he worships Me with all his heart.

Knows Me thus—That is to say, knows the individualized soul as one with the Supreme Self.

He knows all—Because the Supreme Self is the Self of all beings.

इति गुह्यतमं शास्त्रमिदमुक्तं मयानघ।
एतद्बुद्ध्वा बुद्धिमान्स्यात्कृतकृत्यश्च भारत॥ २०॥

20. Thus, O sinless one, has this most profound teaching been imparted by Me. By knowing it a man becomes wise, O Bhārata, and fulfils all his duties.

Most profound teaching etc.—The teachings of the Gītā and the whole Vedānta have been summed up in the fifteenth chapter.

Fulfils all his duties—Whatever duty one has to do in life will have been done when Brahman is realized.

ॐ तत्सदिति श्रीमद्भगवद्गीतासूपनिषत्सु
ब्रह्मविद्यायां योगशास्त्रे श्रीकृष्णार्जुन संवादे
पुरुषोत्तमयोगो नाम पञ्चदशोऽध्यायः॥ १५॥

Thus in the Bhagavad Gītā, the Essence of the Upaniṣads, the Science of Brahman, the Scripture of Yoga, the Dialogue between Śrī *Kṛṣṇa and Arjuna, ends the Fifteenth Chapter, entitled:* THE WAY TO THE SUPREME SELF

CHAPTER 16

THE DIVISION OF DIVINE AND DEMONIAC TREASURES

[दैवासुरसम्पद्विभागयोगः]

श्रीभगवानुवाच।

अभयं सत्त्वसंशुद्धिर्ज्ञानयोगव्यवस्थितिः।
दानं दमश्च यज्ञश्च स्वाध्यायस्तप आर्जवम्॥ १॥

अहिंसा सत्यमक्रोधस्त्यागः शान्तिरपैशुनम्।
दया भूतेष्वलोलुप्त्वं मार्दवं ह्रीरचापलम्॥ २॥

तेजः क्षमा धृतिः शौचमद्रोहो नातिमानिता।
भवन्ति सम्पदं दैवीमभिजातस्य भारत॥ ३॥

1-3. *The Lord said:* Fearlessness, purity of heart, steadfastness in knowledge and yoga; charity, self-control, and sacrifice; study of the scriptures, austerity, and uprightness;

Non-violence, truth, and freedom from anger; renunciation, tranquility, and aversion to slander; compassion to beings and freedom from covetousness; gentleness, modesty, and absence of fickleness;

Courage, forgiveness, and fortitude; purity, and freedom from malice and overweening pride—these belong to him who is born with divine treasures.

Purity of heart—Freedom from deception, dissimulation, falsehood, and the like, in one's dealings with others.

Knowledge and yoga—Knowledge consists in understanding the nature of spiritual things, such as the Self, the Lord, and so on, as taught by the scriptures and the teacher. Yoga consists in making what has been thus learnt an object of direct experience through meditation and self-control.

Freedom from anger—Even when reviled or beaten by others.

Freedom from covetousness—Remaining unaffected even when the senses enjoy their objects.

Absence of fickleness—Abstention from speaking or moving the hands and feet when there is no necessity for it.

Fortitude—A state of mind that sustains both body and mind when they are tired or dejected.

A person endowed with these attributes enjoys happiness and peace.

The sixteenth chapter begins with a description of the spiritual treasures endowed with which one attains the wisdom hinted at in the end of the last chapter.

A description of the demoniac attributes:

दम्भो दर्पोऽभिमानश्च क्रोधः पारुष्यमेव च।
अज्ञानं चाभिजातस्य पार्थ सम्पदमासुरीम्॥४॥

4. Ostentation, arrogance, and self-conceit; anger, rudeness, and ignorance—these belong to him who is born to the heritage of the demons.

The effects of the two natures described above:

दैवी सम्पद्विमोक्षाय निबन्धायासुरी मता।
मा शुचः सम्पदं दैवीमभिजातोऽसि पाण्डव॥५॥

5. The divine treasures are said to be for the purpose of liberation, and the heritage of the demons, for bondage. Grieve not, O Pāṇḍava you are born with divine treasures.

द्वौ भूतसर्गौ लोकेऽस्मिन्दैव आसुर एव च।
दैवो विस्तरशः प्रोक्त आसुरं पार्थ मे शृणु॥६॥

6. There are two types of beings created in this world: the divine and the demoniac. The divine have been described at length. Hear now from Me, O Pārtha, concerning the demoniac.

The traits of demoniac persons:

प्रवृत्तिं च निवृत्तिं च जना न विदुरासुराः।
न शौचं नापि चाचारो न सत्यं तेषु विद्यते॥७॥

7. Men of demoniac nature know not what to do and what to refrain from doing. Purity is not in them, nor good conduct, nor truth.

What to do etc.—What acts are helpful for the attainment of the goal of life and what are detrimental.

असत्यमप्रतिष्ठं ते जगदाहुरनीश्वरम्।
अपरस्परसम्भूतं किमन्यत्कामहैतुकम्॥८॥

8. They say: "The world is devoid of truth, without a moral basis, and without a God. It is brought about the union of male and female, and lust alone is its cause: what else?"

Devoid of truth—As the life and dealings of demoniac persons are based on falsehood, so also, they say, is the very nature of the world. The scriptures or the words of holy men regarding the world and the Soul are untrue.

Moral basis—According to which right alone endures and falsehood perishes.

God—Who rules the world according to the moral standard.

This is the view of the materialists.

एतां दृष्टिमवष्टभ्य नष्टात्मानोऽल्पबुद्धयः।
प्रभवन्त्युग्रकर्माणः क्षयाय जगतोऽहिताः॥९॥

9. Holding such a view, these lost souls of little understanding and fierce deeds rise as the enemies of the world for its destruction.

Little understanding—Since it concerns itself only with sense-objects.

काममाश्रित्य दुष्पूरं दम्भमानमदान्विताः।
मोहाद्गृहीत्वासद्ग्राहान्प्रवर्तन्तेऽशुचिव्रताः॥१०॥

10. Giving themselves up to insatiable desires, full of hypocrisy, pride, and arrogance, they hold false views through delusion and act with impure resolve.

चिन्तामपरिमेयां च प्रलयान्तामुपाश्रिताः ।
कामोपभोगपरमा एतावदिति निश्चिताः ॥ ११ ॥

आशापाशशतैर्बद्धाः कामक्रोधपरायणाः ।
ईहन्ते कामभोगार्थमन्यायेनार्थसञ्चयान् ॥ १२ ॥

11-12. Beset with innumerable cares, which will end only with death, looking on the gratification of desire as their highest goal, and feeling sure that this is all;

Bound by a hundred ties of hope, given up wholly to lust and wrath, they strive, by unjust means, to amass wealth for the satisfaction of their passions.

इदमद्य मया लब्धमिमं प्राप्स्ये मनोरथम् ।
इदमस्तीदमपि मे भविष्यति पुनर्धनम् ॥ १३ ॥

असौ मया हतः शत्रुर्हनिष्ये चापरानपि ।
ईश्वरोऽहमहं भोगी सिद्धोऽहं बलवान्सुखी ॥ १४ ॥

आढ्योऽभिजनवानस्मि कोऽन्योऽस्ति सदृशो मया ।
यक्ष्ये दास्यामि मोदिष्य इत्यज्ञानविमोहिताः ॥ १५ ॥

अनेकचित्तविभ्रान्ता मोहजालसमावृताः ।
प्रसक्ताः कामभोगेषु पतन्ति नरकेऽशुचौ ॥ १६ ॥

13-16. "This I have gained today, and that longing I will fulfil. This wealth is mine, and that also shall be mine in future;

"That enemy I have slain, and others, too, I will slay. I am the lord of all; I enjoy; I am prosperous, mighty, and happy;

"I am rich; I am of high birth. Who else is equal to me? I will offer sacrifice, I will give, I will rejoice." Thus, deluded by ignorance,

Bewildered by many fancies, entangled in the meshes of delusion, addicted to the gratification of lust, they fall into a loathsome hell.

Even their worship and sacrifice are for self-glorification.

आत्मसम्भाविताः स्तब्धा धनमानमदान्विताः ।
यजन्ते नामयज्ञैस्ते दम्भेनाविधिपूर्वकम् ॥ १७ ॥

17. Self-honoured, haughty, filled with the pride and the intoxication of wealth, they ostentatiously perform sacrifices, which are so only in name, in utter disregard of precepts.

Self-honoured—Not honoured by righteous people.

अहङ्कारं बलं दर्पं कामं क्रोधं च संश्रिताः।
मामात्मपरदेहेषु प्रद्विषन्तोऽभ्यसूयकाः॥१८॥

18. Possessed of egotism, power, and pride, and also of lust and wrath, these people, envious by nature, hate Me in the bodies of others and in their own.

Me—The Lord, who is the inmost Soul of all beings.

The fate of those who hate the Lord dwelling in living beings:

तानहं द्विषतः क्रूरान्संसारेषु नराधमान्।
क्षिपाम्यजस्रमशुभानासुरीष्वेव योनिषु॥१९॥

19. These cruel haters, these evil—doers, these vilest of men, I hurl always into the wombs of the demons in the cycle of births and deaths.

Wombs of the demons—That is to say, demoniac people are born in their next life as ferocious animals, such as tigers and boars.

आसुरीं योनिमापन्ना मूढा जन्मनि जन्मनि।
मामप्राप्यैव कौन्तेय ततो यान्त्यधमां गतिम्॥२०॥

20. Having fallen into the wombs of the demons and being deluded from birth to birth, they never attain Me, O son of Kuntī, but go farther down to the lowest state.

The idea behind the text seems to be this: The demoniac nature leads to a series of evil results inimical to all human progress. A man should therefore try to shake it off while he is yet a free agent and while he has not yet passed into a birth that would completely shut him off from the divine light.

This graphic description regarding the nature of the demoniac persons and their dire fate must not be pressed to carry more than it means. The creation of the two types in the world (XVI, 6) does not mean absolute creation but only creation at the beginning of a cycle. The creation itself is without beginning. The devas (souls with spiritual attributes) and asuras (souls with demoniac attributes), representing the forces of good and evil, are ever present in the relative world of the three guṇas. Both are necessary to the evolution of the relative universe. It is not meant that human souls are so created by God from the beginning that they must be either good or evil. Nor is it meant that there is a rigid spiritual predestination, that some are rejected from the beginning by the Lord and blinded by Him so that they may be thrust down to eternal perdition. Souls are born with spiritual or demoniac attributes in accordance with the law of karma. The power of the Lord, which acts like a light, may be used for a good or an evil purpose, according to man's nature. But all souls, the asuras as well as the devas, are eternal portions of the Lord (XV, 7) and all will one day realize their spiritual heritage. The soul, under the influence of rajas and tamas, is deprived of light, sattva, and falls a victim to the perversities of its lower nature. If it does not abandon its ways of error, it is eventually born in a subhuman body, as an asura, endowed with demoniac attributes. Turning its vision away from Light and Truth, it goes on falling, because of the force of the misdirected divine power, till it finds itself in the lowest pit of the relative world, called hell. But since it is a portion of the Divine, nay, in reality one with the Lord Himself, it cannot be consigned for eternity to this state of self-forgetfulness. One day it understands and turns to the Light. And then the other teaching of the Gītā (IX, 30) comes in—that even the greatest sinner, through his spiritual fervour, may follow the path of sattva and ultimately attain perfection and freedom.

The three great demoniac attributes that are the cause of all evils:

त्रिविधं नरकस्येदं द्वारं नाशनमात्मनः ।
कामः क्रोधस्तथा लोभस्तस्मादेतत्त्रयं त्यजेत् ॥ २१ ॥

21. Three are the gateways of this hell leading to the ruin of the self—lust, wrath, and greed. Therefore let man renounce these three.

Ruin of the self—They make the self unfit for any noble. endeavour.

The great result that follows from their renunciation:

एतैर्विमुक्तः कौन्तेय तमोद्वारैस्त्रिभिर्नरः ।
आचरत्यात्मनः श्रेयस्ततो याति परां गतिम् ॥ २२ ॥

22. The man who has escaped these three gates of darkness, O son of Kuntī, practises what is good for himself and thus attains the Supreme Goal.

Gates of darkness—Leading to hell, which is full of pain and delusion.

The scriptures are the authority as to what is to be given up and what is to be followed.

यः शास्त्रविधिमुत्सृज्य वर्तते कामकारतः।
न स सिद्धिमवाप्नोति न सुखं न परां गतिम्॥२३॥

23. He who discards the injunctions of the scriptures and acts upon the impulse of desire attains neither perfection nor happiness nor the Supreme Goal.

Scriptures—Here the word signifies the Vedas, which teach us the nature of God, the soul, the hereafter, and the relationship of man to man—all based on the intuitive experiences of the seers. Morality and ethics, taught from the standpoint of expediency or formulated by unaided reason, break down under the stress of circumstances. They must be based on such spiritual experiences as the realization of the divinity of the soul, the oneness of existence, and the Fatherhood of God, and then be formulated through reason.

तस्माच्छास्त्रं प्रमाणं ते कार्याकार्यव्यवस्थितौ।
ज्ञात्वा शास्त्रविधानोक्तं कर्म कर्तुमिहार्हसि॥२४॥

24. Therefore let the scriptures be your authority in determining what ought to be done and what ought not to be done. Having learnt the injunctions of the scriptures, you should do your work in the world.

Do your work—That is to say, one should perform one's duty following the precepts of karmayoga.

The duties laid down in the scriptures purify a man's heart and enable him to acquire right knowledge and attain liberation.

ॐ तत्सदिति श्रीमद्भगवद्गीतासूपनिषत्सु
ब्रह्मविद्यायां योगशास्त्रे श्रीकृष्णार्जुनसंवादे
दैवासुरसम्पद्विभागयोगो नाम षोडशोऽध्यायः॥१६॥

Thus in the Bhagavad Gītā, the Essence of the Upaniṣads, the Science of Brahman, the Scripture of Yoga, the Dialogue between Śrī *Kṛṣṇa and Arjuna. ends the Sixteenth Chapter, entitled:* THE DIVISION OF DIVINE AND DEMONIAC TREASURES

CHAPTER 17

THE THREEFOLD DIVISION OF FAITH

[श्रद्धात्रयविभागयोगः]

अर्जुन उवाच।

ये शास्त्रविधिमुत्सृज्य यजन्ते श्रद्धयान्विताः।
तेषां निष्ठा तु का कृष्ण सत्त्वमाहो रजस्तमः ॥ १ ॥

1. *Arjuna said:* When men sacrifice to the gods with faith but discard the injunctions of the scriptures, what is the nature of their devotion, O Kṛṣṇa? Is it sattva, rajas, or tamas?

Scriptures—These contain the wisdom won by the collective experience of a race: its culture, religion, science, and progressive discovery of the best rule of life. Opposed to the injunctions of the scriptures is the impulse of personal desire, which, according to the character of the individual, may give rise to beneficial or harmful results. *See* note on XVI, 23.

Discard the injunctions etc.—The text refers to those who abandon the scriptural injunctions out of laziness, or because of the difficulty inherent in strictly complying with them, and worship the gods with faith created by their observance of the conduct of the leaders of society.

Devotion—The untranslatable Sanskrit word "niṣṭhā" means the unswerving devotion that gives a man faith in an ideal and impels him to realize it in action.

Is it sattva etc.—Is the worship offered by them based on sattva, rajas, or tamas?

At the end of the preceding chapter Śrī Kṛṣṇa said that he who discards the scriptural injunctions and acts according to the promptings of his desires cannot attain the highest Knowledge. Arjuna asks about the fate of those who worship with faith but who do not know the scriptures or are indifferent to their rules.

श्रीभगवानुवाच।
त्रिविधा भवति श्रद्धा देहिनां सा स्वभावजा।
सात्त्विकी राजसी चैव तामसी चेति तां शृणु॥ २॥

2. *The Lord said*: The faith of men, born of their individual natures, is of three kinds. It is characterized by sattva, rajas, or tamas. Hear now concerning it.

Born of their individual natures—The nature of man consists of latent tendencies created by his actions—good or bad—in his past lives. The faith of each man takes the shape, colour, and quality given to it by his nature (svabhāva), the stuff of his being, his innate substance. Man acts according to his nature; he cannot easily change it. One can transform a worldly nature into a spiritual nature only with the help of insight gained through the study of the scriptures and an indomitable determination.

Three kinds—Like all things in Prakṛti or Nature.

The threefold faith:

सत्त्वानुरूपा सर्वस्य श्रद्धा भवति भारत।
श्रद्धामयोऽयं पुरुषो यो यच्छ्रद्धः स एव सः॥ ३॥

3. The faith of each man is in accordance with his natural disposition. A man, O Bhārata, is made of his faith; what his faith is, that verily he is.

Natural disposition—That is to say, in accordance with sattva, rajas, or tamas predominating in his nature.

What his faith is etc.—If, on account of the righteous actions of his past lives, a man is born with a nature predominating in sattva, then his faith is also characterized by sattva. The same applies to rajas and tamas.

The word "śraddhā," usually translated as "faith," is not a mechanical belief in or acceptance of the words of a holy man or book. It is an affirmative and reverent attitude toward super-sensuous truths. Through faith a man is intuitively convinced of the existence of the Reality underlying the universe, and his capacity for realizing that Reality. It is not imposed from outside, but is produced by the tendencies that are the results of his past action. The intensity of this faith accounts for the passion with which he pursues an undertaking. This faith is a man's appeal to himself, or to something potent and compelling in himself or in universal reality, for his way to fullness and perfection. So a man is made of his faith; he is that faith and that faith is he. The truth he sees is determined for him by his faith. If a man's innate tendencies are characterized by sattva, then his faith will direct him to the pursuit of knowledge and happiness. If they are characterized by rajas, then his faith will direct him to the pursuit of action, ending in pain and suffering. And if they are characterized by tamas, then his faith will lead him to ignorance and delusion.

The nature of faith is to be inferred from its characteristic effects, namely, the worship of the gods and the like.

यजन्ते सात्त्विका देवान्यक्षरक्षांसि राजसाः ।
प्रेतान्भूतगणांश्चान्ये यजन्ते तामसा जनाः ॥४॥

4. Men in whom sattva prevails worship the gods; men in whom rajas prevails worship demigods and demons; and men in whom tamas prevails worship ghosts and disembodied spirits.

Gods—"Deva," the word in the text, means literally a shining being; a superhuman being endowed with a preponderance of sattva; a benign deity full of noble qualities. *See* note on III, 11-12.

Demigods and demons—The words in the text are "yakṣas" and "rākṣasas." They denote two classes of supernatural beings of fierce and cruel nature.

Disembodied spirits—According to Hindu tradition, a brāhmin who, while on earth, neglects his brāhminical duties becomes after death a disembodied spirit, or preta. The word means, in general, an evil spirit worshipped by certain persons for the fulfilment of morbid, earthly desires

Aspirants seeking peace and happiness worship benign gods, who are of the nature of sattva. Those who desire materialistic enjoyments and physical pleasures worship. fierce deities, who are embodiments of rajas. And people under the influence of tamas are drawn to ghosts and evil spirits, endowed with the traits of inertia, delusion, and morbidity. Different beings, embodying sattva, rajas, or tamas, exist, and worshippers are drawn to them according to their faith and inclination.

When worshipped with faith, they answer the prayers of their devotees and fulfil their respective desires. From the Vedāntic point of view these deities are different manifestations of the Lord. From the Lord alone comes all fulfilment.

Rare is the man whose worship is characterized by sattva. Most men perform their worship under the impulsion of faith characterized by rajas and tamas.

अशास्त्रविहितं घोरं तप्यन्ते ये तपो जनाः ।
दम्भाहङ्कारसंयुक्ताः कामरागबलान्विताः ॥५॥

कर्षयन्तः शरीरस्थं भूतग्राममचेतसः ।
मां चैवान्तःशरीरस्थं तान्विद्ध्यासुरनिश्चयान् ॥६॥

5-6. Those vain and conceited men who, impelled by the force of their lust and attachment, subject themselves to severe austerities not ordained by the scriptures,

And, fools that they are, torture all their bodily organs, and Me, too, who dwell within the body—know that they are fiendish in their resolves.

Austerities—Which cause pain to themselves and other living beings.

Me—The Lord, who is the witness of man's thoughts and deeds. To disregard the Lord's injunctions is to injure the Lord Himself.

आहारस्त्वपि सर्वस्य त्रिविधो भवति प्रियः ।
यज्ञस्तपस्तथा दानं तेषां भेदमिमं शृणु ॥७॥

7. Even the food that is dear to all is of the three kinds. Likewise are the sacrifices, austerities, and gifts. Hear now the distinctions between them.

The division of food, sacrifice, austerity, and gift according to the three guṇas is described in order that the aspirants may eat the right food, perform the right sacrifice, practise the right austerity, and make the right gift so as to secure increase in the element of sattva.

The food characterized by the three guṇas according to its effect on the body and mind of the eater:

आयुःसत्त्वबलारोग्यसुखप्रीतिविवर्धनाः ।
रस्याः स्निग्धाः स्थिरा हृद्या आहाराः सात्त्विकप्रियाः ॥८॥

8. Food that promotes longevity, vitality, strength, health, pleasure, appetite, and that is succulent, oleaginous, substantial, and agreeable, is favoured by people endowed with sattva.

Vitality—Mental vigour.

Substantial—Whose essence nourishes the body for a long time.

Agreeable—Pleasant to look at.

People desirous of increasing sattva should eat food characterized by these qualities and avoid what is described in the two following verses.

कट्वम्ललवणात्युष्णतीक्ष्णरूक्षविदाहिनः।
आहारा राजसस्येष्टा दुःखशोकामयप्रदाः॥९॥

9. Food that is excessively bitter, sour, salty, hot, acrid, dry, and burning is liked by people endowed with rajas. It causes pain, grief, and disease.

Excessively—This word should be understood with all the seven characteristics.

Pain—At the time the food is eaten.

Grief—The after-effect in the form of mental distress.

यातयामं गतरसं पूति पर्युषितं च यत्।
उच्छिष्टमपि चामेध्यं भोजनं तामसप्रियम्॥१०॥

10. And food that is ill cooked, tasteless, putrid, stale, unclean, and left over, is favoured by people endowed with tamas.

The three kinds of sacrifice:

अफलाकाङ्क्षिभिर्यज्ञो विधिदृष्टो य इज्यते।
यष्टव्यमेवेति मनः समाधाय स सात्त्विकः॥११॥

11. That sacrifice is of the nature of sattva which is offered according to the scriptural rules by those who expect no reward and who firmly believe that it is their duty to sacrifice.

Sacrifice—The word in the text is "yajña," which means literally the giving of offerings to a deity. In ancient India through this method of worship the devotees communed with the gods. It was obligatory for a householder to perform sacrifice. *See* note on III, 10.

It is their duty etc.—The duty of a man lies in the performance of the worship itself and not in seeking any result from it.

अभिसन्धाय तु फलं दम्भार्थमपि चैव यत्।
इज्यते भरतश्रेष्ठ तं यज्ञं विद्धि राजसम्॥ १२॥

12. But that sacrifice which is performed in expectation of reward and for the sake of ostentation—know that to be of the nature of rajas.

Such a sacrifice may be performed outwardly according to the scriptures, but its motive is ostentation, pride, or a strong lust for its fruit.

विधिहीनमसृष्टान्नं मन्त्रहीनमदक्षिणम्।
श्रद्धाविरहितं यज्ञं तामसं परिचक्षते॥ १३॥

13. And that sacrifice which is not performed according to the scriptural rules, and in which no food is distributed, no hymns are chanted, and no fees paid, and which is devoid of faith, is said to be of the nature of tamas.

No food is distributed—The giving of food to the brāhmins (the custodians of the Hindu spiritual culture) and the poor is an indispensable part of the sacrifice, without which it becomes wholly a self-regarding thing.

No hymns are chanted—That is to say, they are uttered with defective accents, which make them useless to all intents and purposes.

No fees paid—To the priests who officiate at the sacrifice.

The sacrifice characterized by tamas is performed mechanically, either because the act of living demands it, or because it comes in our way, or because others do it, or because of the desire to avoid another greater difficulty that may arise from its non-performance, or for some other unworthy motive.

The three kinds of austerity:

देवद्विजगुरुप्राज्ञपूजनं शौचमार्जवम्।
ब्रह्मचर्यमहिंसा च शारीरं तप उच्यते॥ १४॥

14. Worship of the gods, of the twice-born, of teachers, and of the wise; cleanliness, uprightness, continence, and non-violence—these are said to be the austerity of the body.

Worship of the gods etc.—The objects of this worship are the creators and protectors of India's spiritual culture.

Twice-born—*See* note on I, 7.

Austerity—"Tapas," the word in the text, refers to self-discipline, prescribed by religion in order to bring body and mind under control.

अनुद्वेगकरं वाक्यं सत्यं प्रियहितं च यत्।
स्वाध्यायाभ्यसनं चैव वाङ्मयं तप उच्यते॥ १५॥

15. Words that do not give offence and that are truthful, pleasant, and beneficial, and also the regular recitation of the Vedas—these are said to be the austerity of speech.

The discipline of speech consists in the combination of all the four characteristics mentioned in the text; the purpose will be frustrated if it lacks any of them.

मनः प्रसादः सौम्यत्वं मौनमात्मविनिग्रहः।
भावसंशुद्धिरित्येतत्तपो मानसमुच्यते॥ १६॥

16. Serenity of mind, gentleness, silence, self-control, and purity of heart—these constitute the austerity of the mind.

Silence—The control of thought, which precedes the silence of the tongue.

Purity of heart—*See* note on XVI, 1-3.

The austerities described above classified according to the three guṇas:

श्रद्धया परया तप्तं तपस्तत्त्रिविधं नरैः।
अफलाकाङ्क्षिभिर्युक्तैः सात्त्विकं परिचक्षते॥ १७॥

17. This threefold austerity practised with supreme faith by steadfast men, without the desire for fruit, is said to be of the nature of sattva.

सत्कारमानपूजार्थं तपो दम्भेन चैव यत्।
क्रियते तदिह प्रोक्तं राजसं चलमध्रुवम्॥ १८॥

18. The austerity that is practised in order to gain respect, honour, and reverence, and for ostentation, is said to be of the nature of rajas. Its result is uncertain and transitory.

मूढग्राहेणात्मनो यत्पीडया क्रियते तपः।
परस्योत्सादनार्थं वा तत्तामसमुदाहृतम्॥ १९॥

19. The austerity that is practised with a determination based on foolishness, by means of self-torture, or for the purpose of ruining another is declared to be of the nature of tamas.

The gifts characterized by the three guṇas:

दातव्यमिति यद्दानं दीयतेऽनुपकारिणे।
देशे काले च पात्रे च तद्दानं सात्त्विकं स्मृतम्॥ २०॥

20. That gift which is made to one who can make no return, and with the feeling that it is one's duty to give, and which is given at the right place and time and to a worthy person—such a gift is held to be of the nature of sattva.

Who can make no return—Who cannot do, or who though able is not expected to do, anything in return.

Right place and time—According to the traditional view, a gift becomes very effective when it is made in a holy place. and on an auspicious occasion.

यत्तु प्रत्युपकारार्थं फलमुद्दिश्य वा पुनः।
दीयते च परिक्लिष्टं तद्दानं राजसं स्मृतम्॥ २१॥

21. But that which is given for the sake of recompense or with the expectation of fruit or in a grudging mood is accounted as of the nature of rajas.

Recompense—Expecting a return from the receiver.

Fruit—In heaven or in the next life.

अदेशकाले यद्दानमपात्रेभ्यश्च दीयते।
असत्कृतमवज्ञातं तत्तामसमुदाहृतम्॥ २२॥

22. And the gift that is made without respect or with disdain, at an improper place and time, and to an unworthy person is declared to be of the nature of tamas.

It may appear that all acts of sacrifice, austerity, and giving will be characterized either by rajas or tamas and that no one will be able to practise or perform them in the manner of sattva. Śrī Kṛṣṇa suggests the way of purifying an imperfect action:

ॐतत्सदिति निर्देशो ब्रह्मणस्त्रिविधः स्मृतः।
ब्राह्मणास्तेन वेदाश्च यज्ञाश्च विहिताः पुरा॥ २३॥

23. "Om Tat Sat"—this has been declared as the threefold designation of Brahman. By means of it were created, at the beginning, the Brahmins, the Vedas, and the Sacrifices.

Om—The principal symbol of Brahman both as the Personal God and as the Impersonal. Truth. Each letter—A, U, M—indicates one of Its three manifestations—gross, subtle, or causal—in ascending order, and the syllable as a whole indicates the transcendental state, Turīya, which is identical with the Absolute. Om also means "yes" or affirmation. *See* note on VII, 8.

Tat—Meaning "That," the Indefinable, which can only be indirectly described as "That."

Sat—Meaning Reality, the supreme and unchanging Existence.

Declared—In Vedānta, by the knowers of Brahman. Were created—By Brahmā, or Prajāpati.

When a sacrificial rite or the like is found defective, it will be made faultless by the utterance of one of these three symbols of Brahman.

तस्मादोमित्युदाहृत्य यज्ञदानतपःक्रियाः।
प्रवर्तन्ते विधानोक्ताः सततं ब्रह्मवादिनाम्॥२४॥

24. Therefore the acts of sacrifice, gift, and austerity, enjoined by the scriptures, are always begun by the followers of the Vedas with the utterance of "Om."

तदित्यनभिसन्धाय फलं यज्ञतपःक्रियाः।
दानक्रियाश्च विविधाः क्रियन्ते मोक्षकाङ्क्षिभिः॥२५॥

25. And with the utterance of "Tat," and without seeking any recompense, are the various acts of sacrifice, austerity, and gift performed by those who seek liberation.

The utterance of "Tat" at the beginning of a sacrifice, austerity, or gift purifies the heart and eliminates the desire for fruit.

सद्भावे साधुभावे च सदित्येतत्प्रयुज्यते।
प्रशस्ते कर्मणि तथा सच्छब्दः पार्थ युज्यते॥२६॥

26. The word "Sat" is used to denote reality and goodness; and likewise, O Pārtha, the word "Sat" is used for an auspicious action.

Auspicious action—Such as a marriage-ceremony or the birth of a son.

In expressing the reality of an object that is not absolutely real—such as the birth of a son—and also the goodness of a thing that is not absolutely good or auspicious, the word "Sat," an epithet of Brahman, which alone is absolutely real, good, and auspicious, is used.

यज्ञे तपसि दाने च स्थितिः सदिति चोच्यते।
कर्म चैव तदर्थीयं सदित्येवाभिधीयते॥२७॥

27. Steadfastness in sacrifice, austerity, and gift is also called "Sat"; and so too is any action connected therewith.

Therewith—That is to say, connected with sacrifice, austerity, and gift, or with Brahman, whose triple epithet is "Om Tat Sat."

Imperfectly performed acts of sacrifice, austerity, and gift are made perfect by the utterance, with faith, of "Sat," the name of Brahman.

But without faith everything is futile.

अश्रद्धया हुतं दत्तं तपस्तप्तं कृतं च यत्।
असदित्युच्यते पार्थ न च तत्प्रेत्य नो इह॥२८॥

28. Whatever sacrifice or gift is made, whatever austerity is practised, whatever ceremony is observed—it is all called "asat," "non-existent," if it is done without faith. It is of no account here or hereafter.

Non-existent—That is to say, it is as good as not performed, because it does not bring any result.

Here or hereafter—Though costing much trouble, it is of no use here as it is not approved by the wise, nor can it produce any good effect hereafter.

The teaching of this chapter may be thus summed up: There are devotees who are ignorant of the scriptural injunctions and yet endowed with śraddhā, or faith. Their faith, according to its nature, may be characterized as belonging to sattva, rajas, or tamas. These devotees should cultivate pure sattva by avoiding food, worship, gift, and austerity that are of the nature of rajas and tamas. They should be devoted to sattva alone. When their gift, worship, or austerity is found to be defective, it should be purified by uttering "Om," "Tat," and "Sat." This will purify the minds of the devotees and gradually enable them to realize Brahman.

ॐ तत्सदिति श्रीमद्भगवद्गीतासूपनिषत्सु
ब्रह्मविद्यायां योगशास्त्रे श्रीकृष्णार्जुनसंवादे
श्रद्धात्रयविभागयोगो नाम सप्तदशोऽध्यायः॥१७॥

Thus in the Bhagavad Gītā, the Essence of the Upaniṣads, the Science of Brahman, the Scripture of Yoga, the Dialogue between Śrī *Kṛṣṇa and Arjuna, ends the Seventeenth Chapter, entitled:* THE THREEFOLD DIVISION OF FAITH

CHAPTER 18

THE WAY TO LIBERATION THROUGH RENUNCIATION

[मोक्षसंन्यासयोगः]

अर्जुन उवाच।

संन्यासस्य महाबाहो तत्त्वमिच्छामि वेदितुम्।
त्यागस्य च हृषीकेश पृथक्केशिनिषूदन॥ १॥

1. *Arjuna said*: I desire to know the true nature of saṃnyāsa and tyāga, as distinguished from each other, O mighty Hṛṣīkeśa, O Slayer of Keśī.

Saṃnyāṣa and tyāga—Both words are generally used to mean renunciation. They have been thus used in the preceding chapters without distinction.

This chapter gives a summary of the whole Gītā and the Vedic religion and philosophy.

श्रीभगवानुवाच।

काम्यानां कर्मणां न्यासं संन्यासं कवयो विदुः।
सर्वकर्मफलत्यागं प्राहुस्त्यागं विचक्षणाः॥ २॥

2. *The Lord said:* The renunciation of works induced by desire is understood by the sages to be saṃnyāsa, while the surrender of the fruits of all works is called tyāga by the wise.

All works—There are four kinds of action. *See* note on V, 13.

The two words convey the same general idea of renunciation, with a slight distinction.

त्याज्यं दोषवदित्येके कर्म प्राहुर्मनीषिणः ।
यज्ञदानतपःकर्म न त्याज्यमिति चापरे ॥ ३ ॥

3. Some philosophers declare that all works should be relinquished as evil; others say that works of sacrifice, gift, and austerity should not be given up.

As evil—Because it is impossible to do a work without inflicting misery or injury on someone.

The word "karma," meaning action, is generally used in the Gītā in the sense of religious rites and ceremonies, which bring to their performer, directly or indirectly, some result. It also includes works of public welfare, such as building a road or digging a well. In ancient India all activities, even the secular, had some religious bearing or significance.

According to the commentator Śaṅkara, action and knowledge are incompatible. Action denotes a consciousness of diversity, such as the distinction between the agent, the instrument of action, and the result. But a man endowed with Knowledge sees only unity. Action forms the discipline of the karmayogis; they purify their hearts through the selfless work advocated in the Gītā and thus become ready for the Knowledge of Reality. Renunciation, discussed in this and some of the following verses, applies to the karmayogis, who are still unenlightened about the Ultimate Reality and whose spiritual discipline lies through the performance of duties; it does not apply to the saṃnyāsīs, who follow the path of knowledge. (III, 3) The saṃnyāsīs renounce religious rites and ceremonies, philanthropic duties, and other secular activities because these are associated with the idea of a doer, an instrument, and a result. They devote themselves to philosophical discrimination between the Real and the unreal, and to contemplation of the Real. What little action they perform, such as procuring food or studying, is done by them without any attachment, since they know that action pertains to the guṇas. (V, 8—9, 13) The life of the saṃnyāsīs has been described by the Lord as free from all undertakings. Therefore the present verse and also verse 8 of this chapter apply to persons who are ignorant of the true nature of the Self. They are asked to perform selfless duties for the purification of their minds. The injunction about work also applies to those who, through delusion or fear of trouble, may sometimes feel tempted to give up action. Different kinds of renunciation (XVIII, 7-9) and divergent views about it (XVIII, 2, 4-6) are described in connexion with the karmayogis, and not with reference to the saṃnyāsīs.

The incompatibility of the highest Knowledge and the performance of duties is discussed by the translator in the concluding paragraphs of the Introduction of this book.

The different kinds of renunciation apply to the karmayogis.

निश्चयं शृणु मे तत्र त्यागे भरतसत्तम।
त्यागो हि पुरुषव्याघ्र त्रिविधः सम्प्रकीर्तितः॥४॥

4. Learn from Me, O best of the Bhāratas, the truth about relinquishment; for relinquishment is declared to be of three kinds, O tiger among men.

Truth about relinquishment—As asked by Arjuna in XVIII, 1.

The three kinds of relinquishment apply only to the karmayogis, who are ignorant about the Self. The subject is profound and can be taught only by the Lord Himself.

The truth about relinquishment as suggested in the foregoing text:

यज्ञदानतपःकर्म न त्याज्यं कार्यमेव तत्।
यज्ञो दानं तपश्चैव पावनानि मनीषिणाम्॥५॥

5. Acts of sacrifice, gift, and austerity must not be given up, but should be performed. For verily, sacrifice, gift, and austerity purify the wise.

Wise—Who perform actions without desiring any fruit.

एतान्यपि तु कर्माणि सङ्गं त्यक्त्वा फलानि च।
कर्तव्यानीति मे पार्थ निश्चितं मतमुत्तमम्॥६॥

6. Even these works, however, should be done without attachment and desire for fruit. This, O Pārtha, is My conclusive and final judgement.

The proposition stated in XVIII, 4, is now concluded. The word "even" in the text implies that the works of sacrifice, gift, and austerity should be performed by a seeker after liberation, though they cause bondage in the case of one who is attached to his work and desires its fruit.

The three kinds of renunciation:

नियतस्य तु संन्यासः कर्मणो नोपपद्यते।
मोहात्तस्य परित्यागस्तामसः परिकीर्तितः ॥७॥

7. The renunciation of obligatory action is not proper. Its abandonment, from delusion, is declared to be of the nature of tamas.

Obligatory action—Such as daily worship and devotions, which every aspirant must perform. It also includes, for the householder, such duties as feeding animals and showing hospitality to guests. Through the performance of these duties the aspirant's heart becomes pure.

दुःखमित्येव यत्कर्म कायक्लेशभयात्त्यजेत्।
स कृत्वा राजसं त्यागं नैव त्यागफलं लभेत्॥८॥

8. The renunciation of a man who abandons a duty from fear of physical suffering, because it is painful, is of the nature of rajas; it does not bring him the fruit of renunciation.

The fruit of renunciation—That is to say, liberation. It is denied to him because his renunciation is not accompanied by wisdom.

कार्यमित्येव यत्कर्म नियतं क्रियतेऽर्जुन।
सङ्गं त्यक्त्वा फलं चैव स त्यागः सात्त्विको मतः ॥९॥

9. When a man performs an obligatory action only because it ought to be done, and renounces all attachment and the fruit—his renunciation, O Arjuna, is characterized by sattva.

The characteristics of a devotee whose renunciation is of the nature of sattva:

न द्वेष्ट्यकुशलं कर्म कुशले नानुषज्जते।
त्यागी सत्त्वसमाविष्टो मेधावी छिन्नसंशयः ॥१०॥

10. The wise man of renunciation, who is endowed with sattva and whose doubts are dispelled, never hates a duty that is disagreeable nor feels attachment to a duty that is agreeable.

An aspirant performs his duties in the manner described above and gradually removes the impurities of his heart, as a result of which he comes to know that the Self is birthless, deathless, and immutable. Gradually he renounces all actions in thought and becomes devoted to Self-knowledge. Thus attaining freedom from action, he fulfils the purpose of karmayoga.

An unenlightened man identifies himself with the body and thinks the Self to be the active agent. Such a person should perform the prescribed duties but renounce their fruit.

न हि देहभृता शक्यं त्यक्तुं कर्माण्यशेषतः ।
यस्तु कर्मफलत्यागी स त्यागीत्यभिधीयते ॥ ११ ॥

11. It is indeed impossible for an embodied being to renounce action entirely. But he who renounces the fruit of action is regarded as one who has renounced.

Embodied being—One who identifies himself with the body.

Is regarded as one etc.—This is only meant as a glorification of the renunciation of the fruit of action.

The renunciation of all action is possible only for him. who does not identify himself with the body and who knows his Self to be one with the actionless Brahman.

What purpose is served by the renunciation of all action?

अनिष्टमिष्टं मिश्रं च त्रिविधं कर्मणः फलम् ।
भवत्यत्यागिनां प्रेत्य न तु संन्यासिनां क्वचित् ॥ १२ ॥

12. The threefold fruit of action—desirable, undesirable, and mixed—accrues after death to those who have not renounced, but none whatever to the saṃnyāsīs.

Action—Characterized by dharma and adharma. Desirable—Enjoyed in a heavenly body.

Undesirable—Experienced in a subhuman body.

Mixed—Experienced in a human body.

Who have not renounced—Who perform action owing to their ignorance of the Supreme Reality.

Saṃnyāsīs—Those who have renounced the world and its duties and who devote themselves only to Self-knowledge.

The ignorant person identifies himself with the body and considers action, agency, and the accessories to be real; therefore for him the abandonment of action is not possible. But the idea that action, agency, and the accessories are real is due to ignorance of the Supreme Reality.

पञ्चैतानि महाबाहो कारणानि निबोध मे।
साङ्ख्ये कृतान्ते प्रोक्तानि सिद्धये सर्वकर्मणाम्॥ १३॥

अधिष्ठानं तथा कर्ता करणं च पृथग्विधम्।
विविधाश्च पृथक्चेष्टा दैवं चैवात्र पञ्चमम्॥ १४॥

13-14. Learn from Me, O mighty Arjuna, the five causes that bring about the accomplishment of a work, as declared in the philosophy of knowledge, which puts an end to all action:

The body, the doer, the different senses, the many and various functions of the vital breaths, and the presiding deity as the fifth.

Philosophy of knowledge—The word "sāṅkhya in the text refers to Vedānta, in which is expounded everything that should be known about the Reality.

Which puts an end etc.—All action ceases when the Knowledge of the Self is attained through the study of Vedānta. Compare: II, 46; IV, 33, 37.

Body—Through which are manifested desire, hatred, happiness, misery, and so on.

Functions of the vital breaths—Prāṇa (out-breathing), apāna (in-breathing), and the rest.

Presiding deity—An unseen power other than the human factors. Each of the sense-organs is controlled by a reflection of Consciousness called its presiding deity. Thus āditya (the sun) is the presiding deity of the eye, by whose aid it sees and acts; and so on with the other senses.

शरीरवाङ्मनोभिर्यत्कर्म प्रारभते नरः।
न्याय्यं वा विपरीतं वा पञ्चैते तस्य हेतवः॥ १५॥

15. Whatever action a man performs with his body, speech, or mind, whether right or wrong—these five are its causes.

तत्रैवं सति कर्तारमात्मानं केवलं तु यः।
पश्यत्यकृतबुद्धित्वान्न स पश्यति दुर्मतिः॥ १६॥

16. That being so, the man of perverted mind, who, on account of impure understanding, looks on the Self, the Absolute, as the agent—he sees not at all.

यस्य नाहङ्कृतो भावो बुद्धिर्यस्य न लिप्यते।
हत्वाऽपि स इमाँल्लोकान्न हन्ति न निबध्यते॥ १७॥

17. He who is free from the feeling of I-consciousness and whose understanding is undefiled—though he slays these men, he slays not nor is he bound.

Free from the feeling etc.—He knows the five factors mentioned in the fourteenth verse to be the causes of all action, and the Self to be the actionless Witness. This is due to his knowledge of scripture, his training by a competent teacher, and his possession of the sound principles of reasoning.

Whose understanding is undefiled—He does not identify the Self with a good or bad action done by the body or senses at the bidding of the guṇas.

Though he slays—From the standpoint of the ignorant.

He slays not—From the standpoint of Truth.

Nor is he bound—By the results of slaying.

Body and Soul, matter and Spirit, are completely different from each other. The attributes of the one cannot affect the other, just as the water of a mirage cannot moisten a single grain of sand in the desert. Whatever change may take place in the body cannot affect the Spirit.

The teachings of the Gītā may be said to conclude here. At the beginning Śrī Kṛṣṇa stated the proposition: "The Self slays not nor is slain" (II, 19) and gave the immutability of the Self as the reason (II, 20). He also briefly introduced the idea (II, 21) that an enlightened person is not compelled to engage in action and explained it in detail throughout the treatise. Now He concludes the book in the words that the wise man "slays not nor is he bound." The essence of the teachings is this: A saṃnyāsī is free from I-consciousness and identification with the body; he renounces all action because it is brought about by ignorance of the true nature of the Self. Therefore the threefold fruit of action—good, evil, and mixed—does not affect him. It is only an unenlightened man that is affected by it.

The immutable Self is not in any way connected with action. The incitement to action is described:

ज्ञानं ज्ञेयं परिज्ञाता त्रिविधा कर्मचोदना।
करणं कर्म कर्तेति त्रिविधः कर्मसङ्ग्रहः ॥ १८ ॥

18. Knowledge, the object of knowledge, and the knower form the threefold incitement to action; and the instrument, the object, and the doer are the threefold basis of action.

Knowledge etc.—The performance of an action, either to obtain or to avoid a thing, is possible only when there is a conjunction of these three.

Instrument—It is of two kinds: external, such as the different organs of perception, and internal, such as the mind and understanding.

Object—That which is sought for and reached through action by the doer.

Doer—He who sets the organs going.

All actions inhere in these three: the instrument, the object, and the doer; hence they form the bases of action.

ज्ञानं कर्म च कर्ता च त्रिधैव गुणभेदतः।
प्रोच्यते गुणसङ्ख्याने यथावच्छृणु तान्यपि॥ १९॥

19. Knowledge, action, and the doer are declared in the science of the guṇas to be of three kinds, according to the distinction of the guṇas. Hear of them as they are.

Science of the guṇas—Meaning Sāṅkhya philosophy, propounded by Kapila. He is acknowledged by all, including the Vedāntists, as the authority on the science of the guṇas.

Since knowledge, action, and the doer are characterized by the three guṇas, they fall into the category of Prakṛti—Nature, or matter. They have no connexion with the Ātman, or Self.

The threefold character of knowledge:

सर्वभूतेषु येनैकं भावमव्ययमीक्षते।
अविभक्तं विभक्तेषु तज्ज्ञानं विद्धि सात्त्विकम्॥ २०॥

20. The knowledge by which one indestructible Substance is seen in all beings, undivided in the divided—know that that knowledge is of the nature of sattva.

Indestructible Substance—That is to say, Brahman, or the Supreme Reality. It does not change though the outer form undergoes modifications.

All beings—From the highest deity to a blade of grass. Undivided—Permeating in the same manner.

With the help of the knowledge characterized by sattva one sees the non-dual Ātman as forming the inner substance of everything, though there are differences in the degree of Its manifestation.

The knowledge characterized by rajas:

पृथक्त्वेन तु यज्ज्ञानं नानाभावान्पृथग्विधान्।
वेत्ति सर्वेषु भूतेषु तज्ज्ञानं विद्धि राजसम्॥२१॥

21. But that knowledge through which one sees in all beings various entities of different kinds as differing from one another—know that that knowledge is of the nature of rajas.

Entities—Souls.

Of different kinds—Endowed with different characteristics, such as happiness, unhappiness, and the like.

As differing from one another—Different in different bodies.

Finding creatures happy or unhappy, wise or ignorant, ugly or beautiful, a man endowed with the knowledge characterized by rajas thinks that different souls dwell in different bodies.

The knowledge characterized by tamas:

यत्तु कृत्स्नवदेकस्मिन्कार्ये सक्तमहैतुकम्।
अतत्त्वार्थवदल्पं च तत्तामसमुदाहृतम्॥२२॥

22. And the knowledge that is confined to one single effect as if it were the whole, and is without reason, without foundation in truth, and trivial—that knowledge is declared to be of the nature of tamas.

One single effect—Such as the body, which is taken to be the all-pervading Self, or an image, which is regarded as the omnipresent Lord.

Trivial—Because it deals with a trivial object or because it produces an insignificant result.

The Ātman is the all-pervading Spirit. A man endowed with the knowledge characterized by tamas finds the Ātman confined to one body only. Similarly, he thinks of the Lord as confined to a single image or symbol.

The threefold nature of action:

नियतं सङ्गरहितमरागद्वेषतः कृतम्।
अफलप्रेप्सुना कर्म यत्तत्सात्त्विकमुच्यते॥२३॥

23. The action that is obligatory and is done without love or hate by one who desires no fruit and who is free from attachment—that action is characterized by sattva.

यत्तु कामेप्सुना कर्म साहङ्कारेण वा पुनः।
क्रियते बहुलायासं तद्राजसमुदाहृतम् ॥ २४ ॥

24. But the action that is performed with much effort by one who seeks to gratify his desires or who is prompted by a feeling of "I"—that action is declared to be of the nature of rajas.

अनुबन्धं क्षयं हिंसामनपेक्ष्य च पौरुषम्।
मोहादारभ्यते कर्म यत्तत्तामसमुच्यते ॥ २५ ॥

25. Whereas the action that is undertaken through ignorance, without regard to consequences or loss or injury, and without regard to one's ability—that action is said to be of the nature of tamas.

Loss—Of power or wealth.

Injury—To living beings.

The three kinds of doers:

मुक्तसङ्गोऽनहंवादी धृत्युत्साहसमन्वितः।
सिद्ध्यसिद्ध्योर्निर्विकारः कर्ता सात्त्विक उच्यते ॥ २६ ॥

26. The doer who is free from attachment and egoism, who is endowed with fortitude and zeal, and who is unaffected by success and failure—he is said to be of the nature of sattva.

रागी कर्मफलप्रेप्सुर्लुब्धो हिंसात्मकोऽशुचिः।
हर्षशोकान्वितः कर्ता राजसः परिकीर्तितः ॥ २७ ॥

27. The doer who is passionately attached to action and desirous of its fruit, who is greedy, violent, and impure, and who is moved by joy and sorrow—he is declared to be of the nature of rajas.

Moved by joy and sorrow—At the success or failure of the action in which he is engaged.

अयुक्तः प्राकृतः स्तब्धः शठो नैष्कृतिकोऽलसः।
विषादी दीर्घसूत्री च कर्ता तामस उच्यते ॥ २८ ॥

28 The doer who is unsteady, vulgar, and arrogant; deceitful, malicious, and indolent; desponding and procrastinating—he is said to be of the nature of tamas.

The three kinds of understanding and firmness:

बुद्धेर्भेदं धृतेश्चैव गुणतस्त्रिविधं शृणु।
प्रोच्यमानमशेषेण पृथक्त्वेन धनञ्जय॥ २९॥

29. Hear from Me the threefold distinction of understanding and firmness, according to the guṇas, O Dhanañjaya, as I explain them severally and fully.

Understanding—The Sanskrit word "buddhi" means the faculty of discrimination, by which doubt created by the mind is resolved.

प्रवृत्तिं च निवृत्तिं च कार्याकार्ये भयाभये।
बन्धं मोक्षं च या वेत्ति बुद्धिः सा पार्थ सात्त्विकी॥ ३०॥

30. The understanding that determines for a man the path of work and renunciation, right and wrong action; that determines for a man fear and fearlessness, bondage and liberation—that, O Pārtha, is of the nature of sattva.

Right and wrong action—Judged by scriptural injunctions and social ethics.

Fear and fearlessness—That is to say, the cause of fear and of fearlessness, and the cause of bondage and of liberation.

यया धर्ममधर्मं च कार्यं चाकार्यमेव च।
अयथावत्प्रजानाति बुद्धिः सा पार्थ राजसी॥ ३१॥

31. The understanding that gives a distorted apprehension of dharma and adharma, of what ought to be done and what ought not to be done—that, O Pārtha, is of the nature of rajas.

Dharma—*See* note on II, 7.

Adharma—The opposite of dharma.

The influence of rajas on a man's understanding diverts his attention to the satisfaction of the desires to which he is attached and which he finds conducive to his gain and pleasure. From this standpoint of egotistic interest and happiness he sets the standard of right and justice. He will uphold as right or legitimate the means that will best help him to attain his coveted fruit. The influence of rajas is the cause of three fourths of the false and distorted understanding of mankind. Rajas is the great sinner and the positive misleader.

अधर्मं धर्ममिति या मन्यते तमसावृता।
सर्वार्थान्विपरीतांश्च बुद्धिः सा पार्थ तामसी॥ ३२॥

32. The understanding that, being enveloped in darkness, regards adharma as dharma and reverses all values—that, O Pārtha is of the nature of tamas.

The buddhi, or understanding, under the influence of tamas calls light darkness and darkness light, takes what *is* not dharma and upholds it as dharma, persists in the thing that ought not to be done and holds it up to us as the one right thing to do.

धृत्या यया धारयते मनःप्राणेन्द्रियक्रियाः।
योगेनाव्यभिचारिण्या धृतिः सा पार्थ सात्त्विकी॥३३॥

33. The firmness that is accompanied by unswerving concentration, and by which one controls the activities of the mind, the prāṇas, and the senses—that, O Pārtha is of the nature of sattva.

Unswerving concentration—Concentration through yoga on the ideal of Brahman.

Controls the activities of the mind etc.—That is to say, restrains them from rushing into what is opposed to dharma.

One can effectively restrain the activities of the mind, the prāṇas, and the senses only by that firmness which is acquired through concentration on Brahman. An ordinary firmness, not so acquired, gives way under the stress of circumstances.

यया तु धर्मकामार्थान्धृत्या धारयतेऽर्जुन।
प्रसङ्गेन फलाकाङ्क्षी धृतिः सा पार्थ राजसी॥३४॥

34. But the firmness by which one holds fast to dharma, pleasure, and wealth, desiring the fruit of each through an intense attachment—that, O Pārtha is of the nature of rajas.

Dharma—The aim of observing dharma is the enjoyment of happiness both here and hereafter.

यया स्वप्नं भयं शोकं विषादं मदमेव च।
न विमुञ्चति दुर्मेधा धृतिः सा पार्थ तामसी॥३५॥

35. And the firmness by which a stupid person does not give up his sleep, fear, grief, despondency, and sensuality—that, O Pārtha is of the nature of tamas.

Does not give up etc.—That is to say, is inordinately addicted to sleep and the rest, regarding these to be the only worth-while objects to be pursued.

After stating the threefold division of action and also of the several factors connected therewith, Śrī Kṛṣṇa describes the threefold division of happiness, which is the goal of action:

सुखं त्विदानीं त्रिविधं शृणु मे भरतर्षभ।
अभ्यासाद्रमते यत्र दुःखान्तं च निगच्छति॥३६॥

यत्तदग्रे विषमिव परिणामेऽमृतोपमम्।
तत्सुखं सात्त्विकं प्रोक्तमात्मबुद्धिप्रसादजम्॥३७॥

36-37. And now hear from Me, O Bhārata prince, the three kinds of happiness:

That in which a man comes to rejoice by practice and in which he reaches the end of pain, and that which is like poison at first but like nectar in the end—that happiness, born of the clear knowledge of the Self, is said to be of the nature of sattva.

By practice—The happiness characterized by sattva does not, like sensuous enjoyment, produce an immediate result. Like poison at first—Because it has to be attained through the knowledge of Truth, renunciation of worldly objects, meditation, and concentration. All these require arduous. endeavour at the beginning.

Born of the clear knowledge of the Self—Because Self-knowledge removes from the mind the impurity of rajas and tamas and endows it with clarity and serenity.

The source of this happiness is not in external things, but within every man. The yogis enjoy it through their communion with the inmost Self.

विषयेन्द्रियसंयोगाद्यत्तदग्रेऽमृतोपमम्।
परिणामे विषमिव तत्सुखं राजसं स्मृतम्॥३८॥

38. That which arises from the contact of the senses with their objects, and which is like nectar at first but like poison in the end—that happiness is said to be of the nature of rajas.

Like nectar at first—This is one of the characteristics of all sensuous happiness.

Like poison in the end—Because it leads to loss of strength, vigour, complexion, wisdom, intelligence, wealth, and energy.

यदग्रे चानुबन्धे च सुखं मोहनमात्मनः।
निद्रालस्यप्रमादोत्थं तत्तामसमुदाहृतम्॥३९॥

39. But that which deludes the soul at the beginning and even after its termination, and which springs from sleep, sloth, and error—that happiness is declared to be of the nature of tamas.

The topic is concluded:

न तदस्ति पृथिव्यां वा दिवि देवेषु वा पुनः।
सत्त्वं प्रकृतिजैर्मुक्तं यदेभिः स्यात्त्रिभिर्गुणैः ॥४०॥

40. There is no creature here on earth, nor among the gods in heaven, who is free from the three guṇas born of Prakṛti

The whole relative universe, with its various material entities, and actions, instruments of action, and results, is characterized by the guṇas and set up by avidyā, or ignorance. Hence it may seem that the cessation of relative existence is not possible and liberation cannot be attained. Śrī Kṛṣṇa says to Arjuna that man should worship the Lord through the performance of the duties for which he is qualified. Thus he will obtain divine grace, and through it, liberation.

ब्राह्मणक्षत्रियविशां शूद्राणां च परन्तप।
कर्माणि प्रविभक्तानि स्वभावप्रभवैर्गुणैः ॥४१॥

41. The duties of brāhmins, kṣatriyas, vaiśyas, and śūdras have been assigned according to the guṇas born of Nature.

Assigned—Allotted to each class. The scriptures allot different duties to the different castes, taking into consideration the preponderance of the guṇas in their respective natures.

Guṇas born of Nature—The word "Nature" (svabhāva) may mean māyā, the power of the Lord, consisting of the three guṇas. According to the guṇas of Nature, the different castes are endowed with different attributes. A brāhmins nature consists mostly of sattva; a kṣatriya's of rajas and sattva, the latter being under the influence of the former; a vaiśya's of rajas and tamas, tamas being under the influence of rajas; and a śūdra's of tamas and rajas, rajas being under the influence of tamas.

Or the text may be explained in a different way: The manifestation of the guṇas cannot be without a cause. The cause is the nature (svabhāva) of the man himself, formed by the tendencies (saṃskāras) acquired as a result of his desires, actions, and associations in his past lives.

The Gītā lays the utmost emphasis on svadharma—the dharma, or duty, of an individual—as determined by his svabhāva, his inner nature formed as a result of his own past actions. When a man's outer action is determined by his svabhāva, it is the right and healthful thing, the authentic movement of his soul. Arjuna is asked by Śrī Kṛṣṇa to fight because it is his svadharma, the very stuff of his kṣatriya nature. One's own dharma, however defective, is better for oneself than the well performed dharma of another. It is desirable to risk one's life in the performance of one's dharma; for to follow another's dharma is dangerous to the soul and contrary to the natural way of evolution; it is a thing imposed from outside and therefore a hindrance to one's achievement of the true stature of one's spirit. Work undertaken at the bidding of one's dharma should be laid as an offering at the feet of the Lord; the fruit of the work belongs to the Lord Himself. The ideal of svadharma determined by one's svabhāva and not imposed from outside is the philosophical basis of the Hindu caste-system, which is mainly responsible for the cohesion and integrity of Hindu society during the past several thousand years.

शमो दमस्तपः शौचं क्षान्तिरार्जवमेव च।
ज्ञानं विज्ञानमास्तिक्यं ब्रह्मकर्म स्वभावजम्॥४२॥

42. Control of the mind, control of the senses, austerity, cleanliness, forbearance, and uprightness, as also knowledge, realization, and faith—these are the duties. of a brāhmin, born of his own nature.

Austerity Described in XVII, 14—16.

Realization—Of the nature of God, the soul, and so on, described in the scriptures.

Faith—In the hereafter as described in the scriptures.

शौर्यं तेजो धृतिर्दाक्ष्यं युद्धे चाप्यपलायनम्।
दानमीश्वरभावश्च क्षात्रं कर्म स्वभावजम्॥४३॥

43. Heroism, high spirit, firmness, resourcefulness, dauntlessness in battle, generosity, and sovereignty—these are the duties of a kṣatriya, born of his own nature.

Resourcefulness—The performance, without confusion, of duties that present themselves quite unexpectedly and demand ready action.

Sovereignty—The temperament of a ruler and leader.

कृषिगौरक्ष्यवाणिज्यं वैश्यकर्म स्वभावजम्।
परिचर्यात्मकं कर्म शूद्रस्यापि स्वभावजम्॥४४॥

44. Agriculture, cattle—rearing, and trade are the duties of a vaiśya, born of his own nature. And the duty of a śūdra, born of his own nature, is action consisting of service.

Consisting of service—Rendered to members of the other castes.

These duties rightly performed bring happiness hereafter and make their performers fit for higher knowledge.

स्वे स्वे कर्मण्यभिरतः संसिद्धिं लभते नरः।
स्वकर्मनिरतः सिद्धिं यथा विन्दति तच्छृणु॥४५॥

45. Man attains high perfection by devotion to his own duty. Hear from Me, O Arjuna, how perfection is attained by him who is devoted to his own duty.

High perfection—Which consists in the fitness of the body and senses for devotion to knowledge.

But the mere performance of a duty does not bring perfection.

यतः प्रवृत्तिर्भूतानां येन सर्वमिदं ततम्।
स्वकर्मणा तमभ्यर्च्य सिद्धिं विन्दति मानवः॥४६॥

46. By worshipping Him from whom all beings proceed and by whom the whole universe is pervaded—by worshipping Him through the performance of duty does a man attain perfection.

Him—The Supreme Lord, who is the Inner Guide of each soul and who pervades the universe as Spirit and Energy.

The veil of māyā, creating the notion of duties, actions, and so on, separates man from the Lord. The working-out of one's own karma, according to the law of one's being, is the means by which the veil of māyā can be rent and the Lord realized. Duty performed as an act of worship to the Lord, without desire for the result, accomplishes this end, through His grace.

श्रेयान्स्वधर्मो विगुणः परधर्मात्स्वनुष्ठितात्।
स्वभावनियतं कर्म कुर्वन्नाप्नोति किल्बिषम्॥४७॥

47. Better is one's own dharma, though imperfect, than the dharma of another well performed. He who does the duty ordained by his own nature incurs no sin.

As a poisonous substance does not injure the worm born in that substance, so he who does even an unpleasant duty ordained by his own dharma incurs no evil. That is the only real thing for him. All other duties are alien to his nature. Throughout all of Śrī Kṛṣṇa's exhortation to Arjuna about duty it should not be forgotten that duty must be performed as an act of worship. From our work we must not seek any personal gain; we must regard ourselves only as instruments for the fulfilment of a divine purpose. For Arjuna, participation in the cruel battle is more desirable than the life of a recluse living on alms and inflicting no injury on others. Such a life would be entirely alien to Arjuna's inborn nature.

An unenlightened man cannot remain inactive even for one moment. Work prompted by one's own nature is not harmful. Further, all actions have some measure of defect. Therefore,

सहजं कर्म कौन्तेय सदोषमपि न त्यजेत्।
सर्वारम्भा हि दोषेण धूमेनाग्निरिवावृताः॥४८॥

48. One ought not to give up the work to which one is born, O son of Kuntī, though it has its imperfections; for all undertakings are beset with imperfections, as fire with smoke.

All undertakings—Duties belonging to oneself or others.

Beset with imperfections—Because all actions are associated with the three guṇas.

Fire with smoke—As in the case of fire the wise man disregards the smoke and utilizes its heat and light to destroy cold and darkness, so also in the case of actions one should be indifferent to their unavoidable imperfections and employ their virtues for self-purification.

Action is the property of the guṇas, be they regarded as real or falsely set up by avidyā, or ignorance. It is ascribed to the Self through ignorance; hence an ignorant person cannot desist from action even for a moment. On the other hand, he who has realized the actionless Self can renounce action altogether, inasmuch as his ignorance has been dispelled by Self-knowledge.

It has been said (XVIII, 45) *that the result of karmayoga is the attainment of fitness for devotion to knowledge. The consummation of knowledge is perfection in the form of absolute freedom from action.*

असक्तबुद्धिः सर्वत्र जितात्मा विगतस्पृहः।
नैष्कर्म्यसिद्धिं परमां संन्यासेनाधिगच्छति॥४९॥

49. He whose mind is not attached to anything, who has subdued his heart, and who is free from all longing—he, by renunciation, attains supreme perfection, which is freedom from action.

Anything—Son, wife, wealth, and other objects of attachment.

Longing—For body, life, or pleasures.

Renunciation—Saṃnyāsa. He knows the Self to be identical with the actionless Brahman.

Supreme perfection—As contrasted with the perfection one attains through karmayoga. *See* XVIII, 45.

He…attains etc.—This may also be interpreted to mean: He attains the supreme state, in which he remains as the actionless Self.

How does a man who is fitted for devotion to Self-knowledge by the practice of karmayoga attain the perfection known as freedom from action?

सिद्धिं प्राप्तो यथा ब्रह्म तथाप्नोति निबोध मे।
समासेनैव कौन्तेय निष्ठा ज्ञानस्य या परा॥५०॥

50. Learn from Me in brief, O son of Kuntī, how one who has reached such perfection realizes Brahman, which is the supreme consummation of knowledge.

Perfection—Fitness of the body, mind, and senses to pursue the path of knowledge. The body and the organs acquire it through the grace of God, who is pleased with a devotee when he performs his duty as an act of worship.

Brahman—The Knowledge of Brahman is the same as the Knowledge of the Ātman, or Self.

Consummation of knowledge—The constant dwelling of the mind on Brahman without any break or interruption.

How is this consummation attained?

बुद्ध्या विशुद्धया युक्तो धृत्यात्मानं नियम्य च।
शब्दादीन्विषयांस्त्यक्त्वा रागद्वेषौ व्युदस्य च॥५१॥

विविक्तसेवी लघ्वाशी यतवाक्कायमानसः।
ध्यानयोगपरो नित्यं वैराग्यं समुपाश्रितः॥५२॥

अहङ्कारं बलं दर्पं कामं क्रोधं परिग्रहम्।
विमुच्य निर्ममः शान्तो ब्रह्मभूयाय कल्पते॥५३॥

51-53. Endowed with a pure understanding, restraining the self with firmness, turning away from sound and other objects, and abandoning love and hatred;

Dwelling in solitude, eating but little, controlling the speech, body, and mind, ever engaged in meditation and concentration, and cultivating freedom from passion;

Forsaking conceit and power, pride and lust, wrath and possessions, tranquil in heart, and free from ego—he becomes worthy of becoming one with Brahman.

Pure understanding—An understanding (buddhi) that is free from doubt and delusion, and unswerving in its devotion *to* the goal. The pure buddhi, because it reflects Consciousness undistortedly, is the same as Brahman.

The self—The body and the senses.

Turning away from sound etc.—Relinquishing all luxuries, all objects except the minimum that is necessary for the bare sustenance of the body.

Abandoning love and hatred—Giving up love and hatred even for objects that are necessary for the bare sustenance of the body.

Dwelling in solitude etc.—Solitude and the control of food are conducive to serenity of mind, because they eliminate distraction, drowsiness, and other evils.

Ever engaged—The word "ever" implies that the aspirant for Self-knowledge gives up all other rituals and ceremonies and practises only meditation and concentration.

Meditation—Upon the true nature of the Self.

Concentration—One-pointedness of the mind on the Self. Freedom from passion—For objects here and hereafter.

Power—That power which is combined with lust and passion.

Forsaking . . . possessions—This is the characteristic of a paramahaṃsa saṃnyāsī, a monk of the highest order, who does not keep with him the slightest possessions, even for the bare sustenance of his body.

Worthy of becoming etc.—An aspirant endowed with the virtues stated in the text attains the supreme perfection of total identity with Brahman.

The result of undeviating union with Brahman:

ब्रह्मभूतः प्रसन्नात्मा न शोचति न काङ्क्षति।
समः सर्वेषु भूतेषु मद्भक्तिं लभते पराम्॥५४॥

54. Having become Brahman and being tranquil in heart, he neither grieves nor desires. He treats alike all beings and attains supreme devotion to Me.

Having become Brahman—Firmly grounded in the conviction that he is Brahman.

He neither grieves nor desires—Because of his absence of identification with the body, senses, and mind.

Treats alike—He regards the pleasure and pain of others as if they were his own.

Supreme devotion—Mentioned in VII, 17.

भक्त्या मामभिजानाति यावान्यश्चास्मि तत्त्वतः ।
ततो मां तत्त्वतो ज्ञात्वा विशते तदनन्तरम् ॥ ५५ ॥

55. By that devotion he knows Me, knows what, in truth, I am and who I am. Then, having known Me in truth, he forthwith enters into Me.

What, in truth, I am—He knows that the Lord alone is the essence of the diverse manifestations caused by His māyā.

Who I am—He knows that the Lord is devoid of all names and forms caused by māyā and is of the nature of the Absolute.

Having known Me in truth—Having known that the Lord is non-dual, unborn, un-decaying, unchanging, and of the nature of Spirit and Consciousness.

Enters into Me—The acts of knowing and entering are not two separate and consecutive actions; they are one and the same. To know the Lord truly is to be completely absorbed in Him.

Supreme devotion (XVIII, 54), which is the consummation of knowledge, is attained by the aspirant when his knowledge of the unity of the individual self and the transcendental Self—realized through the instructions of the scriptures and the teacher and also through his practice of such disciplines as purity, humility, non-violence, and so on—is accompanied by the renunciation of all activity associated. with the notion of a doer and a result, and also when such knowledge is corroborated by his own experience. Through such devotion he creates an uninterrupted mental current by which he remains ever aware of his identity with the Supreme Self. It is obvious that work that assumes a distinction between the doer, the instrument, and the result must be renounced by a man who wants to maintain such a current.

The liberation described above may also be attained through the performance of one's duties.

सर्वकर्माण्यपि सदा कुर्वाणो मद्व्यपाश्रयः।
मत्प्रसादादवाप्नोति शाश्वतं पदमव्ययम्॥५६॥

56. Even though engaged in all kinds of action, a man who has taken refuge in Me reaches, by My grace, the eternal and imperishable Abode.

All kinds of action—Including even forbidden action.

Taken refuge in Me—Performing his duty to please the Lord alone and not to earn any result for himself.

चेतसा सर्वकर्माणि मयि संन्यस्य मत्परः।
बुद्धियोगमुपाश्रित्य मच्चित्तः सततं भव॥५७॥

57. Surrendering, in thought, all actions to Me, regarding Me as the Supreme Goal, and practising steadiness of mind, fix your heart, O Arjuna, constantly on Me.

Surrendering etc.—As stated in IV, 24 and IX, 27.

मच्चित्तः सर्वदुर्गाणि मत्प्रसादात्तरिष्यसि।
अथ चेत्त्वमहङ्कारान्न श्रोष्यसि विनङ्क्ष्यसि॥५८॥

58. Fixing your heart on Me, you will overcome every difficulty by My grace; but if from self-conceit you do not listen to Me, you shall perish utterly.

यदहङ्कारमाश्रित्य न योत्स्य इति मन्यसे।
मिथ्यैष व्यवसायस्ते प्रकृतिस्त्वां नियोक्ष्यति॥५९॥

59. If, indulging in self—conceit, you say to yourself, "I will not fight," vain is your resolution. Your nature will compel you.

Nature—The kṣatriya nature, with a preponderance of rajas.

स्वभावजेन कौन्तेय निबद्धः स्वेन कर्मणा।
कर्तुं नेच्छसि यन्मोहात्करिष्यस्यवशोऽपि तत्॥६०॥

60. Bound by your own karma, O son of Kuntī, which is born of your very nature, what through delusion you seek not to do, you shall do even against your will.

Karma—Such as heroism, high spirit, and so on, mentioned in XVIII, 43.

ईश्वरः सर्वभूतानां हृद्देशेऽर्जुन तिष्ठति।
भ्रामयन्सर्वभूतानि यन्त्रारूढानि मायया॥ ६१॥

61. The Lord dwells in the hearts of all beings, O Arjuna, and by His māyā causes them to revolve as though mounted on a machine.

Arjuna—The word also means "white" and signifies a man of pure heart.

Mounted on a machine—As marionettes are moved by a wire-puller seated behind the screen, so also the created beings move and act on the stage of the world, under the control of the Lord seated in the hearts of all. Compare: IX, 10.

तमेव शरणं गच्छ सर्वभावेन भारत।
तत्प्रसादात्परां शान्तिं स्थानं प्राप्स्यसि शाश्वतम्॥ ६२॥

62. Take refuge in Him alone with all your soul, O Bhārata. By His grace will you gain Supreme Peace and the Everlasting Abode.

Take refuge in Him alone—Give up self-conceit, for all creatures are under the control of the Supreme Lord.

इति ते ज्ञानमाख्यातं गुह्याद्गुह्यतरं मया।
विमृश्यैतदशेषेण यथेच्छसि तथा कुरु॥ ६३॥

63. Thus has wisdom more profound than all profundities been declared to you by Me. Reflect upon it fully and act as you will.

It—The teaching of the Gītā.

Act as you will—The scriptures serve the purpose of telling man what he should do and what he should not. It is up to man himself to choose the right and reject the wrong.

सर्वगुह्यतमं भूयः शृणु मे परमं वचः।
इष्टोऽसि मे दृढमिति ततो वक्ष्यामि ते हितम्॥ ६४॥

64. Again listen to My supreme word, the profoundest of all. You are well beloved of Me; therefore I will tell you what is for your good.

मन्मना भव मद्भक्तो मद्याजी मां नमस्कुरु।
मामेवैष्यसि सत्यं ते प्रतिजाने प्रियोऽसि मे॥६५॥

65. Fix your heart on Me, give your love to Me, worship Me, bow down before Me; so shall you come to Me. This is My pledge to you, for you are dear to Me.

The devotee who looks upon the Lord as his aim, means, and end is certain to reach the Lord. The Lord's promise cannot but be fulfilled. Since liberation is the result of whole-souled devotion to the Lord, one should look upon Him alone as the highest and sole Refuge.

सर्वधर्मान्परित्यज्य मामेकं शरणं व्रज।
अहं त्वा सर्वपापेभ्यो मोक्षयिष्यामि मा शुचः॥६६॥

66. Abandon all dharmas and come to Me alone for shelter. I will deliver you from all sins; do not grieve.

Dharmas—Dharma, righteous action, here includes what is unrighteous also. All action, righteous or unrighteous, creates bondage and therefore is incompatible with the supreme liberation taught here. Śrī Kṛṣṇa lays down renunciation of all action as the condition of liberation.

Me—The Lord, the Self of all, dwelling in all as their inmost essence.

For shelter—For there is none else except the Lord.

I will deliver you—By revealing the true nature of the Lord, which is beyond the multiplicity of the relative world.

All sins—That is to say, the bondage imposed on men in the form of dharma and adharma. Forgetfulness of the true nature of the Lord, through His māyā, creates the illusion of good and evil, pain and pleasure, and the other pairs of opposites, which impel men to action for the acceptance of the one and the rejection of the other.

The conclusion of the Gītā, according to the commentator Śaṅkara, is that supreme liberation, which also is the highest. Bliss, is not possible either through work (ritualistic, philanthropic, or any kind of work associated with the idea of a doer, means of action, and result) or through a conjunction of work and knowledge; it is possible only through Self-knowledge, or the Knowledge of Brahman. Action is possible. only in a relative world of multiplicity. The perception of the manifold is due to avidyā, or ignorance, on account of which man feels an urge to action. Ignorance is without beginning and so also is the urge to action. As by darkness one cannot destroy darkness, so by means of action one cannot remove ignorance and attain the highest Bliss. As light alone can destroy darkness, so the Knowledge of the Self—the Knowledge that makes one realize that the Self is unborn, immortal, incorporeal, ever pure, ever free, and untouched by time, space, and causation—destroys ignorance and with it the illusory notion of one's duty in the world of multiplicity. Indeed, Knowledge removes the illusion of the very existence of the relative universe and reveals the Reality, which is One and without a second. Further, eternal Bliss cannot be the *effect* of action or anything else; in that case it must have a beginning and cannot be eternal. This Bliss, or liberation, is said to be produced by Knowledge only in a figurative sense, inasmuch as Knowledge destroys ignorance, and this destruction is simultaneous with the revelation of the ever existent Reality.

The teachings of the Gītā are concluded. Now the Lord lays down the rules for their handing down:

इदं ते नातपस्काय नाभक्ताय कदाचन।
न चाशुश्रूषवे वाच्यं न च मां योऽभ्यसूयति॥६७॥

67. You must not speak about it to one who is not austere in life or who is without devotion, nor to one who does not wish to hear, nor to one who speaks ill of Me.

It—The instruction embodied in the Gītā.

Without devotion—To God or to his teacher.

Who does not wish to hear—The word in the text may also mean "who does not render service to the guru."

Who speaks ill of Me—Who regards Me, Kṛṣṇa, as an ordinary man and does not recognize My divine nature.

The merit of teaching the Gītā to the Lord's devotees:

य इदं परमं गुह्यं मद्भक्तेष्वभिधास्यति।
भक्तिं मयि परां कृत्वा मामेवैष्यत्यसंशयः॥६८॥

68. He who, with supreme devotion to Me, teaches this deeply profound philosophy to those who are devoted to Me shall without question come to Me.

Teaches—The teacher of the Gītā must have the faith that through his teaching he is rendering service to the Lord, the Supreme Teacher.

Devotion to the Lord is the condition for being a student or a teacher of the Gītā.

न च तस्मान्मनुष्येषु कश्चिन्मे प्रियकृत्तमः ।
भविता न च मे तस्मादन्यः प्रियतरो भुवि ॥ ६९ ॥

69. There is none among men who can do anything more pleasing to Me than he; nor shall there be another on earth dearer to Me than he.

He—Who explains the teachings of the Gītā to the Lord's devotees.

The result of the study of the Gītā:

अध्येष्यते च य इमं धर्म्यं संवादमावयोः ।
ज्ञानयज्ञेन तेनाहमिष्टः स्यामिति मे मतिः ॥ ७० ॥

70. And he who will study this sacred dialogue of ours—by him shall I have been worshipped through knowledge as a sacrifice; such is My judgement.

Knowledge as a sacrifice—Various kinds of sacrifice (yajña) have been described in the fourth chapter of the Gītā, and it has been pointed out (IV, 33) that the sacrifice through knowledge is the best of all.

The result of hearing the Gītā:

श्रद्धावाननसूयश्च शृणुयादपि यो नरः ।
सोऽपि मुक्तः शुभाँल्लोकान्प्राप्नुयात्पुण्यकर्मणाम् ॥ ७१ ॥

71. And the man who hears this, full of faith and free from malice—even he, liberated from sin, shall attain the happy regions of the righteous.

Even he—That a more meritorious result awaits him who understands the teachings of the Gītā need not be pointed out.

The Divine Teacher wants to know whether or not the pupil has understood the teachings of the Gītā. If not, He will find some other means to bring conviction to Arjuna's mind.

कच्चिदेतच्छ्रुतं पार्थ त्वयैकाग्रेण चेतसा ।
कच्चिदज्ञानसम्मोहः प्रनष्टस्ते धनञ्जय ॥ ७२ ॥

72. Has it been heard by you, O Pārtha, with an undivided mind? Has your delusion, born of ignorance, been destroyed, O Dhanañjaya?

The teacher works hard to explain the scriptures, and the student works hard to understand the teaching. The effort on the part of both aims at the destruction of the student's ignorance.

अर्जुन उवाच।

नष्टो मोहः स्मृतिर्लब्धा त्वत्प्रसादान्मयाच्युत।
स्थितोऽस्मि गतसन्देहः करिष्ये वचनं तव॥७३॥

73. *Arjuna said:* My delusion is gone. I have regained my memory through Your grace, O Kṛṣṇa. I am firm; I am free from doubt. I will act according to Your word.

Delusion—Born of ignorance, the cause of the evil of worldly existence.

Memory—Regarding the true nature of the Self.

I am firm—Arjuna is ready to fight to carry out Kṛṣṇa's command.

The purpose of the study of the scriptures is the destruction of delusion, which is at once followed by Self-knowledge.

The teaching of the Gītā is over. The rest is only the conclusion of the main narrative.

सञ्जय उवाच।

इत्यहं वासुदेवस्य पार्थस्य च महात्मनः।
संवादमिममश्रौषमद्भुतं रोमहर्षणम्॥७४॥

74. *Sañjaya said:* Thus did I hear this wonderful dialogue between Kṛṣṇa and the high-souled Arjuna, which caused my hair to rise.

Sañjaya says this to the blind king Dhṛtarāṣṭra

व्यासप्रसादाच्छ्रुतवानेतद्गुह्यमहं परम्।
योगं योगेश्वरात्कृष्णात्साक्षात्कथयतः स्वयम्॥७५॥

75. Through the grace of Vyāsa I heard this supreme and profound yoga direct from Kṛṣṇa, the Lord of yoga, Himself teaching it.

Through the grace etc.—Through the grace of the sage Vyāsa, Sañjaya had been endowed with divine vision, by which he observed all that happened between Kṛṣṇa and Arjuna on the battle-field and reported it to Dhṛtarāṣṭra

Yoga—The Gītā is called "yoga" because it deals with yoga, or the communion of the soul with the Supreme Self.

राजन्संस्मृत्य संस्मृत्य संवादमिममद्भुतम्।
केशवार्जुनयोः पुण्यं हृष्यामि च मुहुर्मुहुः॥७६॥

76. O King, every time I remember this wonderful and sacred dialogue between Kṛṣṇa and Arjuna, I rejoice again and again and over again.

King—Dhṛtarāṣṭra

तच्च संस्मृत्य संस्मृत्य रूपमत्यद्भुतं हरेः।
विस्मयो मे महान् राजन्हृष्यामि च पुनः पुनः ॥७७॥

77. And as often as I remember that most wonderful form of Kṛṣṇa, great is my astonishment, O King, and I rejoice again and again.

Form—The Universal Form of Kṛṣṇa, described in the eleventh chapter of the Gītā.

The outcome of the battle can no longer be doubted.

यत्र योगेश्वरः कृष्णो यत्र पार्थो धनुर्धरः।
तत्र श्रीर्विजयो भूतिर्ध्रुवा नीतिर्मतिर्मम ॥७८॥

78. The side that has Kṛṣṇa, the Lord of yoga, and the side that has Arjuna, the wielder of the Gāṇḍīva—there surely will be fortune, victory, prosperity, and right conduct. Such is my conviction.

Gāṇḍīva—The mighty bow of Arjuna.

ॐ तत्सदिति श्रीमद्भगवद्गीतासूपनिषत्सु
ब्रह्मविद्यायां योगशास्त्रे श्रीकृष्णार्जुनसंवादे
मोक्षसंन्यासयोगो नाम अष्टादशोऽध्यायः ॥१८॥

Thus in the Bhagavad Gītā, the Essence of the Upaniṣads, the Science of Brahman, the Scripture of Yoga, the Dialogue between Śrī Kṛṣṇa and Arjuna, ends the Eighteenth Chapter, entitled: THE WAY TO LIBERATION THROUGH RENUNCIATION

शान्ताकारं भुजगशयनं पद्मनाभं सुरेशम्।
विश्वाधारं गगनसदृशं मेघवर्णं शुभाङ्गम्।
लक्ष्मीकान्तं कमलनयनं योगिभिर्ध्यानगम्यम्।
वन्दे विष्णुं भवभयहरं सर्वलोकैकनाथम्॥

Here ends the Śrīmad Bhagavad Gītā.
Om. Peace! Peace! Peace be unto all!
Om Tat Sat. .

ॐ

GLOSSARY

A	The first of the Sanskrit letters; all sounds are based on this sound.
Acyuta	(Lit., the Changeless One) An epithet of Kṛṣṇa.
adharma	*(Lit.*, the opposite of dharma) Impiety or unrighteousness. *See* dharma.
Ādityas	Twelve deities constituting a group.
Airāvata	The name of the celestial elephant born out of the churning of the ocean by the gods and demons and given to Indra for his use.
ākāśa	The first of the five material elements that constitute the universe; often translated as "space" or "ether."
amṛta	(Lit., immortal) The elixir of immortality.
apāna	A modification of the vital breath, by the action of which the unassimilated food and drink go downward; the movement of the out—going breath.
asura	Demon.
aśvattha	The holy fig tree.
Aświns	According to Hindu mythology they are the twin sons of the Sun—god, and the physicians *of* the gods in heaven,
Ātman	The Self, or Soul; denotes also the Supreme Soul, which, according to the Non-dualistic Vedānta, is one with the individual soul.

avidyā	A term of Vedānta philosophy meaning ignorance, either in its cosmic or in its individual form
Bhārata	A descendant of King Bharata, the son of Śakuntalā and Duṣyanta. In honour of Bharata, India is called Bhārata or Bhāratavarṣa. In the Gītā the word refers occasionally to Dhṛtarāṣṭra and frequently to Arjuna, both of whom were descended from the ancient King Bharata.
Brahmā	The Creator God; the First Person of the Hindu Trinity, the other two being Viṣṇu and Śiva.
Brahmacārī	A celibate religious student who lives with his teacher and devotes himself to the practice of spiritual discipline.
Brahman	The Absolute; the Supreme Reality of Vedānta philosophy.
Brahma-sūtras	An authoritative text-book on Vedānta philosophy, ascribed to Vyāsa.
brāhmin	The priestly caste.
Bṛhaspati	The preceptor and priest of the gods.
buddhi	The determinative faculty of the mind, which makes decisions.
conch	The conch-shell, used in India as a trumpet.
cycle	A world period. *See* note on VIII, 17.
Daityas	(*Lit.*, the sons of Diti) The demons, who challenged the power of the gods.
deva	(*Lit.*, shining one) A god. *See* note on III, 11-12.
Devarṣī	One who is at the same time a god and a ṛṣi, or seer of Truth.
Dhanañjaya	A name of Arjuna, given in honour of his having subdued the kings of India and acquired their wealth.
dharma	(*Lit.*, that which holds together) The inmost constitution of a thing, the law of its inner being, which hastens its growth and without which it ceases to exist. The dharma of a man is not imposed from outside, but is acquired by him as a result of his actions in his past lives. Thus every man, in a special sense, has his own dharma, which de-

	termines his conduct, his righteousness, and his sense of right and wrong. *See* note on II, 7.
Dhṛtarāṣṭra	The elder brother of King Pāṇḍu, and the father of one hundred sons, of whom Duryodhana was the eldest.
Draupadī	The wife of the five sons of Pāṇḍu.
Duryodhana	The eldest son of King Dhṛtarāṣṭra and the leader of the Kauravas.
Dvanda	A compound in Sanskrit grammar in which the meanings of the component parts are fully retained, which is not the case with other compounds.
faith	The untranslatable Sanskrit word "śraddhā" denotes an intuitive conviction of the existence of Truth and also a mental attitude, on the part of the aspirant, consisting primarily of sincerity of purpose, humility, and reverence.
Gandharvas	Members of a class of demigods, regarded as the singers and musicians of the gods.
Gāṇḍīva	The celebrated bow of Arjuna.
Garuḍa	A mythical bird, the carrier of the Lord Viṣṇu.
Gāyatrī	A Vedic metre of twenty-four syllables; also the name of a sacred Vedic verse repeated daily by every brāhmin at the time of his regular devotions.
god	The word in Sanskrit is "deva," literally, "shining one.' "When a human being performs meritorious action on earth, he becomes a god after death and occupies a temporary position in heaven, where he is given charge of a cosmic process. Thus the Hindu scriptures describe the god of fire, the god of wind, the god of the ocean, and so on.
Govinda	(*Lit.*, the Protector of cows) An epithet of Kṛṣṇa.
Guḍākeśa	(*Lit.*, one who has controlled sleep) An epithet of Arjuna.
guṇa	According to Sāṅkhya philosophy, Prakṛti (Nature or matter), in contrast with Puruṣa (Soul), consists of three guṇas—usually translated as "qualities"—known as sattva, rajas, and tamas. Tamas stands for inertia or

	dullness, rajas for activity or restlessness, and sattva for balance or wisdom.
Haṭhayoga	A school of yoga that aims chiefly at physical health and well-being.
Hṛṣīkeśa	(*Lit.*, the Lord, or Director, of the senses) A name of Kṛṣṇa.
Ikṣvāku	The son of Manu and ancestor of the Solar dynasty of kṣatriyas.
Indra	The king of the gods.
Īśvara-form	The Divine Form of the Lord, possessed of omnipotence, omnipresence, infinite wisdom, infinite strength, infinite virtue, and infinite splendour.
Janaka	A king of ancient India, who was endowed with the highest knowledge.
Janārdana	(*Lit.*, the Destroyer of the demon Jana) According to Śaṅkara, an epithet of Kṛṣṇa because He is prayed to for prosperity and liberation.
japa	Repetition of a name of God.
jīva	(*Lit.*, living being) The individual soul; which in essence is one with the Universal Soul.
jīvanmukti	The experience of liberation while one dwells in this world.
jñāna	Knowledge.
Jñānī	A man endowed with jñāna, or knowledge.
Kāmadhuk	The famous cow of the sage Vaśiṣṭha, which fulfilled all desires and yielded milk in abundance.
Kandarpa	The Hindu god of love.
Kapila	Reputed to be the author of Sāṅkhya philosophy.
karma	Action in general; duty; ritualistic worship.
karmayoga	The path of duty leading to union with the Lord. *See* note on "yoga," II, 39.
karmayogi	A follower of karmayoga. *See* karmayoga.
Kāśī	Benares.
Keśava	A name of Kṛṣṇa.

Keśī	The name of a demon.
kṣatriya	The warrior caste.
Kuntī	A wife of King Pāṇḍu; same as Pṛthā.
Kuru	A section of northern India, comprising the country around modern Delhi; a prince of that country. The epithet "chief of the Kurus" is applied in the Gītā to Arjuna. In the *Mahābhārata* this title is used also to denote Dhṛtarāṣṭra and Duryodhana. Kuru was a common ancestor of them all.
Kurukṣetra	A place near modern Delhi.
Kuśa-grass	A kind of grass from which mats for meditation are made.
Kuvera	The god of riches and treasure; also the king of the Yakṣas.
Life-breath	Same as prāṇa. *See* prāṇa.
Mādhava	A name of Kṛṣṇa.
Madhusūdana	(*Lit.*, the Slayer of the demon Madhu) An epithet of Kṛṣṇa.
mahāratha	One able to fight single-handed ten thousand archers.
Manu	The celebrated law-giver of ancient India; the name of a mythical personage regarded as the representative man and the father of the human race. The *Manu saṃhitā*, or *Institutes* of *Manu*, mentions fourteen Manus, who were the fourteen successive progenitors or sovereigns of the earth. The seventh Manu, called Vaivasvat, is supposed to have been born of the sun and is regarded as the progenitor of the present race of human beings.
Maruts	The winds.
māyā	A term of Vedānta philosophy denoting ignorance obscuring the vision of God; the cosmic illusion on account of which the One appears as many, the Absolute as the relative. *See* note on VII, 14.
Meru	A mythical mountain abounding in gold and other treasures.
mokṣa	Liberation.

muni	A sage given to meditation and contemplation.
Nāgas	These form a class of snakes.
Nirvāṇa	(*Lit.*, blowing out—as of a flame) Annihilation of desire, passion, and ego; liberation characterized by freedom and bliss.
Nivṛtti	Renunciation, detachment.
Om	The most sacred word of the Vedas; also written *Aum*. It is the symbol of both the Personal God and the Absolute. *See* note on VII, 8.
organs of action	They are five in number, namely, hands, feet, the organ of speech, and the organs of generation and evacuation.
pairs of opposites	All correlated ideas and sensations, for instance, good and evil, pleasure and pain, heat and cold, light and darkness.
Pāṇḍava	(*Lit.*, son of Pāṇḍu) Generally used in the text to denote Arjuna.
Pāṇḍu	The younger brother of King Dhṛtarāṣṭra and father of Yudhiṣṭhira, Bhīma, Arjuna, Nakula, and Sahadeva.
Pārtha	(*Lit.*, son of Pṛthā) An epithet of Arjuna.
Patañjali	The celebrated author of *Rājayoga*.
Pitṛs	Forefathers.
Prahlāda	The son of Hiraṇyakaśipu, who was an unrighteous demon. Prahlāda was tortured by his father for his great love of God. The Lord, in His Incarnation as Nṛsiṃha, Man-lion, killed the cruel father.
Prajāpati	An epithet of the ten lords of created beings, the first to be created by Brahmā.
Prakṛti	Primordial Nature; the material substratum of the creation, consisting of sattva, rajas, and tamas.
prāṇa	The vital breath, which sustains life in a physical body; the breath. In the books of yoga, prāṇa is described as having five modifications, according to its five different functions. They are: prāṇa (the vital energy that controls breath), apāna (the vital energy that carries downward unassimilated food and drink), samāna (the vital energy

	that carries nutrition all over the body), vyāna (the vital energy that pervades the entire body), and udāna (the vital energy by which the contents of the stomach are ejected through the mouth). According to some writers on yoga, prāṇa and apāna mean, respectively, the in-going and the out-going breath.
Pravṛtti	Desire, the out-going propensity of the mind.
Pṛthā	A wife of King Pāṇḍu same as Kuntī.
Purāṇas	Books of Hindu mythology.
Puruṣa	(*Lit.*, person) A term of Sāṅkhya philosophy denoting the Conscious Principle. The universe evolves from the union of Prakṛti (Nature) and Puruṣa. In Vedānta the word also denotes the Soul and the Absolute.
rajas	*See* guṇa.
rājayoga	A system of yoga ascribed to Patanjali, dealing with concentration and its methods, control of the mind, samādhi, and similar matters.
Rākṣasas	Members of a class of demigods; monsters.
Ṛk	A part of the Vedas.
Rudras	Members of a group of gods, eleven in number, supposed to be collateral manifestations of Siva, who is their leader.
sacrifice	The Sanskrit word "yajña" means a religious rite or worship. It also denotes the offering of oblations to God, or any action performed with a spiritual motive. An additional meaning is the Supreme Lord.
Sādhyas	Members of a particular class of celestial beings.
samādhi	Ecstasy, trance, complete concentration, communion with God.
Sāman	A part of the Vedas.
Sāṅkhya	One of the six systems of Hindu philosophy, ascribed to Kapila.
Saṃsāra	The relative world.
Sañjaya	The reporter who recounted the progress of the battle of Kurukṣetra to the blind King Dhṛtarāṣṭra.

saṃnyāsa	(*Lit.*, complete renunciation) Renunciation practised by saṃnyāsīs, or monks, in the form of giving up all desire for progeny, wealth, and happiness on earth and in heaven after death.
saṃnyāsī	A Hindu monk, who renounces the world in order to realize God.
Sat	Reality, Existence.
sattva	*See* guṇa.
Siddhas	Semi-divine beings of great purity and holiness, endowed with supernatural powers.
Śiva	The Destroyer God; the Third Person of the Hindu Trinity, the other two being Brahmā and Viṣṇu.
Skanda	The commander-in-chief of the armies in heaven.
Soma-juice	A beverage made from the soma-plant and used in various Vedic sacrifices.
Śraddhā	*See* faith.
Subhadrā	A wife of Arjuna.
śūdra	The labouring caste.
tamas	*See* guṇa.
twice-born	The members of the three upper castes—brāhmin, kṣatriya, and vaiśya—whose second birth is said to take place when they are invested with the sacred thread at the time of initiation into spiritual life.
Uccais-śravas	The name of the kingly horse that came out of the ocean when, according to Hindu mythology, it was churned for the amṛta, or elixir of immortality.
upādhis	A term of Vedānta philosophy denoting the limitations imposed upon the Self through ignorance, by which one is bound to worldly life.
Uṣmapās	The manes.
Vaiśeṣika	One of the six systems of Hindu philosophy, ascribed to Kaṇāda.
vaiśya	The commercial and agricultural caste.
Vārṣṇeya	(*Lit.*, one belonging to the clan of the Vṛṣṇis) An epithet of Kṛṣṇa.

Varuṇa	The lord of the ocean; usually associated with Mitra.
Vāsudeva	(*Lit.*, the Son of Vāsudeva) A name of Kṛṣṇa.
Vasus	Members of a class of deities, usually eight in number.
Vedānta	A system of philosophy discussed mainly in the Upaniṣads, the Bhagavad Gītā, and the Brahma-sūtras.
Vedas	The great scriptures of the Hindus and the ultimate authority of the Hindu religion.
Viṣṇu	(*Lit.*, the All-pervading Spirit) A name of the Supreme Lord; the Second Person of the Hindu Trinity, the other two being Brahmā and Śiva.
Viśwas	Members of a group of deities, ten in number.
Vivasvat	The Sun-god.
Vṛkodara	(*Lit.*, one having the belly of a wolf) A name of Bhīma, given because of his enormous appetite.
Vyāsa	A celebrated sage, who is reputed to have arranged the Vedas in their present form; he is also believed to be the author of the *Mahābhārata*. The eighteen Purāṇas and the Brahma-sūtras are also ascribed to him.
Yādava	(*Lit.*, One belonging to the race of Yadu) A name of Kṛṣṇa.
Yādavas	The members of the race to which Kṛṣṇa belonged.
yajña	*See* sacrifice.
Yajus	A part of the Vedas.
Yakṣas	Certain demigods.
Yama	The king of death.
yoga	The union of the individual soul and the Supreme Soul; also the discipline by which such union is effected.
yogi	One who practises yoga. *See* yoga.
Yudhiṣṭhira	The eldest son of King Pāṇḍu.

INDEX

* * *